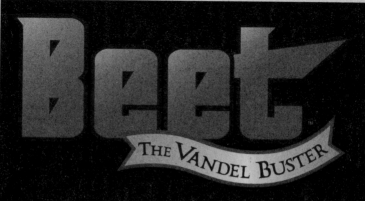

SHONEN JUMP GRAPHIC NOVEL

Beet™ THE VANDEL BUSTER

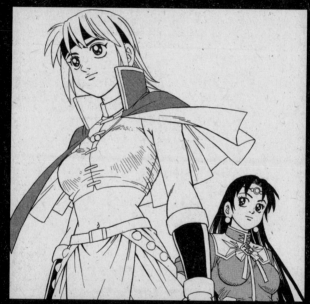

Volume 8

Story by Riku Sanjo

Art by Koji Inada

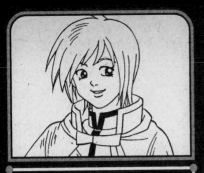

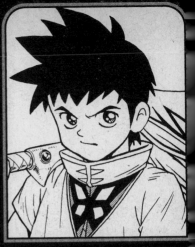

BEET

The hero of this story. Believing in justice, he sets out on a journey to save the world. He received five Saiga weapons from the Zenon Warriors.

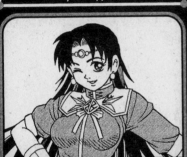

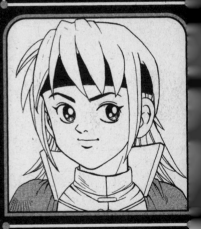

POALA

Beet's childhood friend has an unyeilding spirit. She joins Beet as the second of the Beet Warriors and sets out on the journey with him. She is skilled at Kenjutsu, the art of the samurai sword, as well as the Divine Attack.

KISSU

An old friend of Beet's, he is a prodigy of Divine Attack, and expert in both theory and application.

MILFA

Milfa is one of the Broad Busters, an elite class of high-level Busters. She has an extremely upbeat personality and is a huge fan of the Zenon Warriors.

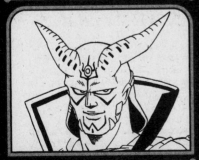

BELTORZE

Known as the "King of Tragedy," he is a seven-star Vandel widely feared by humans.

STORY

CHARACTERS

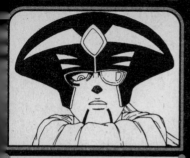

NOA
Called the "Vandel Scholar," he is a seven-star Vandel who has thoroughly mastered research on both Vandels and humans.

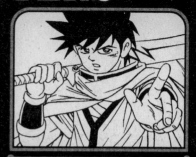

ZENON
Beet's older brother.
No one has seen him since the Zenon Warriors violent battle with Beltorze.

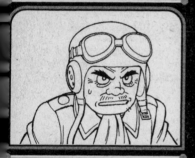

GUNTRY
A pilot from Bekatrute.
He's willing to risk his life for a big sloppy kiss.

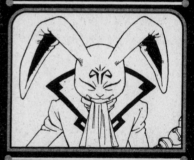

SHAGIE
The "world's busiest Vandel," he is in charge of evaluating and supervising all Vandels. He is the Chief of the Dark House of Sorcery.

"Vandels"... In this story, that's what we call evil creatures with magical powers. One day they appeared on the surface of the Earth, releasing monsters and destroying whole nations. People called this seemingly endless era "The Dark Age." Beet, a young boy who believes in justice, binds himself with a contract to become a Vandel Buster. Early in his career, Beet stumbles into a battle between the Zenon Warriors and a Vandel named Beltorze, where he suffers a fatal injury. He miraculously survives by receiving the Saiga of the Zenon Warriors.

Carrying on the Zenon Warriors' dream of peace, Beet sets out with his friends Poala and Kissu on a quest to destroy all Vandels. By combining their efforts, the three Beet Warriors succeed in defeating Grineed, a seven-star Vandel and lord of the Black Horizon. But Kissu's dark past as a servant of Grineed catches up to him. To atone for his crimes, the Beet Warriors agree to head for Gransista, home of the Buster headquarters, with Broad Buster Milfa. As they prepare to travel across an expanse of ocean, a five-star Vandel suddenly blocks their way...

Beet™ THE VANDEL BUSTER

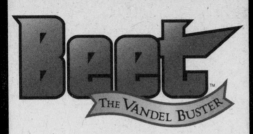

8

Chapter 27: Put the Ocean Devils to Rout!!

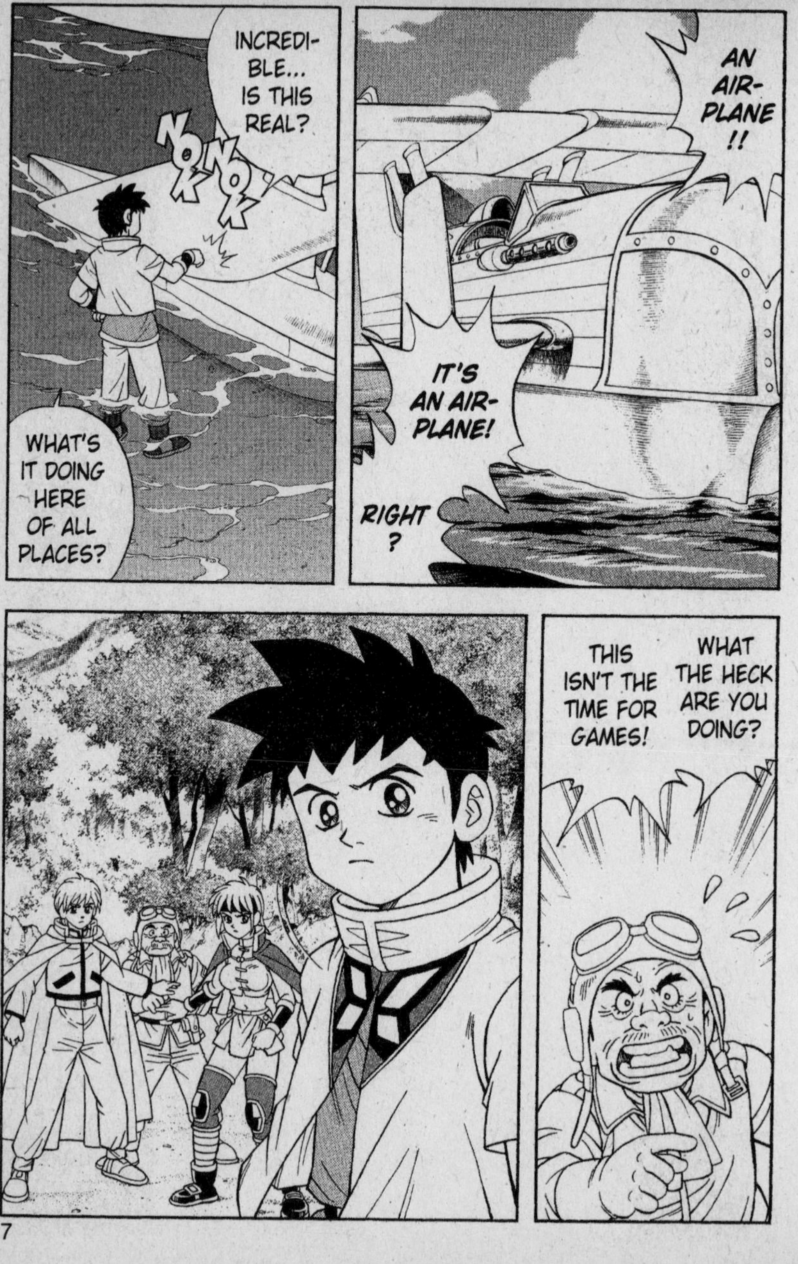
AN AIR-PLANE!!
IT'S AN AIR-PLANE!
RIGHT?
INCREDI-BLE... IS THIS REAL?
NOK NOK
WHAT'S IT DOING HERE OF ALL PLACES?
WHAT THE HECK ARE YOU DOING?
THIS ISN'T THE TIME FOR GAMES!

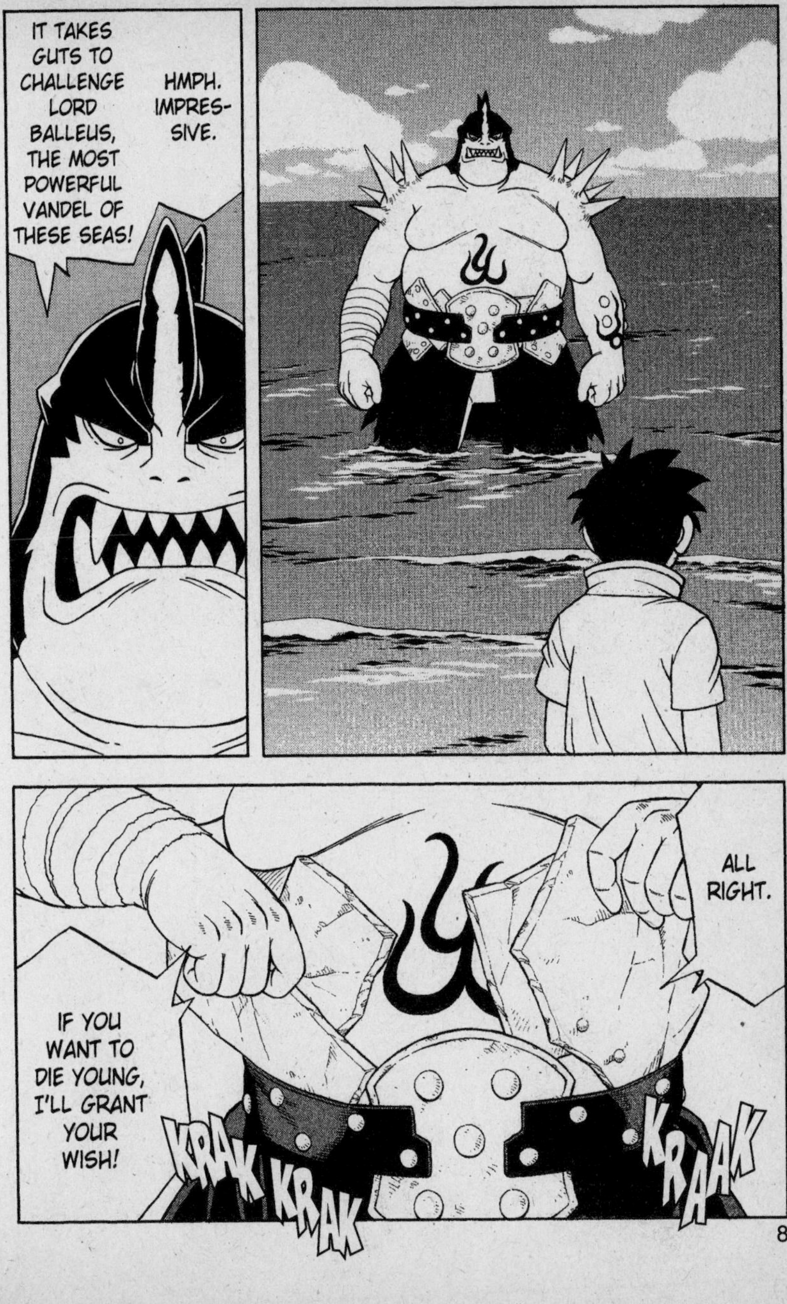
HMPH. IMPRES-SIVE.
IT TAKES GUTS TO CHALLENGE LORD BALLEUS, THE MOST POWERFUL VANDEL OF THESE SEAS!
ALL RIGHT.
KRAAK
IF YOU WANT TO DIE YOUNG, I'LL GRANT YOUR WISH!
KRAK KRAK
KRAK

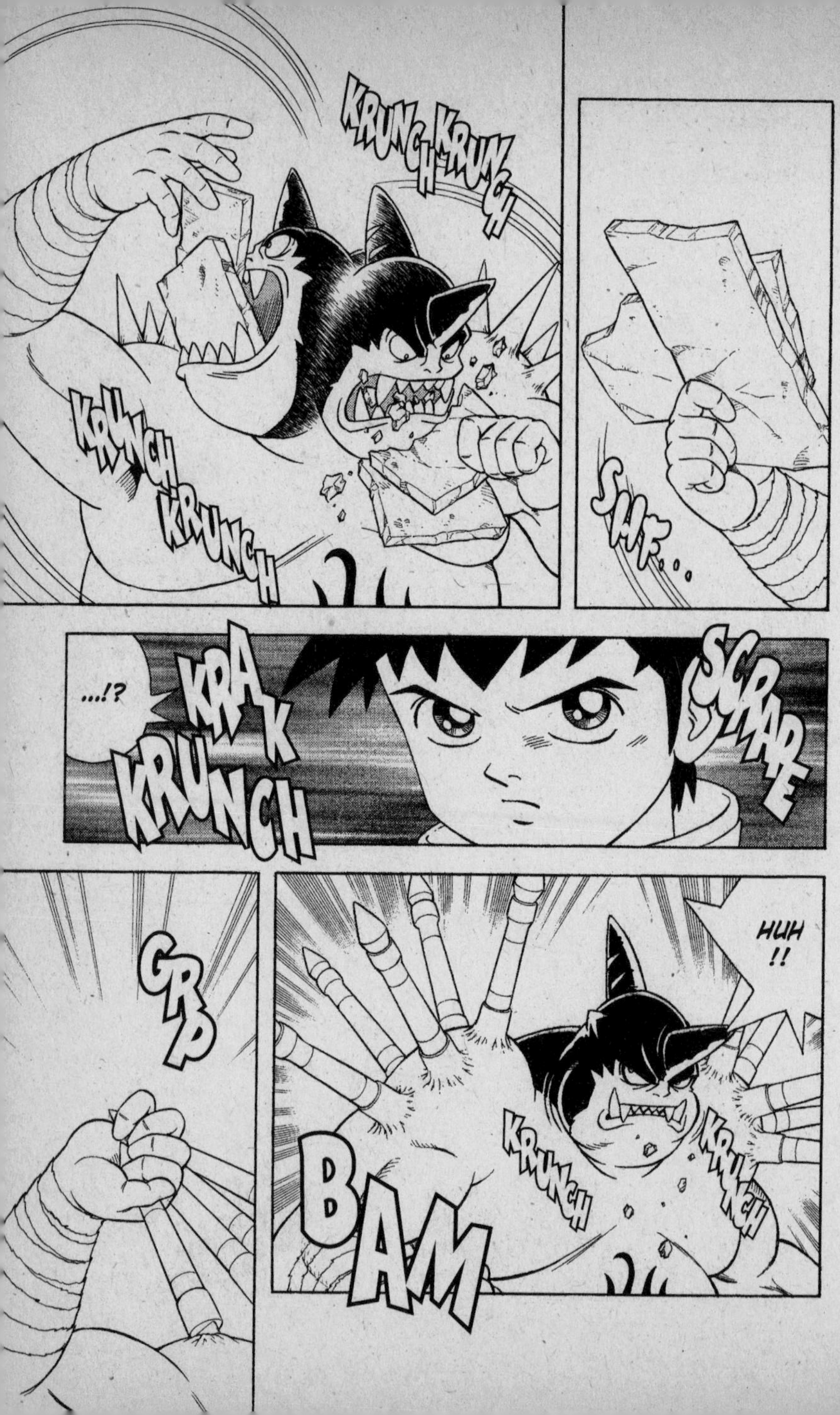
SWF...
KRUNCH KRUNCH
KRUNCH KRUNCH
SCRAPE
KRAK
...!?
KRUNCH
HUH !!
KRUNCH
KRUNCH
BAM
GRP

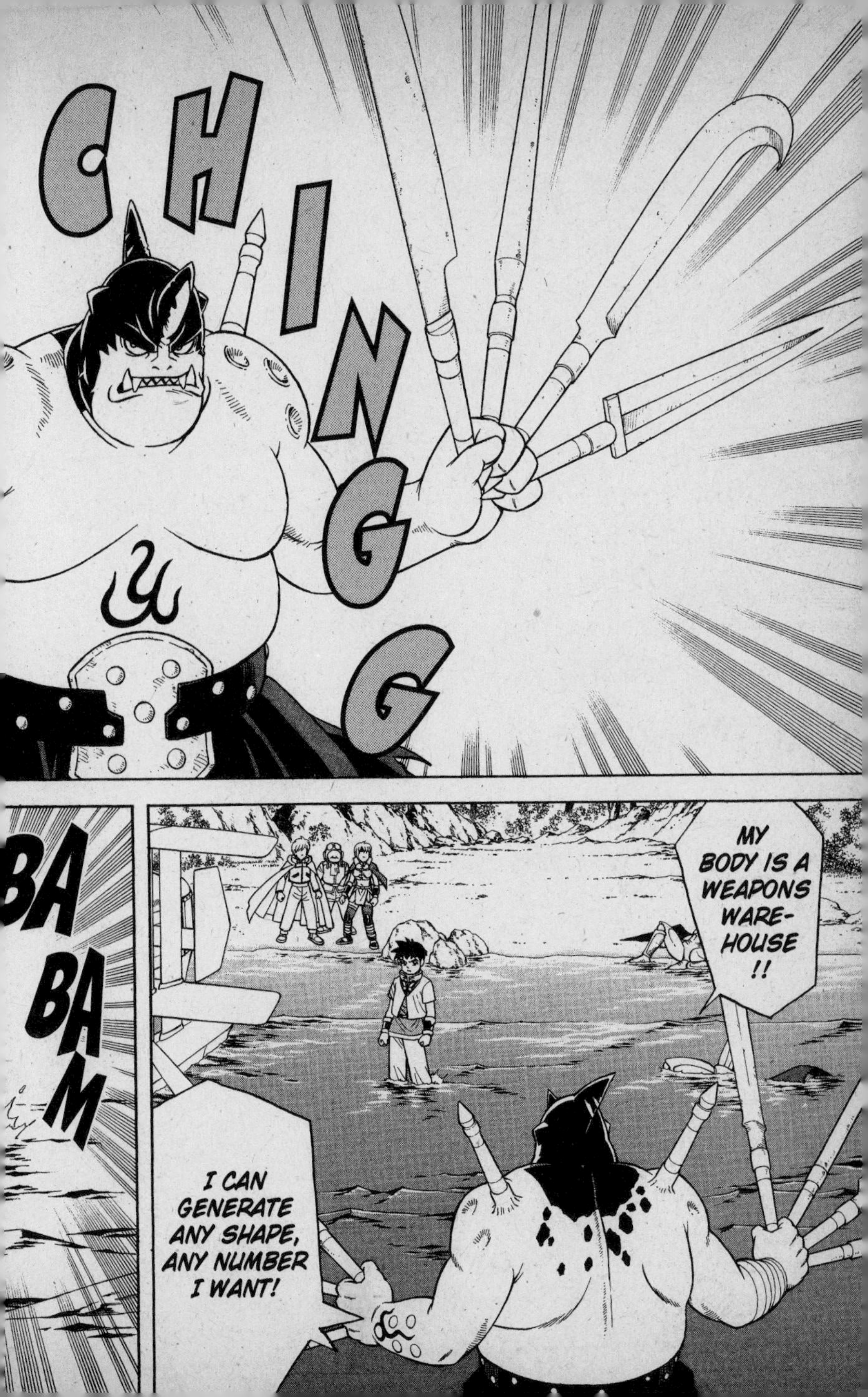
CHING
MY BODY IS A WEAPONS WARE-HOUSE !!
I CAN GENERATE ANY SHAPE, ANY NUMBER I WANT!
BA BA BAM

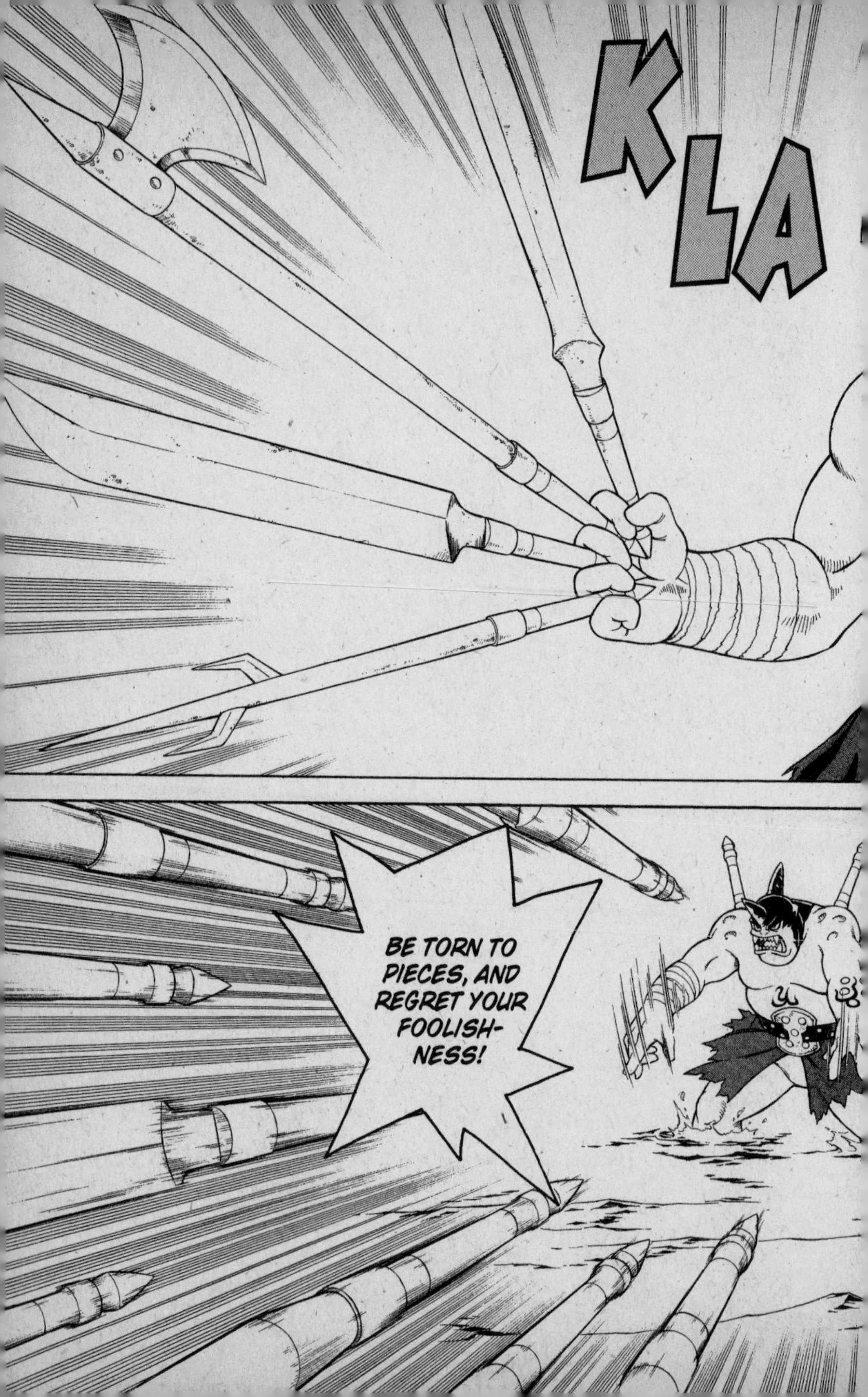
KLA
BE TORN TO PIECES, AND REGRET YOUR FOOLISH-NESS!

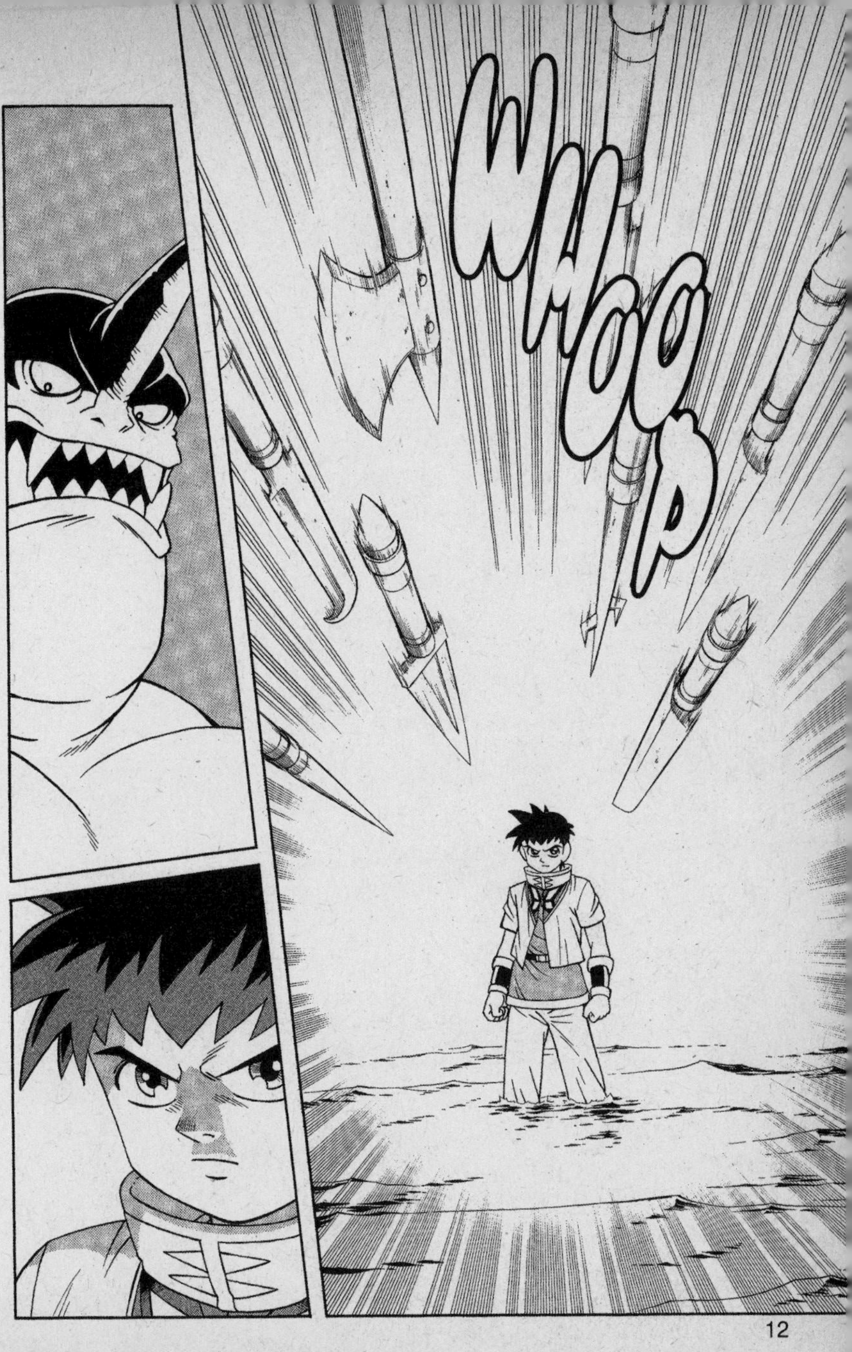
WHOOOP

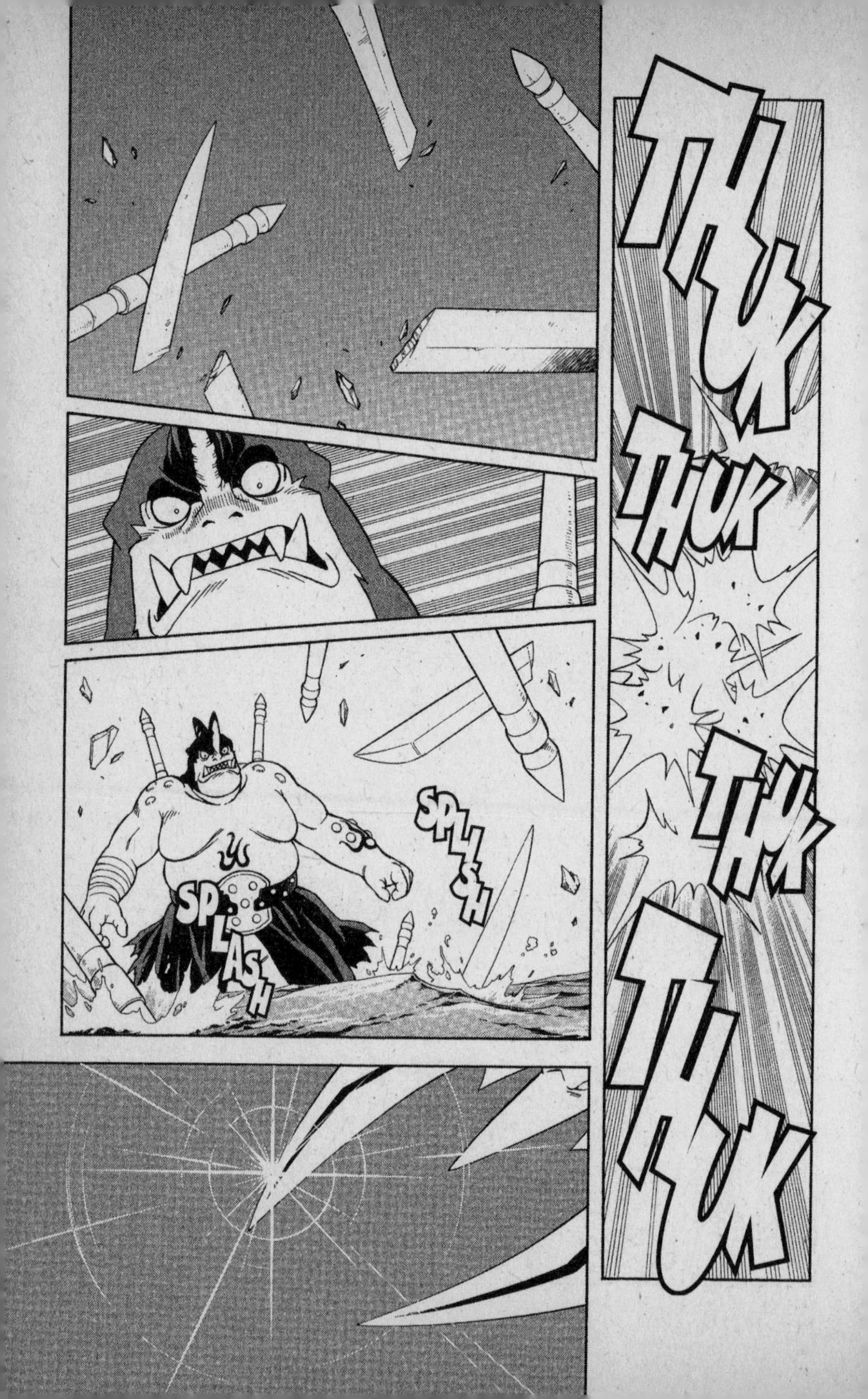
THUK
THUK
THUK
THUK
SPLASH
SPLASH

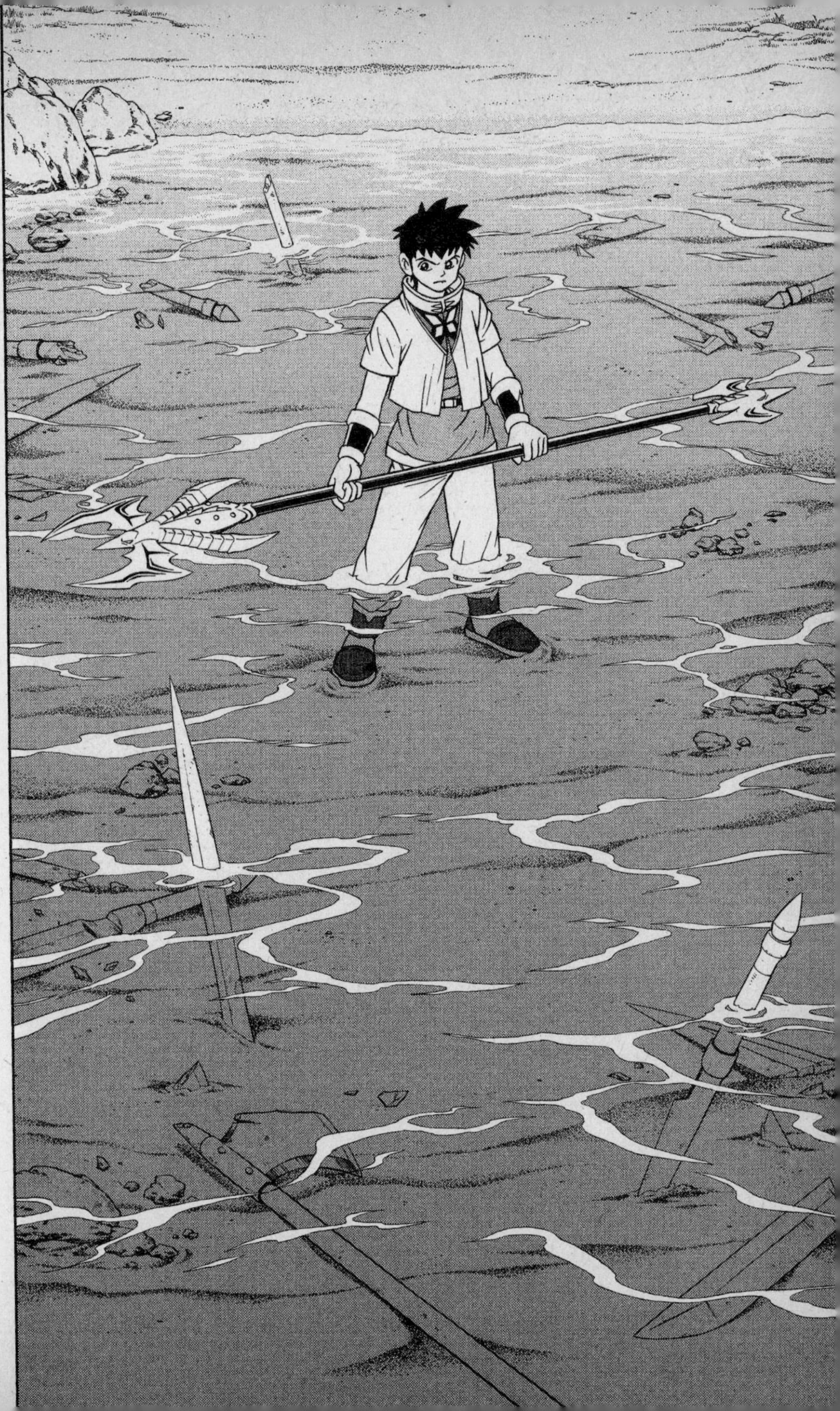

READ THIS WAY

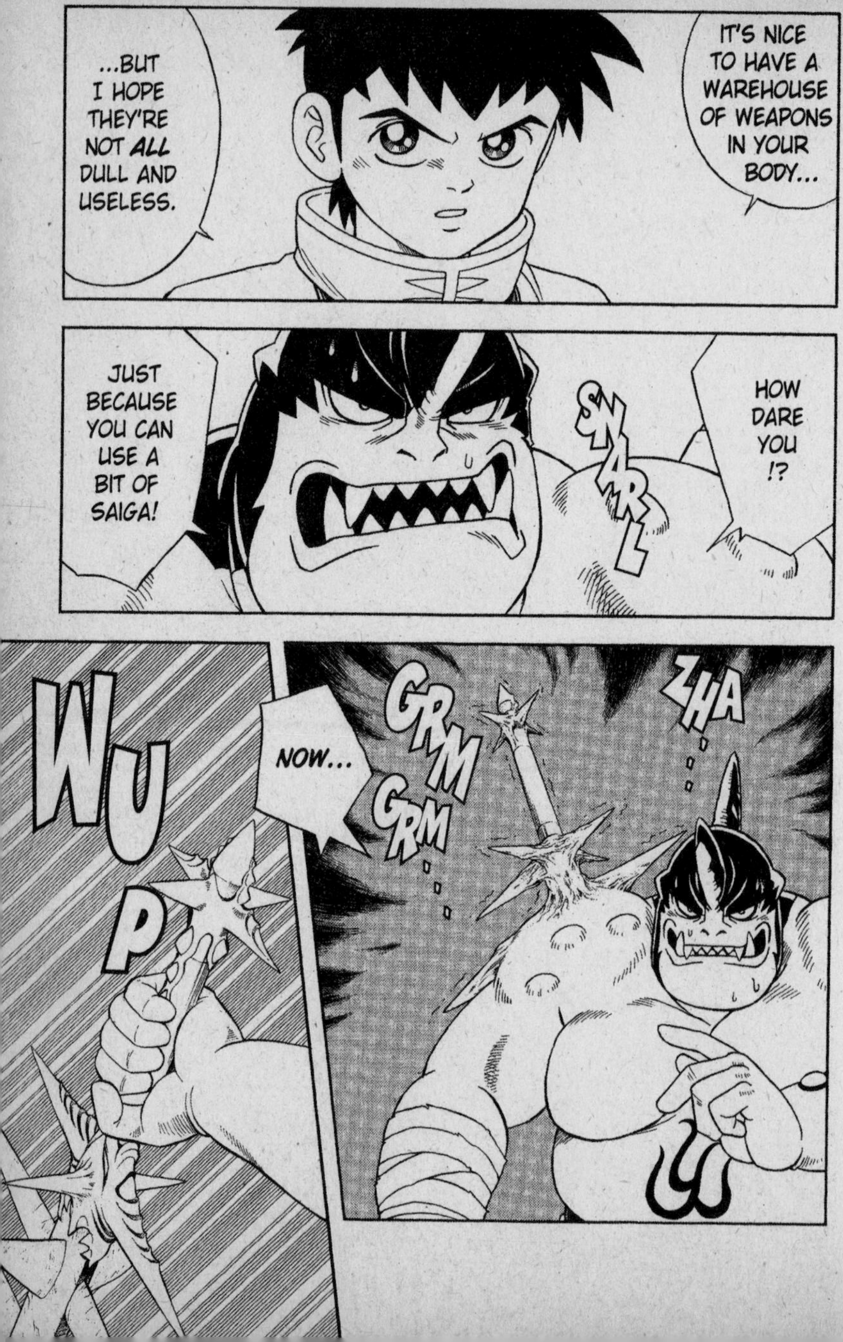
IT'S NICE TO HAVE A WAREHOUSE OF WEAPONS IN YOUR BODY...
...BUT I HOPE THEY'RE NOT ALL DULL AND USELESS.
HOW DARE YOU !?
SNARL
JUST BECAUSE YOU CAN USE A BIT OF SAIGA!
ZHA
GRM GRM
NOW...
WUP

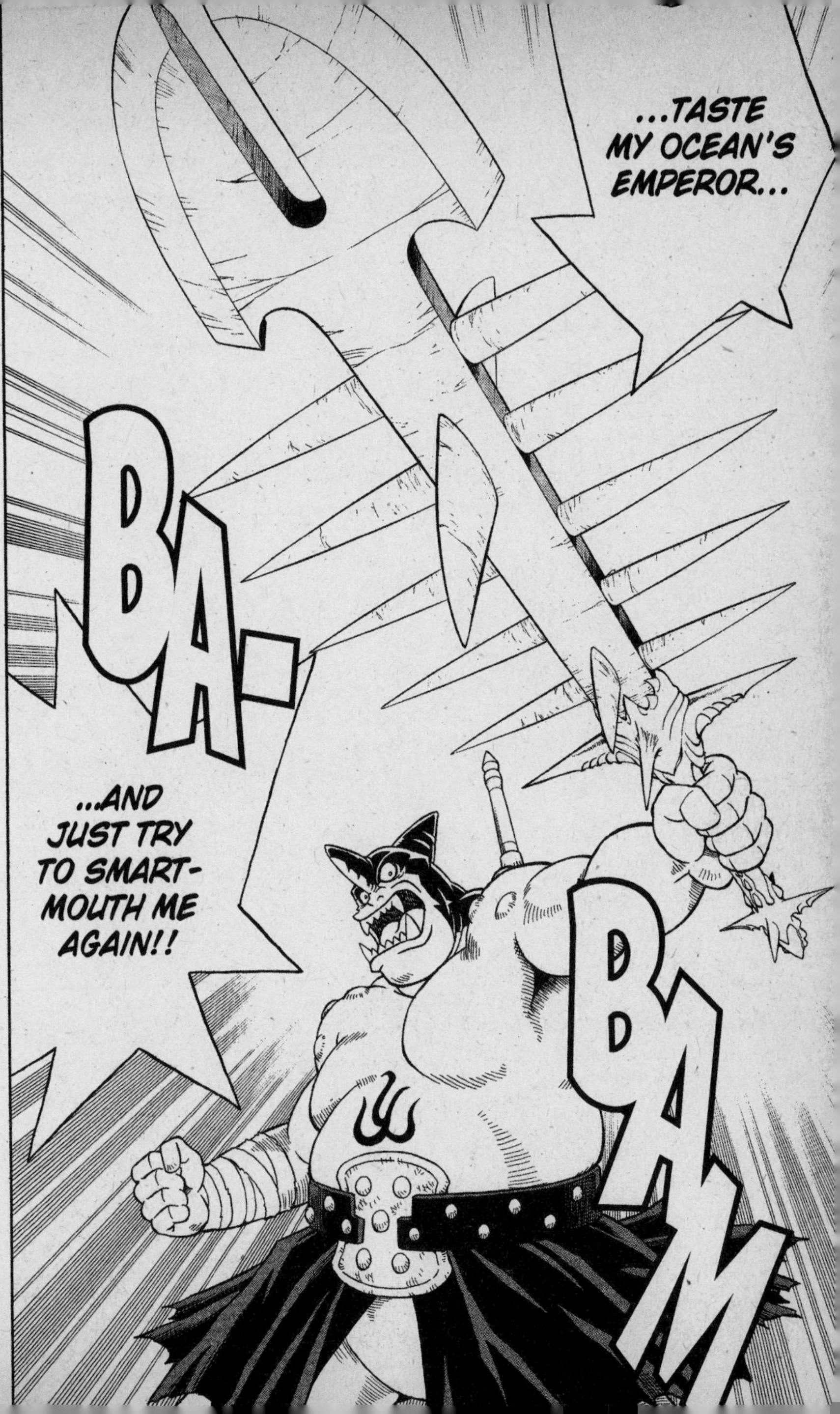
...TASTE MY OCEAN'S EMPEROR...
BA-
...AND JUST TRY TO SMART-MOUTH ME AGAIN!!
BAM

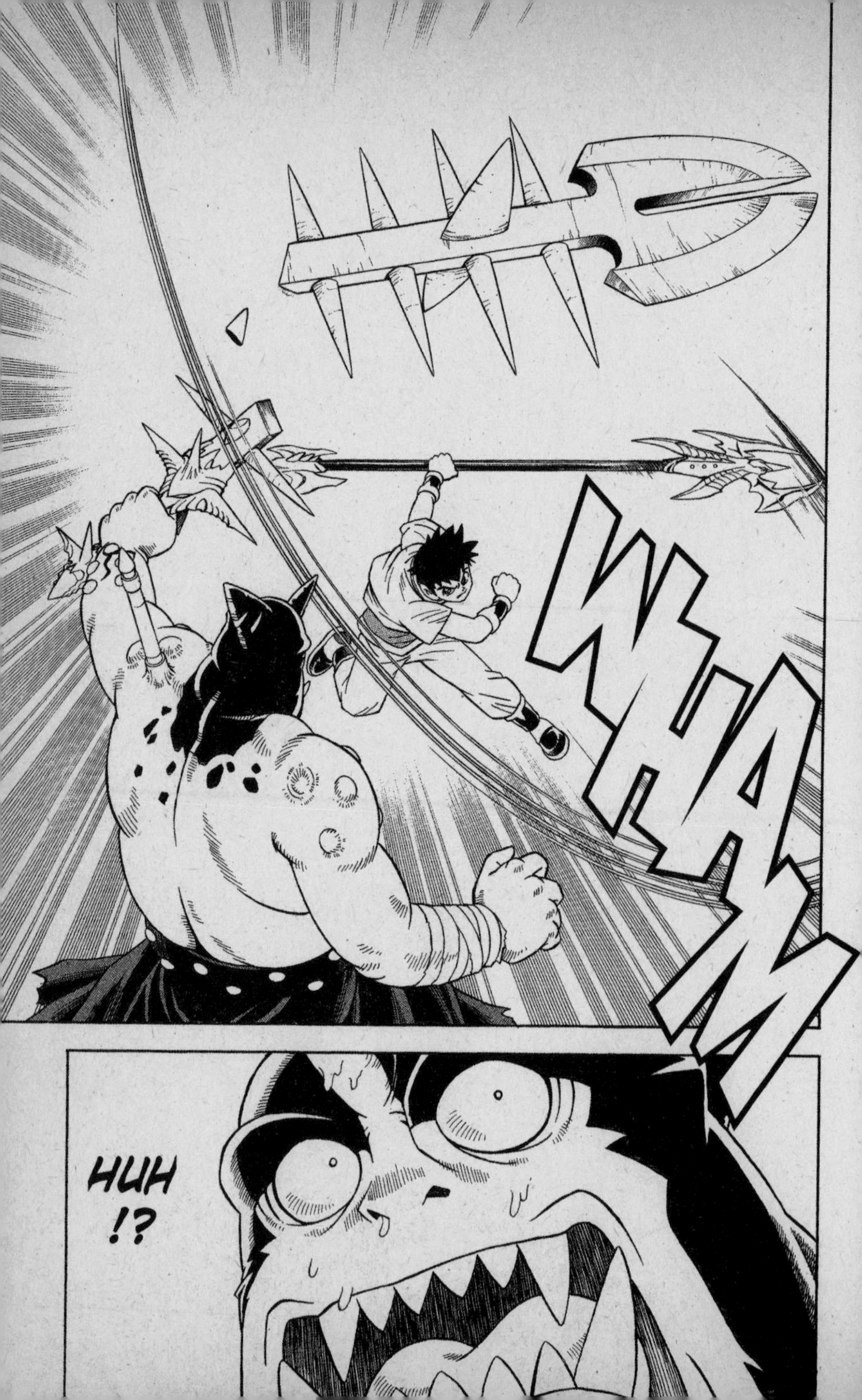
WHAM
HUH
!?

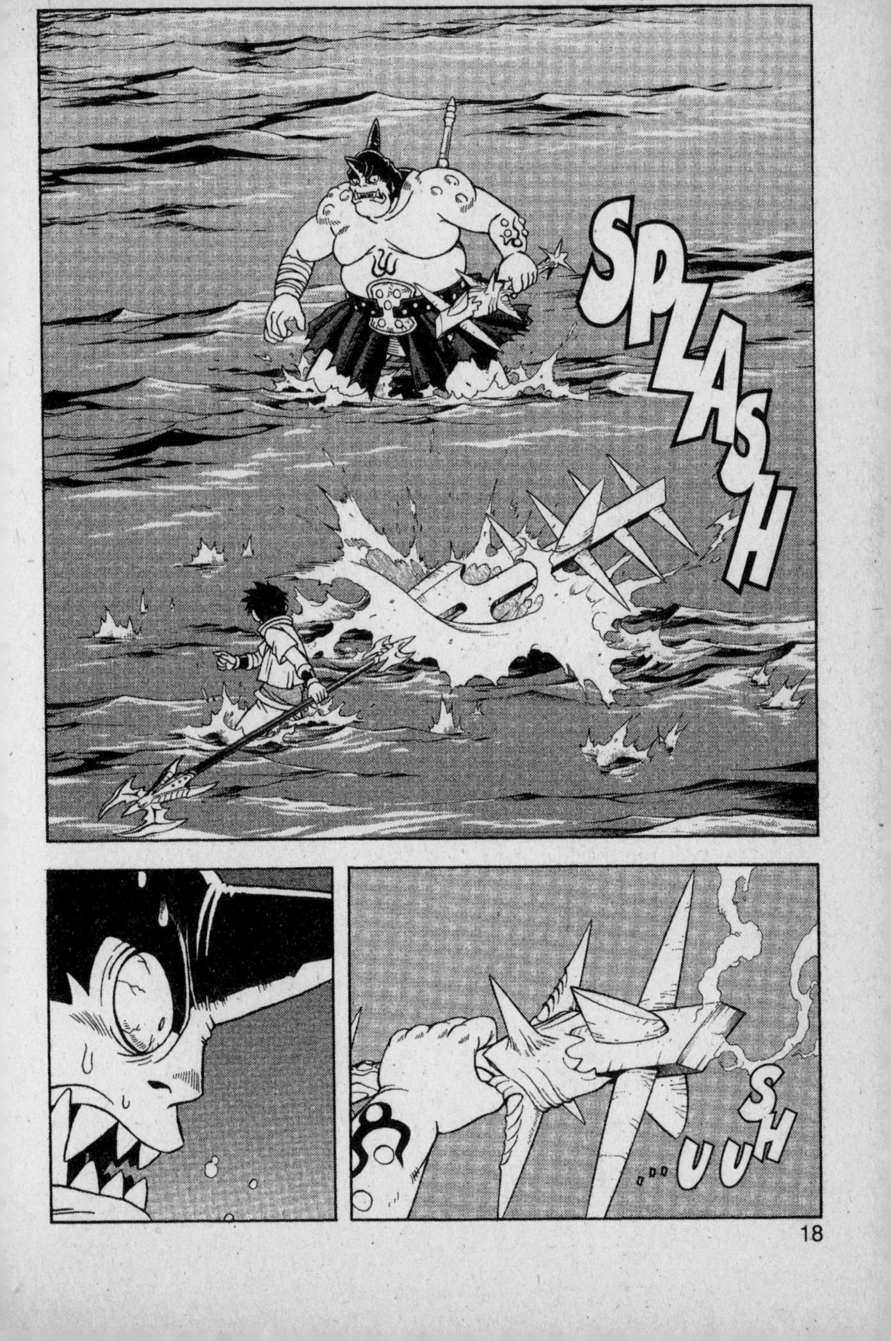
SPLASH
SHUU...

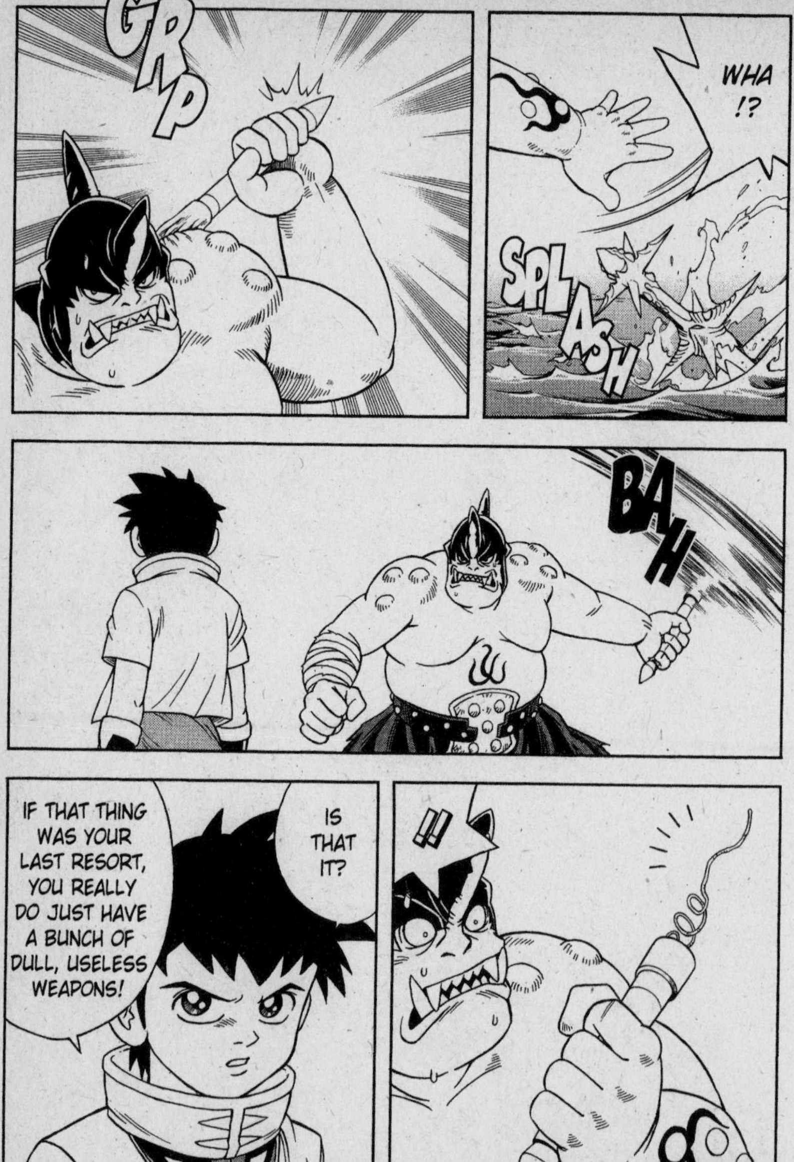
WHA !?
SPLASH
GRP
BAH
!!
IS THAT IT?
IF THAT THING WAS YOUR LAST RESORT, YOU REALLY DO JUST HAVE A BUNCH OF DULL, USELESS WEAPONS!

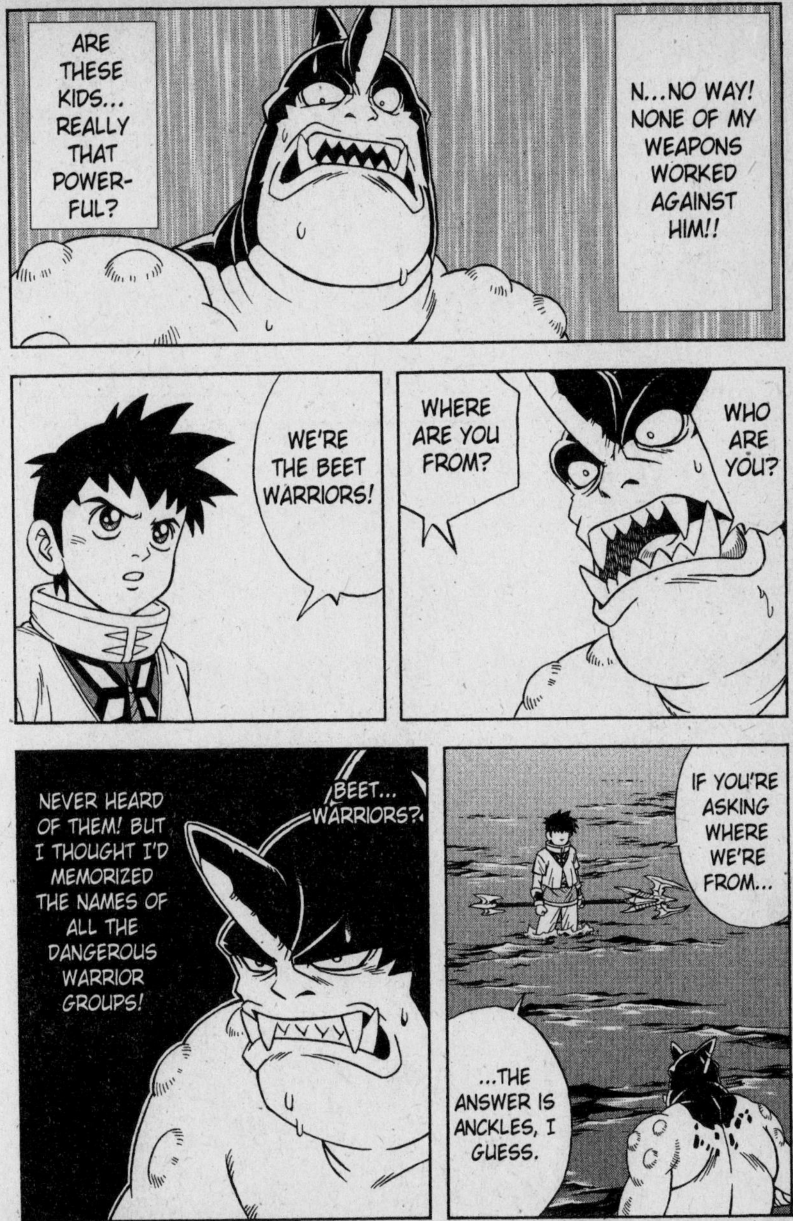
N...NO WAY! NONE OF MY WEAPONS WORKED AGAINST HIM!!
ARE THESE KIDS... REALLY THAT POWER-FUL?
WHO ARE YOU?
WHERE ARE YOU FROM?
WE'RE THE BEET WARRIORS!
IF YOU'RE ASKING WHERE WE'RE FROM...
...THE ANSWER IS ANCKLES, I GUESS.
BEET... WARRIORS?
NEVER HEARD OF THEM! BUT I THOUGHT I'D MEMORIZED THE NAMES OF ALL THE DANGEROUS WARRIOR GROUPS!

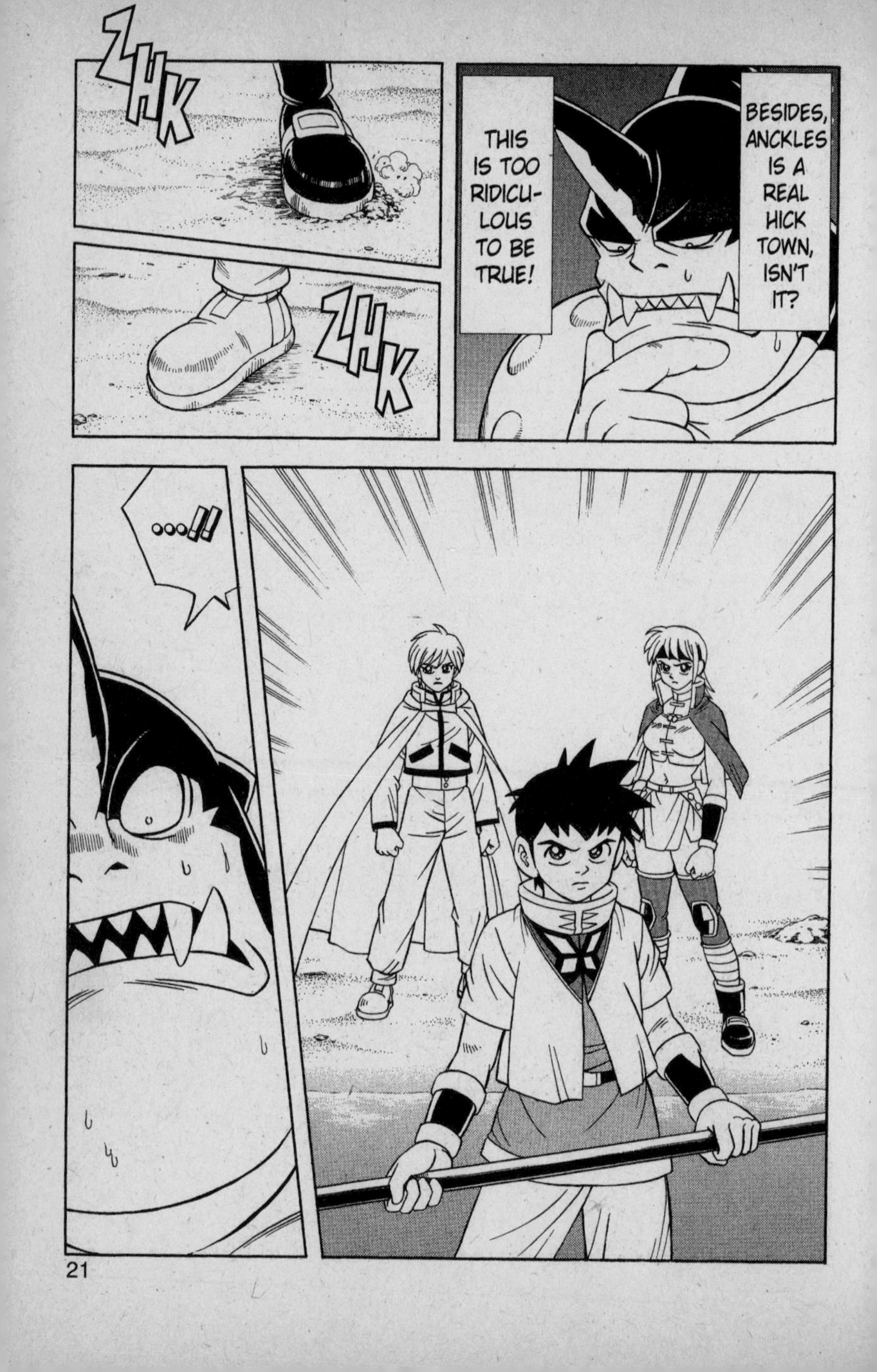
BESIDES, ANCKLES IS A REAL HICK TOWN, ISN'T IT?
THIS IS TOO RIDICU-LOUS TO BE TRUE!
ZHK
ZHK
...!!

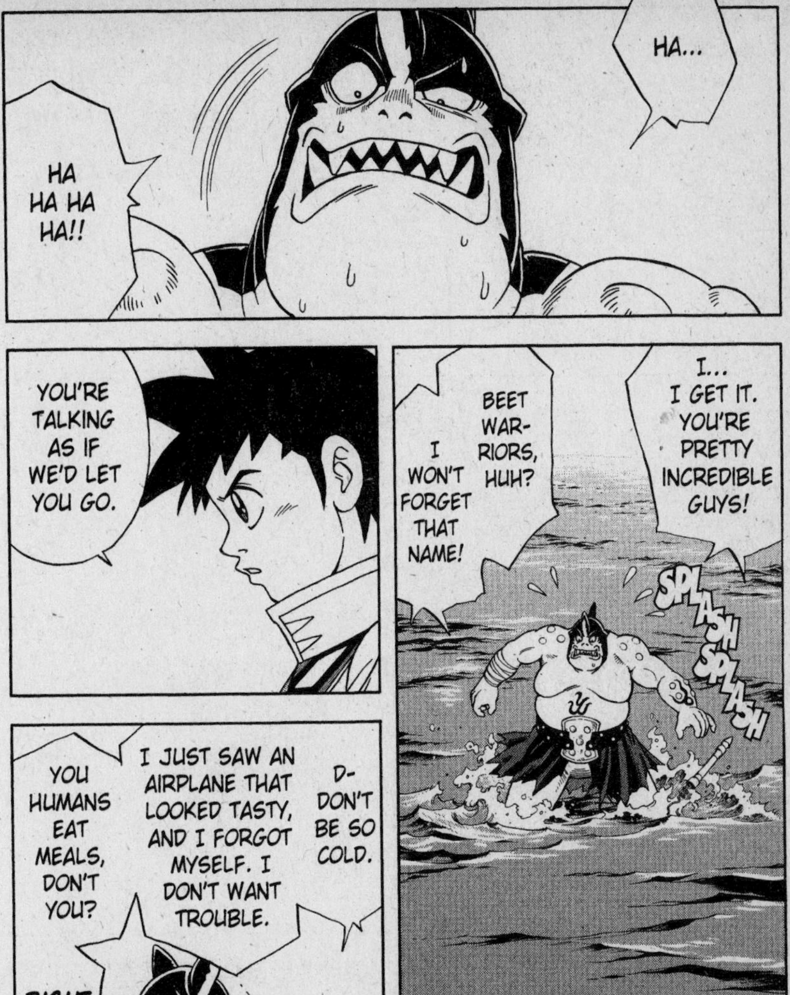
HA...
HA HA HA HA!!
I... I GET IT. YOU'RE PRETTY INCREDIBLE GUYS!
BEET WAR-RIORS, HUH?
I WON'T FORGET THAT NAME!
SPLASH SPLASH
YOU'RE TALKING AS IF WE'D LET YOU GO.
D- DON'T BE SO COLD.
I JUST SAW AN AIRPLANE THAT LOOKED TASTY, AND I FORGOT MYSELF. I DON'T WANT TROUBLE.
YOU HUMANS EAT MEALS, DON'T YOU?
RIGHT !?

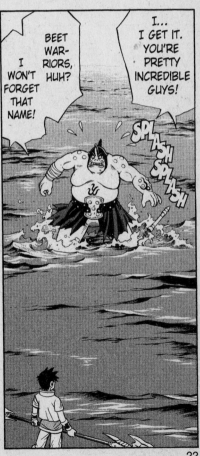

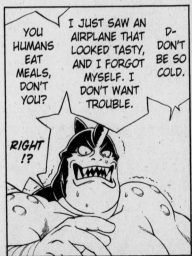

READ THIS WAY

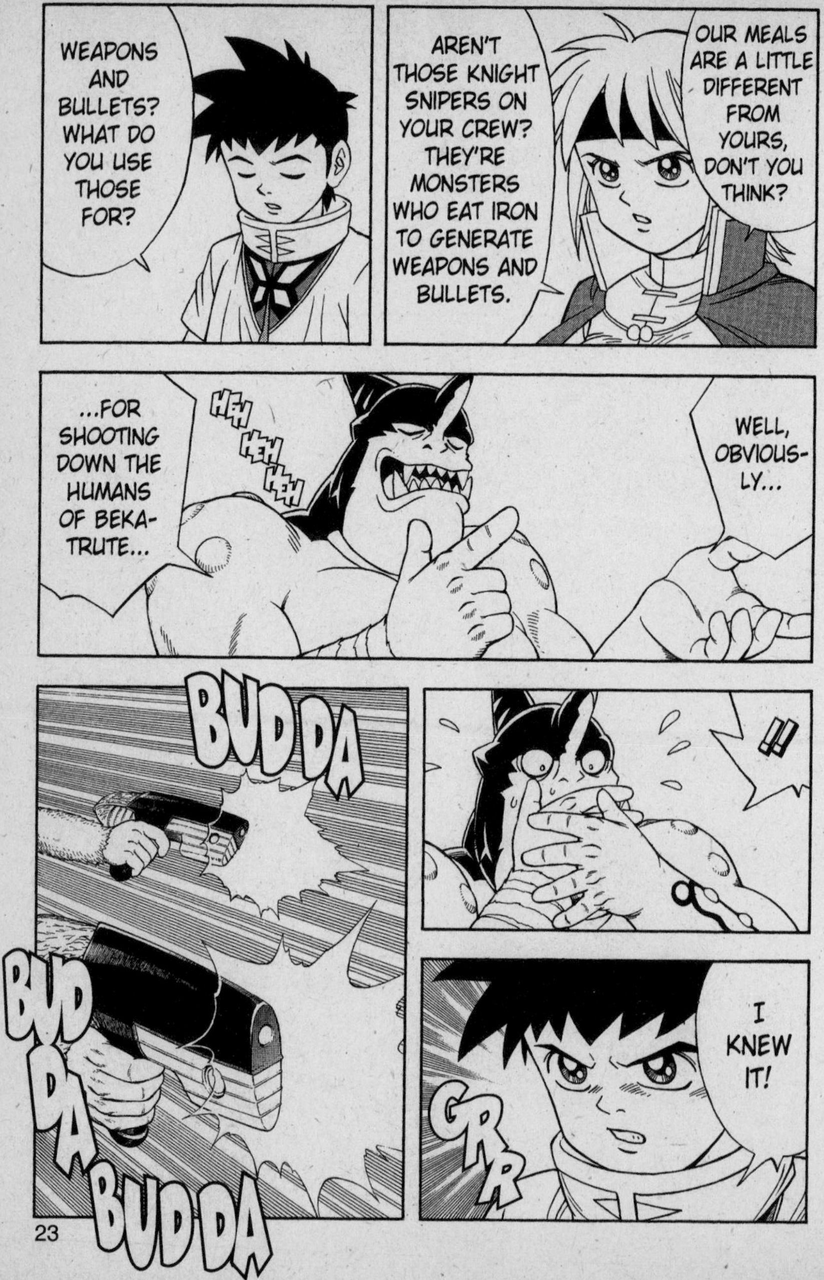
OUR MEALS ARE A LITTLE DIFFERENT FROM YOURS, DON'T YOU THINK?
AREN'T THOSE KNIGHT SNIPERS ON YOUR CREW? THEY'RE MONSTERS WHO EAT IRON TO GENERATE WEAPONS AND BULLETS.
WEAPONS AND BULLETS? WHAT DO YOU USE THOSE FOR?
WELL, OBVIOUSLY...
HEH HEH HEH
...FOR SHOOTING DOWN THE HUMANS OF BEKA-TRUTE...
!!
I KNEW IT!
GRR
BUD DA
BUD DA BUD DA

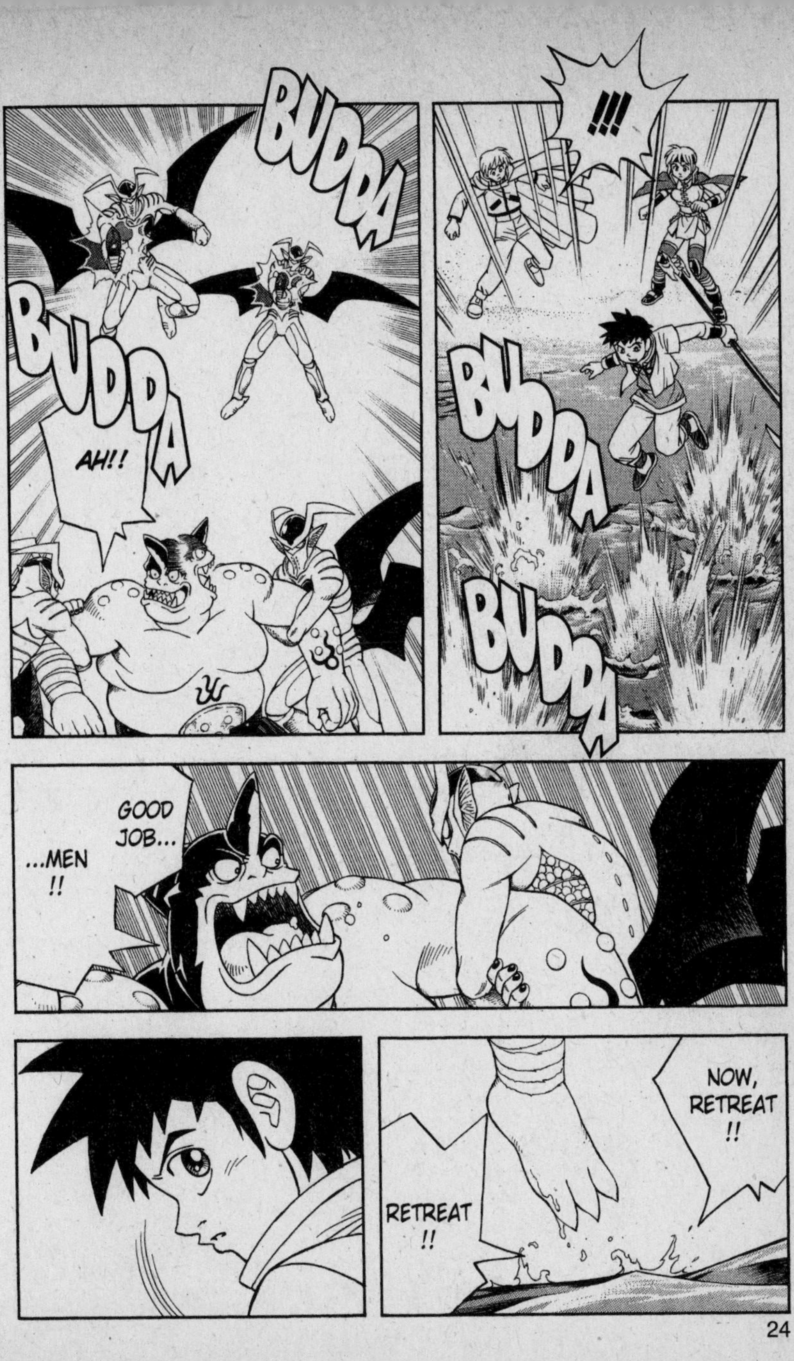
!!!
BUDDA
BUDDA
BUDDA
BUDDA
AH!!
GOOD JOB...
...MEN !!
NOW, RETREAT !!
RETREAT !!

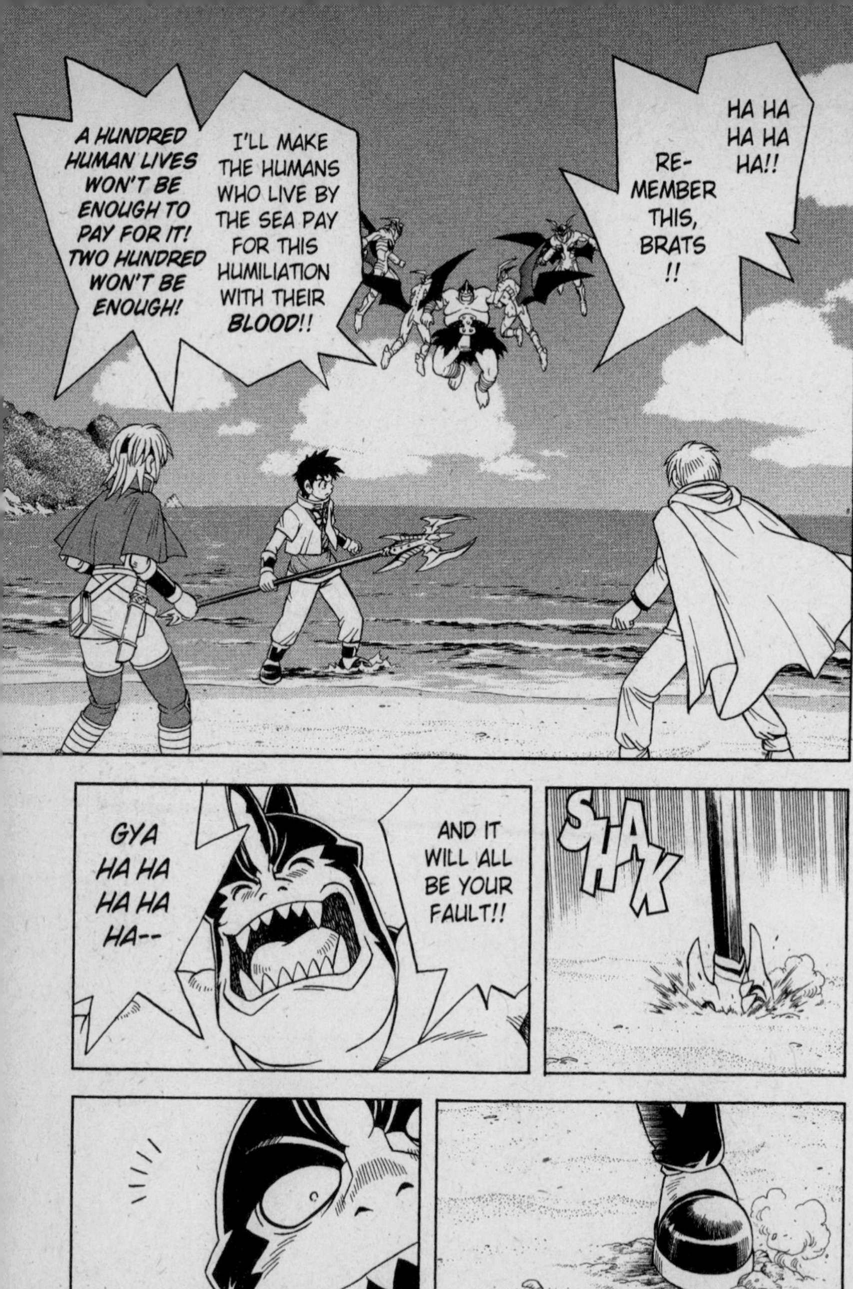
RE-MEMBER THIS, BRATS!!
HA HA HA HA HA!!
I'LL MAKE THE HUMANS WHO LIVE BY THE SEA PAY FOR THIS HUMILIATION WITH THEIR BLOOD!!
A HUNDRED HUMAN LIVES WON'T BE ENOUGH TO PAY FOR IT! TWO HUNDRED WON'T BE ENOUGH!
SHAK
AND IT WILL ALL BE YOUR FAULT!!
GYA HA HA HA HA HA--

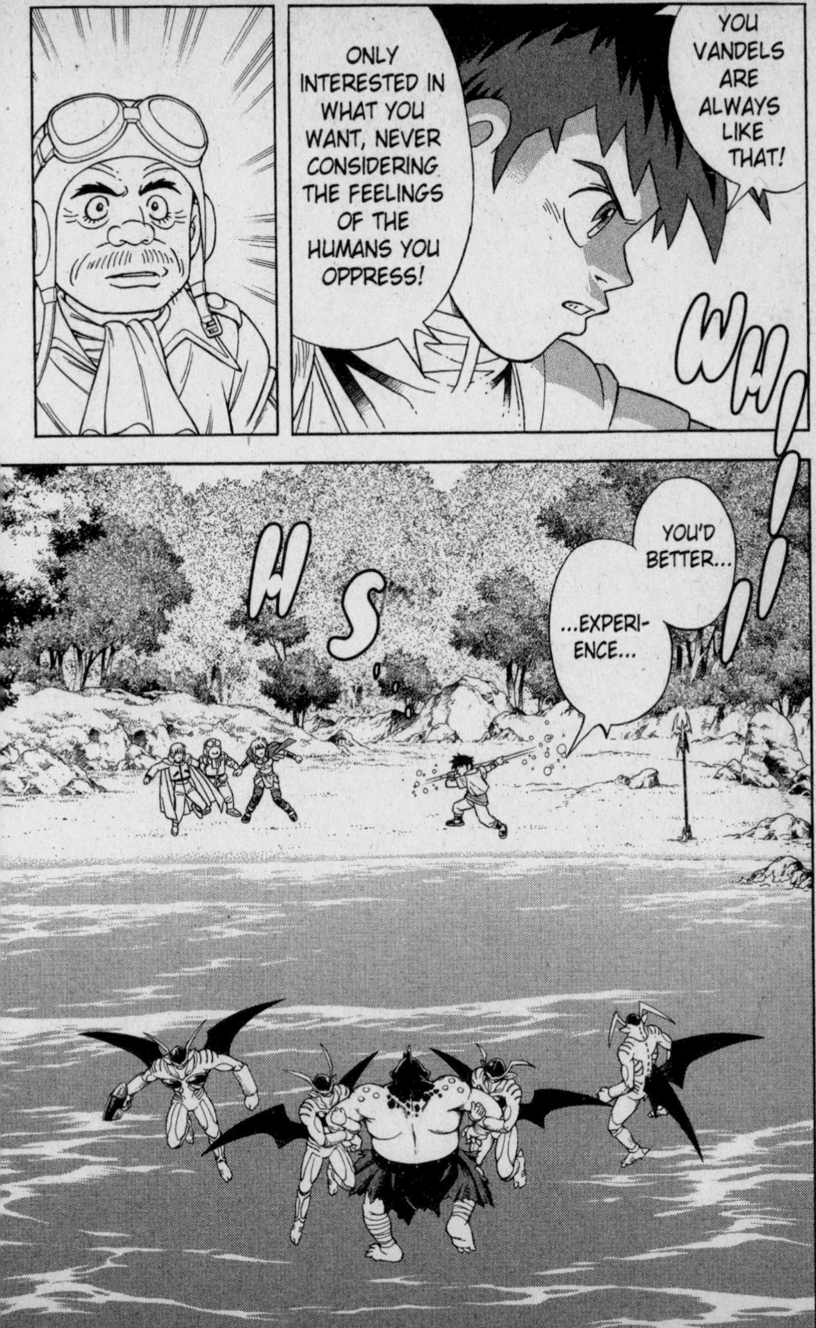
YOU VANDELS ARE ALWAYS LIKE THAT!
ONLY INTERESTED IN WHAT YOU WANT, NEVER CONSIDERING THE FEELINGS OF THE HUMANS YOU OPPRESS!
WHI
YOU'D BETTER...
...EXPERIENCE...
HS

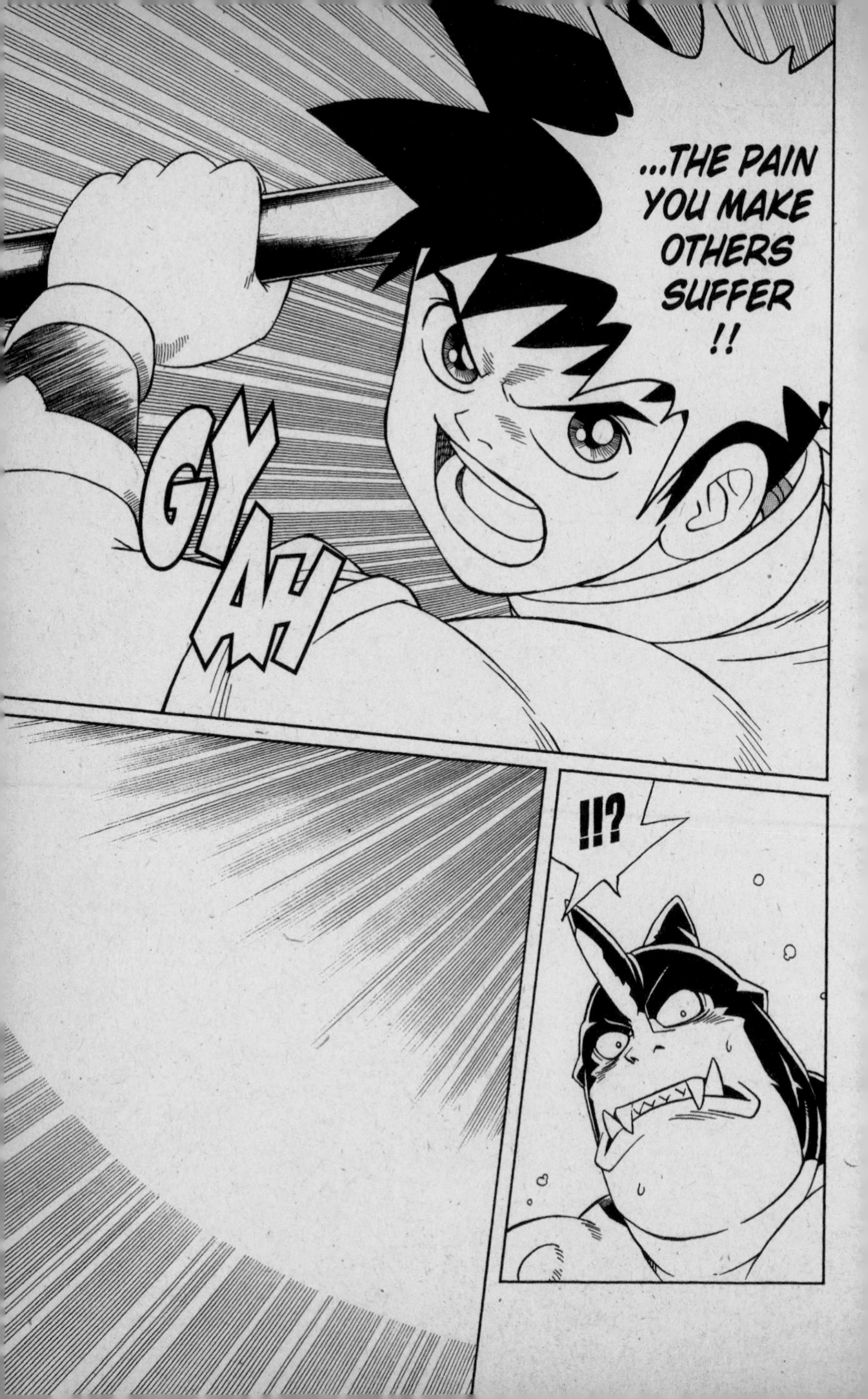
...THE PAIN YOU MAKE OTHERS SUFFER !!
GYAAH
!!?

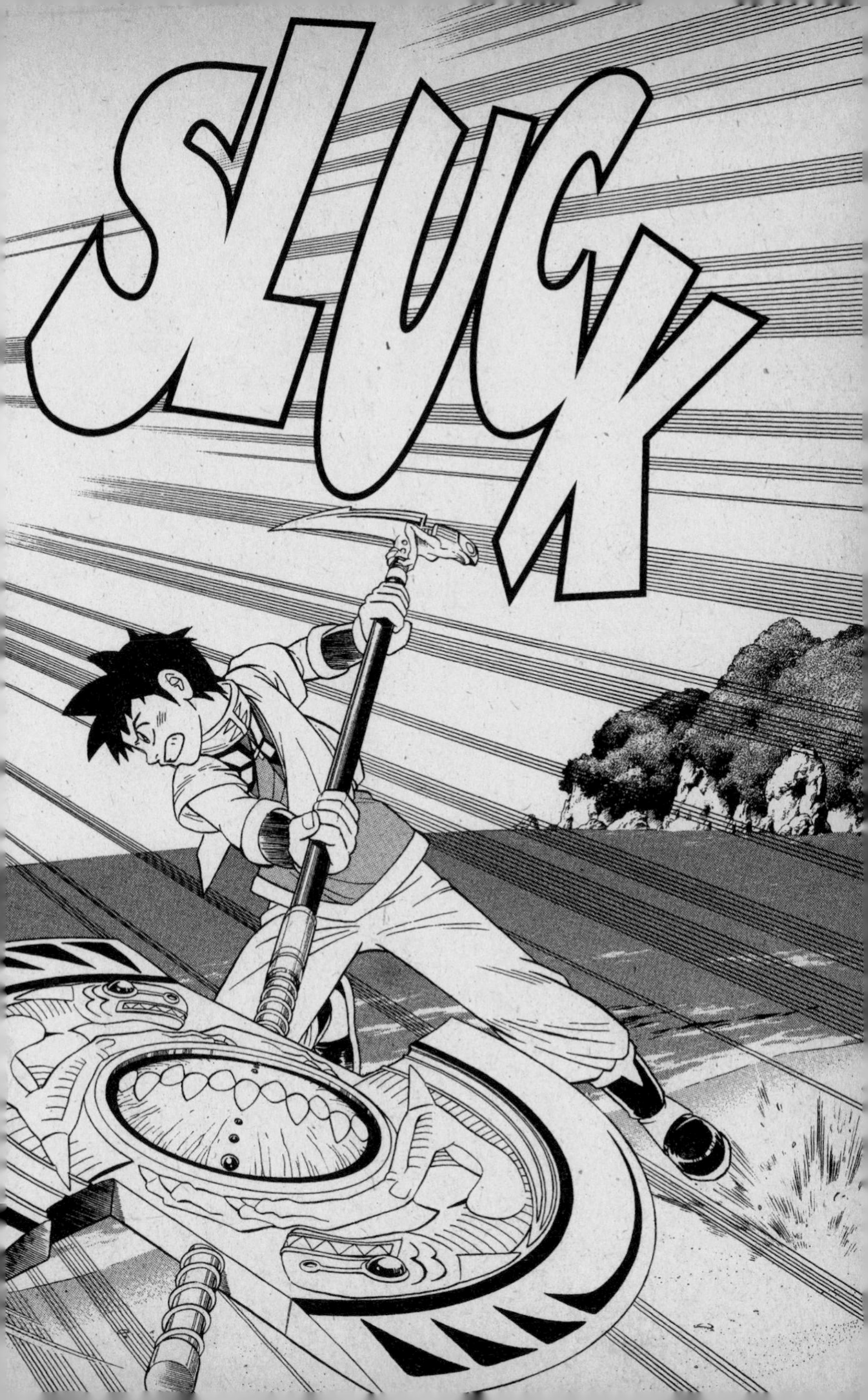
SLUG

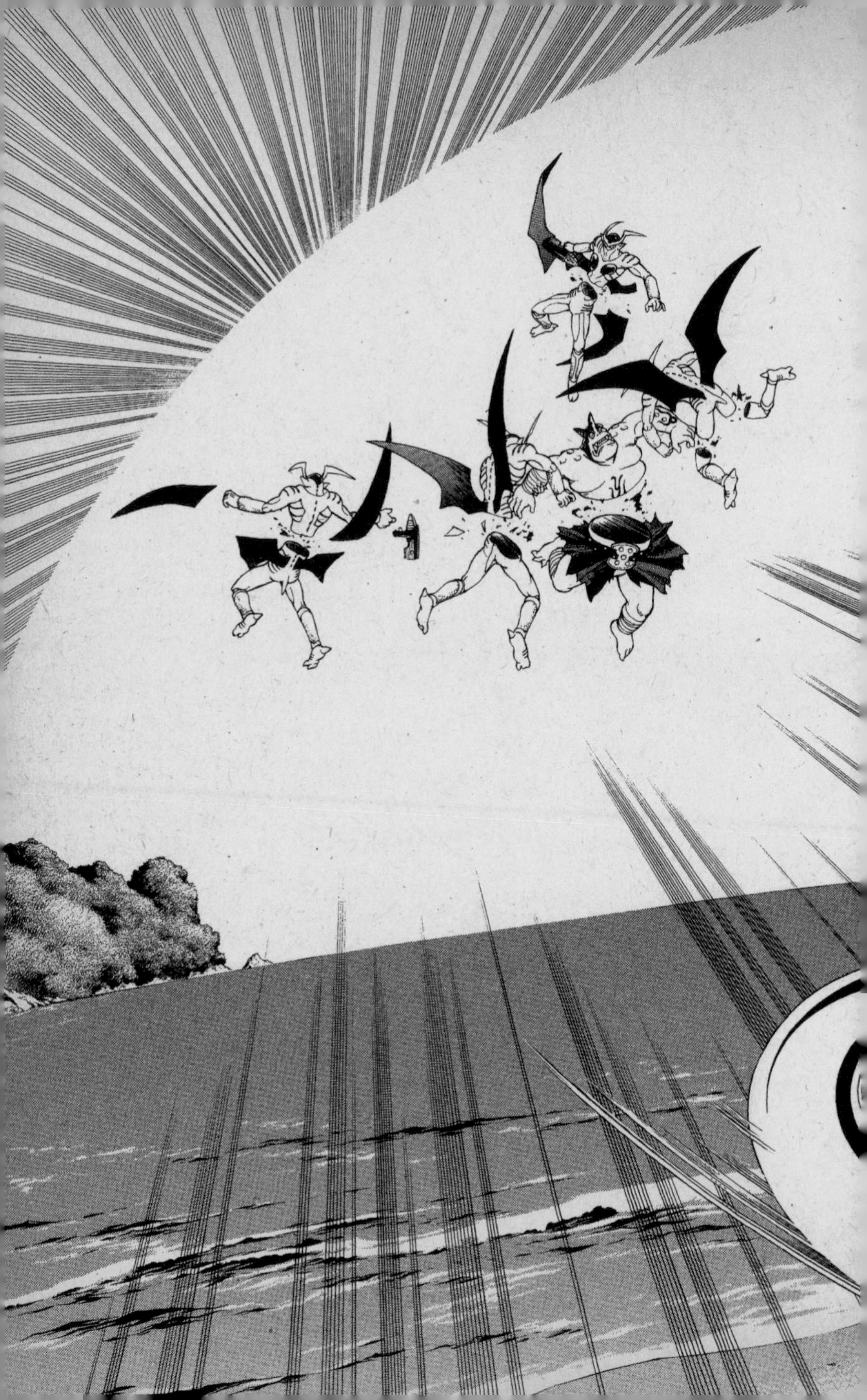

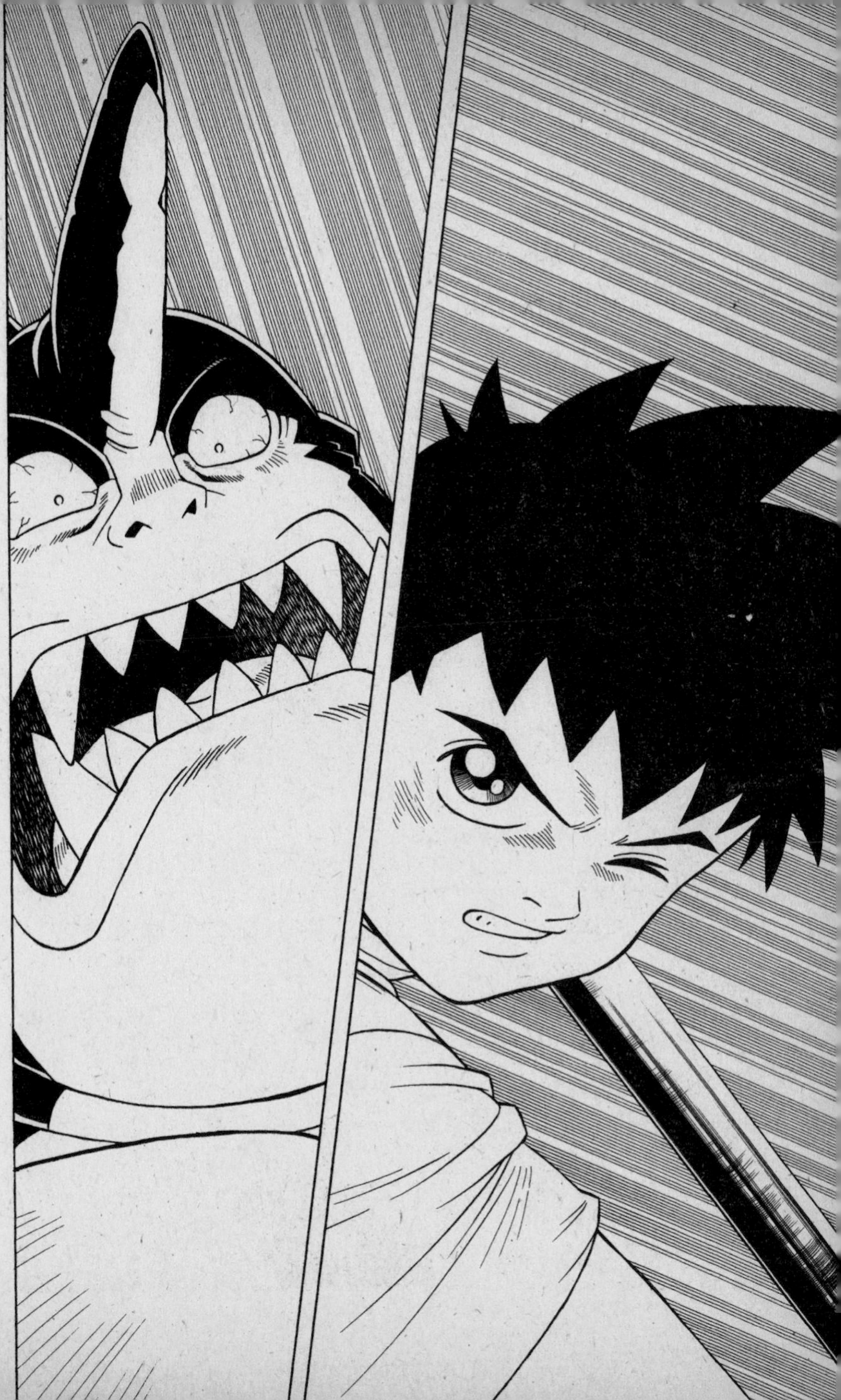

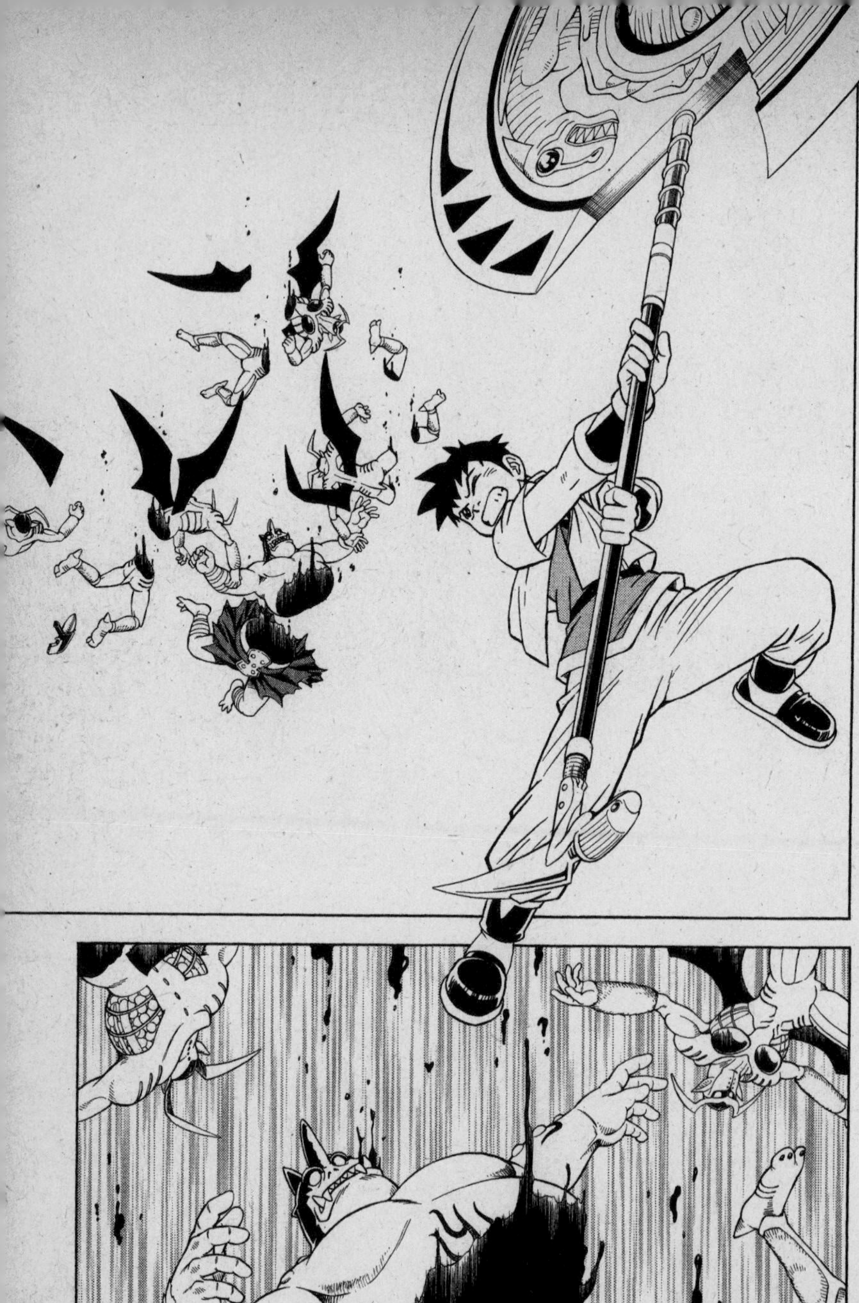

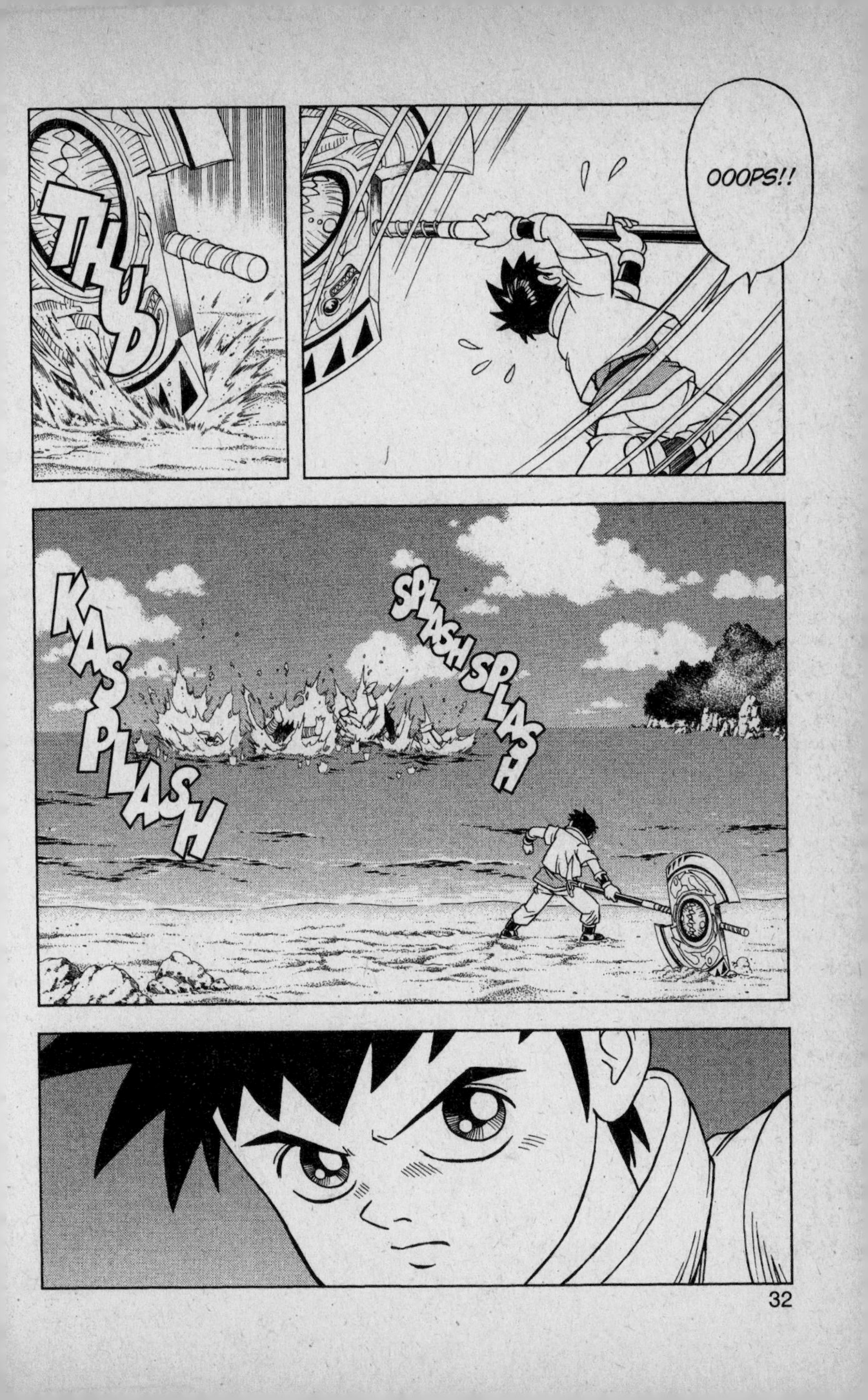
OOOPS!!
THUD
SPLASH SPLASH
KASPLASH

READ THIS WAY

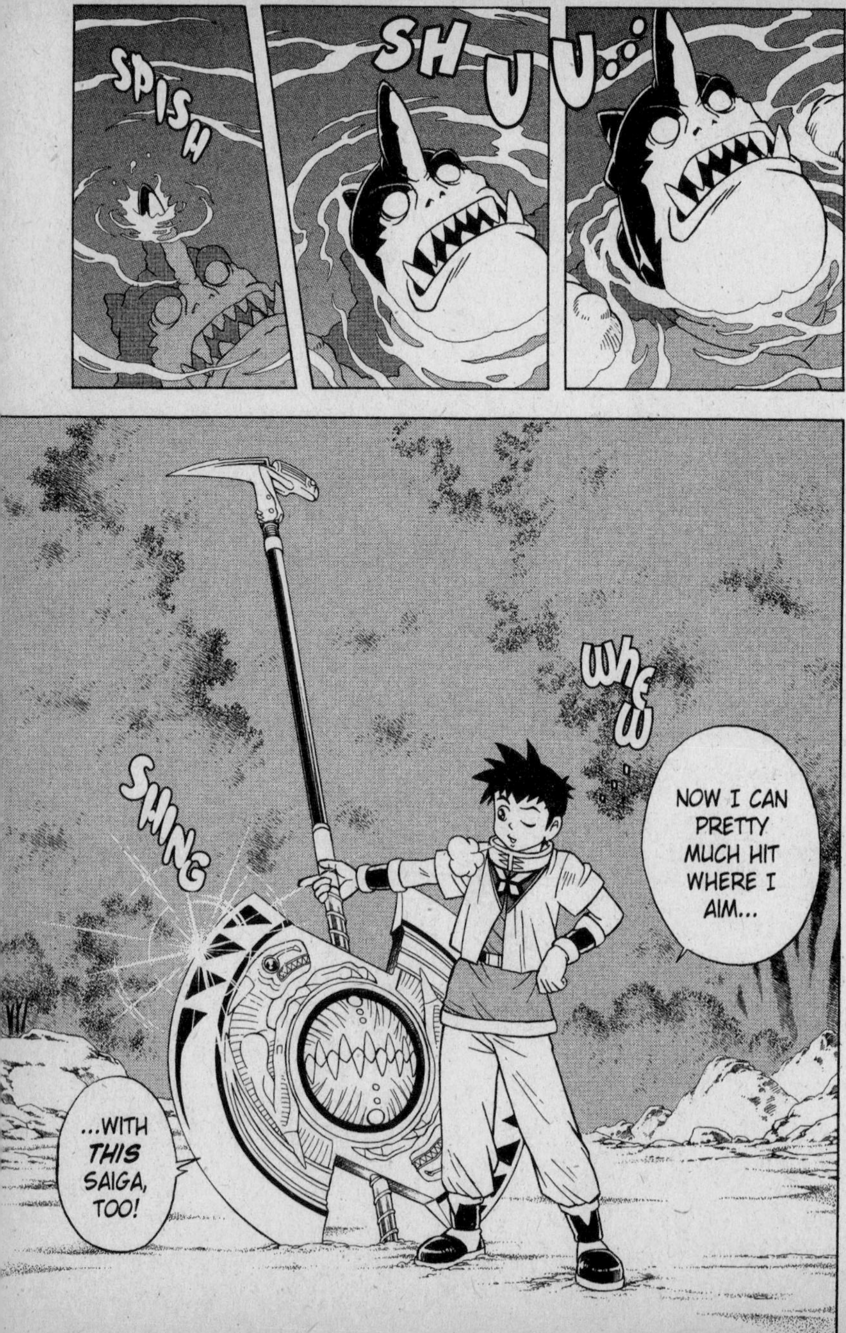
SHUUU
SPISH
WHEW
NOW I CAN PRETTY MUCH HIT WHERE I AIM...
SHING
...WITH *THIS* SAIGA, TOO!

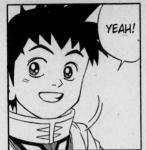

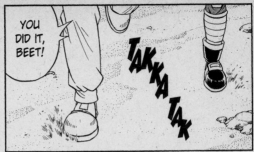

YOU DID IT, BEET!
TAKKA TAK
YEAH!
THUP
FOR A FIVE-STAR VANDEL, HE WAS FAIRLY EASY TO BEAT, WASN'T HE?
AFTER BATTLING GRINEED ... IT MUST MEAN WE'RE GETTING STRONGER OURSELVES. RIGHT?
YOU COULD BE RIGHT!
HA HA

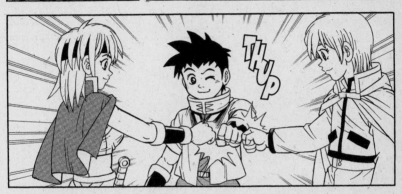

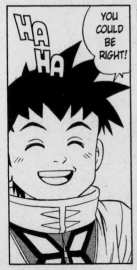

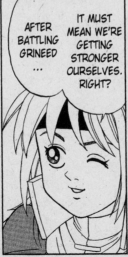

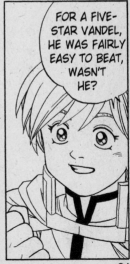

READ THIS WAY

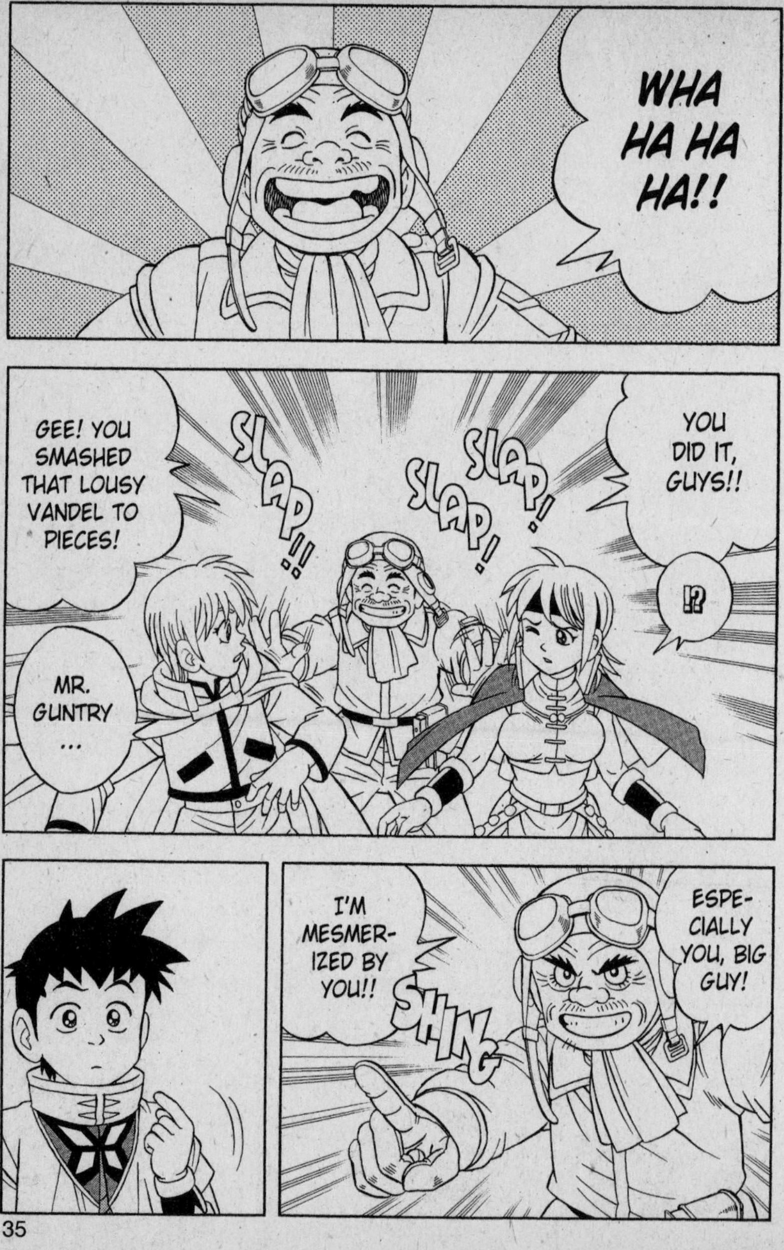
WHA HA HA HA!!
YOU DID IT, GUYS!!
SLAP!
SLAP!
SLAP!!!
GEE! YOU SMASHED THAT LOUSY VANDEL TO PIECES!
!?
MR. GUNTRY ...
ESPE-CIALLY YOU, BIG GUY!
SHING
I'M MESMER-IZED BY YOU!!

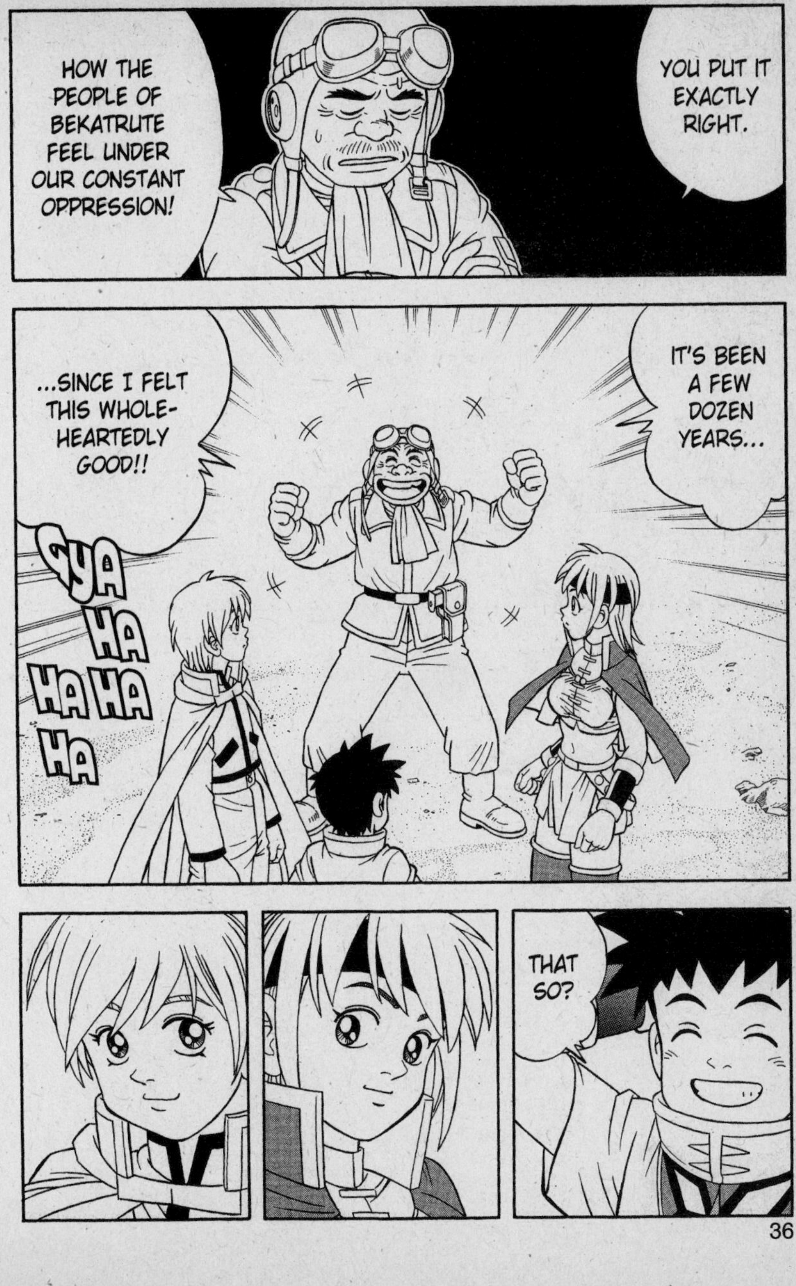
YOU PUT IT EXACTLY RIGHT.
HOW THE PEOPLE OF BEKATRUTE FEEL UNDER OUR CONSTANT OPPRESSION!
IT'S BEEN A FEW DOZEN YEARS...
...SINCE I FELT THIS WHOLE-HEARTEDLY GOOD!!
GYA HA HA HA HA
THAT SO?

READ THIS WAY

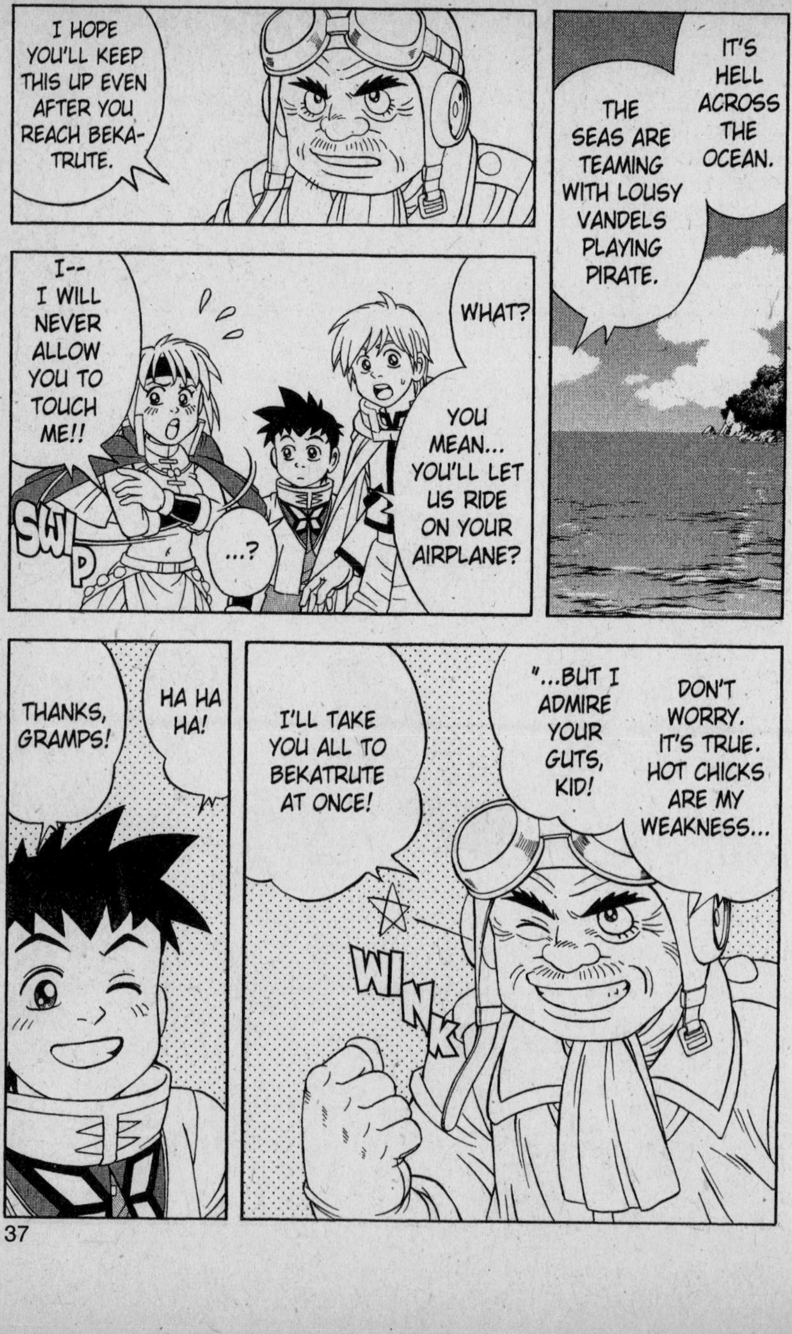
IT'S HELL ACROSS THE OCEAN.
THE SEAS ARE TEAMING WITH LOUSY VANDELS PLAYING PIRATE.
I HOPE YOU'LL KEEP THIS UP EVEN AFTER YOU REACH BEKA-TRUTE.
WHAT?
YOU MEAN... YOU'LL LET US RIDE ON YOUR AIRPLANE?
...?
I-- I WILL NEVER ALLOW YOU TO TOUCH ME!!
SWIP
DON'T WORRY. IT'S TRUE. HOT CHICKS ARE MY WEAKNESS...
"...BUT I ADMIRE YOUR GUTS, KID!
I'LL TAKE YOU ALL TO BEKATRUTE AT ONCE!
WINK
HA HA HA!
THANKS, GRAMPS!

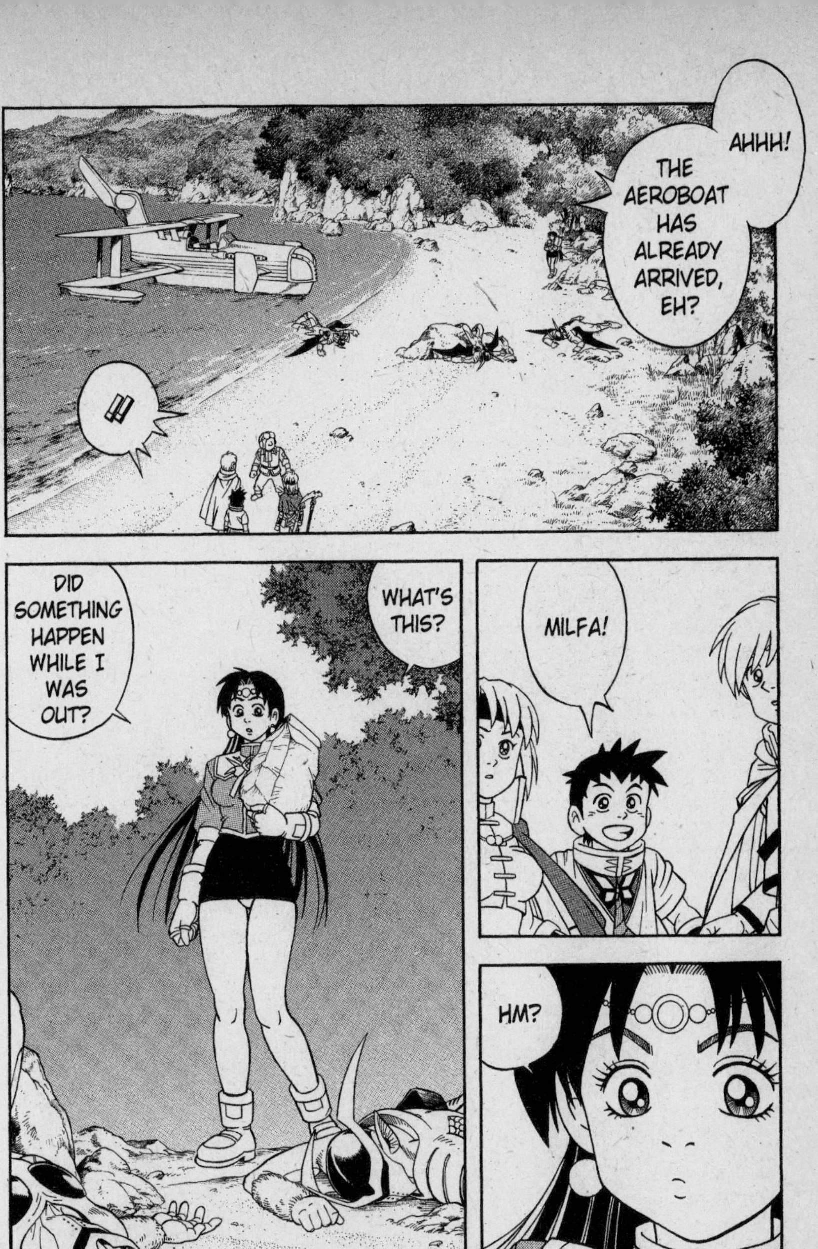
AHHH!
THE AEROBOAT HAS ALREADY ARRIVED, EH?
!!
MILFA!
HM?
WHAT'S THIS?
DID SOMETHING HAPPEN WHILE I WAS OUT?

READ THIS WAY

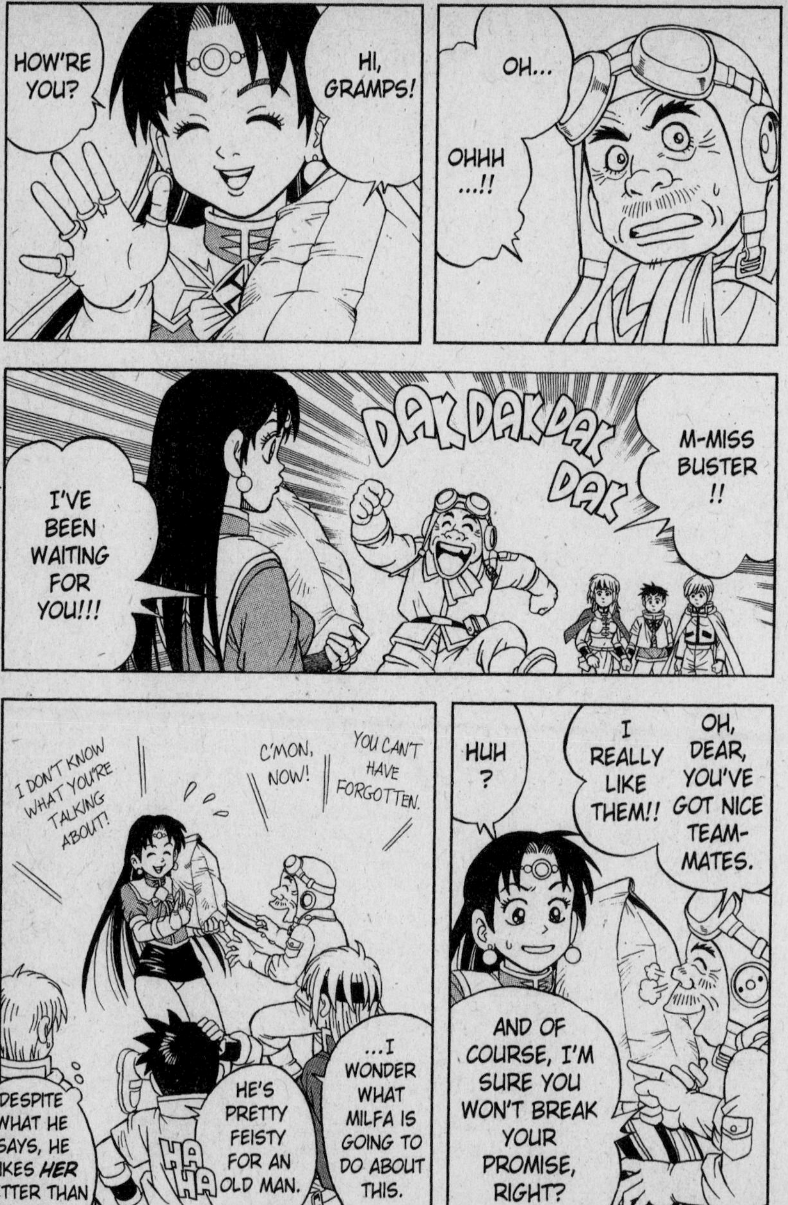
OH...
OHHH ...!!
HI, GRAMPS!
HOW'RE YOU?
M-MISS BUSTER !!
DAK DAK DAK DAK DAK
I'VE BEEN WAITING FOR YOU!!!
OH, DEAR, YOU'VE GOT NICE TEAM-MATES.
I REALLY LIKE THEM!!
HUH ?
AND OF COURSE, I'M SURE YOU WON'T BREAK YOUR PROMISE, RIGHT?
YOU CAN'T HAVE FORGOTTEN.
C'MON, NOW!
I DON'T KNOW WHAT YOU'RE TALKING ABOUT!
...I WONDER WHAT MILFA IS GOING TO DO ABOUT THIS.
HE'S PRETTY FEISTY FOR AN OLD MAN.
HA HA
DESPITE WHAT HE SAYS, HE LIKES *HER* BETTER THAN HE LIKES US...

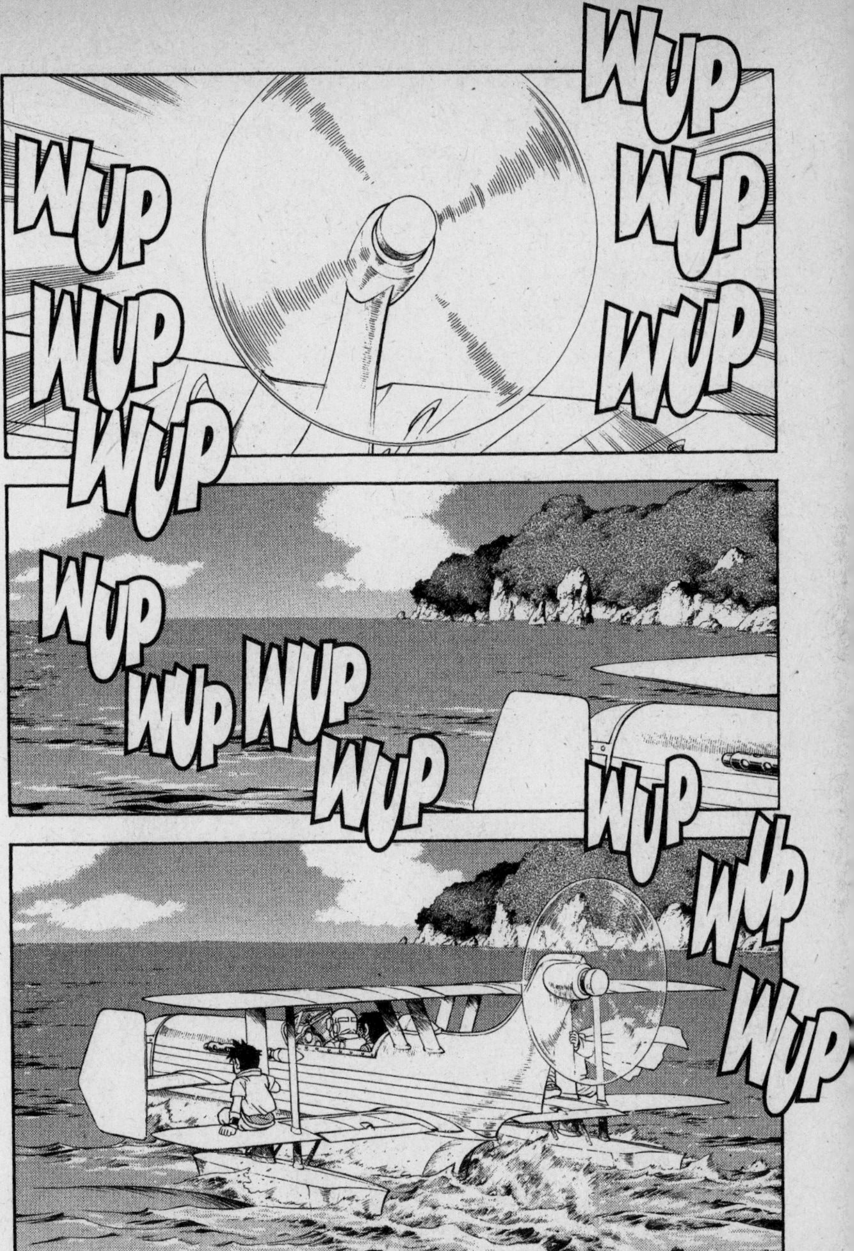
WUP
WUP
WUP
WUP
WUP
WUP
WUP
WUP
WUP
WUP
WUP
WUP
WUP
WUP
WUP

READ THIS WAY

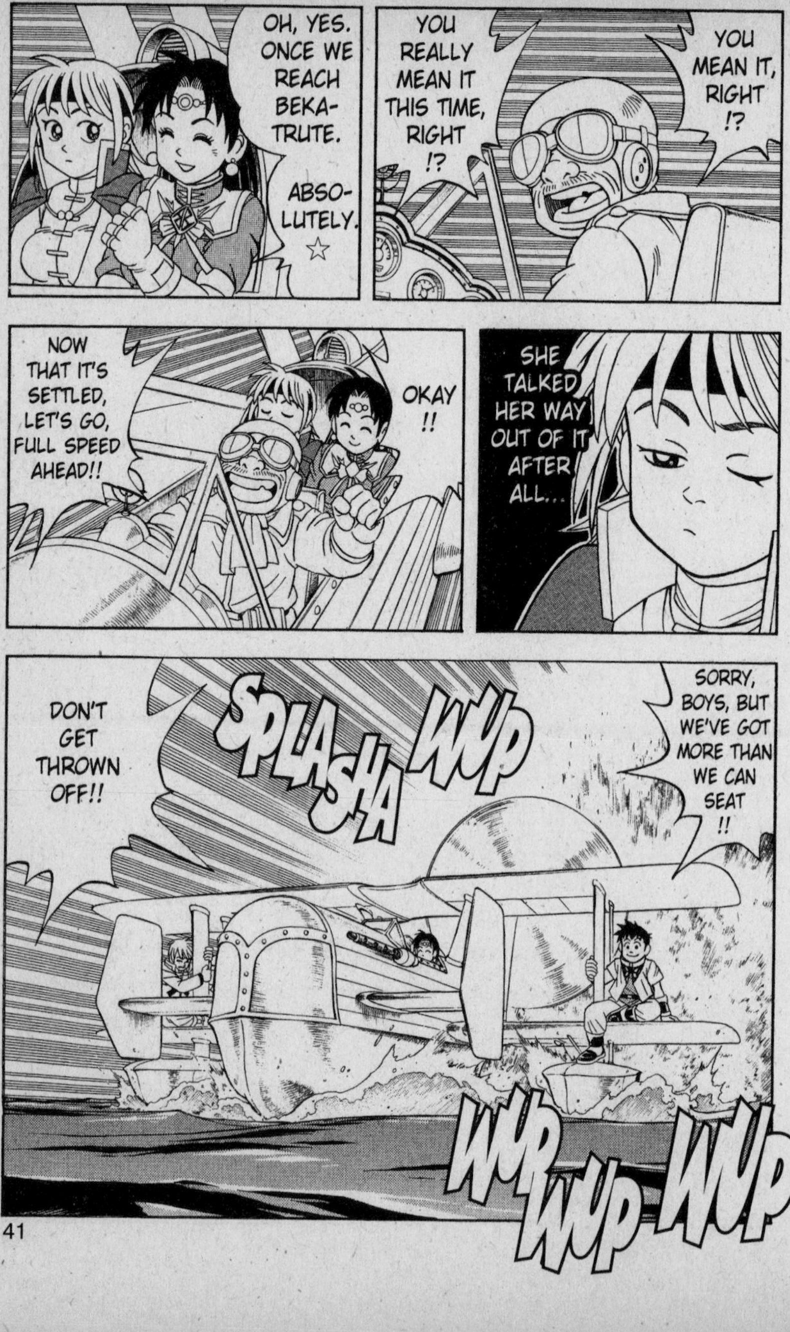

YOU MEAN IT, RIGHT !?
YOU REALLY MEAN IT THIS TIME, RIGHT !?
OH, YES. ONCE WE REACH BEKA-TRUTE.
ABSO-LUTELY. ☆
SHE TALKED HER WAY OUT OF IT AFTER ALL...
NOW THAT IT'S SETTLED, LET'S GO, FULL SPEED AHEAD!!
OKAY !!
SORRY, BOYS, BUT WE'VE GOT MORE THAN WE CAN SEAT !!
WUP
SPLASHA
DON'T GET THROWN OFF!!
WUP
WUP
WUP

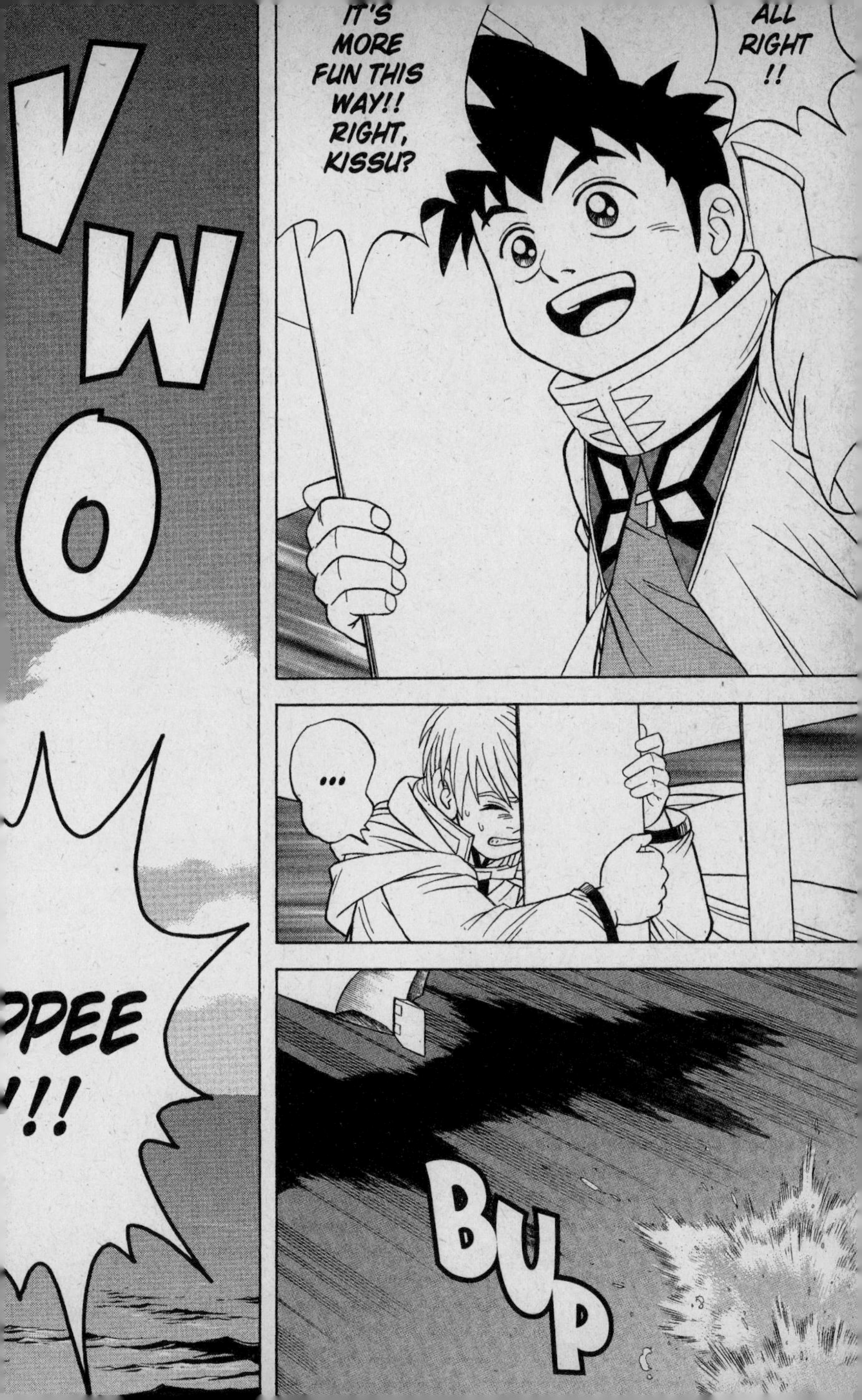
ALL RIGHT !!
IT'S MORE FUN THIS WAY!! RIGHT, KISSU?
...
BUP
VWO
PEE !!

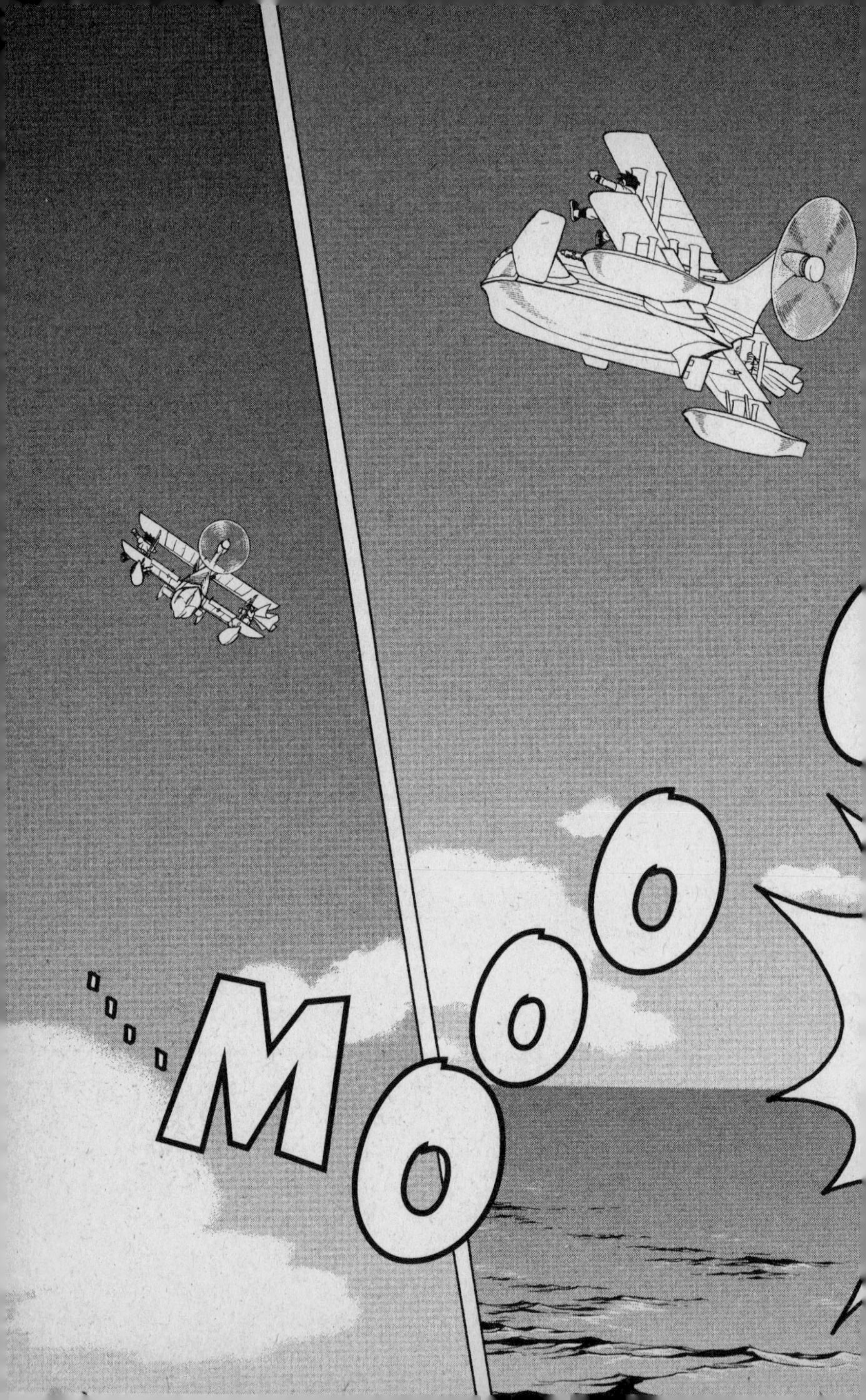
MOOO

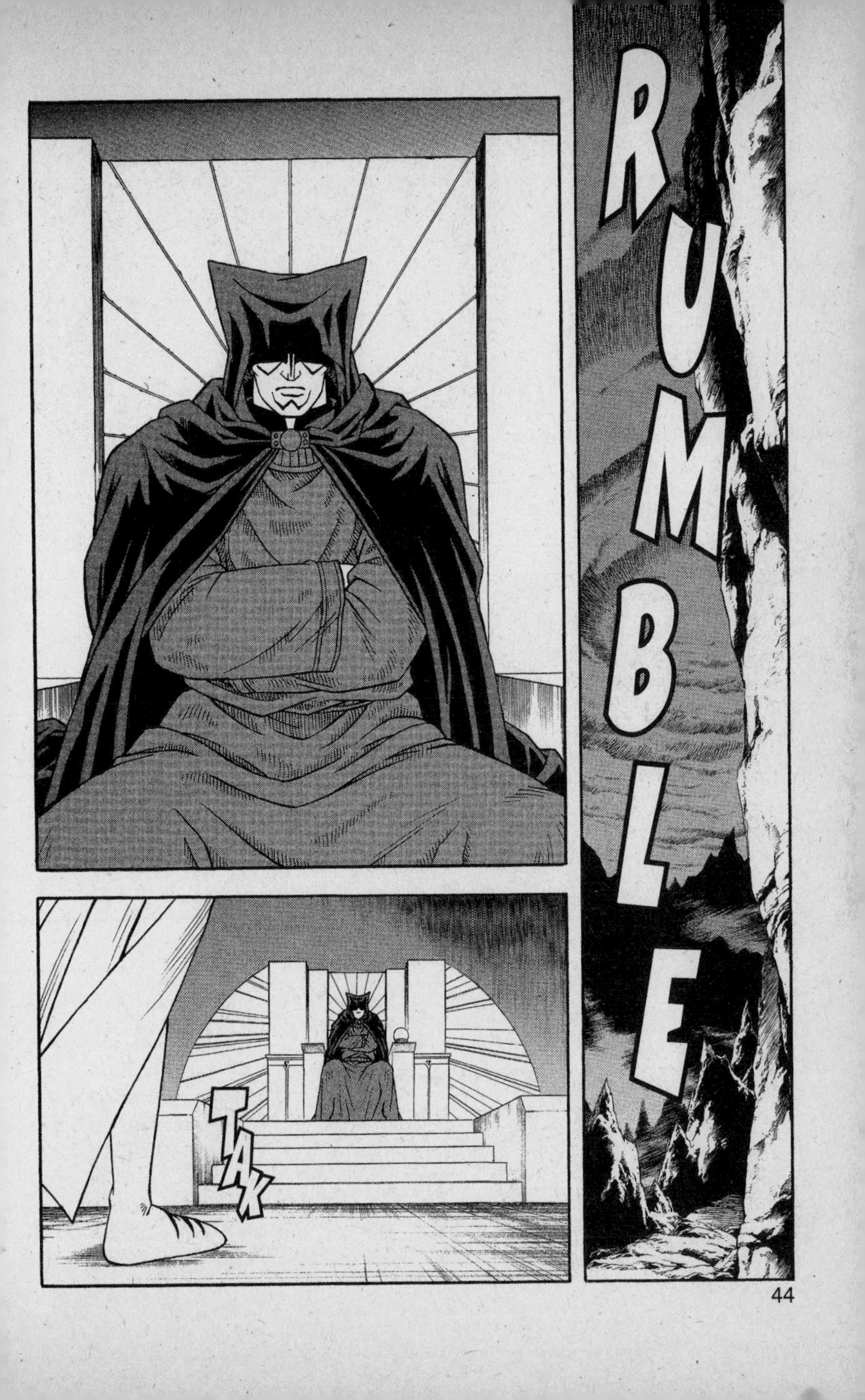
RUMBLE
TAK

READ THIS WAY

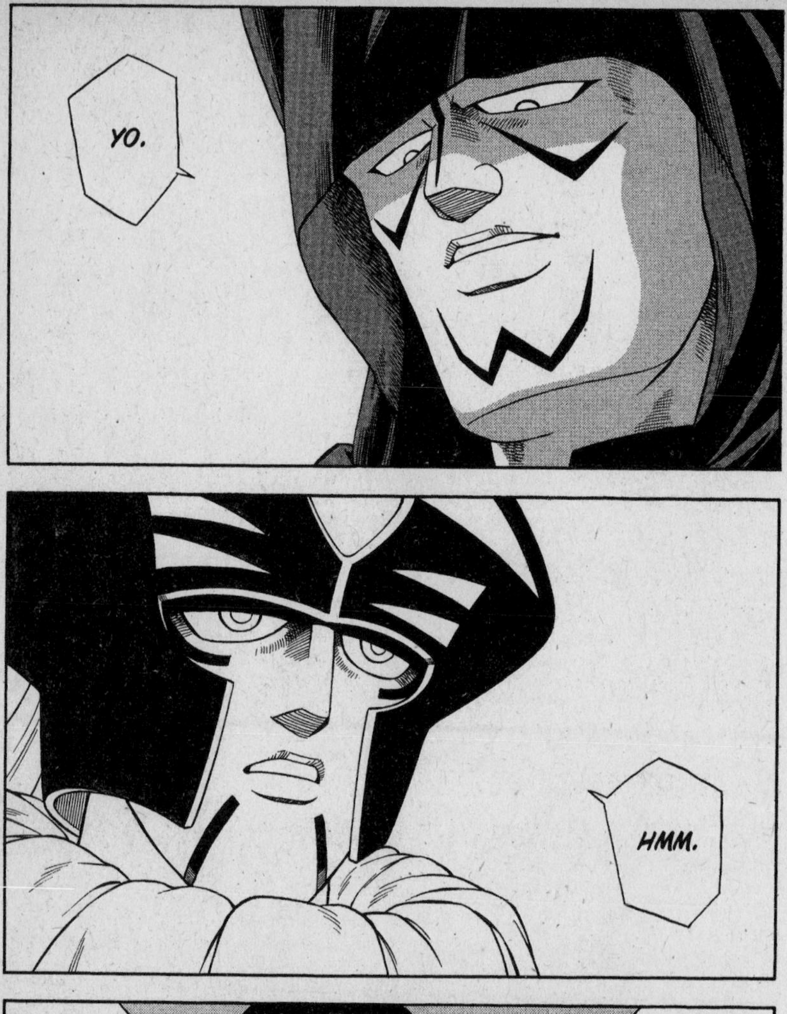
YO.
HMM.
IT LOOKS LIKE YOU'VE INCREASED YOUR POWER EVEN MORE.
IT ALMOST SCARES ME...

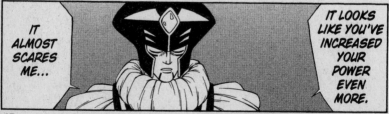

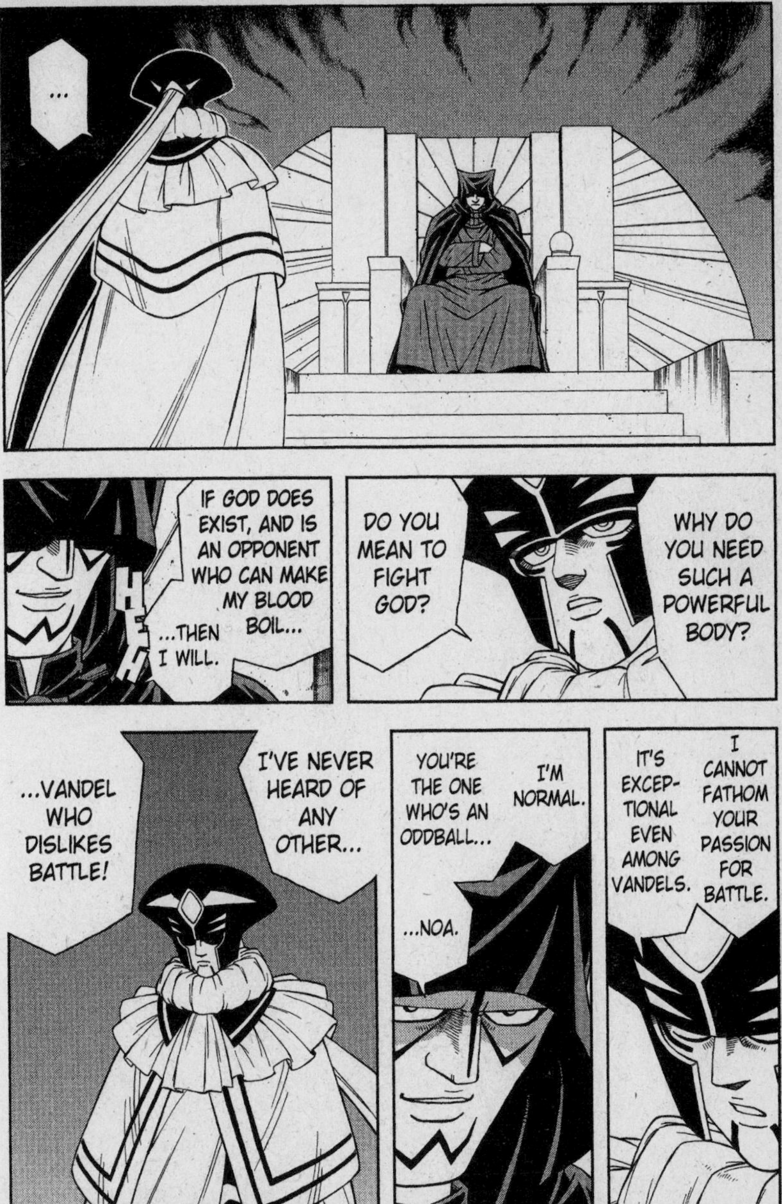
...
WHY DO YOU NEED SUCH A POWERFUL BODY?
DO YOU MEAN TO FIGHT GOD?
IF GOD DOES EXIST, AND IS AN OPPONENT WHO CAN MAKE MY BLOOD BOIL...
...THEN I WILL.
I CANNOT FATHOM YOUR PASSION FOR BATTLE.
IT'S EXCEP-TIONAL EVEN AMONG VANDELS.
I'M NORMAL.
YOU'RE THE ONE WHO'S AN ODDBALL...
...NOA.
I'VE NEVER HEARD OF ANY OTHER...
...VANDEL WHO DISLIKES BATTLE!

READ THIS WAY

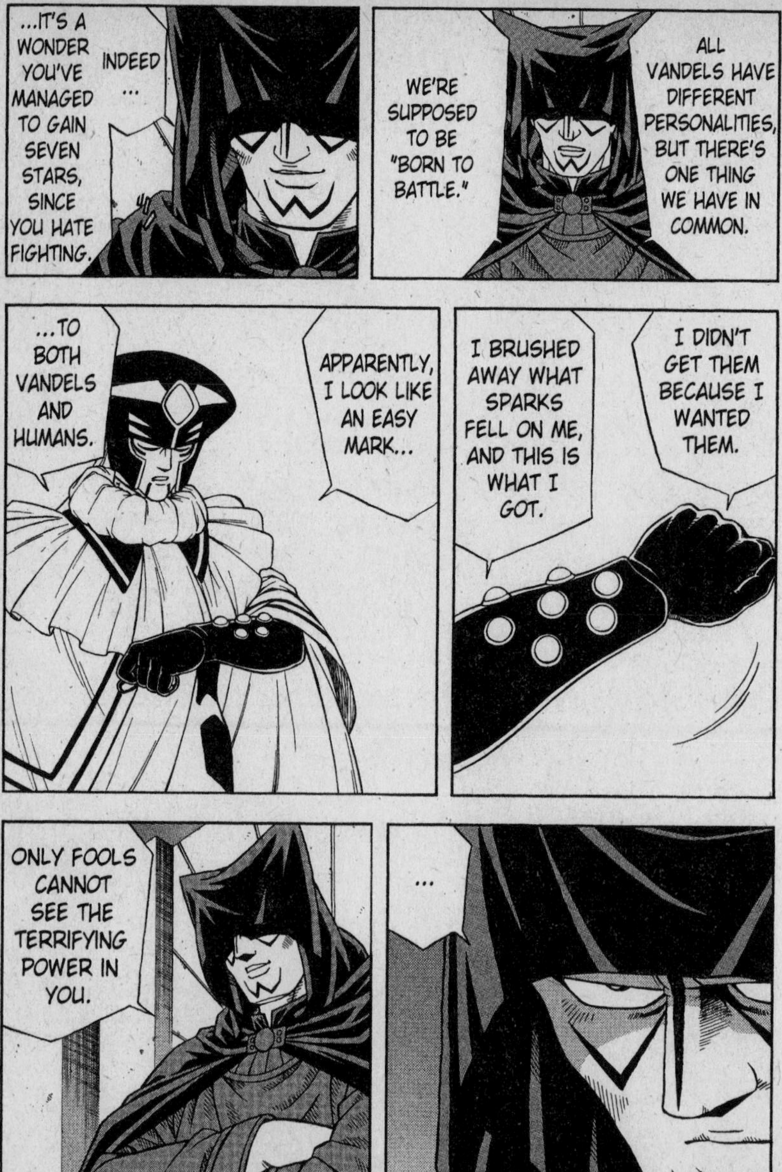
ALL VANDELS HAVE DIFFERENT PERSONALITIES, BUT THERE'S ONE THING WE HAVE IN COMMON.
WE'RE SUPPOSED TO BE "BORN TO BATTLE."
INDEED...
...IT'S A WONDER YOU'VE MANAGED TO GAIN SEVEN STARS, SINCE YOU HATE FIGHTING.
I DIDN'T GET THEM BECAUSE I WANTED THEM.
I BRUSHED AWAY WHAT SPARKS FELL ON ME, AND THIS IS WHAT I GOT.
APPARENTLY, I LOOK LIKE AN EASY MARK...
...TO BOTH VANDELS AND HUMANS.
...
ONLY FOOLS CANNOT SEE THE TERRIFYING POWER IN YOU.

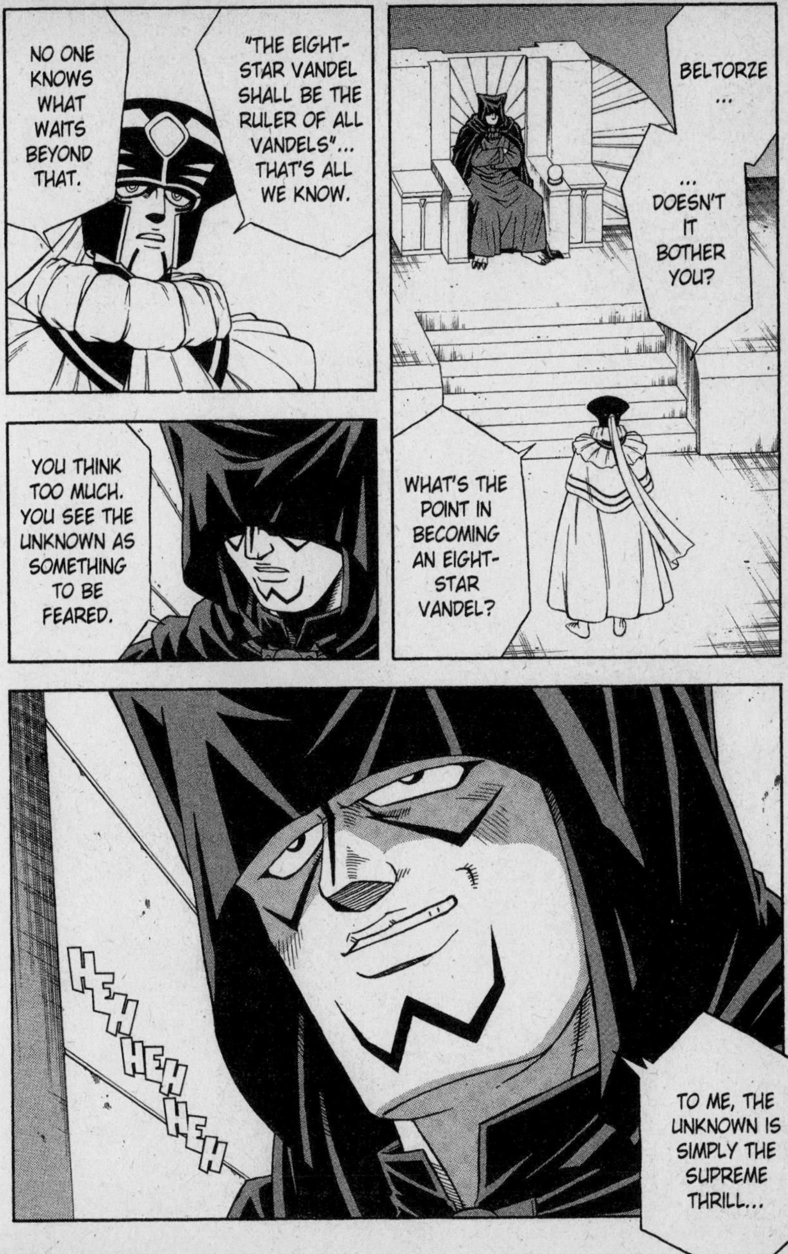
BELTORZE ...
... DOESN'T IT BOTHER YOU?
WHAT'S THE POINT IN BECOMING AN EIGHT-STAR VANDEL?
"THE EIGHT-STAR VANDEL SHALL BE THE RULER OF ALL VANDELS"... THAT'S ALL WE KNOW.
NO ONE KNOWS WHAT WAITS BEYOND THAT.
YOU THINK TOO MUCH. YOU SEE THE UNKNOWN AS SOMETHING TO BE FEARED.
HEH HEH HEH
TO ME, THE UNKNOWN IS SIMPLY THE SUPREME THRILL...

READ THIS WAY

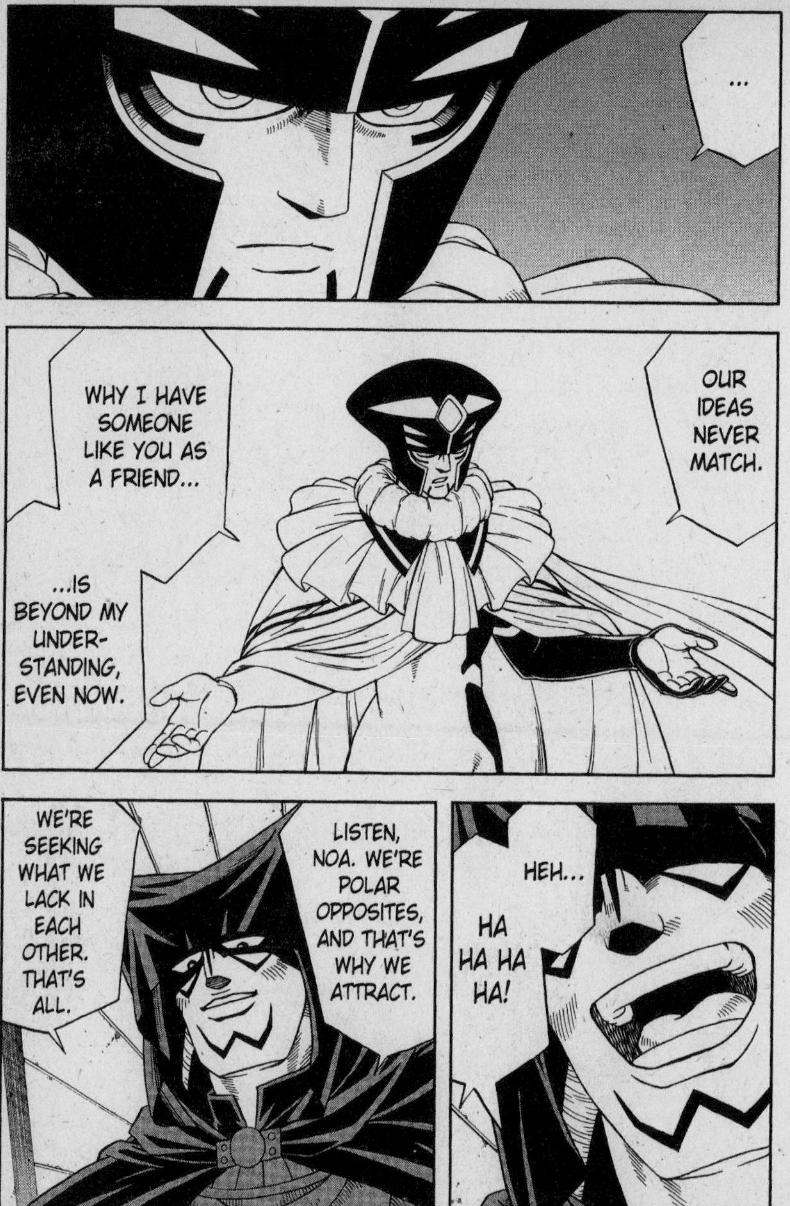
...
OUR IDEAS NEVER MATCH.
WHY I HAVE SOMEONE LIKE YOU AS A FRIEND...
...IS BEYOND MY UNDER-STANDING, EVEN NOW.
HEH...
HA HA HA HA!
LISTEN, NOA. WE'RE POLAR OPPOSITES, AND THAT'S WHY WE ATTRACT.
WE'RE SEEKING WHAT WE LACK IN EACH OTHER. THAT'S ALL.

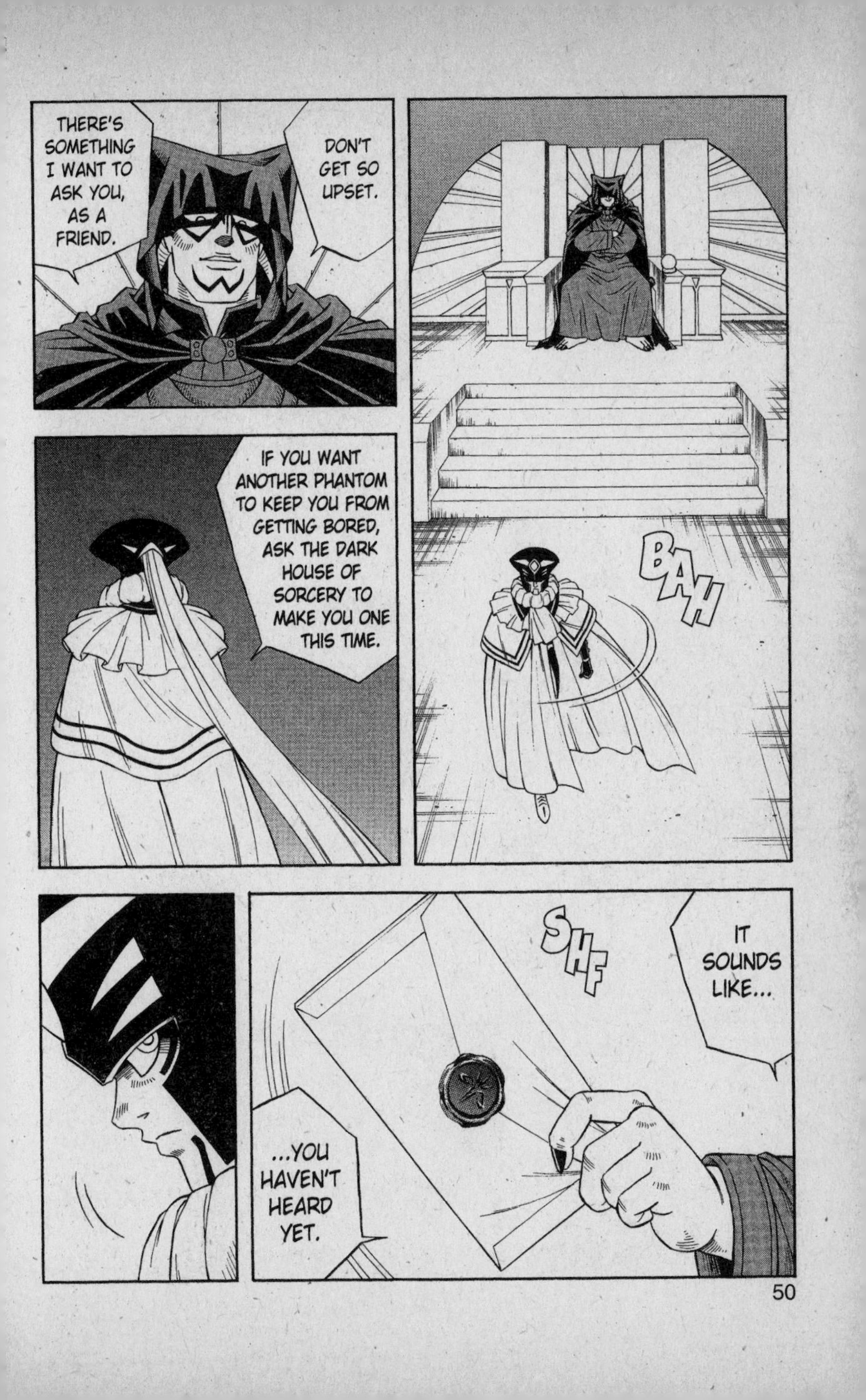
BAH
DON'T GET SO UPSET.
THERE'S SOMETHING I WANT TO ASK YOU, AS A FRIEND.
IF YOU WANT ANOTHER PHANTOM TO KEEP YOU FROM GETTING BORED, ASK THE DARK HOUSE OF SORCERY TO MAKE YOU ONE THIS TIME.
SHF
IT SOUNDS LIKE...
...YOU HAVEN'T HEARD YET.

READ THIS WAY

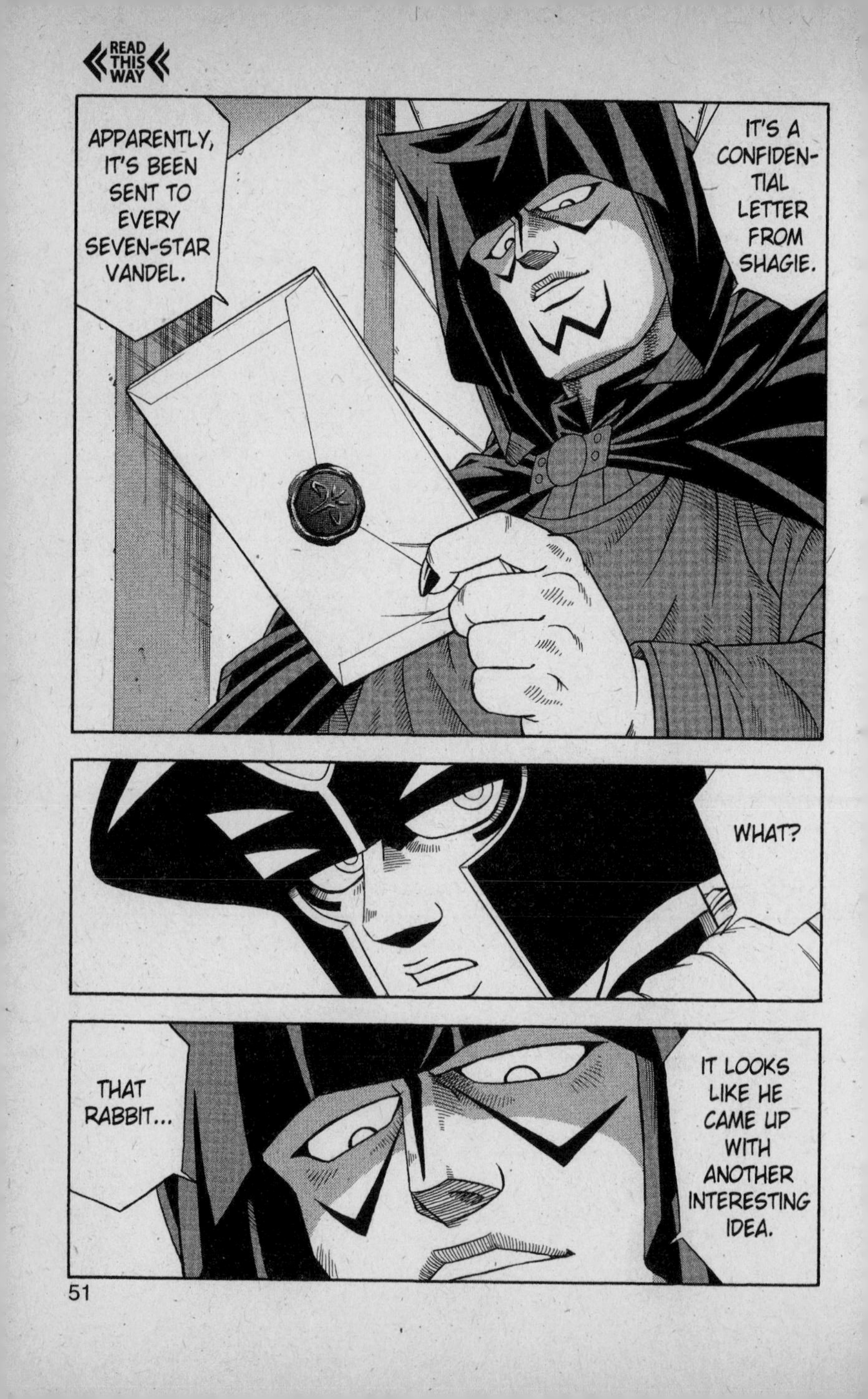
IT'S A CONFIDEN-TIAL LETTER FROM SHAGIE.
APPARENTLY, IT'S BEEN SENT TO EVERY SEVEN-STAR VANDEL.
WHAT?
IT LOOKS LIKE HE CAME UP WITH ANOTHER INTERESTING IDEA.
THAT RABBIT...

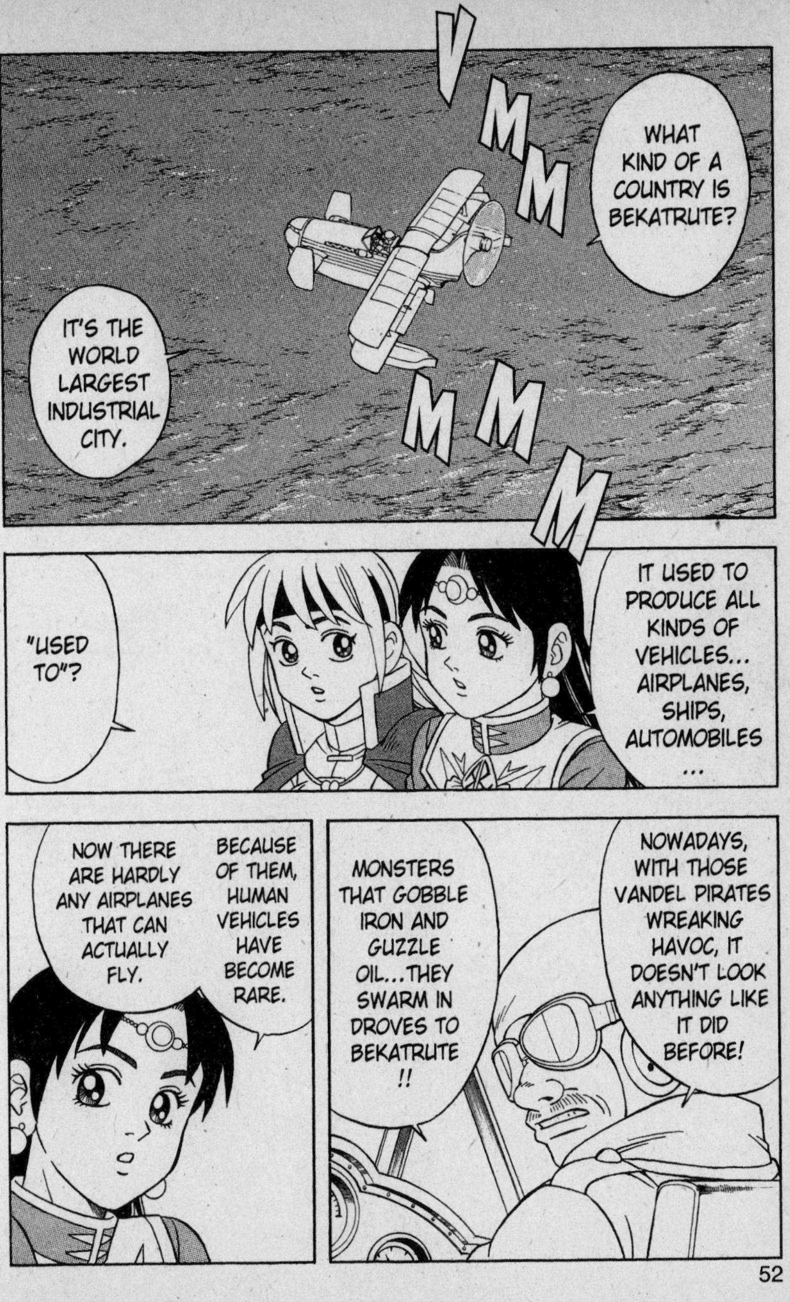
WHAT KIND OF A COUNTRY IS BEKATRUTE?
VMMMMM
IT'S THE WORLD LARGEST INDUSTRIAL CITY.
IT USED TO PRODUCE ALL KINDS OF VEHICLES... AIRPLANES, SHIPS, AUTOMOBILES ...
"USED TO"?
NOWADAYS, WITH THOSE VANDEL PIRATES WREAKING HAVOC, IT DOESN'T LOOK ANYTHING LIKE IT DID BEFORE!
MONSTERS THAT GOBBLE IRON AND GUZZLE OIL...THEY SWARM IN DROVES TO BEKATRUTE !!
BECAUSE OF THEM, HUMAN VEHICLES HAVE BECOME RARE.
NOW THERE ARE HARDLY ANY AIRPLANES THAT CAN ACTUALLY FLY.

READ THIS WAY

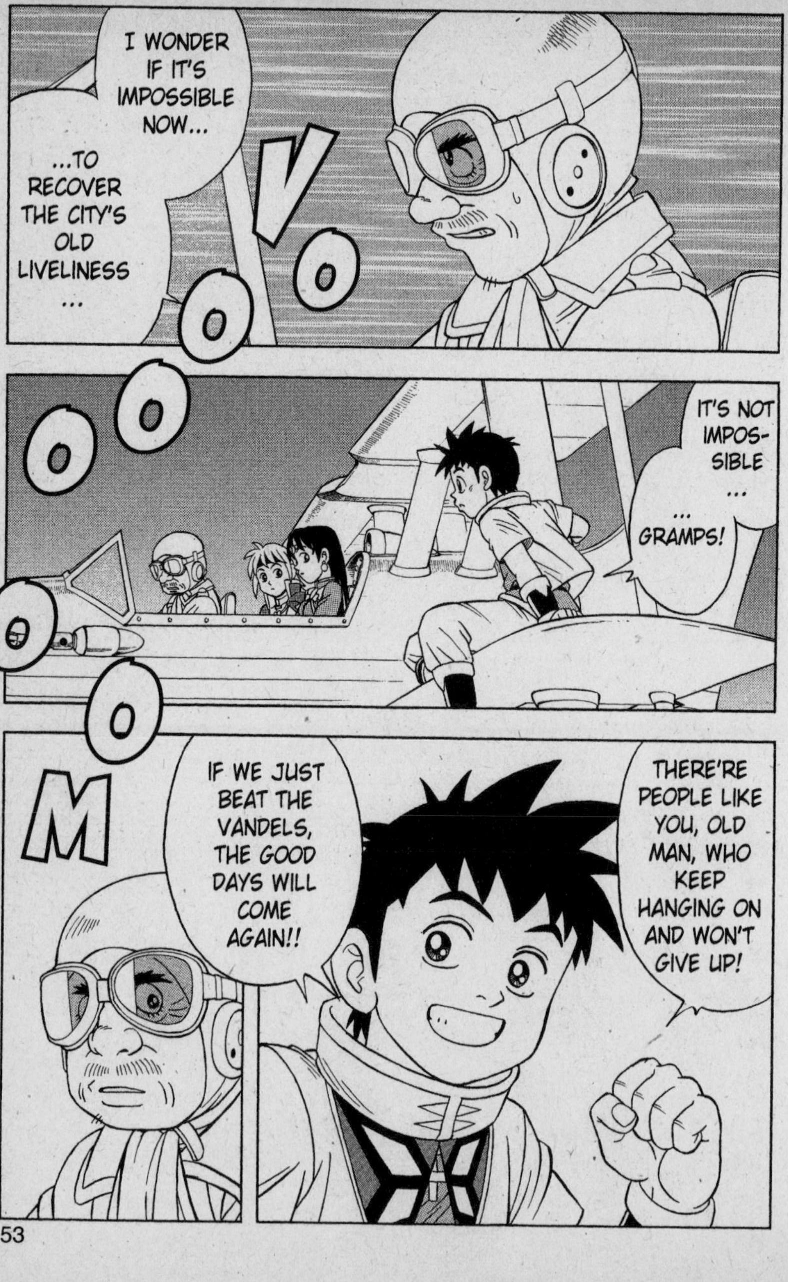

I WONDER IF IT'S IMPOSSIBLE NOW...
...TO RECOVER THE CITY'S OLD LIVELINESS ...
VOOOOOOM
IT'S NOT IMPOSSIBLE ...
... GRAMPS!
THERE'RE PEOPLE LIKE YOU, OLD MAN, WHO KEEP HANGING ON AND WON'T GIVE UP!
IF WE JUST BEAT THE VANDELS, THE GOOD DAYS WILL COME AGAIN!!

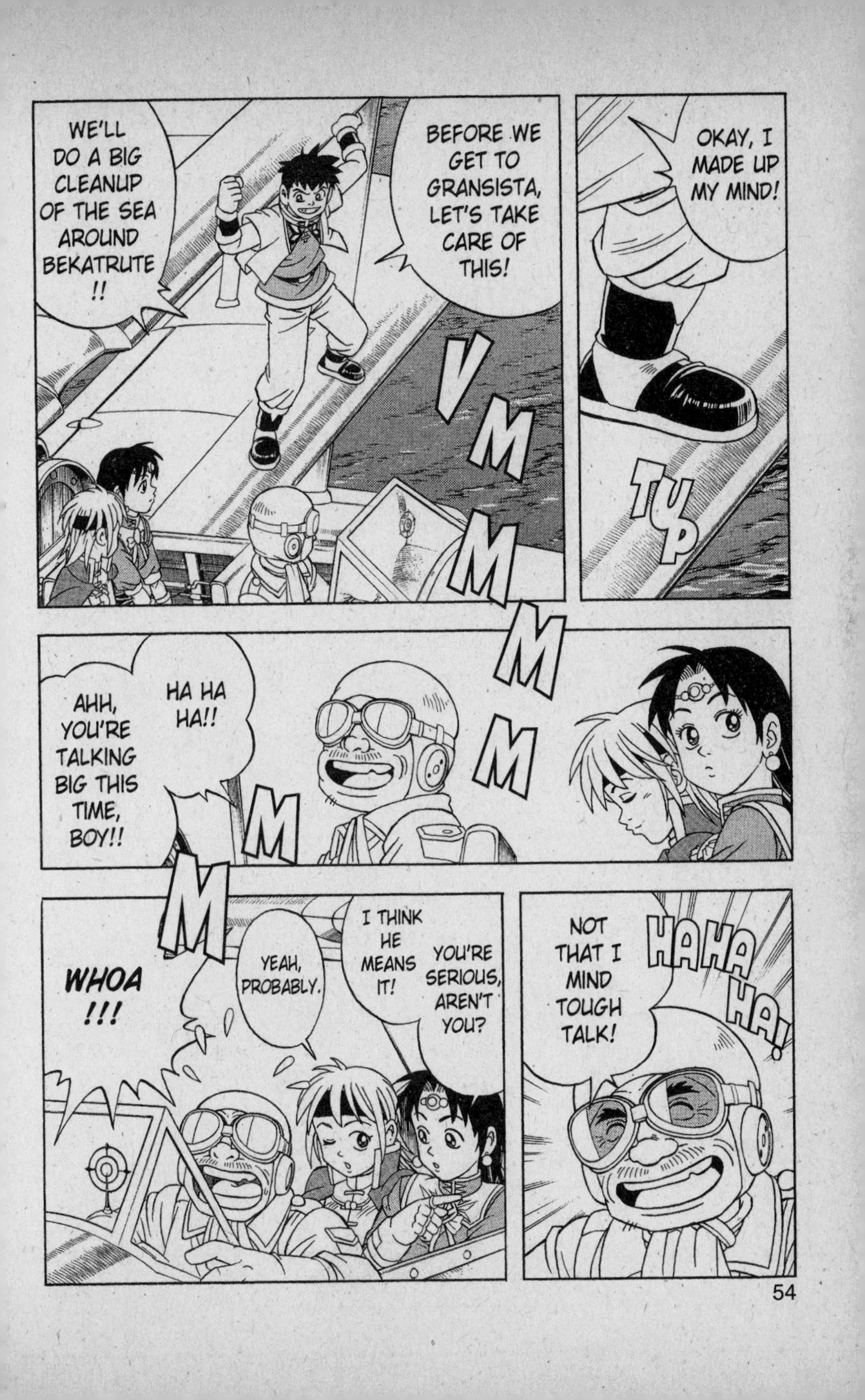
OKAY, I MADE UP MY MIND!
TUP
BEFORE WE GET TO GRANSISTA, LET'S TAKE CARE OF THIS!
WE'LL DO A BIG CLEANUP OF THE SEA AROUND BEKATRUTE !!
VMMMMMMM
HA HA HA!!
AHH, YOU'RE TALKING BIG THIS TIME, BOY!!
HAHAHA HA!
NOT THAT I MIND TOUGH TALK!
YOU'RE SERIOUS, AREN'T YOU?
I THINK HE MEANS IT!
YEAH, PROBABLY.
WHOA !!!

READ THIS WAY

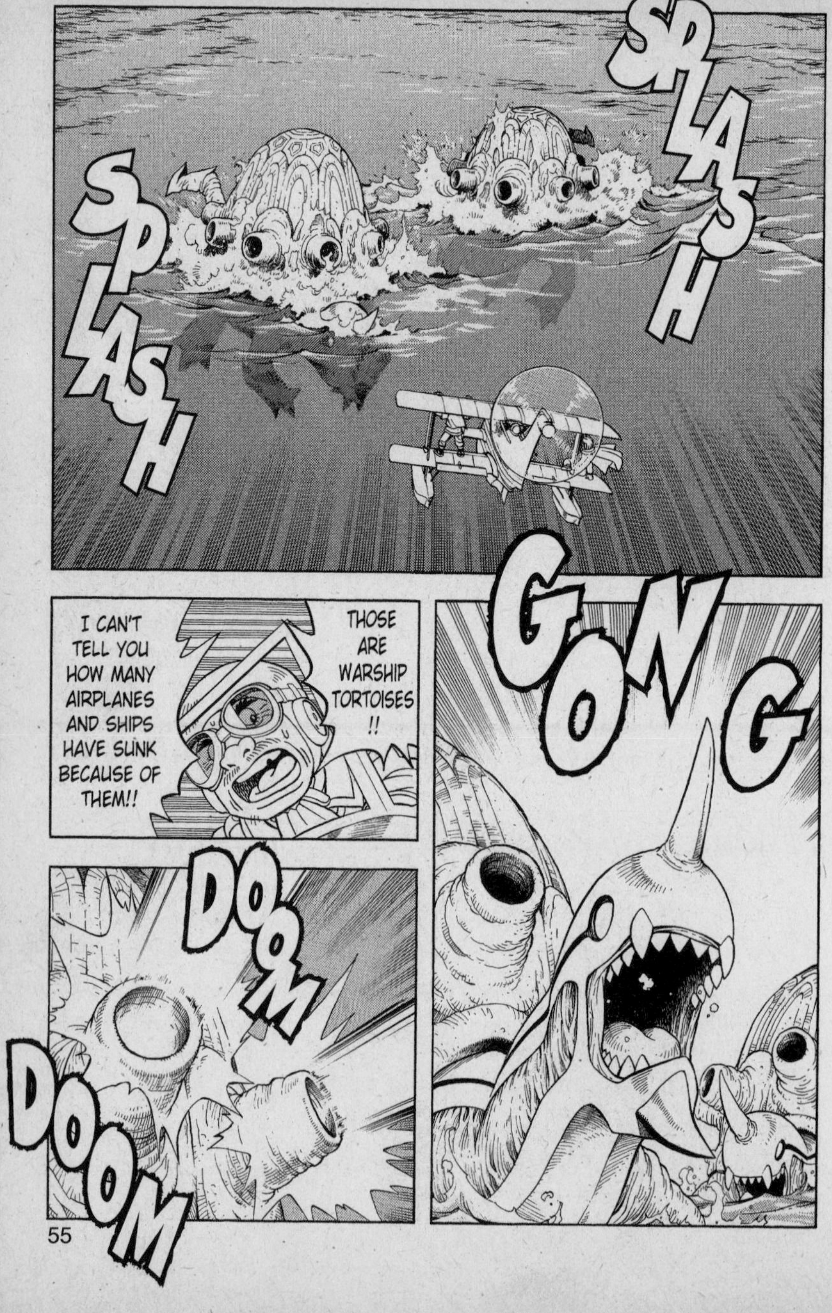

SPLASH
SPLASH
GONG
THOSE ARE WARSHIP TORTOISES!!
I CAN'T TELL YOU HOW MANY AIRPLANES AND SHIPS HAVE SUNK BECAUSE OF THEM!!
DOOM
DOOM

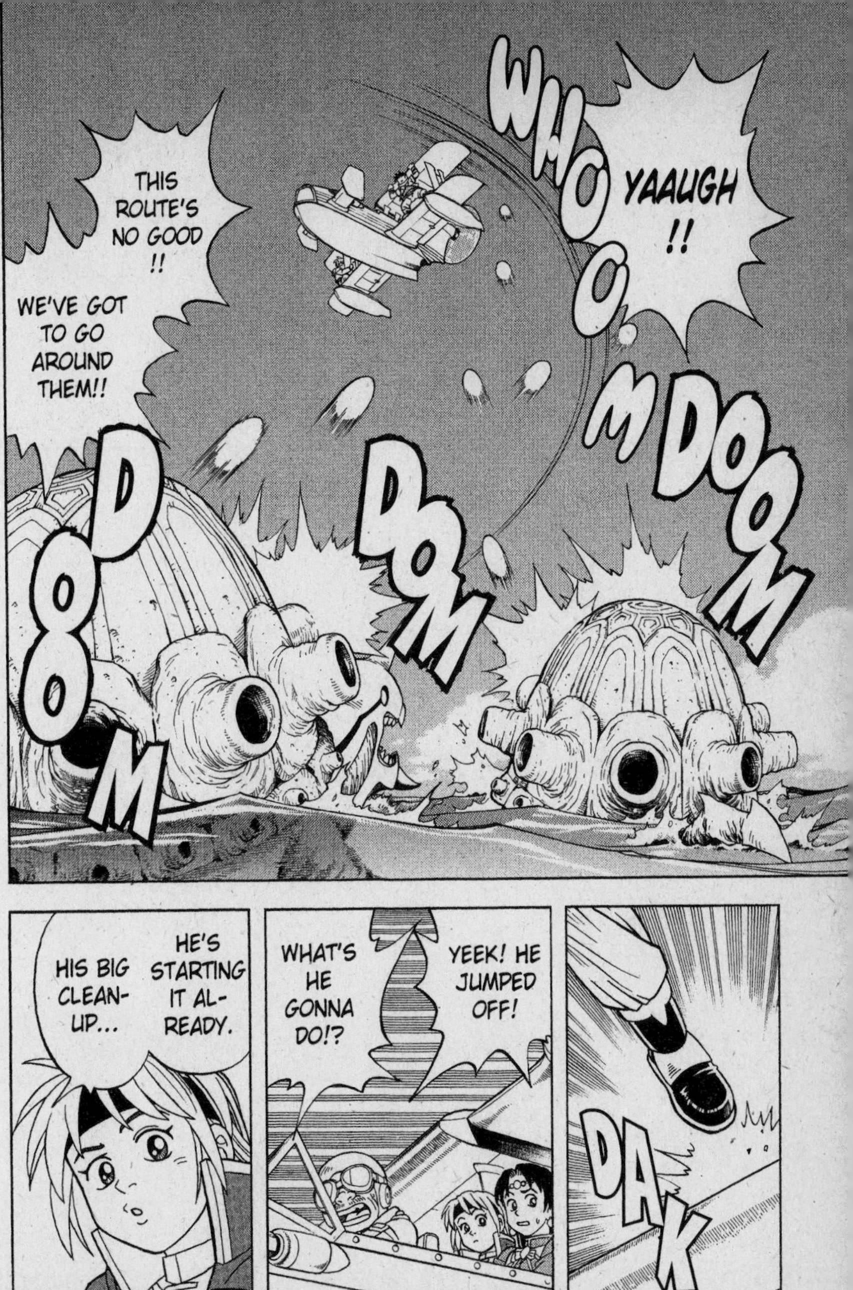
YAAUGH !!
WHOOOM
THIS ROUTE'S NO GOOD !!
WE'VE GOT TO GO AROUND THEM!!
DOOOM
DOOM
DOOOM
DAK
YEEK! HE JUMPED OFF!
WHAT'S HE GONNA DO!?
HE'S STARTING IT AL-READY.
HIS BIG CLEAN-UP...

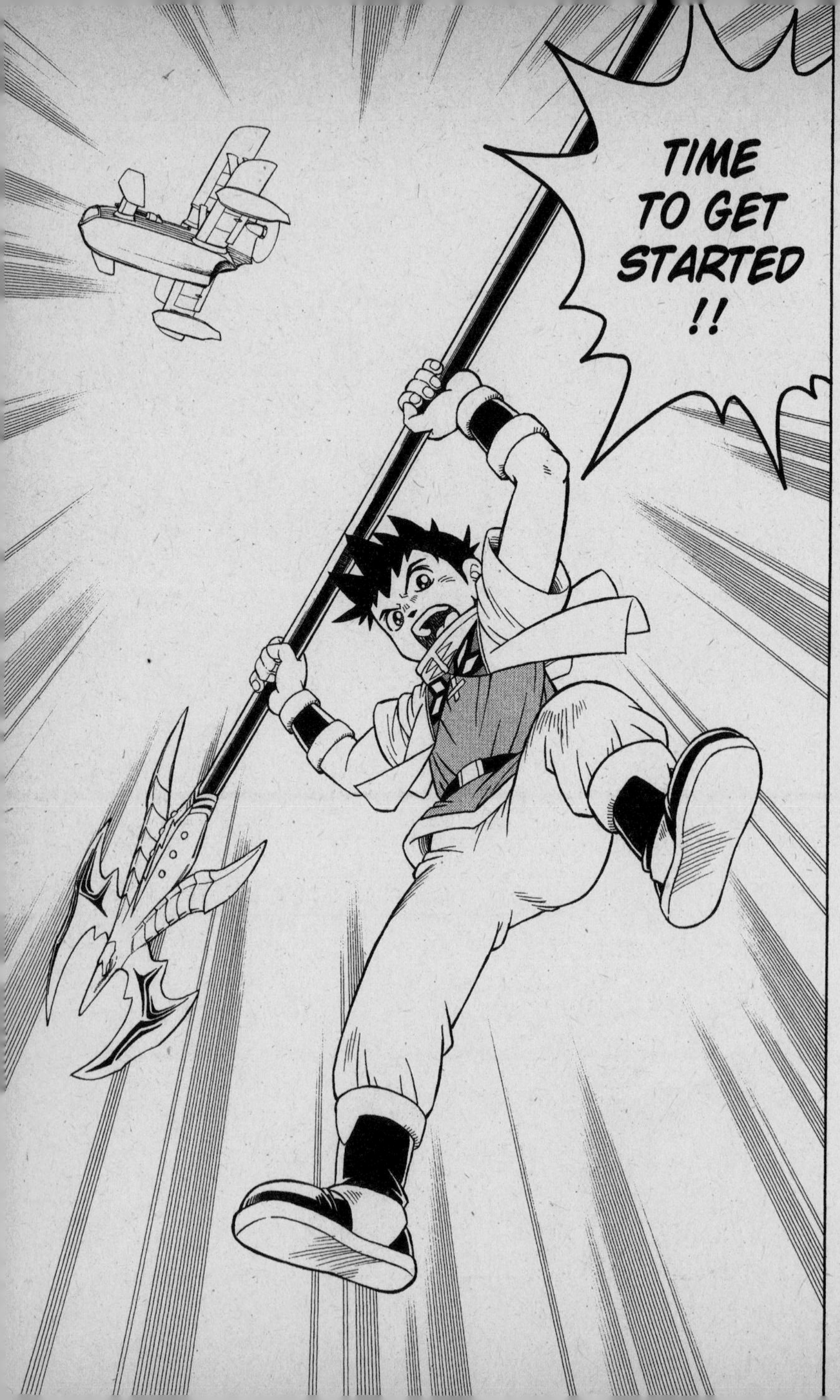
TIME TO GET STARTED !!

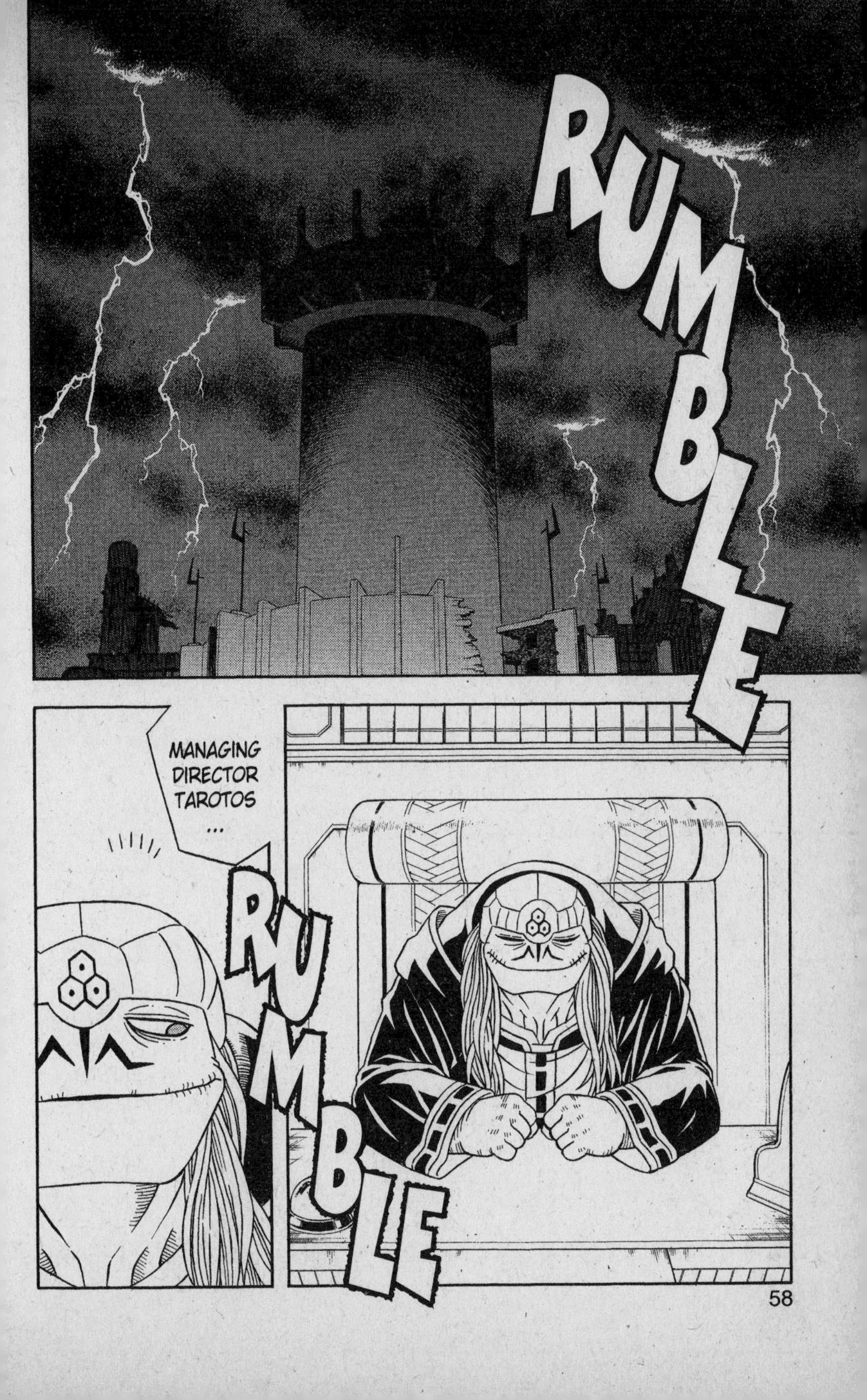
RUMBLE
RUMBLE
MANAGING DIRECTOR TAROTOS ...

READ THIS WAY

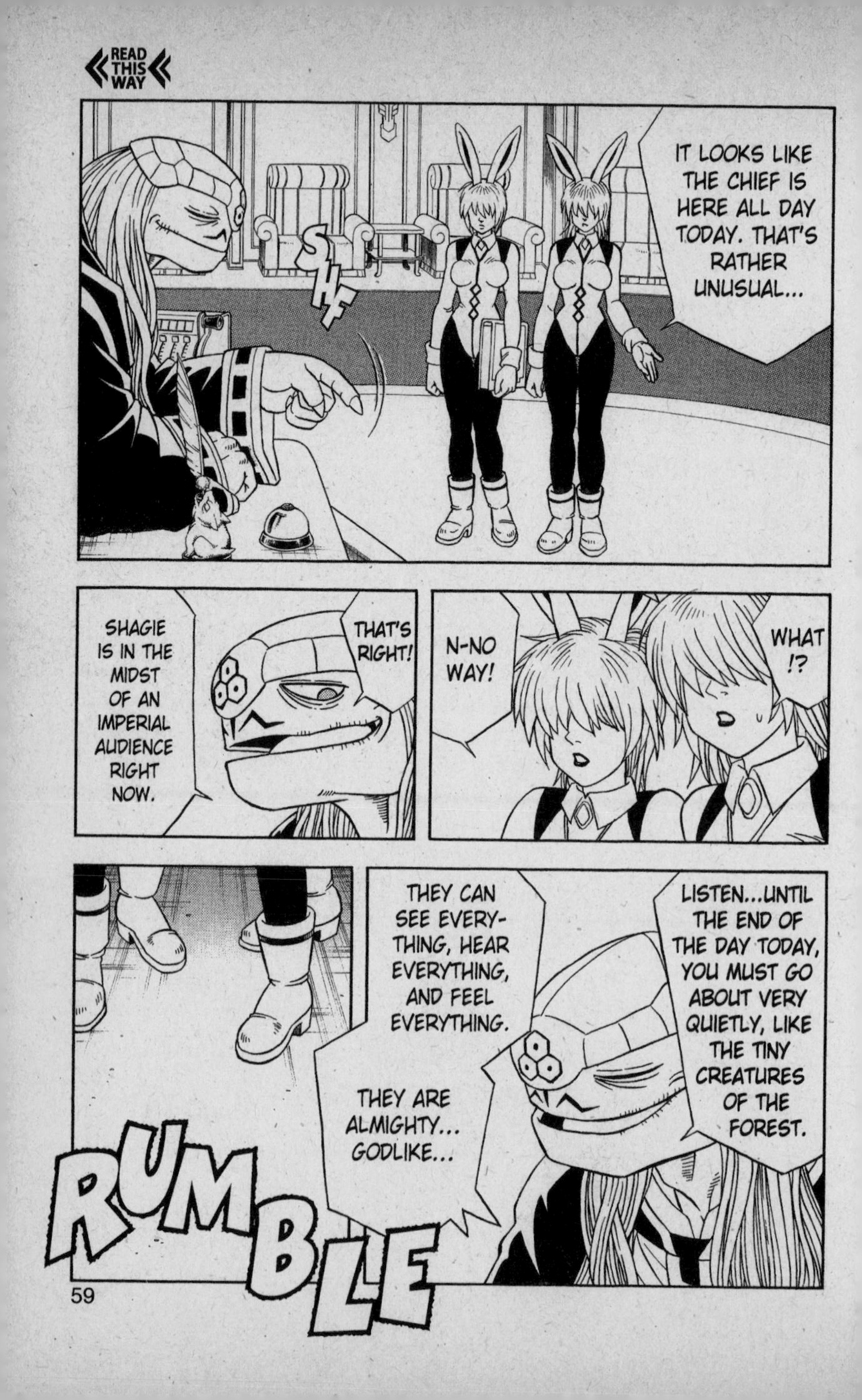
SHF
IT LOOKS LIKE THE CHIEF IS HERE ALL DAY TODAY. THAT'S RATHER UNUSUAL...
WHAT!?
N-NO WAY!
THAT'S RIGHT!
SHAGIE IS IN THE MIDST OF AN IMPERIAL AUDIENCE RIGHT NOW.
LISTEN...UNTIL THE END OF THE DAY TODAY, YOU MUST GO ABOUT VERY QUIETLY, LIKE THE TINY CREATURES OF THE FOREST.
THEY CAN SEE EVERYTHING, HEAR EVERYTHING, AND FEEL EVERYTHING.
THEY ARE ALMIGHTY... GODLIKE...
RUMBLE

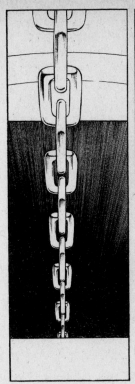
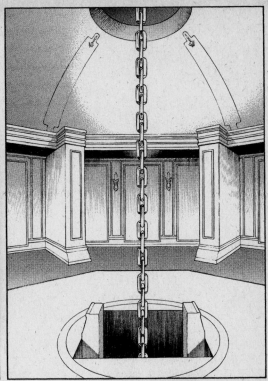
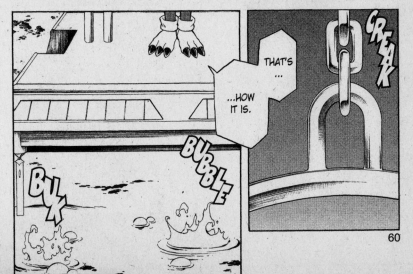

THAT'S
...

...HOW IT IS.

CREAK

BUBBLE

BUK

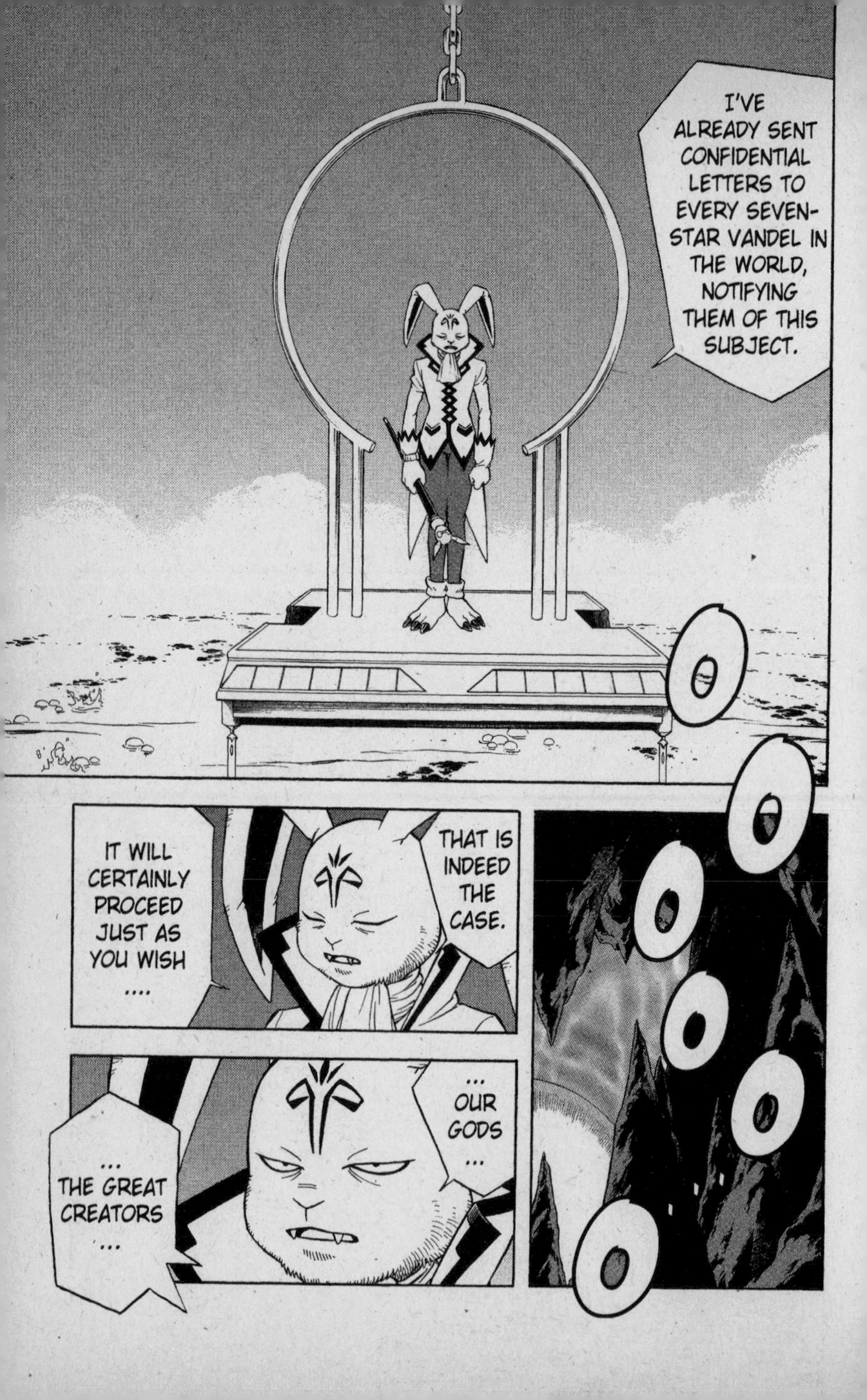
I'VE ALREADY SENT CONFIDENTIAL LETTERS TO EVERY SEVEN-STAR VANDEL IN THE WORLD, NOTIFYING THEM OF THIS SUBJECT.
THAT IS INDEED THE CASE.
IT WILL CERTAINLY PROCEED JUST AS YOU WISH ....
... OUR GODS ...
... THE GREAT CREATORS ...

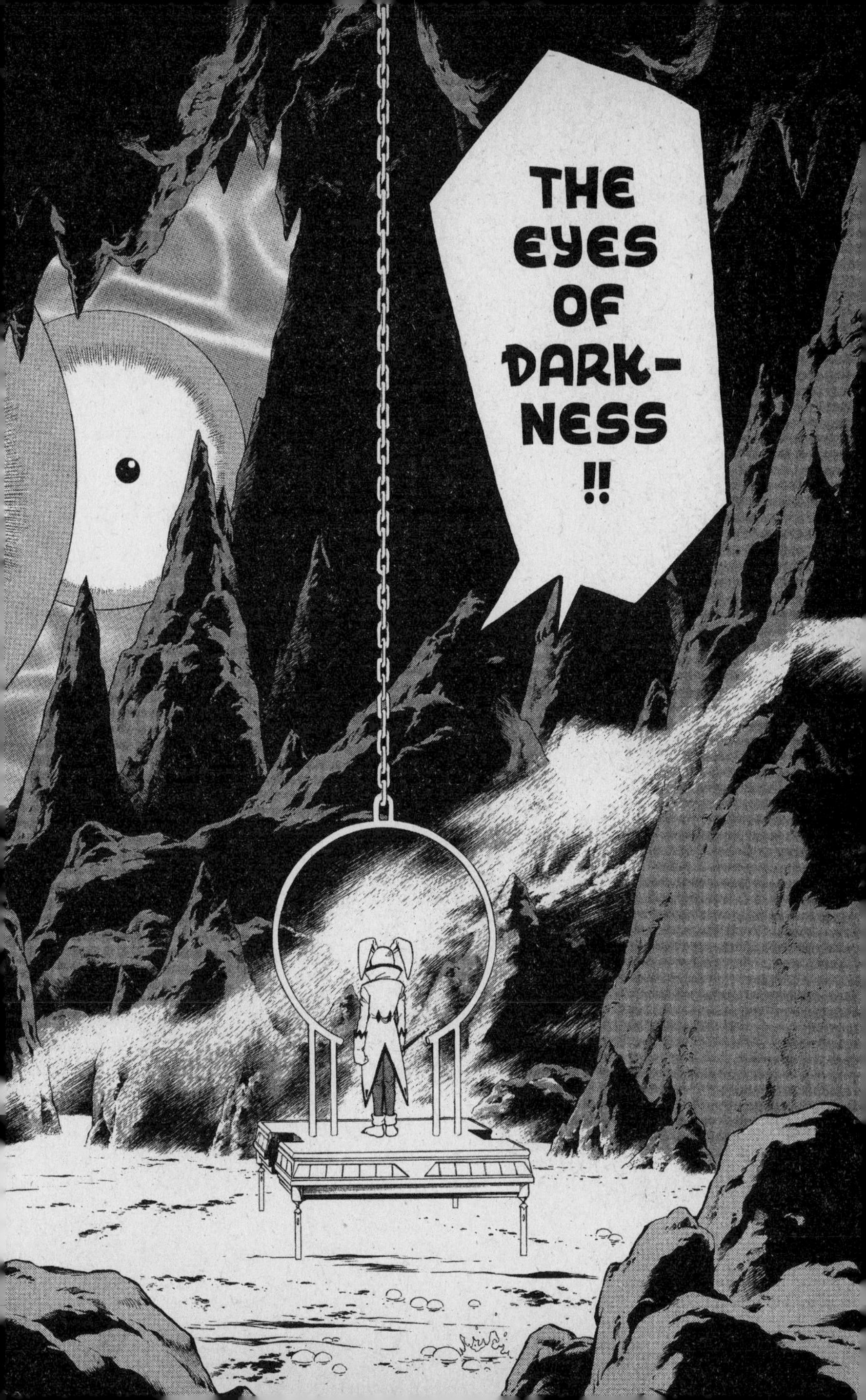
THE EYES OF DARK-NESS !!

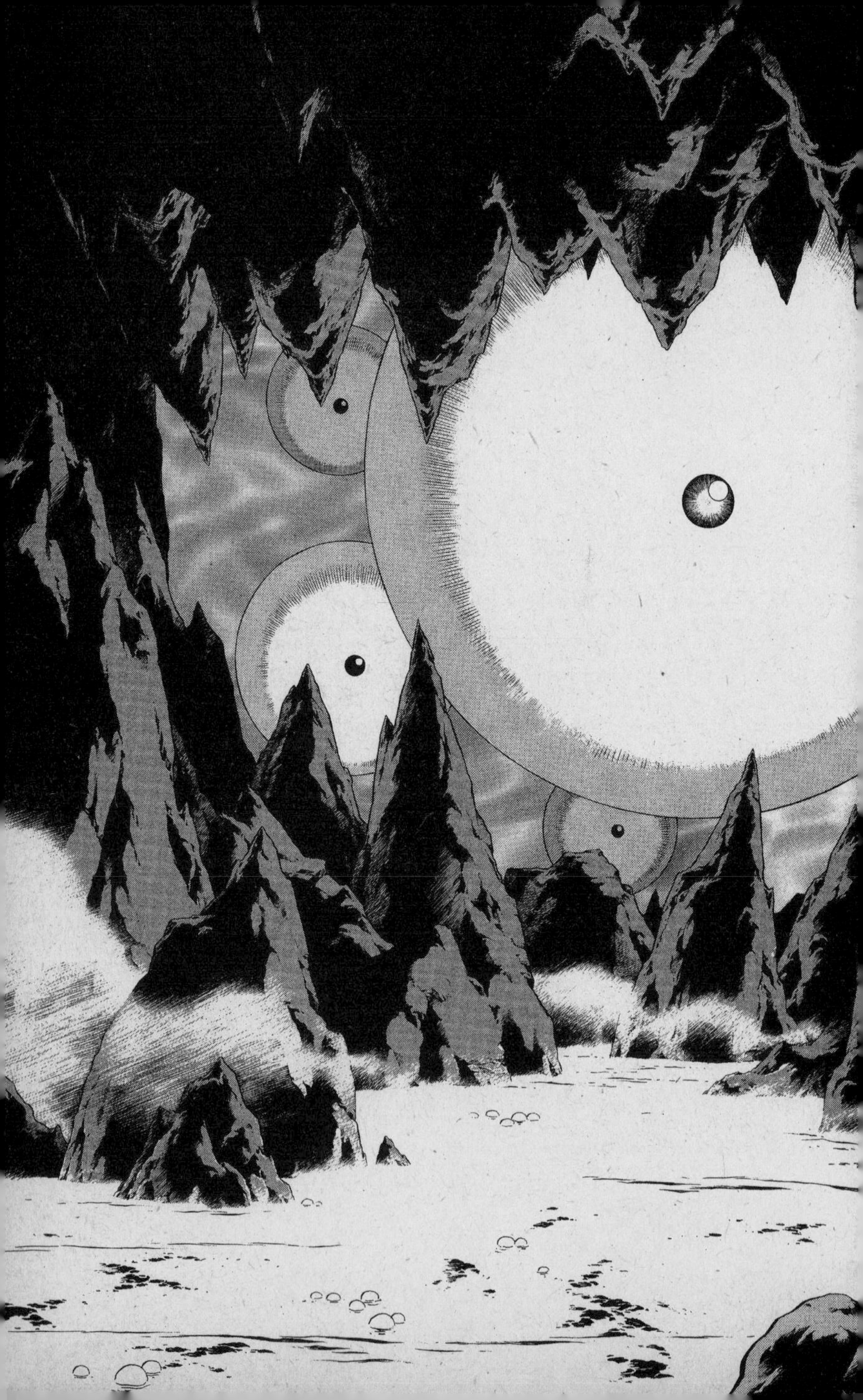

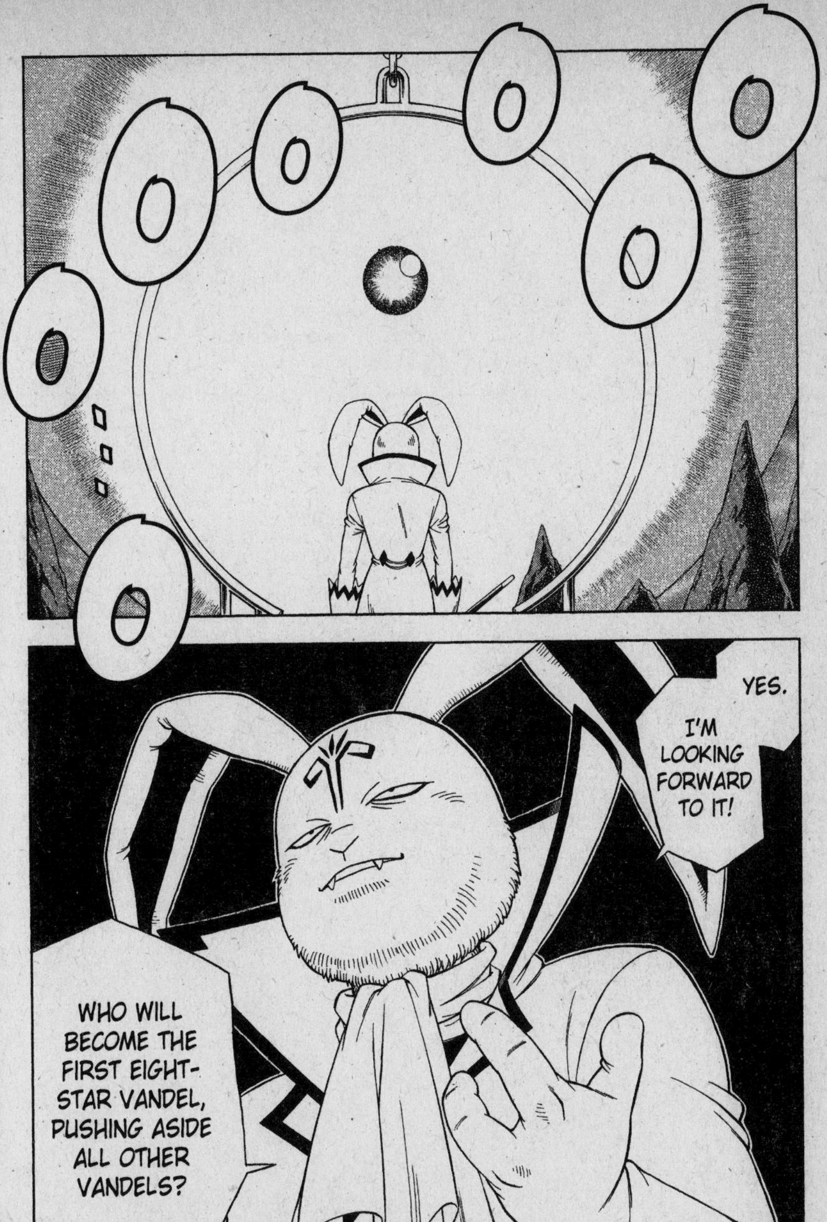
YES.
I'M LOOKING FORWARD TO IT!
WHO WILL BECOME THE FIRST EIGHT-STAR VANDEL, PUSHING ASIDE ALL OTHER VANDELS?

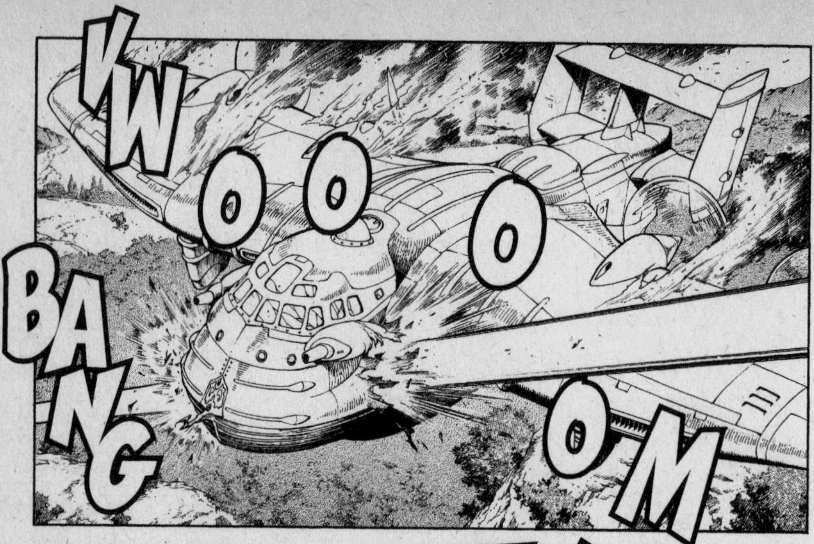
VWOOOOM
BANG

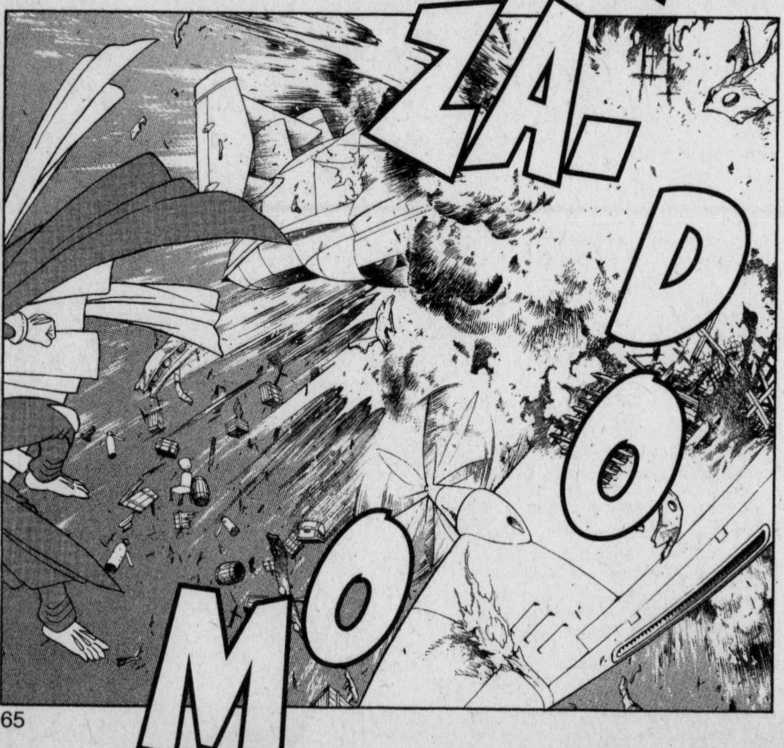
ZA-DOOM

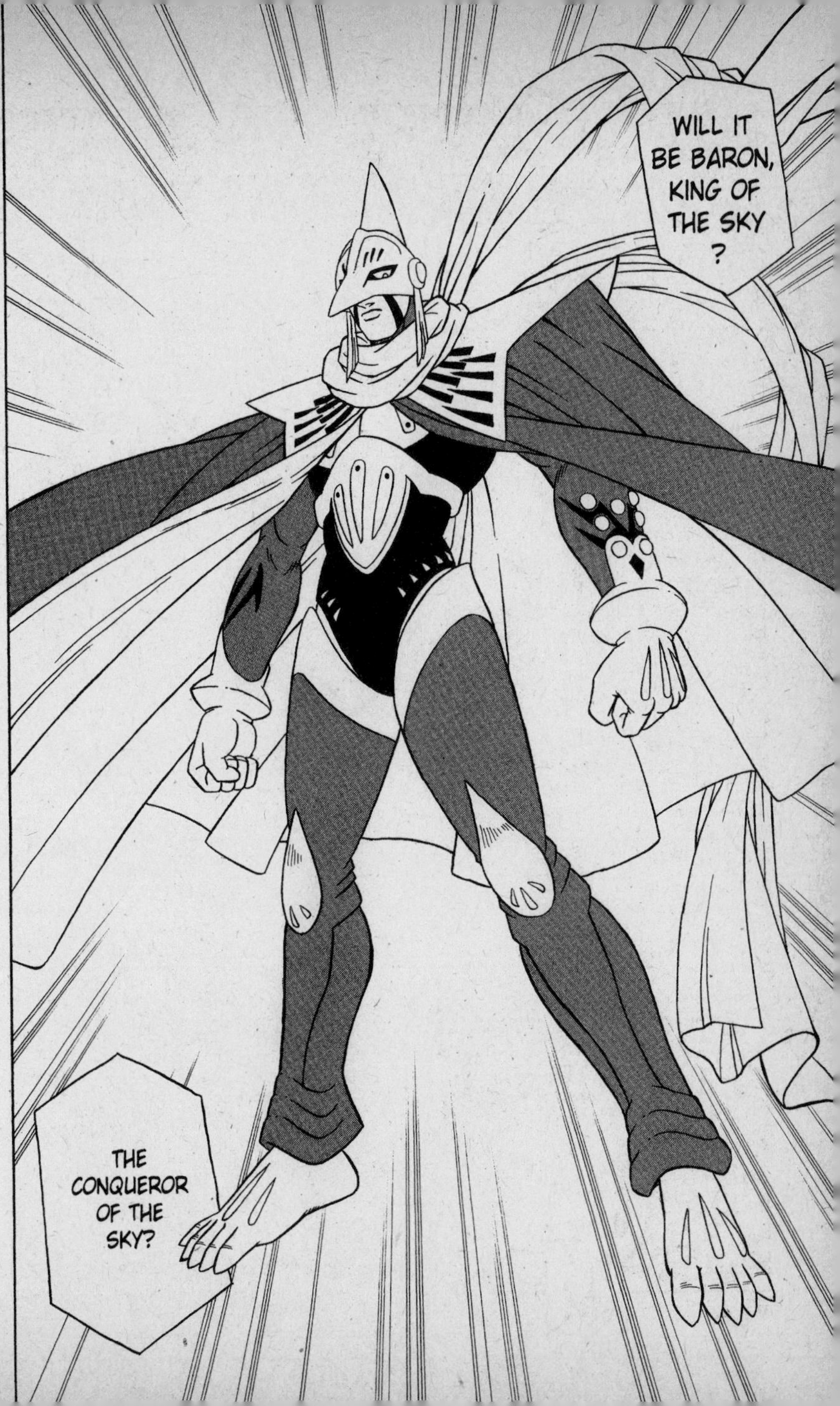
WILL IT BE BARON, KING OF THE SKY ?
THE CONQUEROR OF THE SKY?

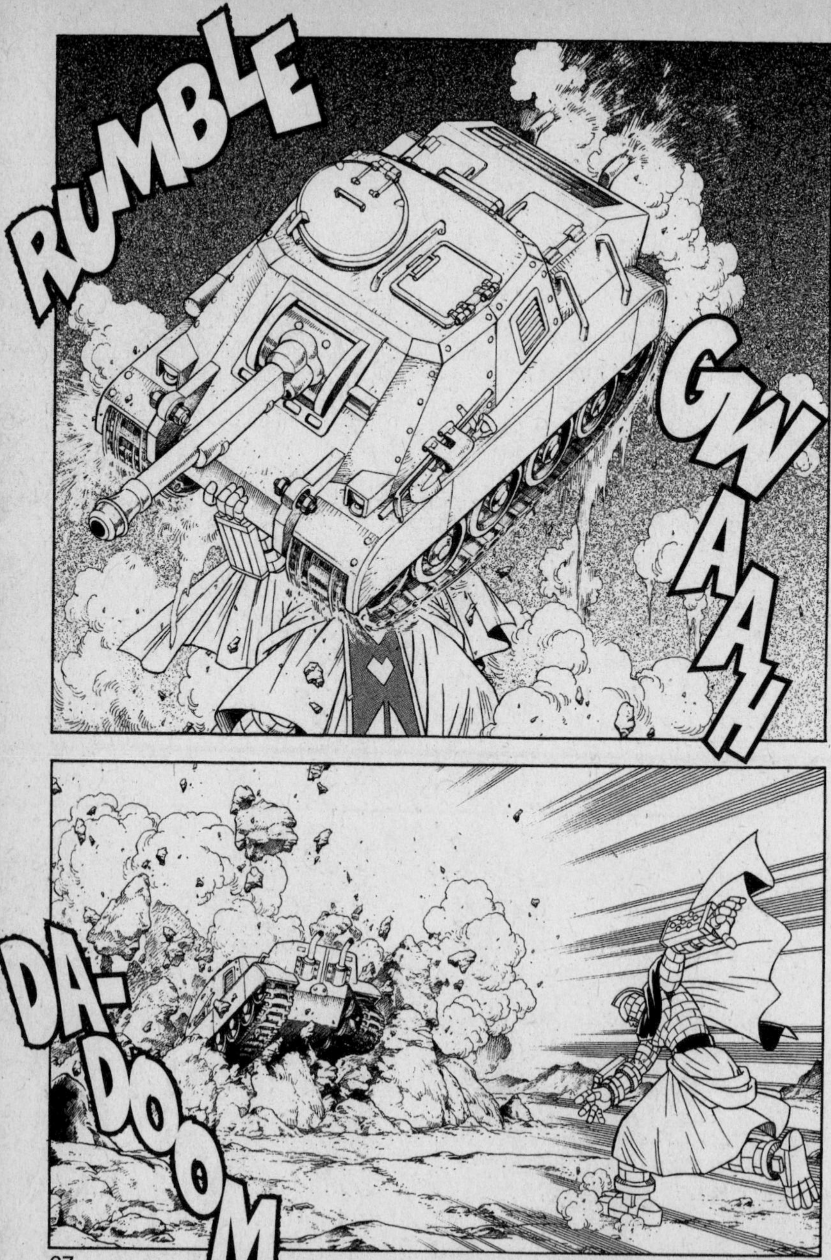
GWAAH
RUMBLE
DA-DOOM

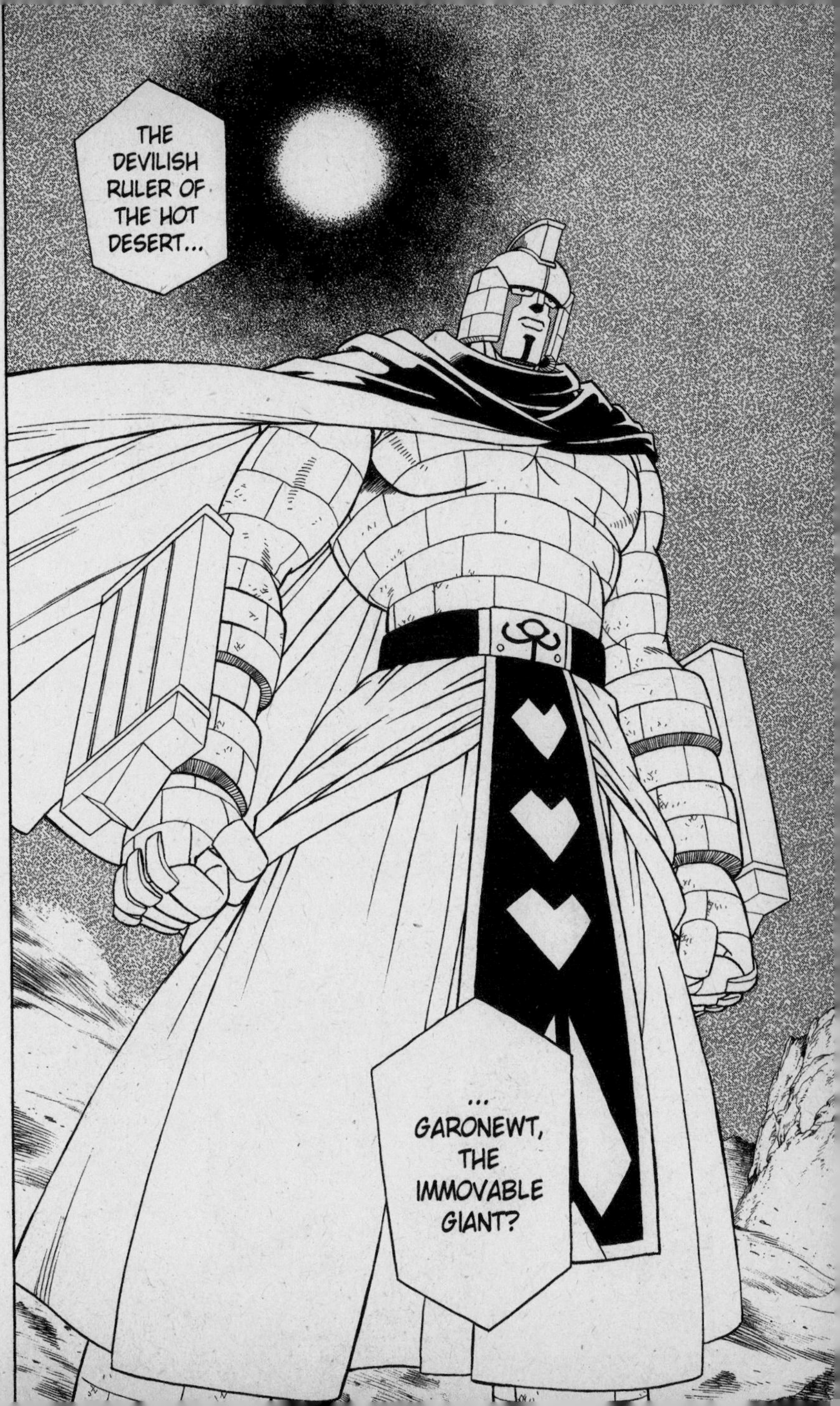
THE DEVILISH RULER OF THE HOT DESERT...
...GARONEWT, THE IMMOVABLE GIANT?

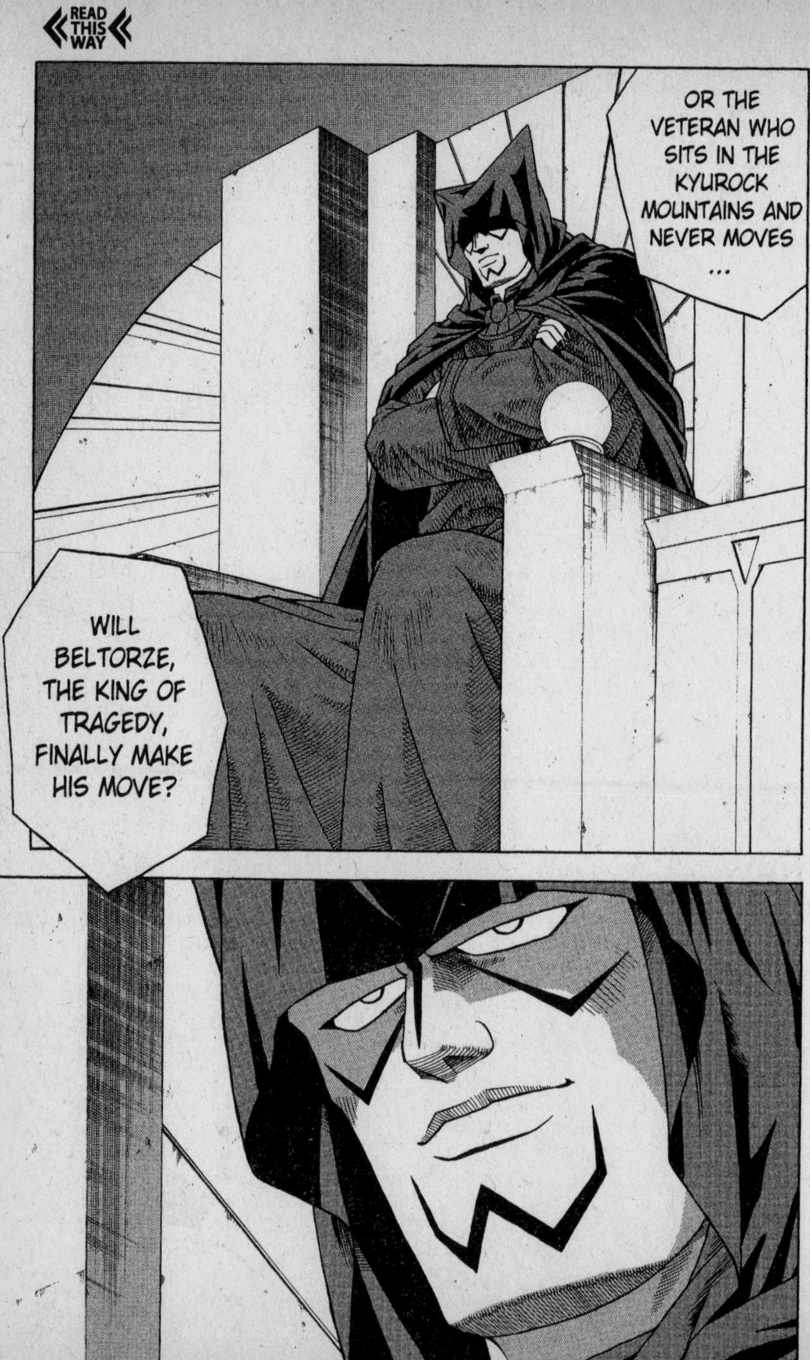
READ THIS WAY
OR THE VETERAN WHO SITS IN THE KYUROCK MOUNTAINS AND NEVER MOVES ...
WILL BELTORZE, THE KING OF TRAGEDY, FINALLY MAKE HIS MOVE?

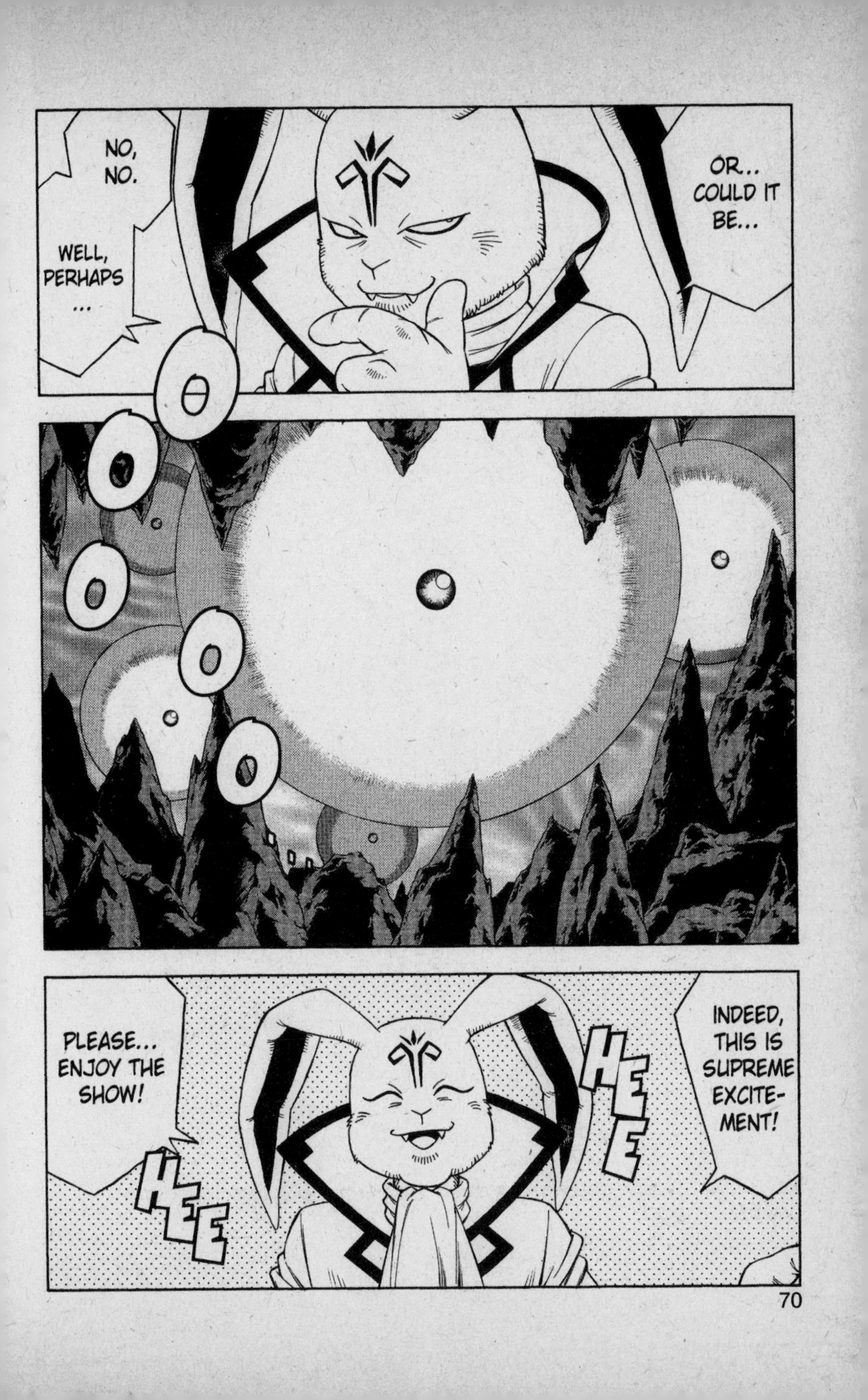
OR... COULD IT BE...
NO, NO.
WELL, PERHAPS...
INDEED, THIS IS SUPREME EXCITE-MENT!
HEE
PLEASE... ENJOY THE SHOW!
HEE

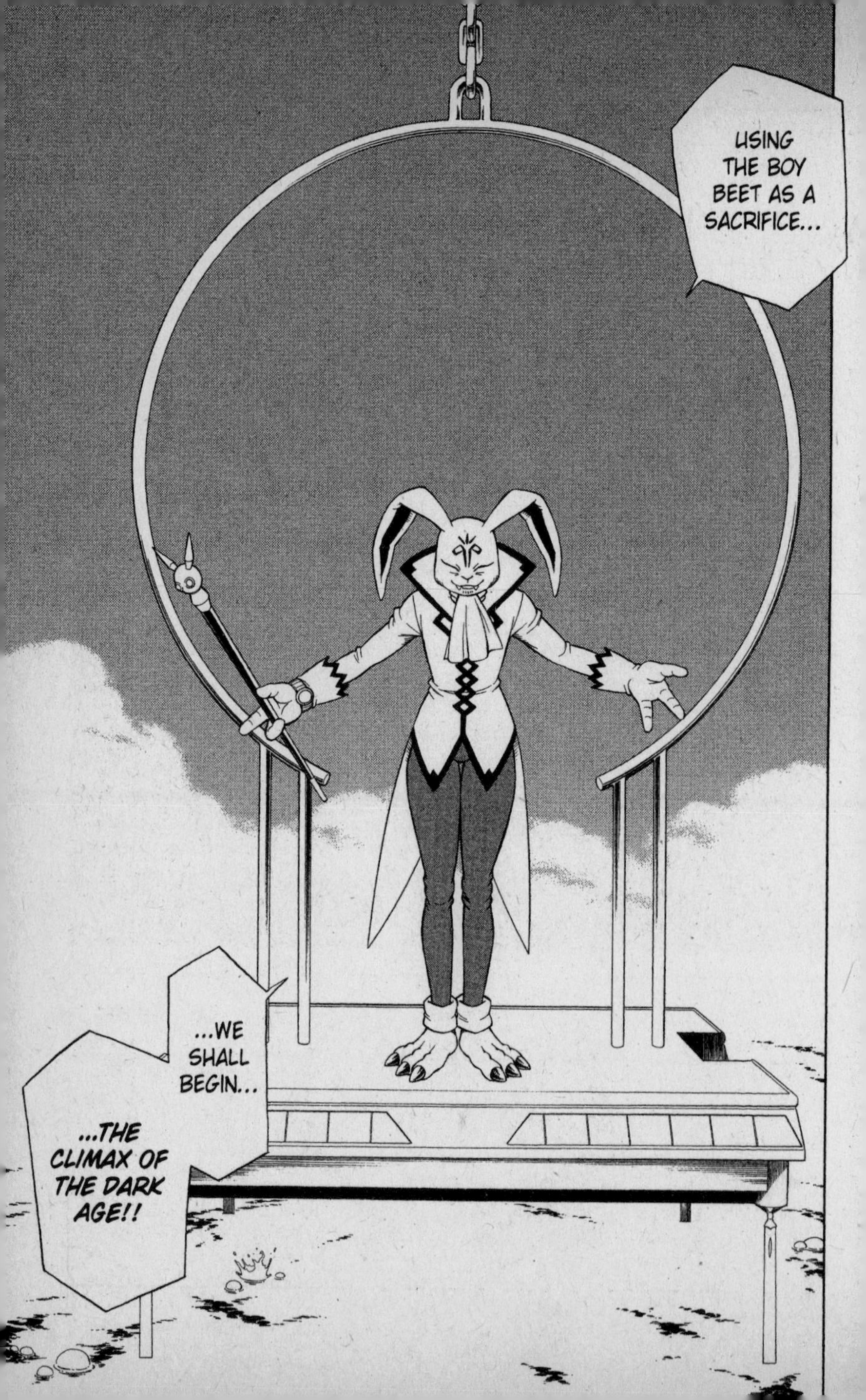
USING THE BOY BEET AS A SACRIFICE...
...WE SHALL BEGIN...
...THE CLIMAX OF THE DARK AGE!!

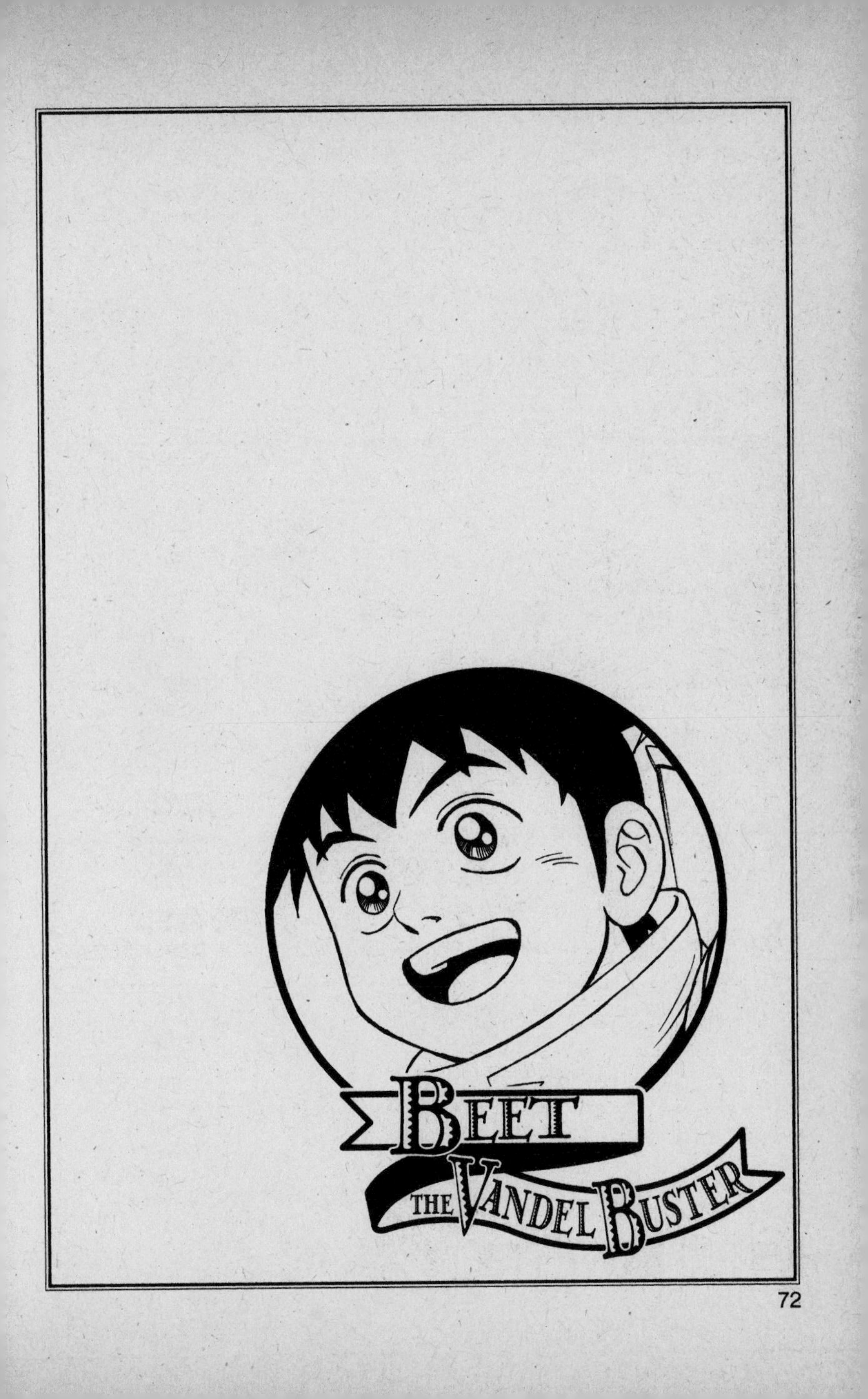
BEET
THE VANDEL BUSTER

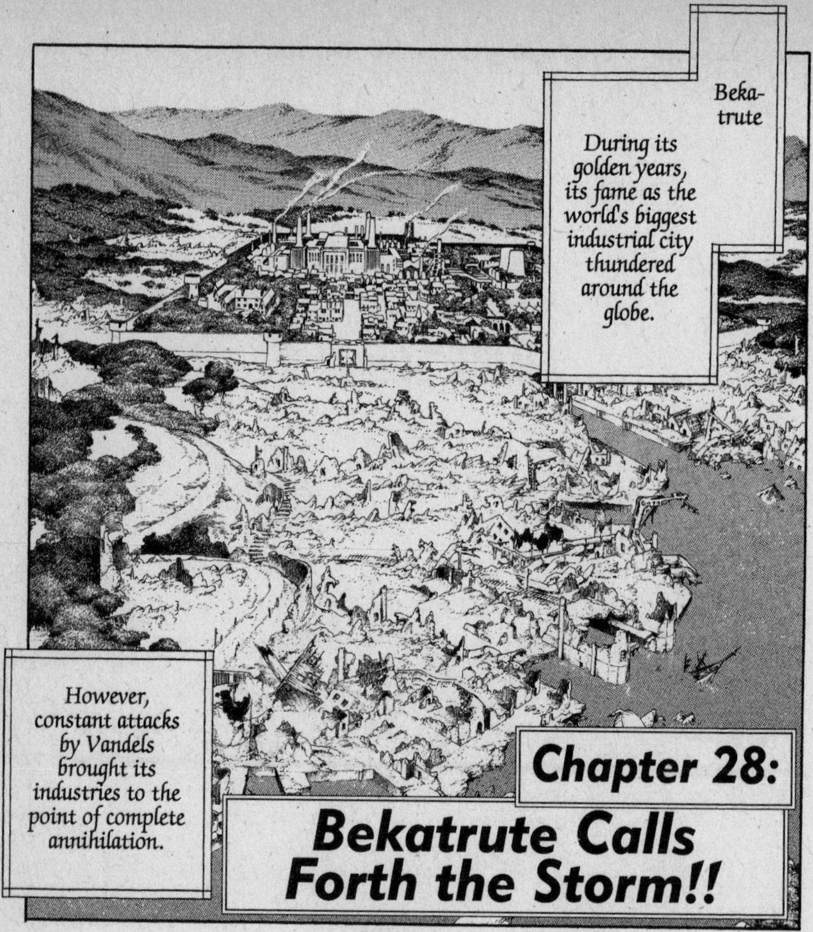
Beka-trute
During its golden years, its fame as the world's biggest industrial city thundered around the globe.
However, constant attacks by Vandels brought its industries to the point of complete annihilation.
Chapter 28:
Bekatrute Calls Forth the Storm!!

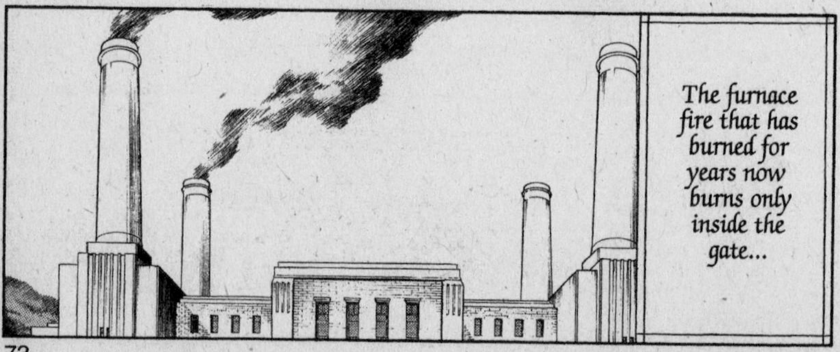
The furnace fire that has burned for years now burns only inside the gate...

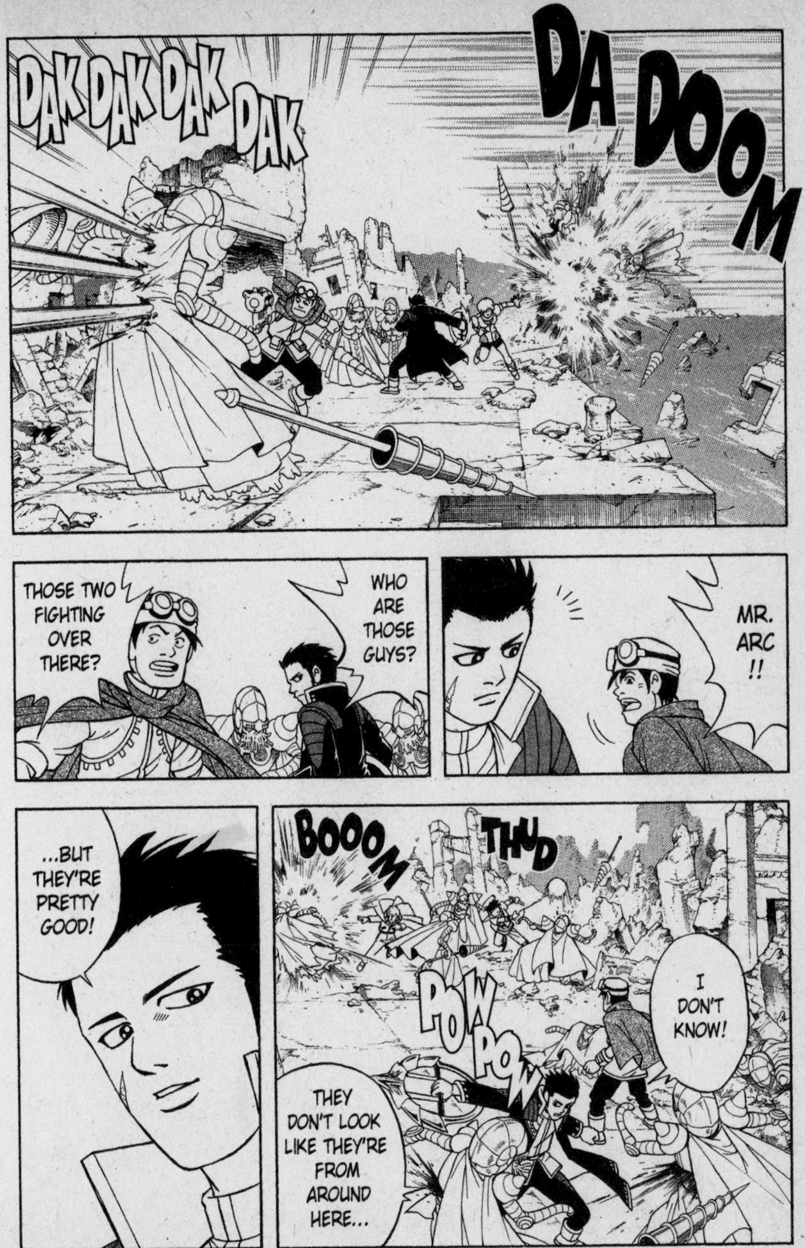
DA DOOM
DAK DAK DAK DAK
MR. ARC !!
WHO ARE THOSE GUYS?
THOSE TWO FIGHTING OVER THERE?
THUD
BOOOM
I DON'T KNOW!
POW POW
THEY DON'T LOOK LIKE THEY'RE FROM AROUND HERE...
...BUT THEY'RE PRETTY GOOD!

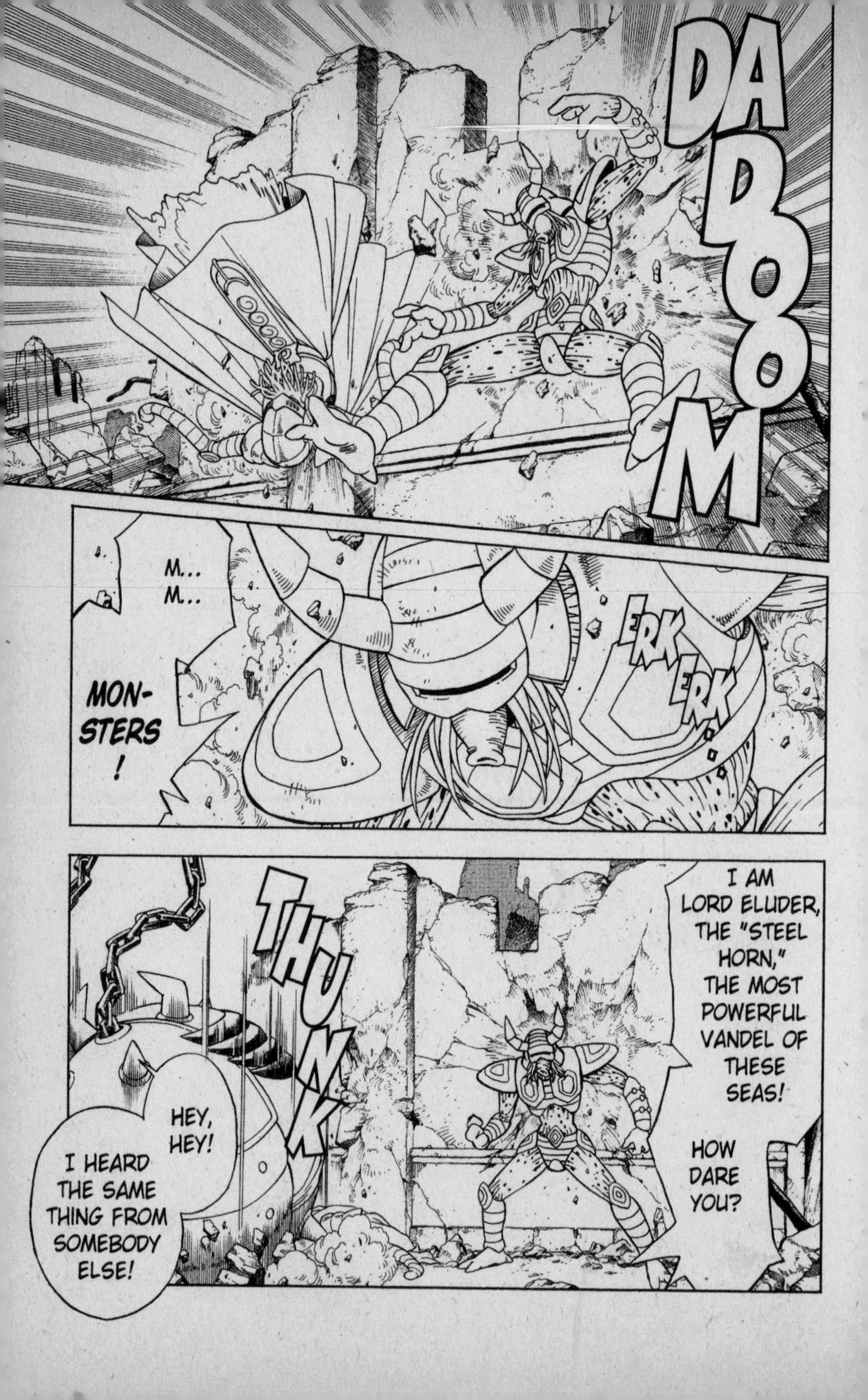
DABOOM
ERK ERK
M... M...
MON- STERS!
I AM LORD ELUDER, THE "STEEL HORN," THE MOST POWERFUL VANDEL OF THESE SEAS!
HOW DARE YOU?
THUNK
HEY, HEY!
I HEARD THE SAME THING FROM SOMEBODY ELSE!

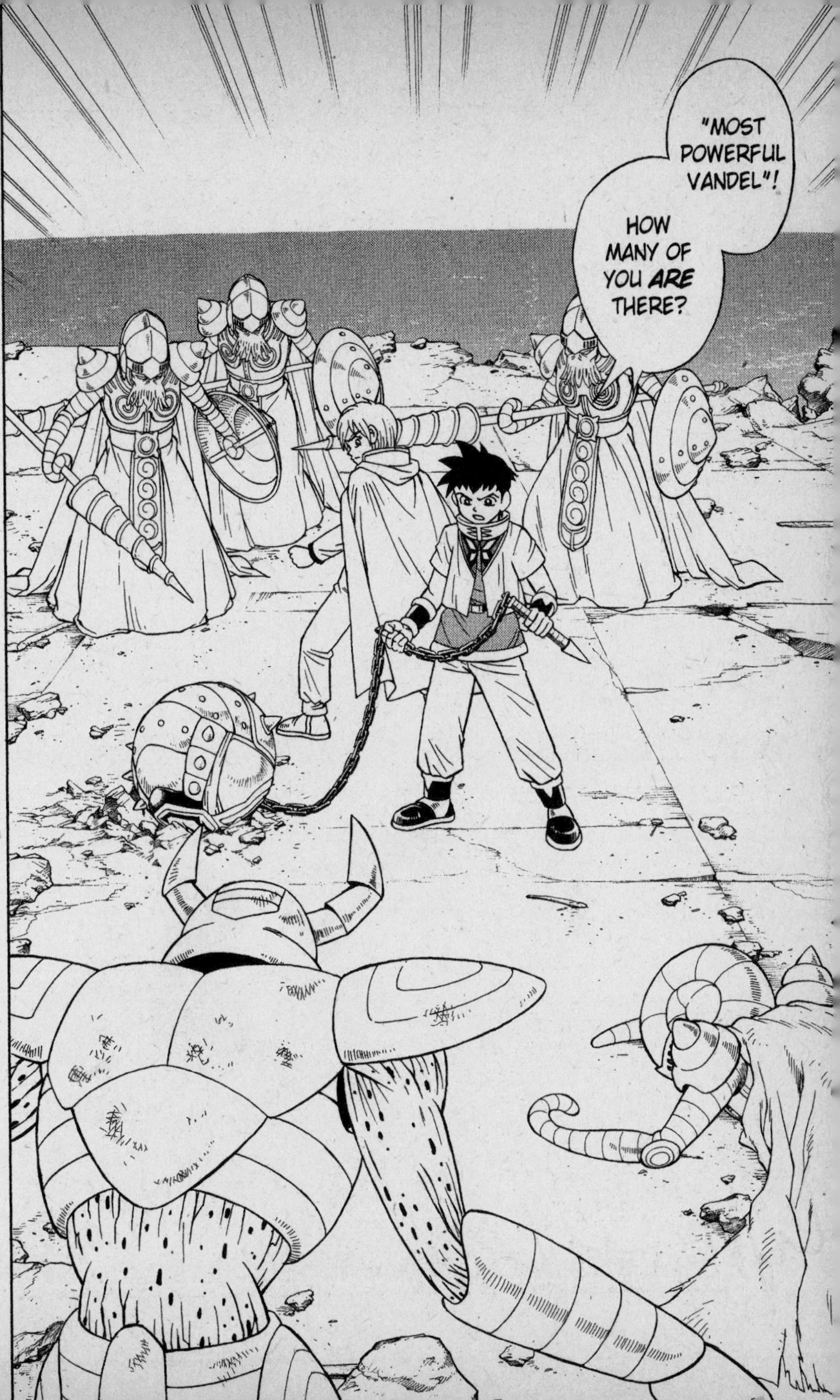
"MOST POWERFUL VANDEL"!
HOW MANY OF YOU ARE THERE?

READ THIS WAY

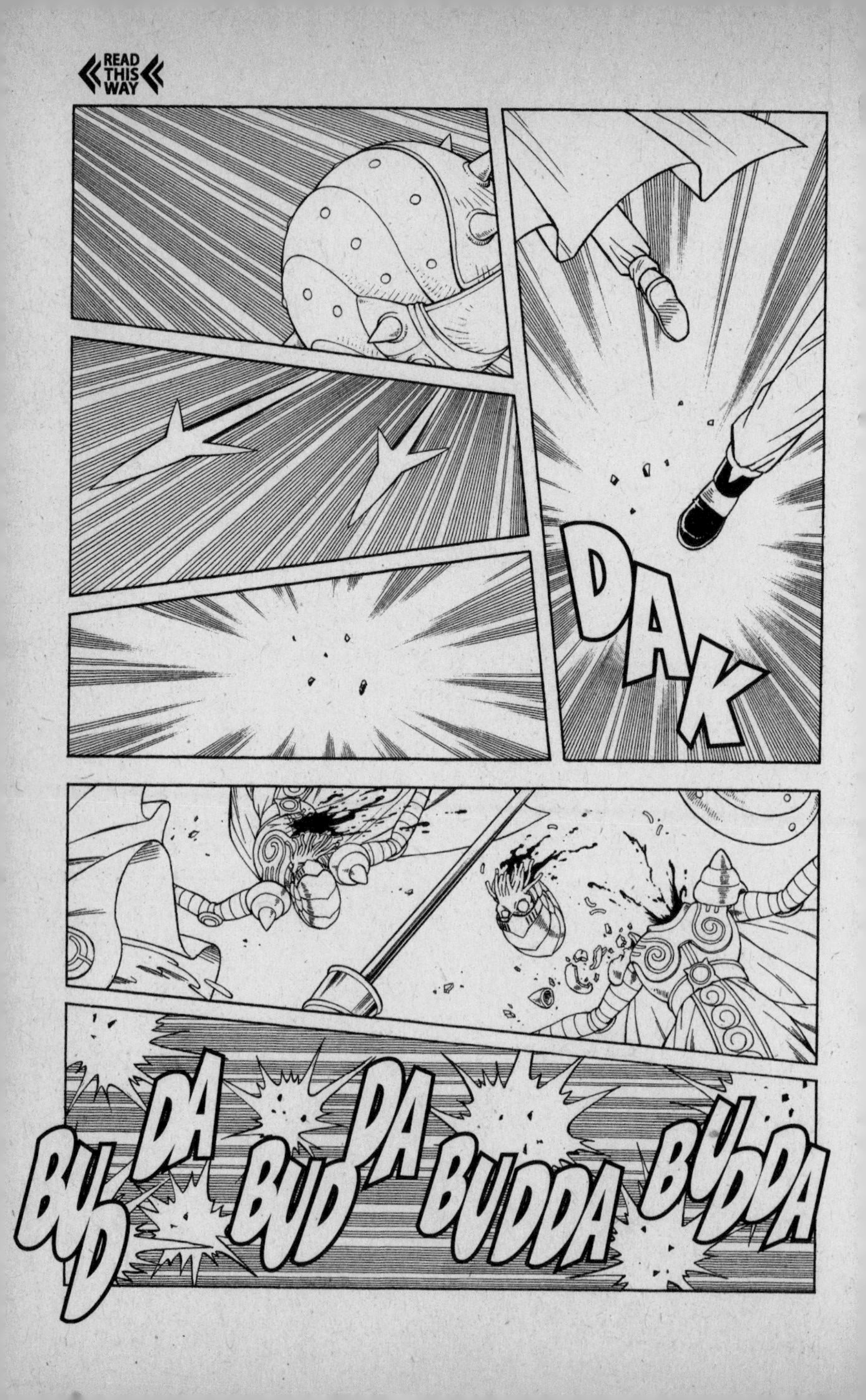
DAK
BUDDA BUDDA BUDDA BUDDA

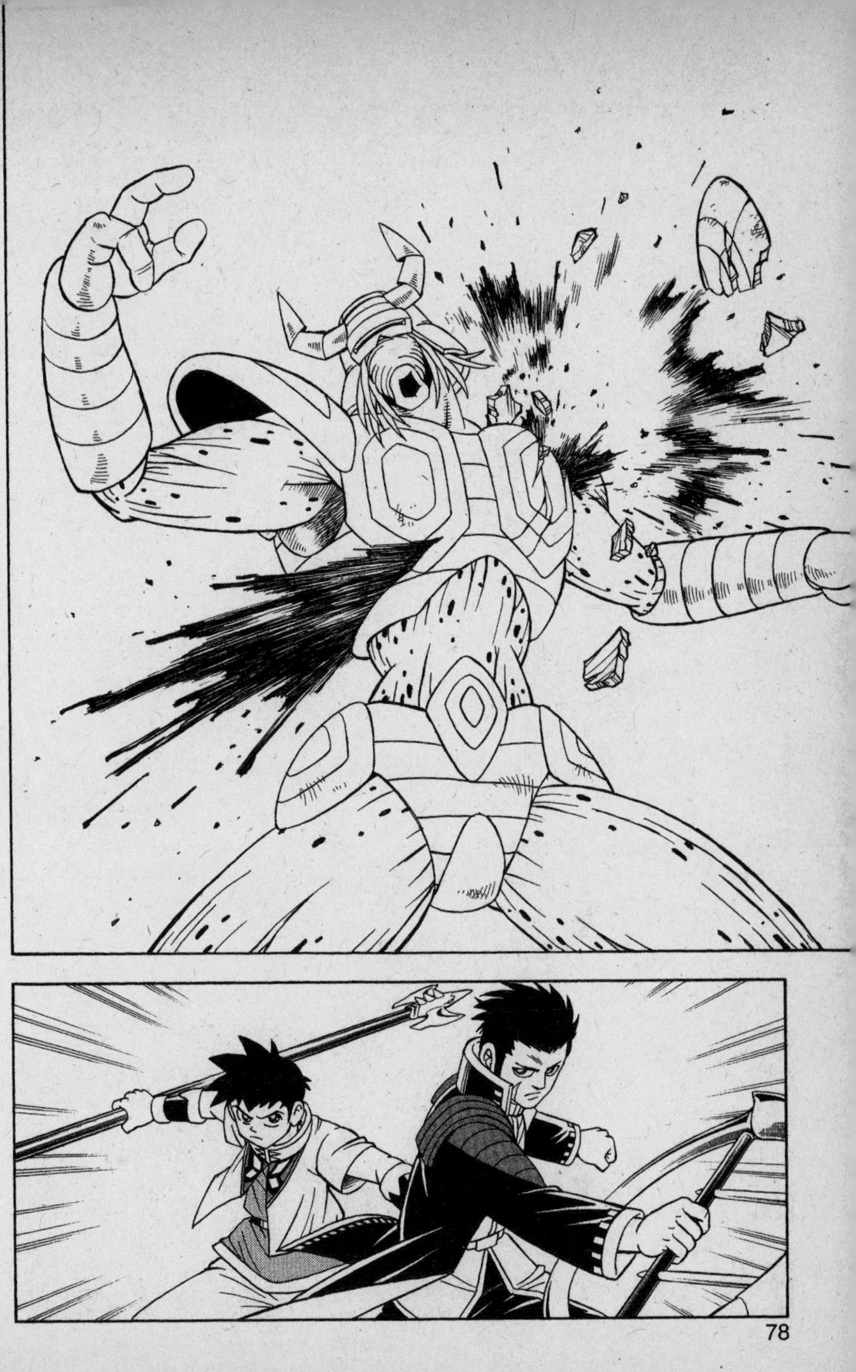

READ THIS WAY

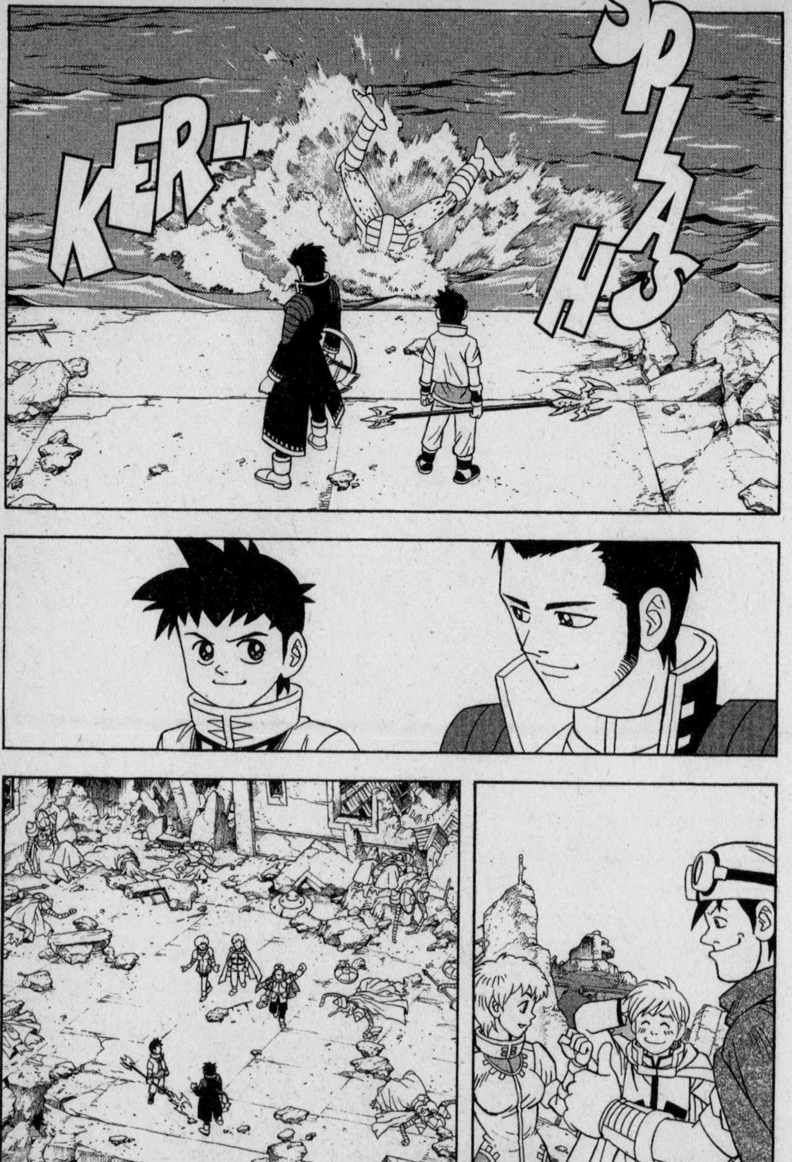
KER-
SPLASH

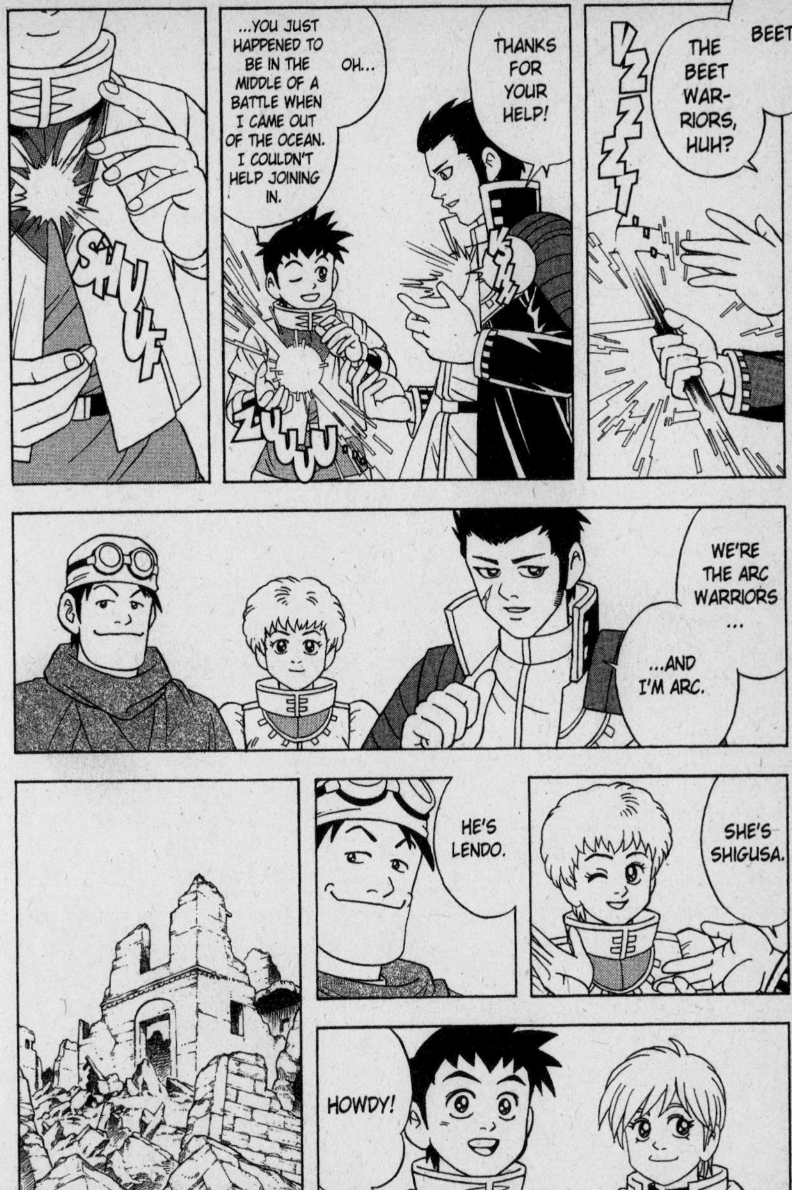
BEET...
THE BEET WAR-RIORS, HUH?
VZZZT
THANKS FOR YOUR HELP!
OH...
...YOU JUST HAPPENED TO BE IN THE MIDDLE OF A BATTLE WHEN I CAME OUT OF THE OCEAN. I COULDN'T HELP JOINING IN.
VSHH
ZUUUU
SHUUF
WE'RE THE ARC WARRIORS...
...AND I'M ARC.
SHE'S SHIGUSA.
HE'S LENDO.
HOWDY!

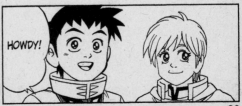

READ THIS WAY

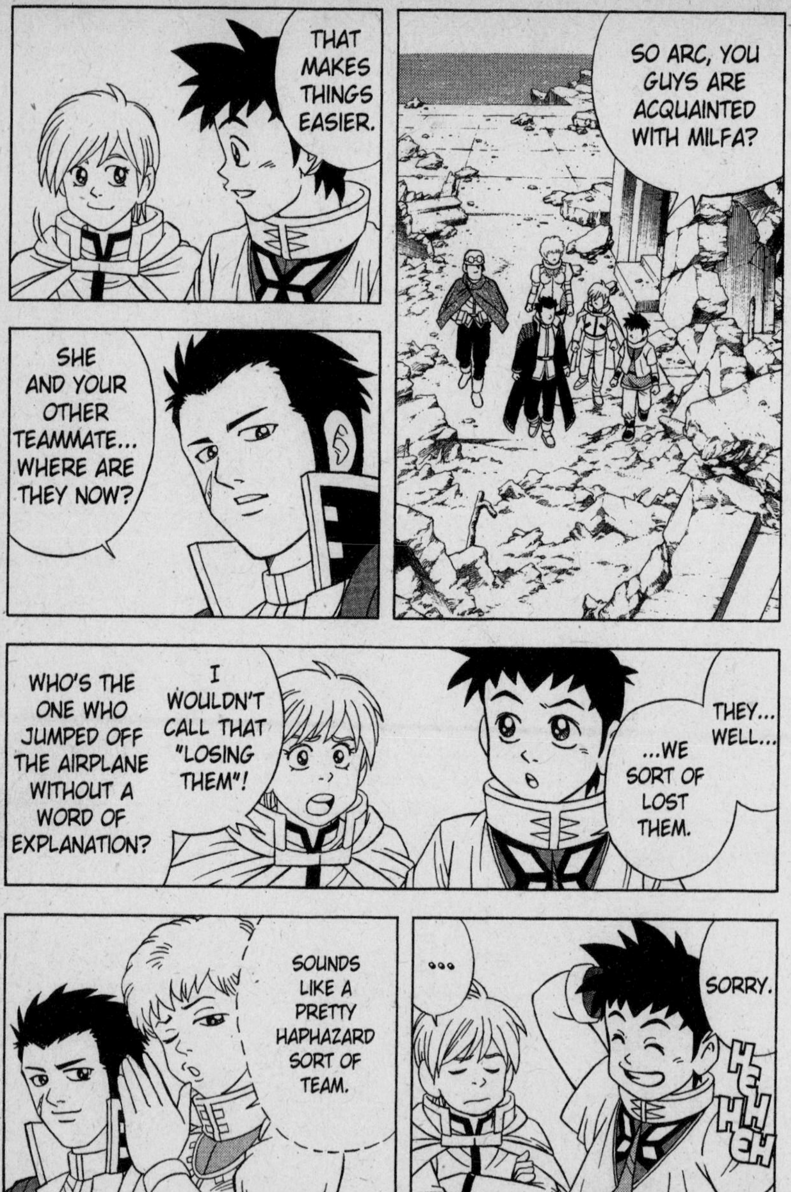

SO ARC, YOU GUYS ARE ACQUAINTED WITH MILFA?
THAT MAKES THINGS EASIER.
SHE AND YOUR OTHER TEAMMATE... WHERE ARE THEY NOW?
THEY... WELL...
...WE SORT OF LOST THEM.
I WOULDN'T CALL THAT "LOSING THEM"!
WHO'S THE ONE WHO JUMPED OFF THE AIRPLANE WITHOUT A WORD OF EXPLANATION?
SORRY.
HEH HEH HEH
...
SOUNDS LIKE A PRETTY HAPHAZARD SORT OF TEAM.

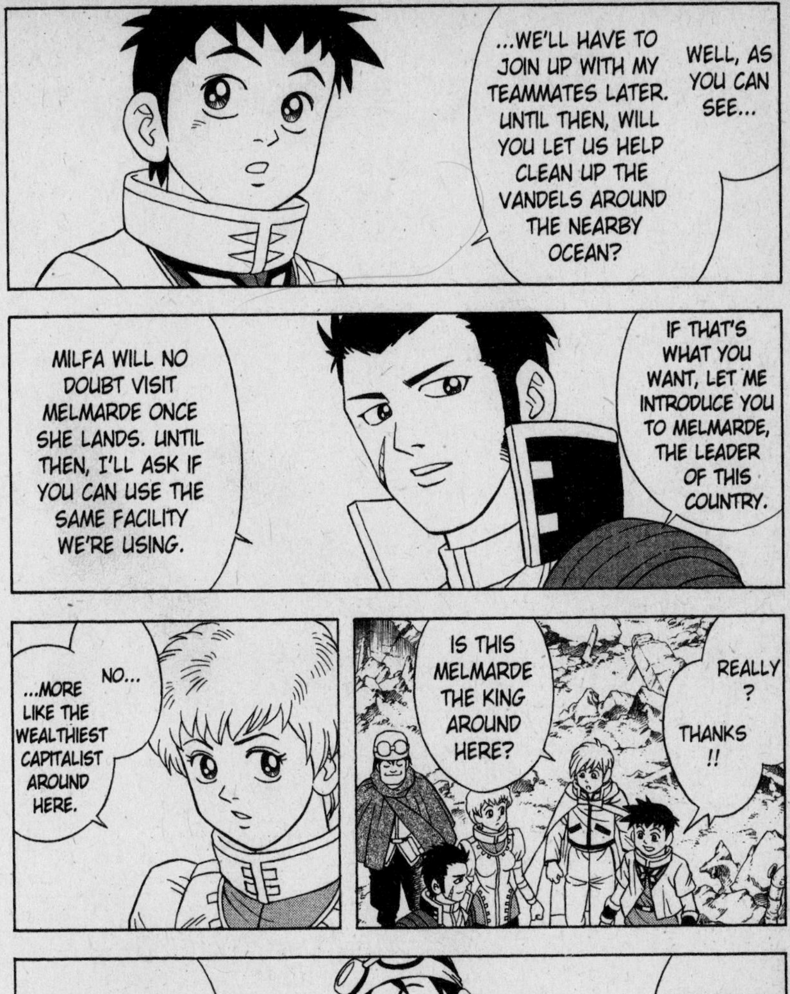
WELL, AS YOU CAN SEE...
...WE'LL HAVE TO JOIN UP WITH MY TEAMMATES LATER. UNTIL THEN, WILL YOU LET US HELP CLEAN UP THE VANDELS AROUND THE NEARBY OCEAN?
IF THAT'S WHAT YOU WANT, LET ME INTRODUCE YOU TO MELMARDE, THE LEADER OF THIS COUNTRY.
MILFA WILL NO DOUBT VISIT MELMARDE ONCE SHE LANDS. UNTIL THEN, I'LL ASK IF YOU CAN USE THE SAME FACILITY WE'RE USING.
REALLY? THANKS!!
IS THIS MELMARDE THE KING AROUND HERE?
NO...
...MORE LIKE THE WEALTHIEST CAPITALIST AROUND HERE.
BEKATRUTE'S GOVERNMENT HAS BEEN DESTROYED.
THE FAMILY THAT USED TO CONTROL THE INDUSTRIES HAS TAKEN OVER THE FUNCTIONS OF LEADERSHIP.

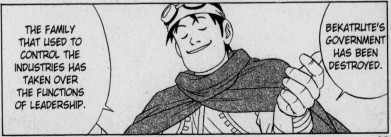

READ THIS WAY

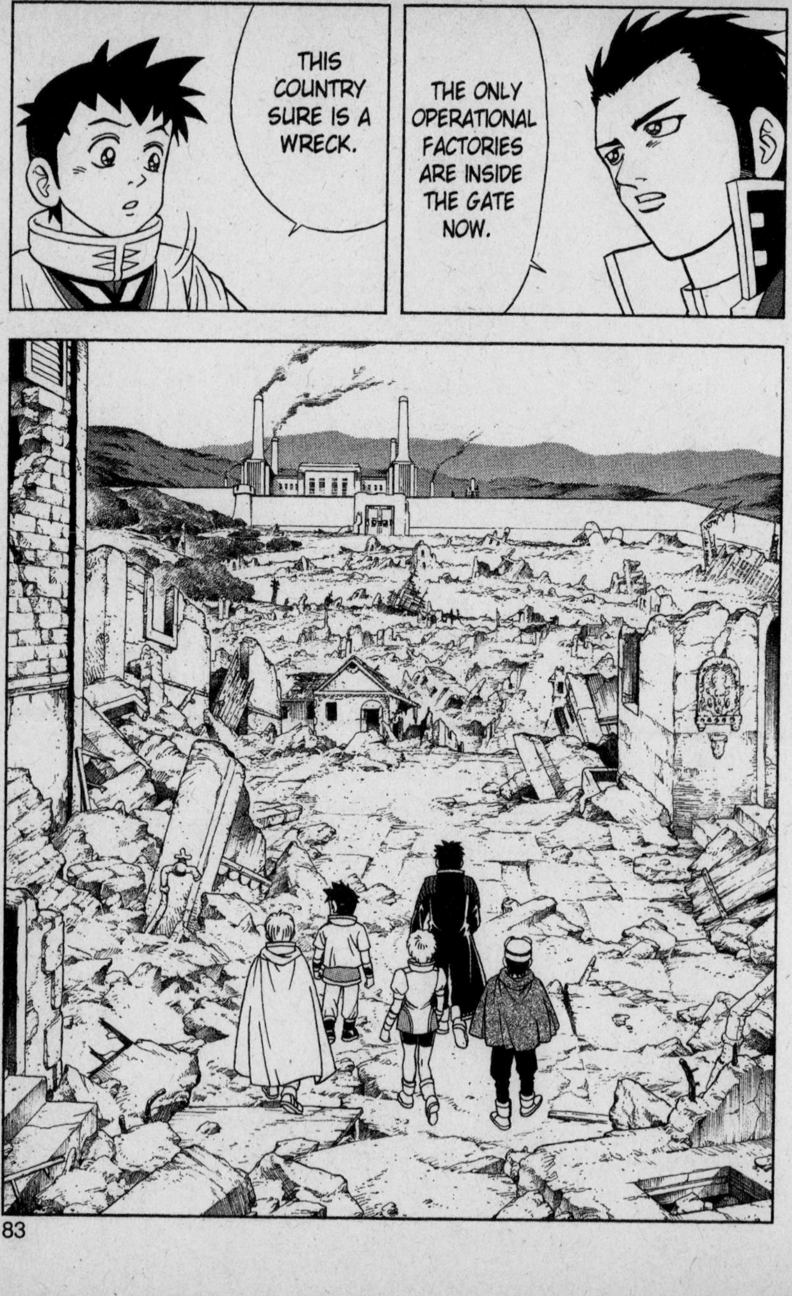
THE ONLY OPERATIONAL FACTORIES ARE INSIDE THE GATE NOW.
THIS COUNTRY SURE IS A WRECK.

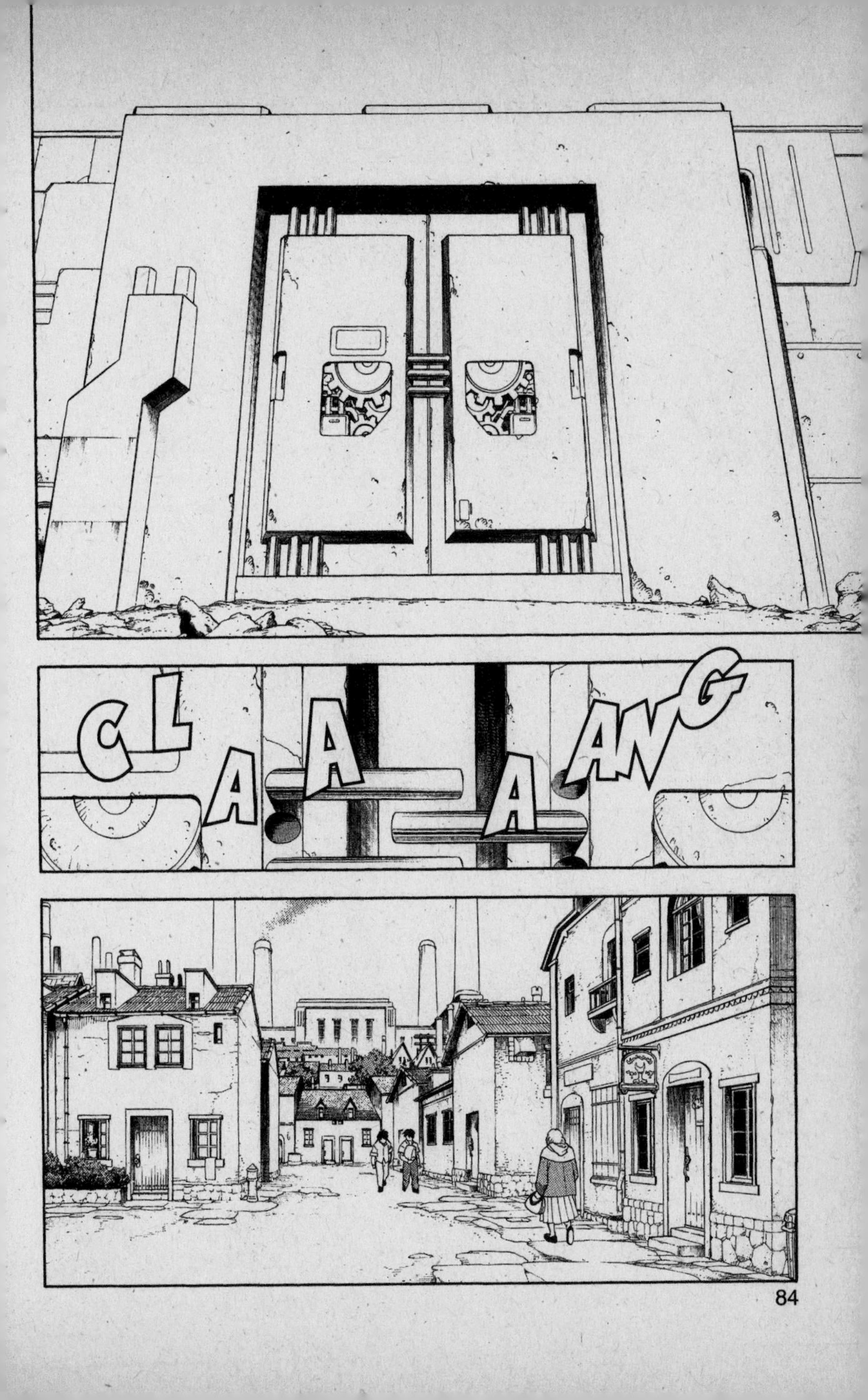
CLAAAANG

READ THIS WAY

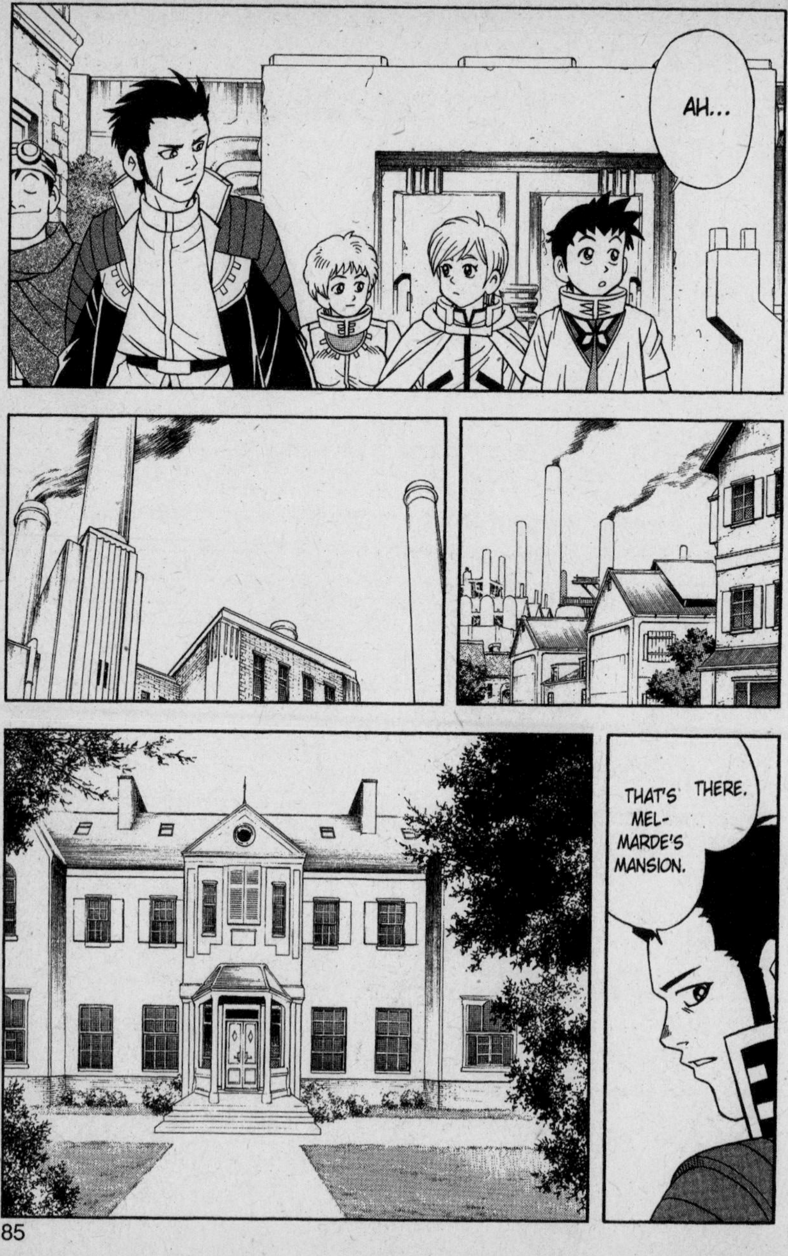
AH...
THERE. THAT'S MEL-MARDE'S MANSION.

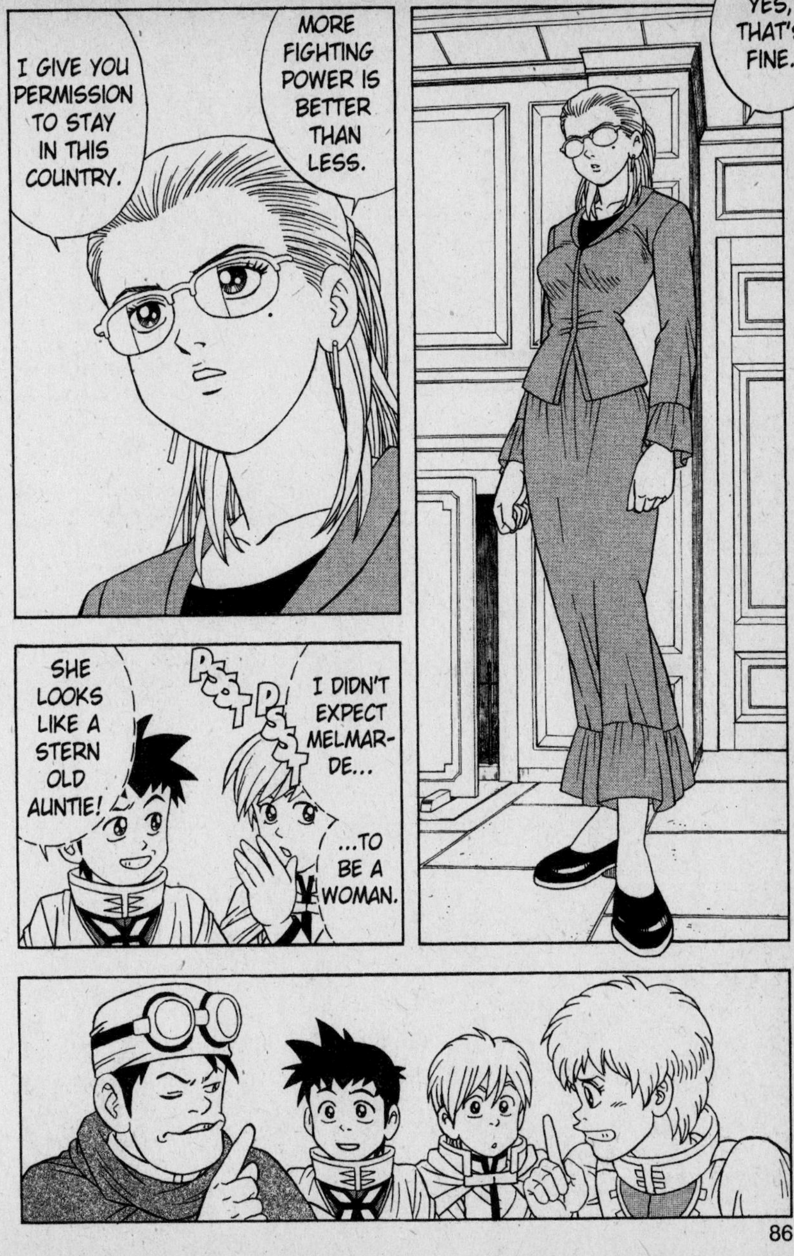
YES, THAT'S FINE.
MORE FIGHTING POWER IS BETTER THAN LESS.
I GIVE YOU PERMISSION TO STAY IN THIS COUNTRY.
I DIDN'T EXPECT MELMARDE...
PSST PSST
SHE LOOKS LIKE A STERN OLD AUNTIE!
...TO BE A WOMAN.

READ THIS WAY

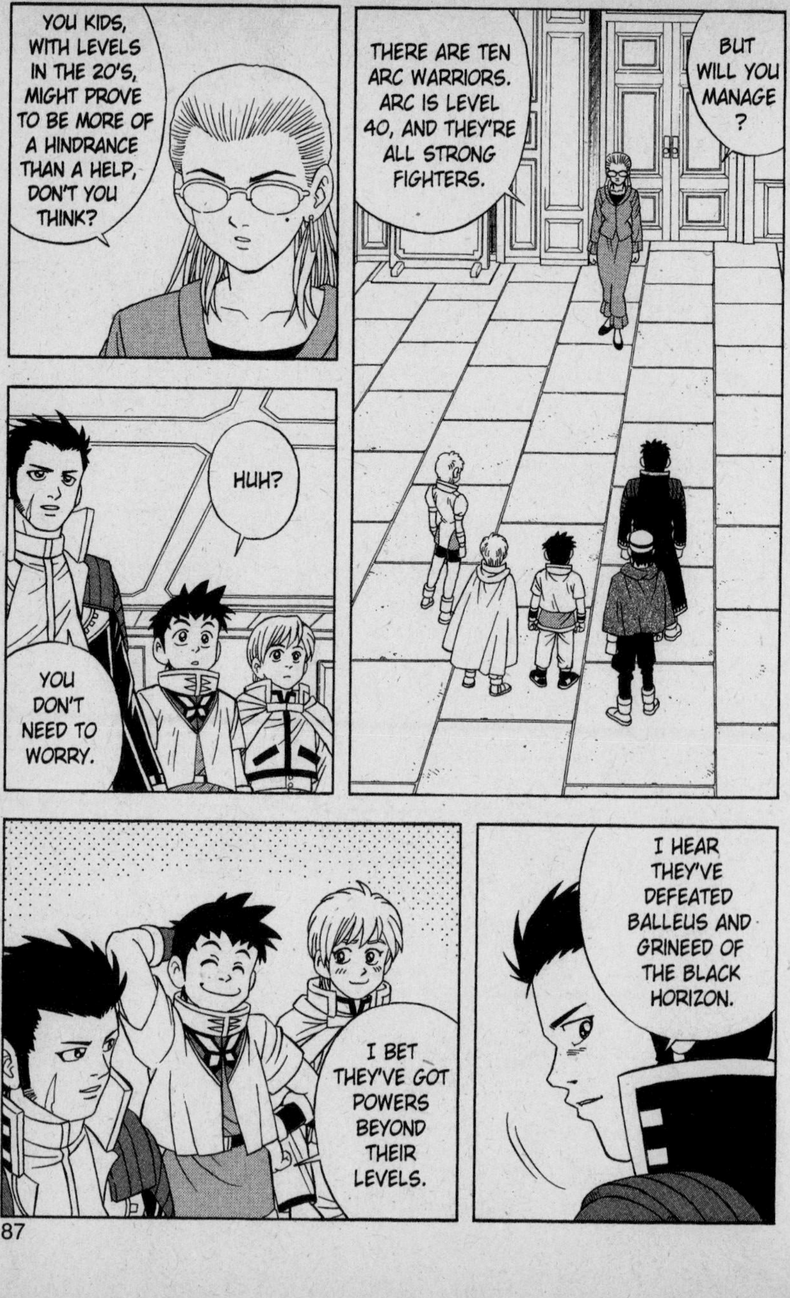
BUT WILL YOU MANAGE?
THERE ARE TEN ARC WARRIORS. ARC IS LEVEL 40, AND THEY'RE ALL STRONG FIGHTERS.
YOU KIDS, WITH LEVELS IN THE 20'S, MIGHT PROVE TO BE MORE OF A HINDRANCE THAN A HELP, DON'T YOU THINK?
HUH?
YOU DON'T NEED TO WORRY.
I HEAR THEY'VE DEFEATED BALLEUS AND GRINEED OF THE BLACK HORIZON.
I BET THEY'VE GOT POWERS BEYOND THEIR LEVELS.

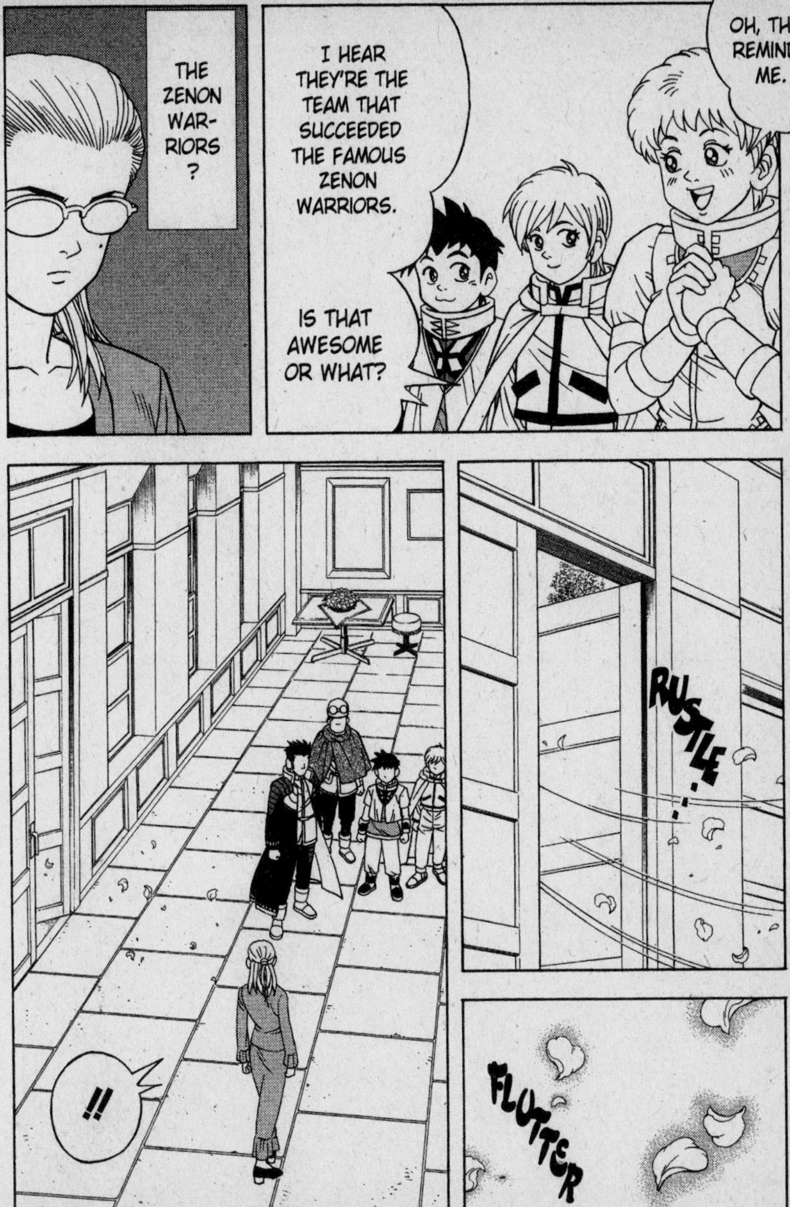
OH, THAT REMINDS ME.
I HEAR THEY'RE THE TEAM THAT SUCCEEDED THE FAMOUS ZENON WARRIORS.
IS THAT AWESOME OR WHAT?
THE ZENON WAR-RIORS ?
RUSTLE...
FLUTTER
!!

READ THIS WAY

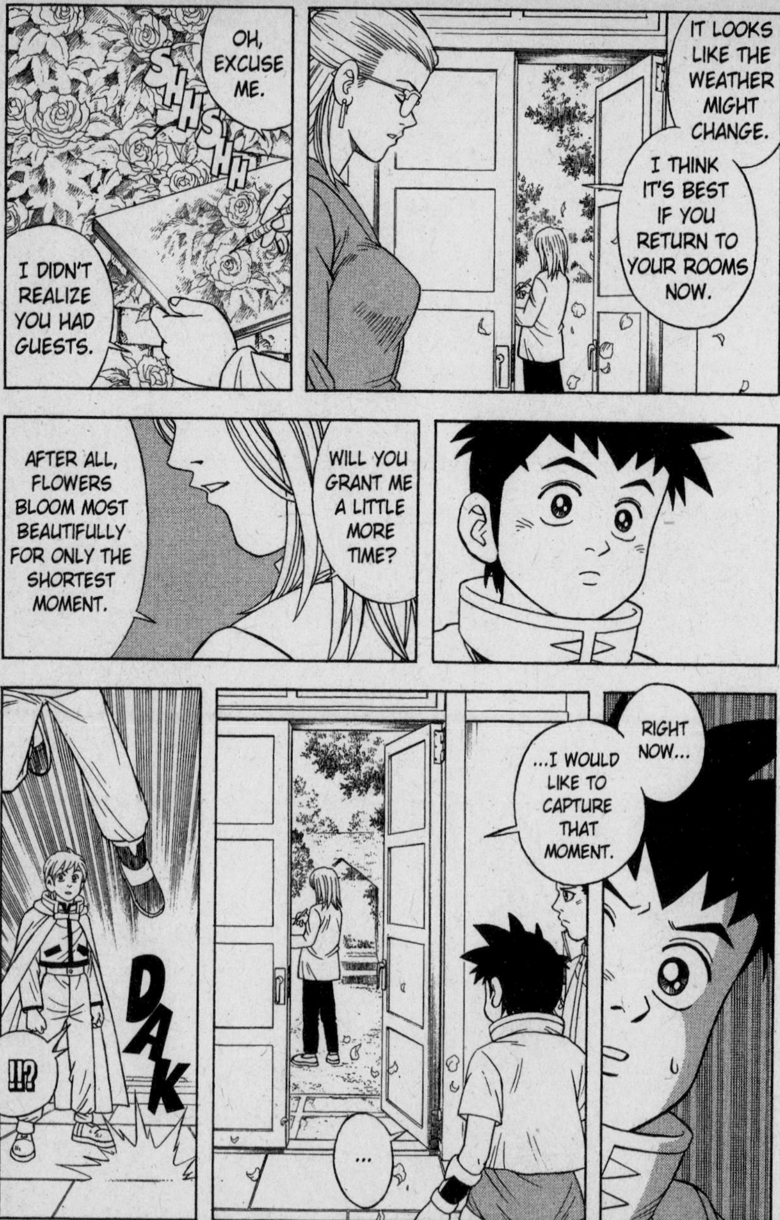
IT LOOKS LIKE THE WEATHER MIGHT CHANGE.
I THINK IT'S BEST IF YOU RETURN TO YOUR ROOMS NOW.
OH, EXCUSE ME.
SHHSHH
I DIDN'T REALIZE YOU HAD GUESTS.
WILL YOU GRANT ME A LITTLE MORE TIME?
AFTER ALL, FLOWERS BLOOM MOST BEAUTIFULLY FOR ONLY THE SHORTEST MOMENT.
RIGHT NOW...
...I WOULD LIKE TO CAPTURE THAT MOMENT.
...
DAK
!!?

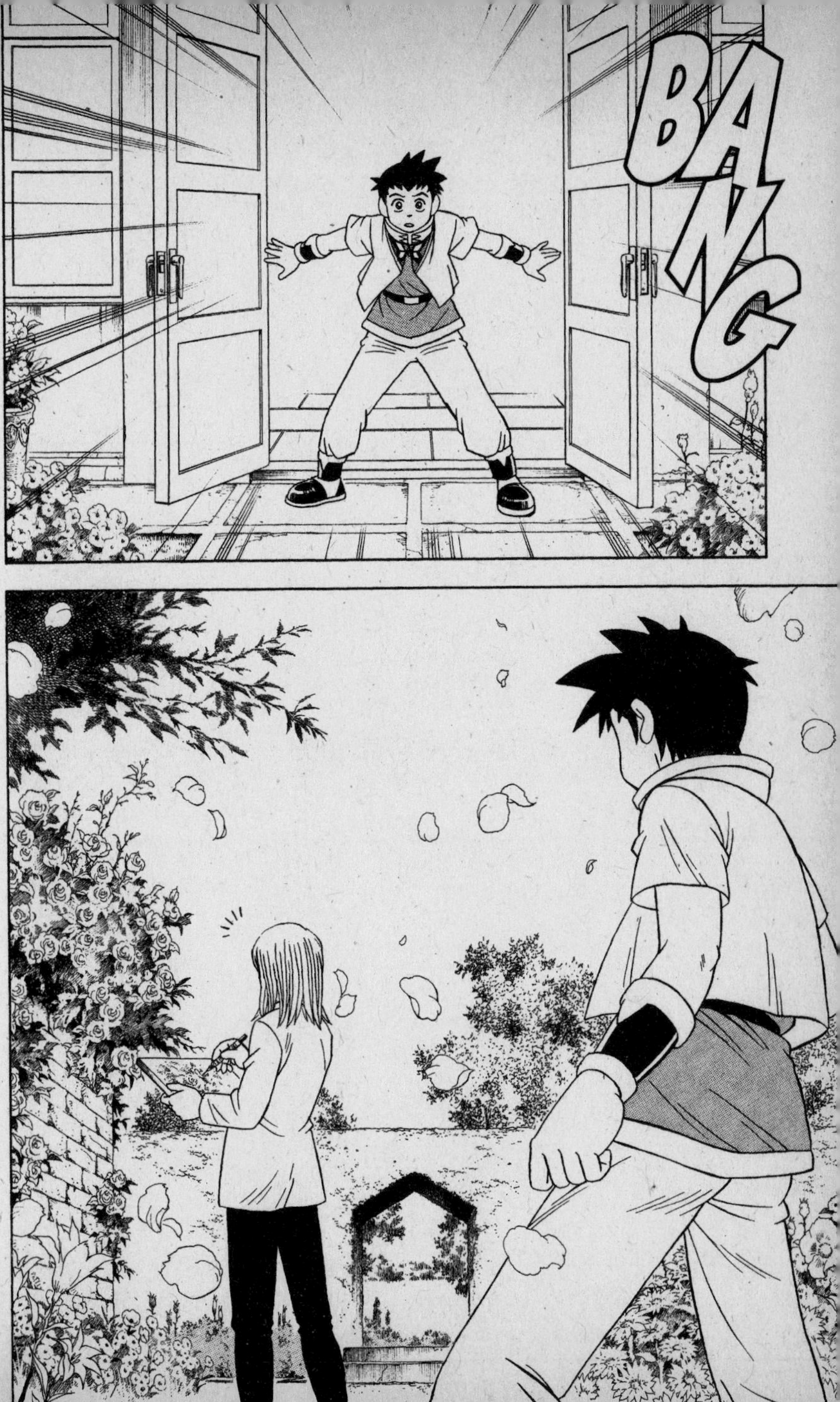
BANG

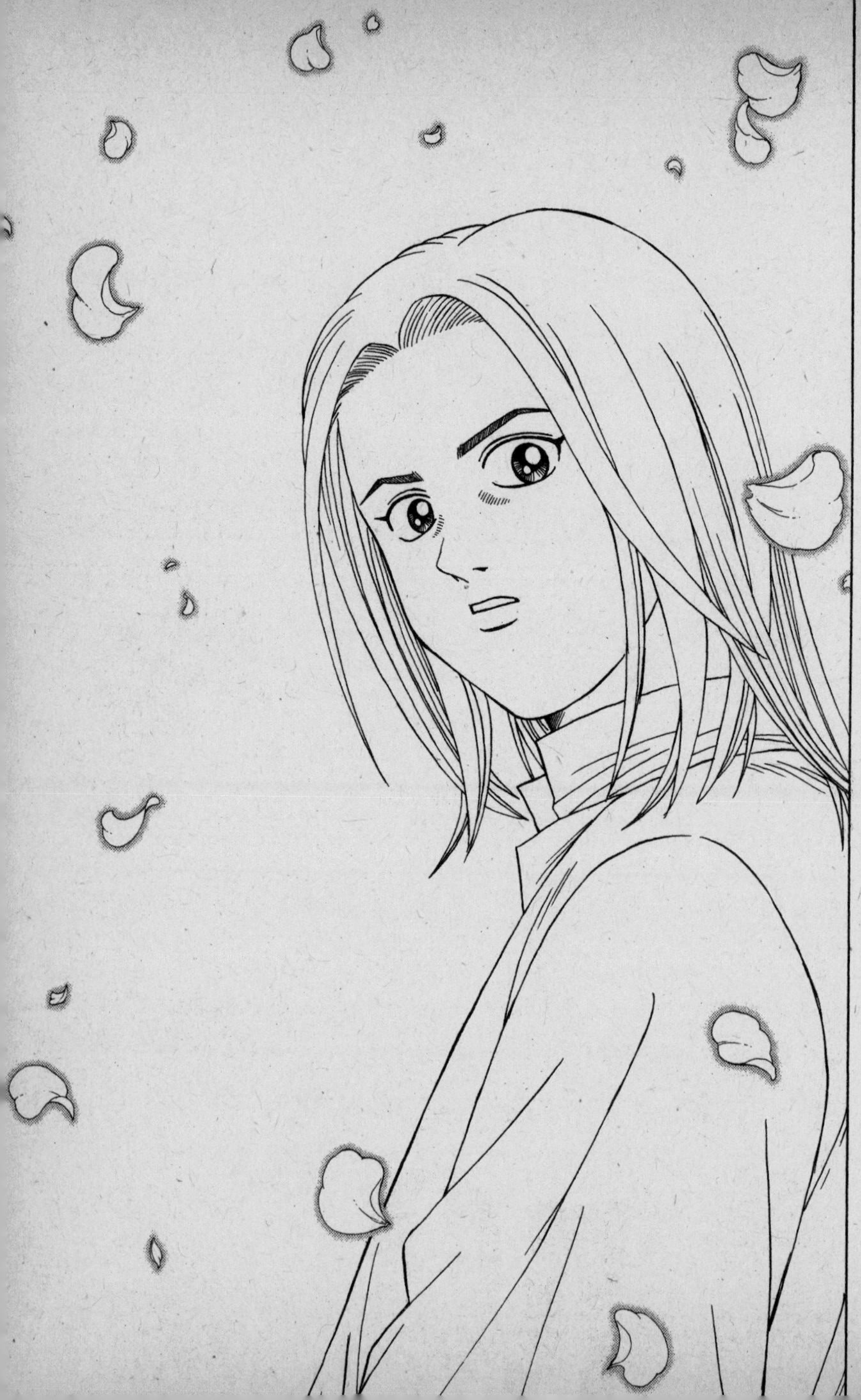

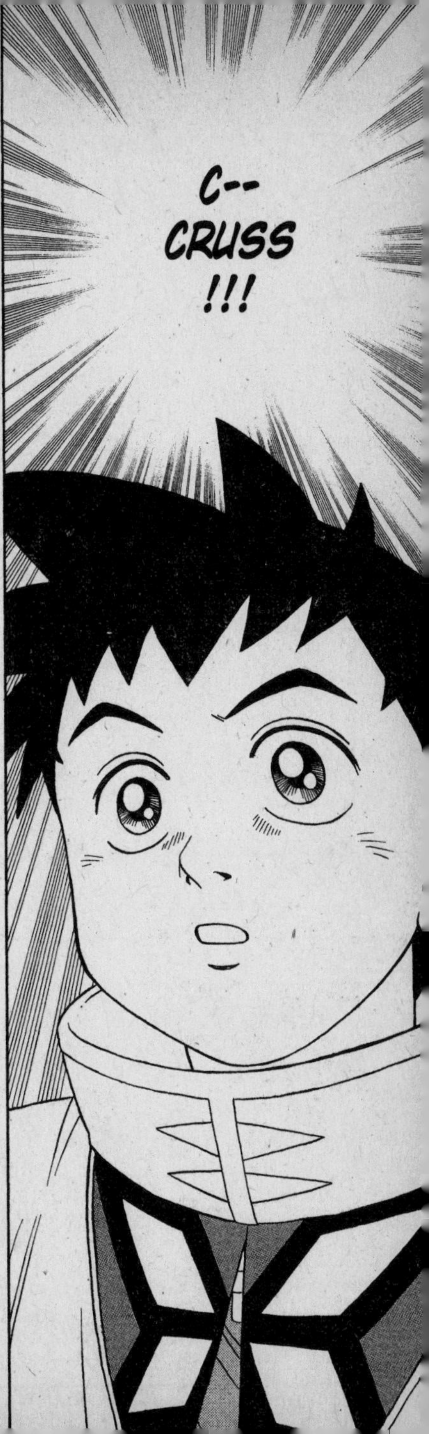
C-- CRUSS !!!
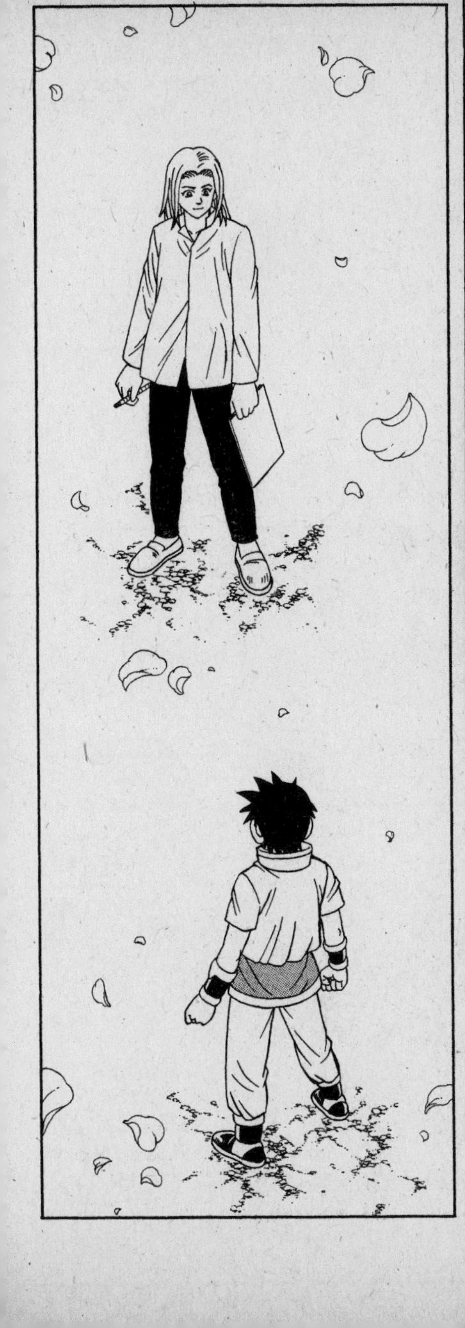

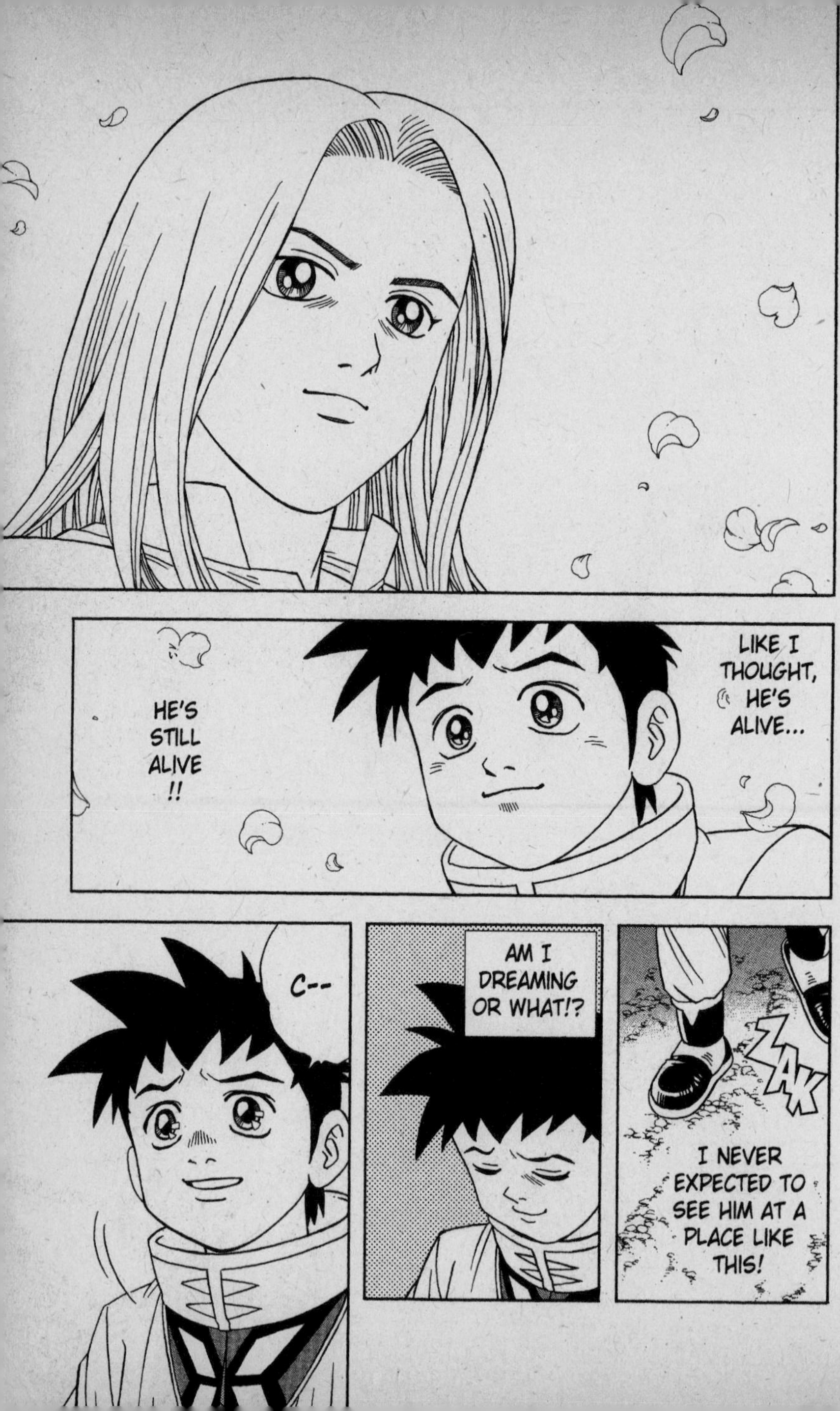
LIKE I THOUGHT, HE'S ALIVE...
HE'S STILL ALIVE!!
ZAK
I NEVER EXPECTED TO SEE HIM AT A PLACE LIKE THIS!
AM I DREAMING OR WHAT!?
C--

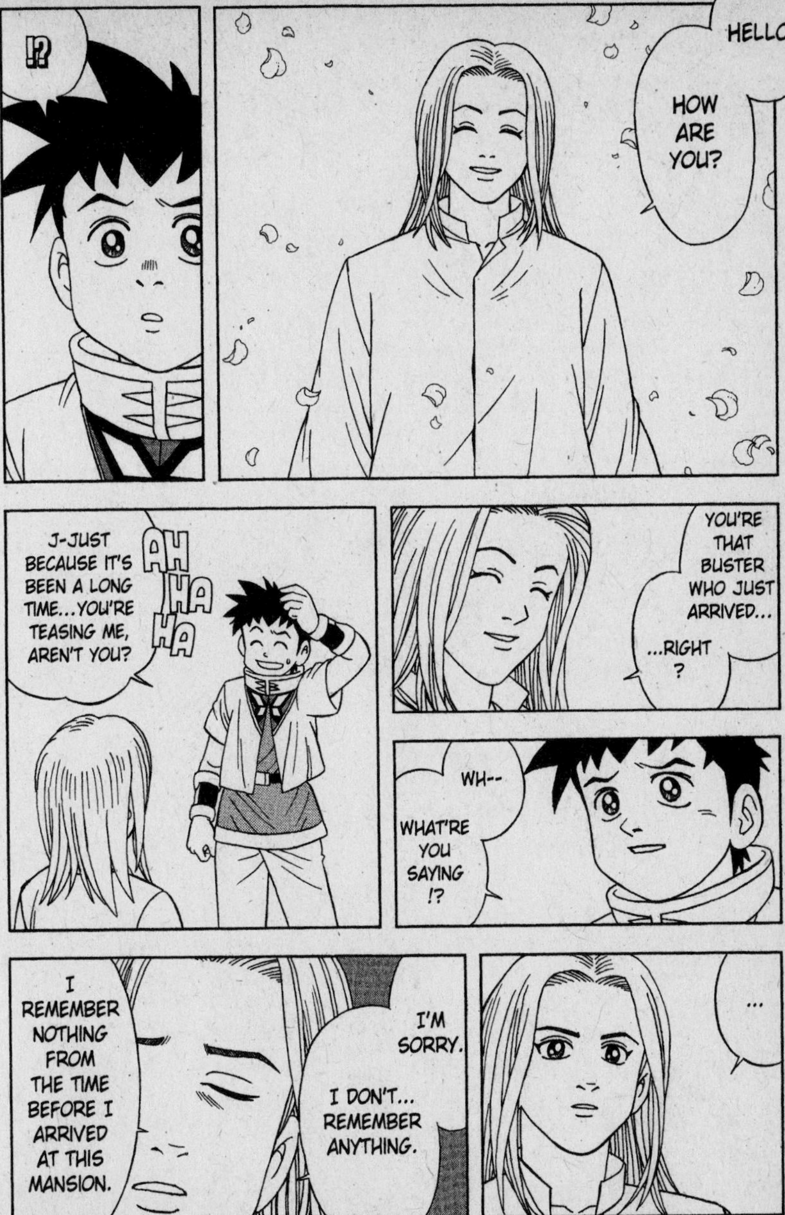
HELLO!
HOW ARE YOU?
!?
YOU'RE THAT BUSTER WHO JUST ARRIVED... ...RIGHT?
WH-- WHAT'RE YOU SAYING!?
AH HA HA
J-JUST BECAUSE IT'S BEEN A LONG TIME...YOU'RE TEASING ME, AREN'T YOU?
...
I'M SORRY. I DON'T... REMEMBER ANYTHING.
I REMEMBER NOTHING FROM THE TIME BEFORE I ARRIVED AT THIS MANSION.

READ THIS WAY

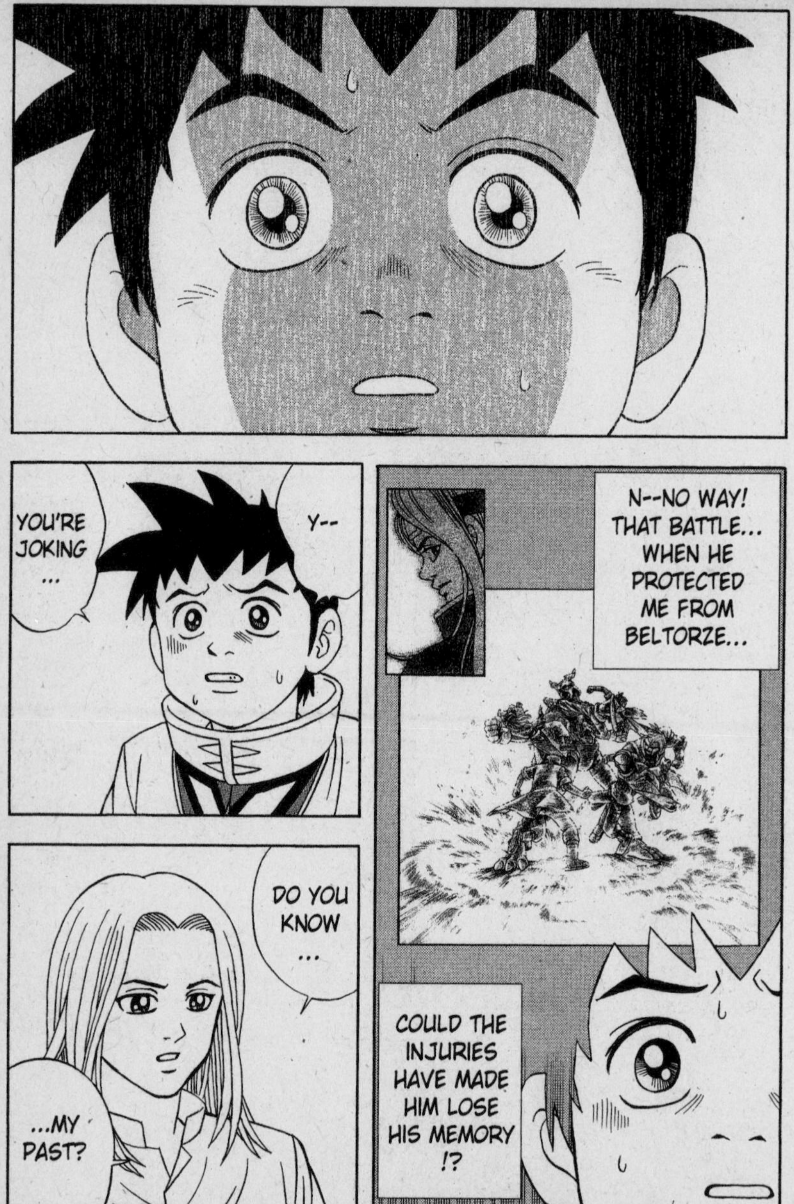

N--NO WAY! THAT BATTLE... WHEN HE PROTECTED ME FROM BELTORZE...
COULD THE INJURIES HAVE MADE HIM LOSE HIS MEMORY!?
Y--
YOU'RE JOKING...
DO YOU KNOW...
...MY PAST?

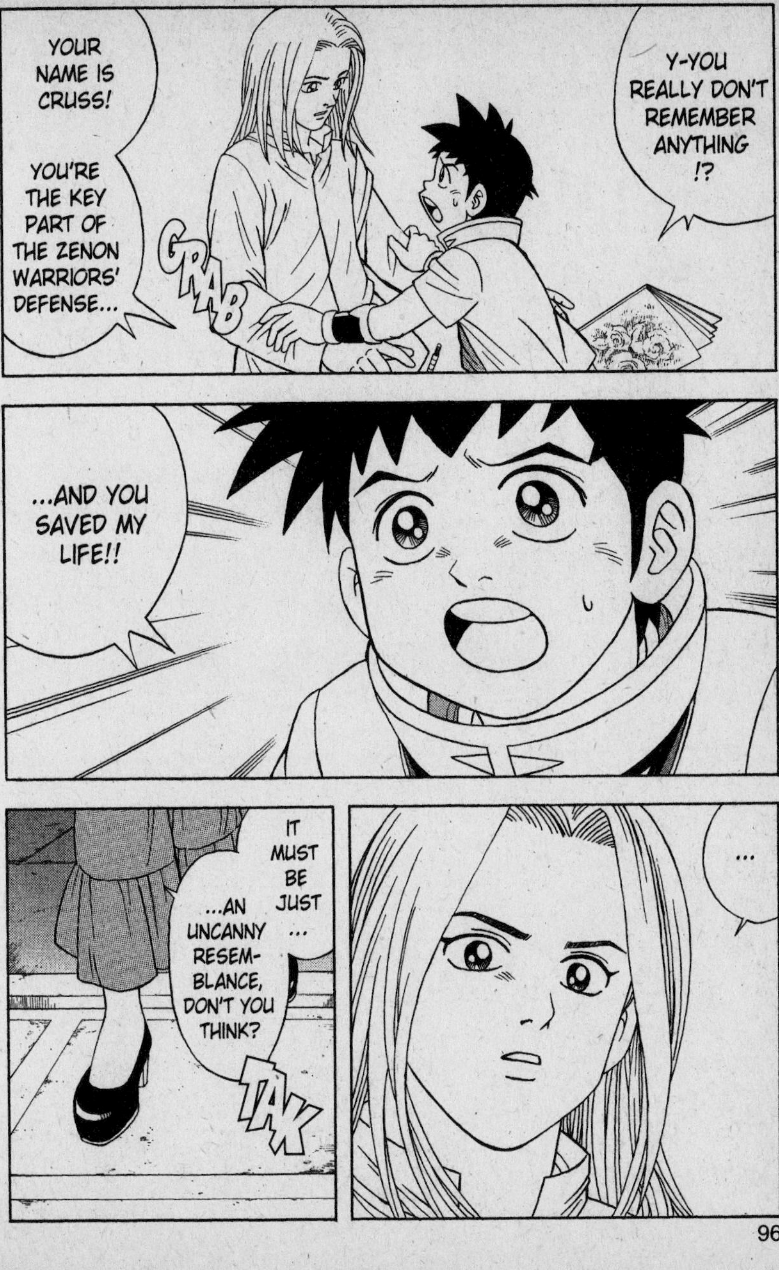
Y-YOU REALLY DON'T REMEMBER ANYTHING !?
YOUR NAME IS CRUSS!
YOU'RE THE KEY PART OF THE ZENON WARRIORS' DEFENSE...
GRAB
...AND YOU SAVED MY LIFE!!
...
IT MUST BE JUST ...
...AN UNCANNY RESEM-BLANCE, DON'T YOU THINK?
TAK

READ THIS WAY

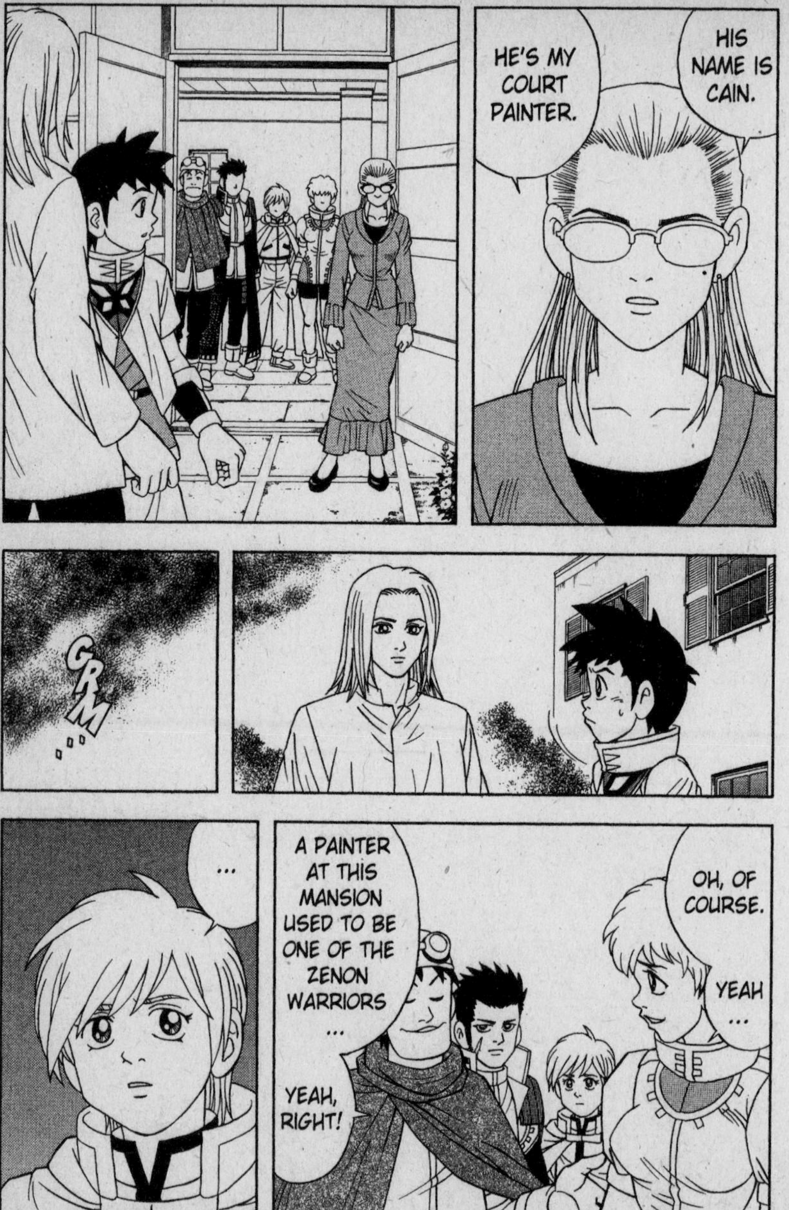
HIS NAME IS CAIN.
HE'S MY COURT PAINTER.
GRM...
OH, OF COURSE.
YEAH ...
A PAINTER AT THIS MANSION USED TO BE ONE OF THE ZENON WARRIORS ...
YEAH, RIGHT!
...

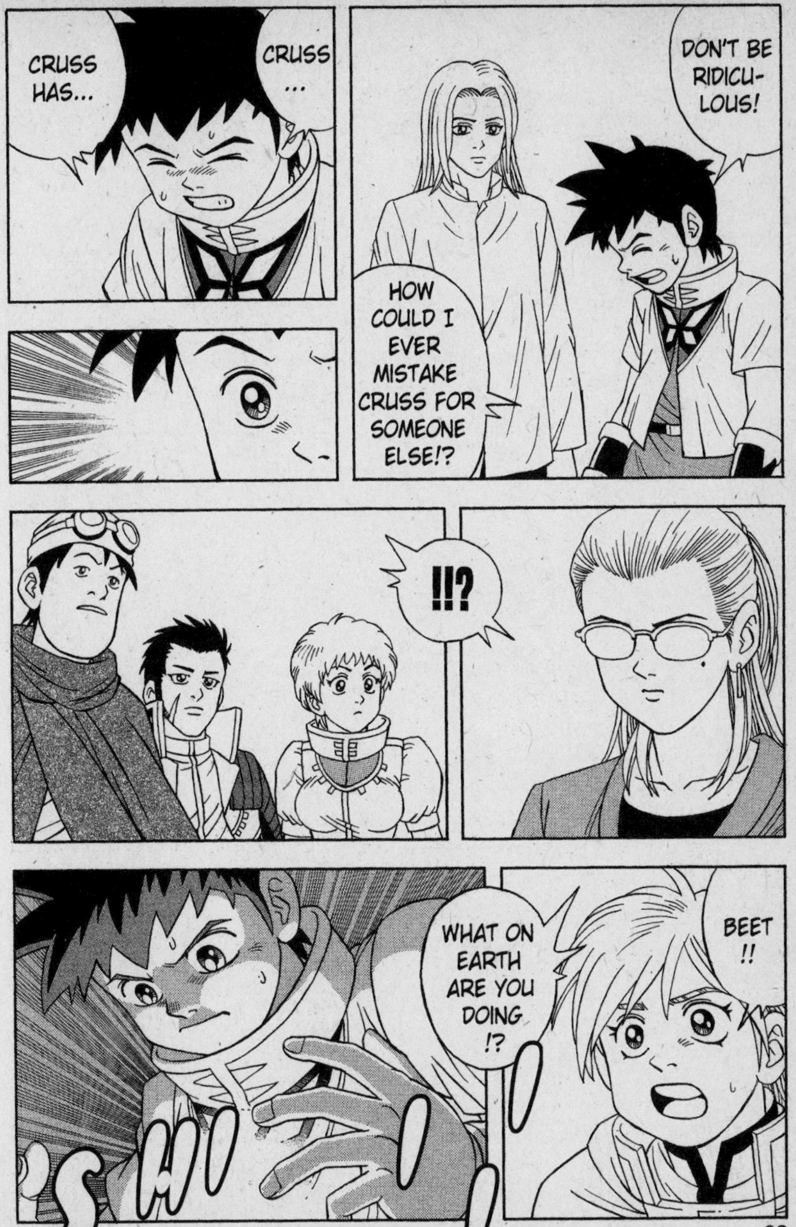

DON'T BE RIDICU-LOUS!
HOW COULD I EVER MISTAKE CRUSS FOR SOMEONE ELSE!?
CRUSS ...
CRUSS HAS...
!!?
BEET !!
WHAT ON EARTH ARE YOU DOING !?

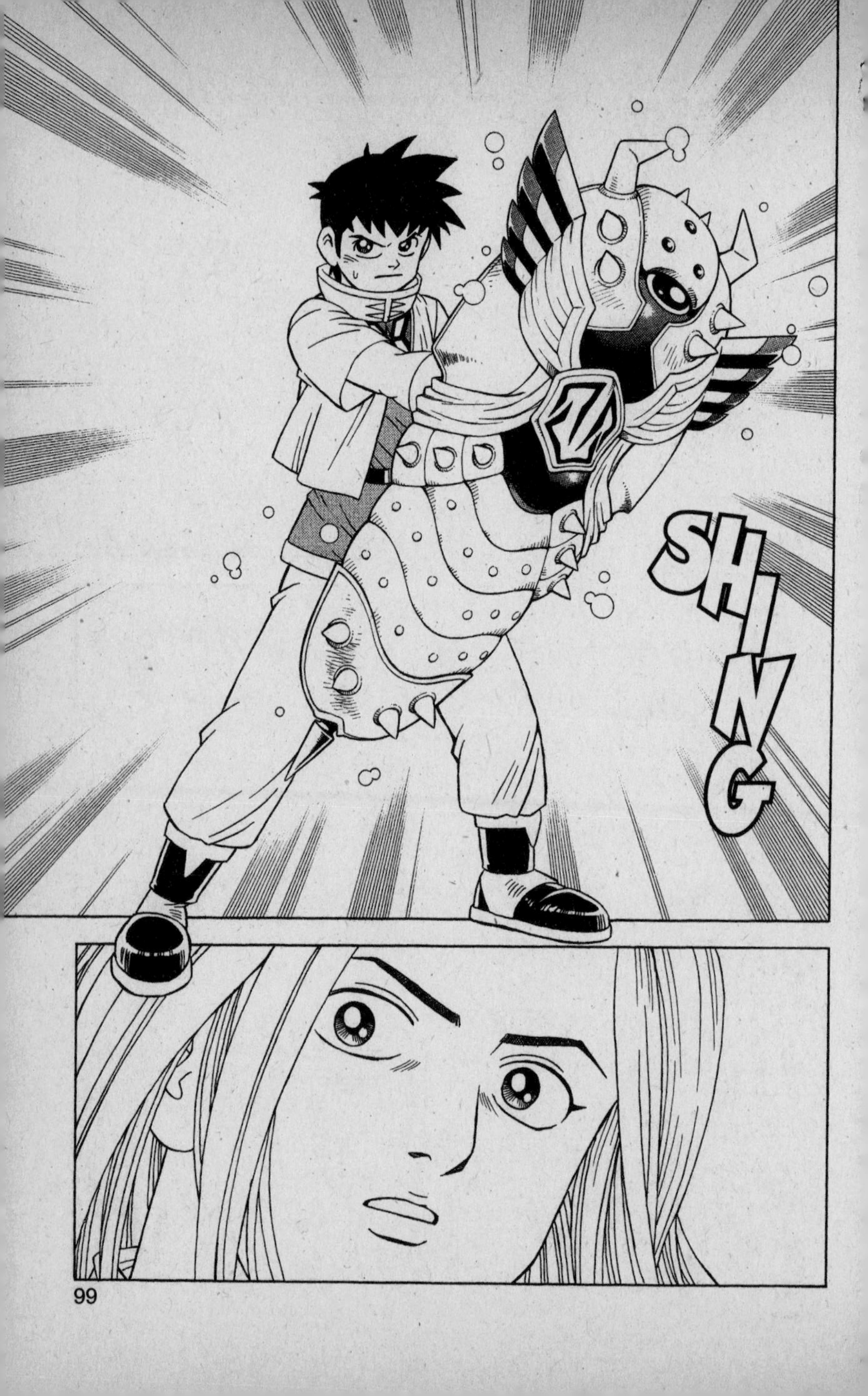
SHING

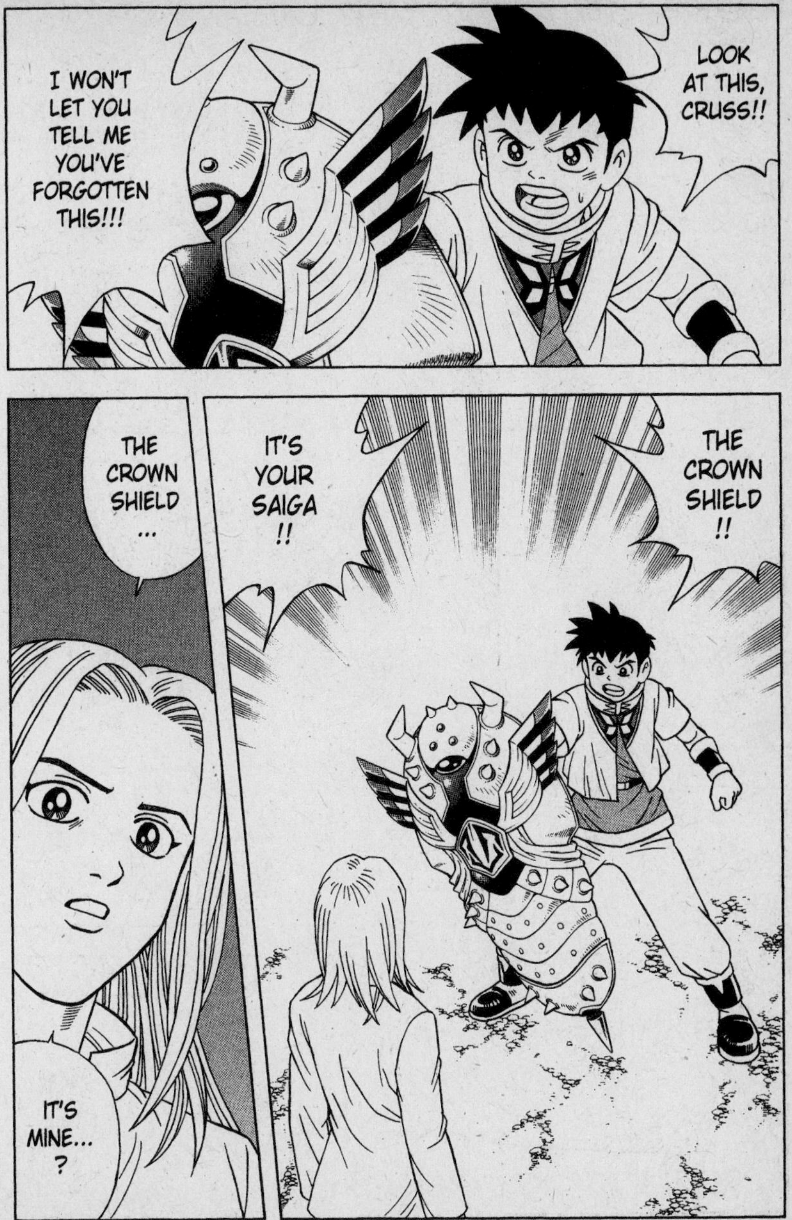
LOOK AT THIS, CRUSS!!
I WON'T LET YOU TELL ME YOU'VE FORGOTTEN THIS!!!
THE CROWN SHIELD !!
IT'S YOUR SAIGA !!
THE CROWN SHIELD ...
IT'S MINE... ?

READ THIS WAY

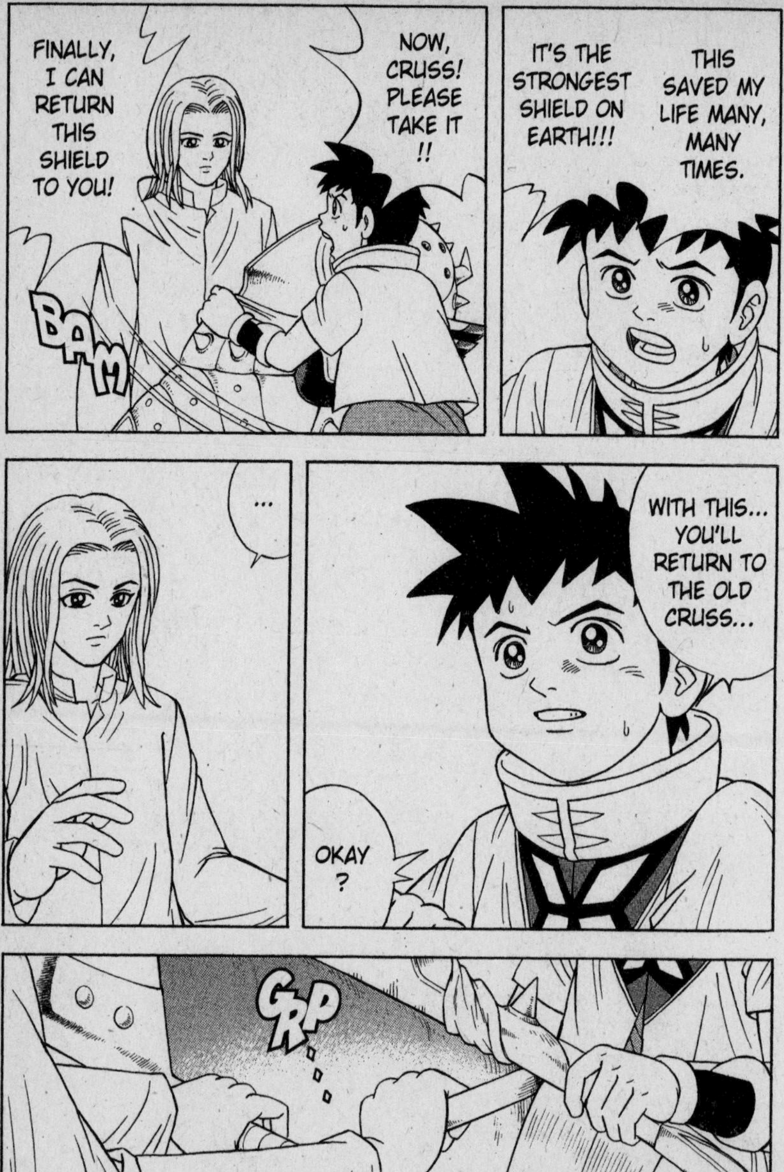
THIS SAVED MY LIFE MANY, MANY TIMES.
IT'S THE STRONGEST SHIELD ON EARTH!!!
NOW, CRUSS! PLEASE TAKE IT !!
FINALLY, I CAN RETURN THIS SHIELD TO YOU!
BAM
WITH THIS... YOU'LL RETURN TO THE OLD CRUSS...
OKAY ?
...
GRP

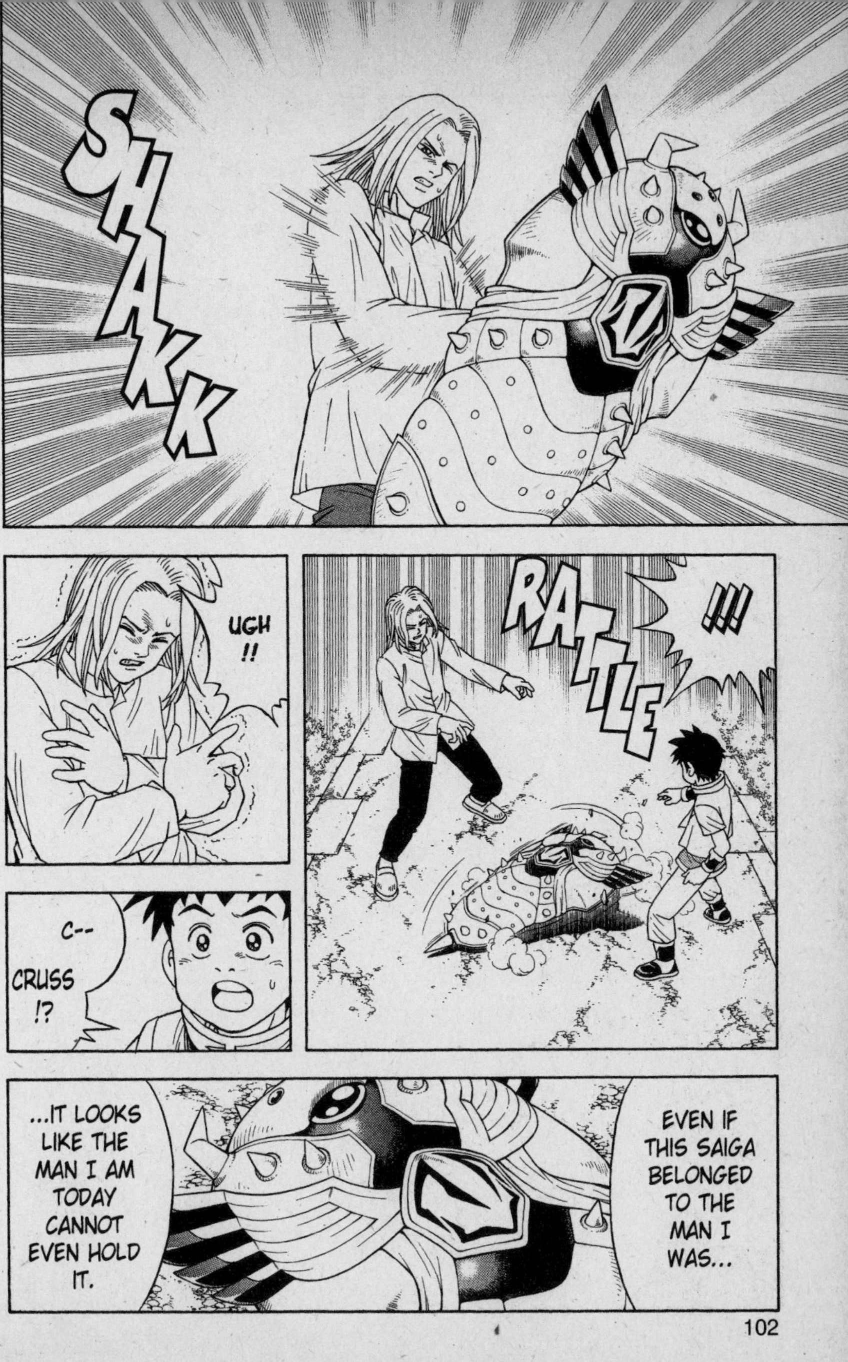
SHAKK
RATTLE !!!
UGH !!
C-- CRUSS !?
EVEN IF THIS SAIGA BELONGED TO THE MAN I WAS...
...IT LOOKS LIKE THE MAN I AM TODAY CANNOT EVEN HOLD IT.

READ THIS WAY

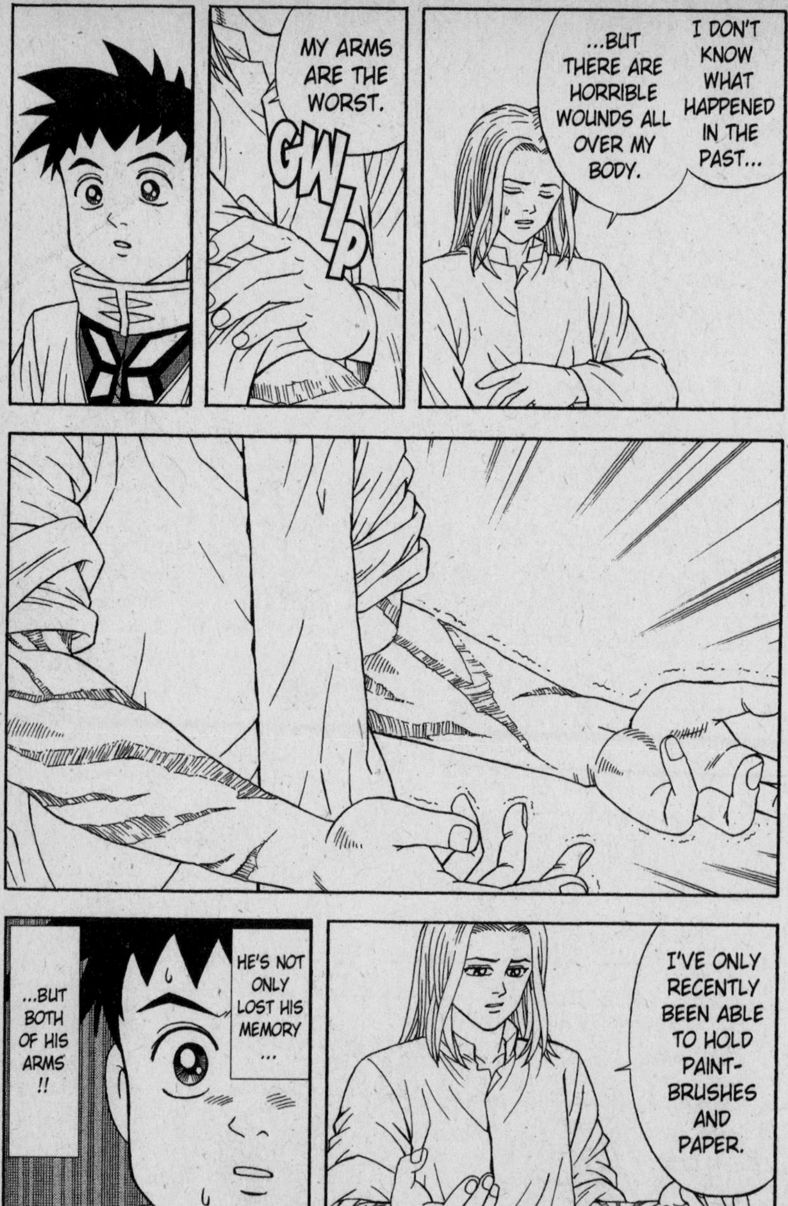
I DON'T KNOW WHAT HAPPENED IN THE PAST...
...BUT THERE ARE HORRIBLE WOUNDS ALL OVER MY BODY.
MY ARMS ARE THE WORST.
GWLIP
I'VE ONLY RECENTLY BEEN ABLE TO HOLD PAINT-BRUSHES AND PAPER.
HE'S NOT ONLY LOST HIS MEMORY ...
...BUT BOTH OF HIS ARMS !!

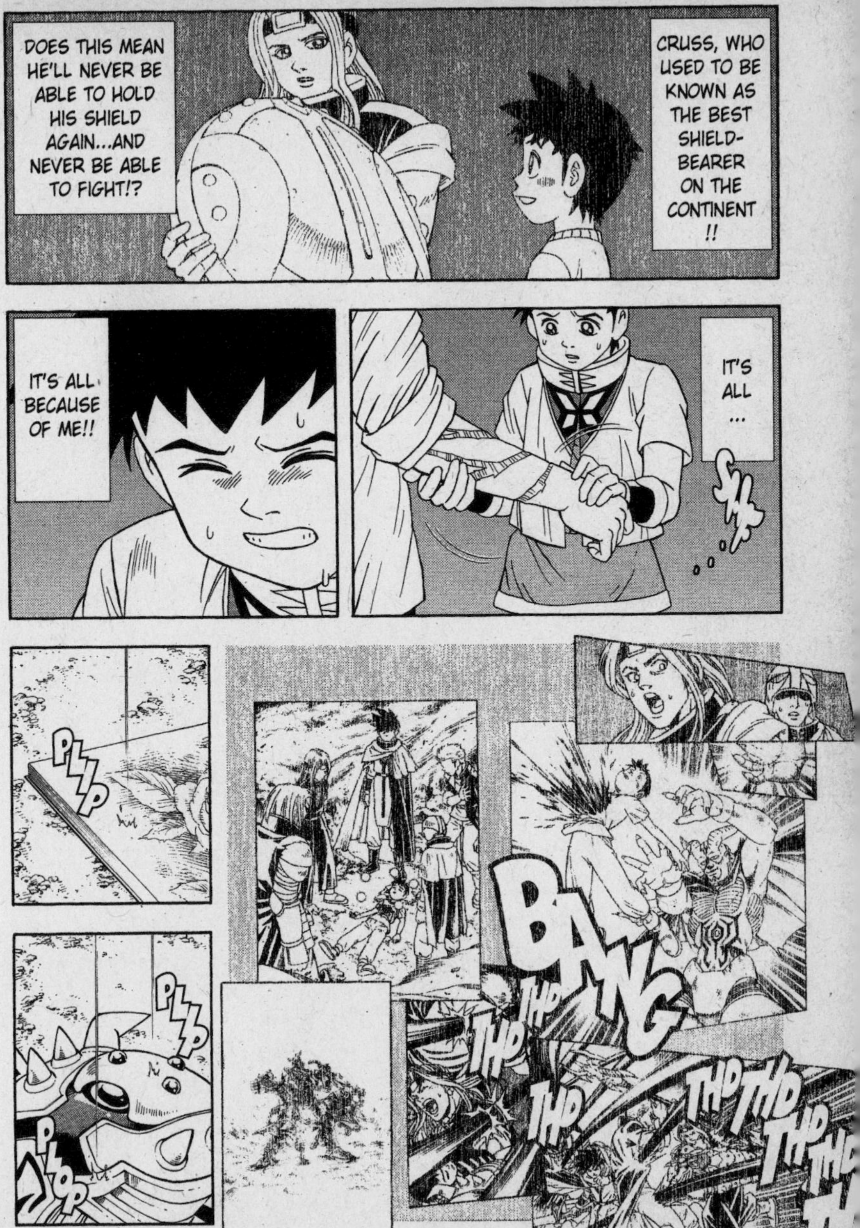
CRUSS, WHO USED TO BE KNOWN AS THE BEST SHIELD-BEARER ON THE CONTINENT !!
DOES THIS MEAN HE'LL NEVER BE ABLE TO HOLD HIS SHIELD AGAIN...AND NEVER BE ABLE TO FIGHT!?
IT'S ALL ...
SHF
IT'S ALL BECAUSE OF ME!!
THD THD
THD THD
THD THD
BANG
THD
THD
PLIP
PLIP
PLOP

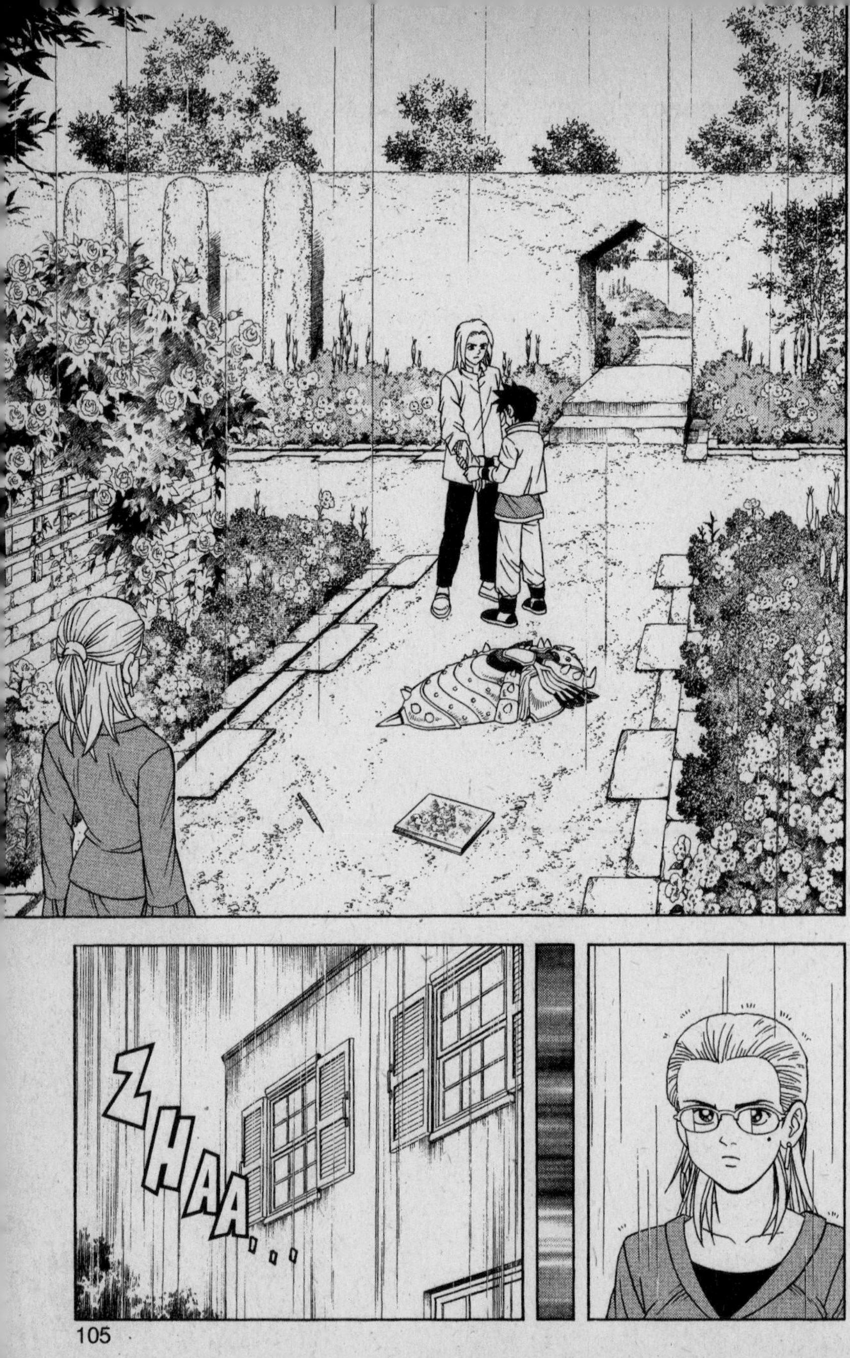
ZHAA...

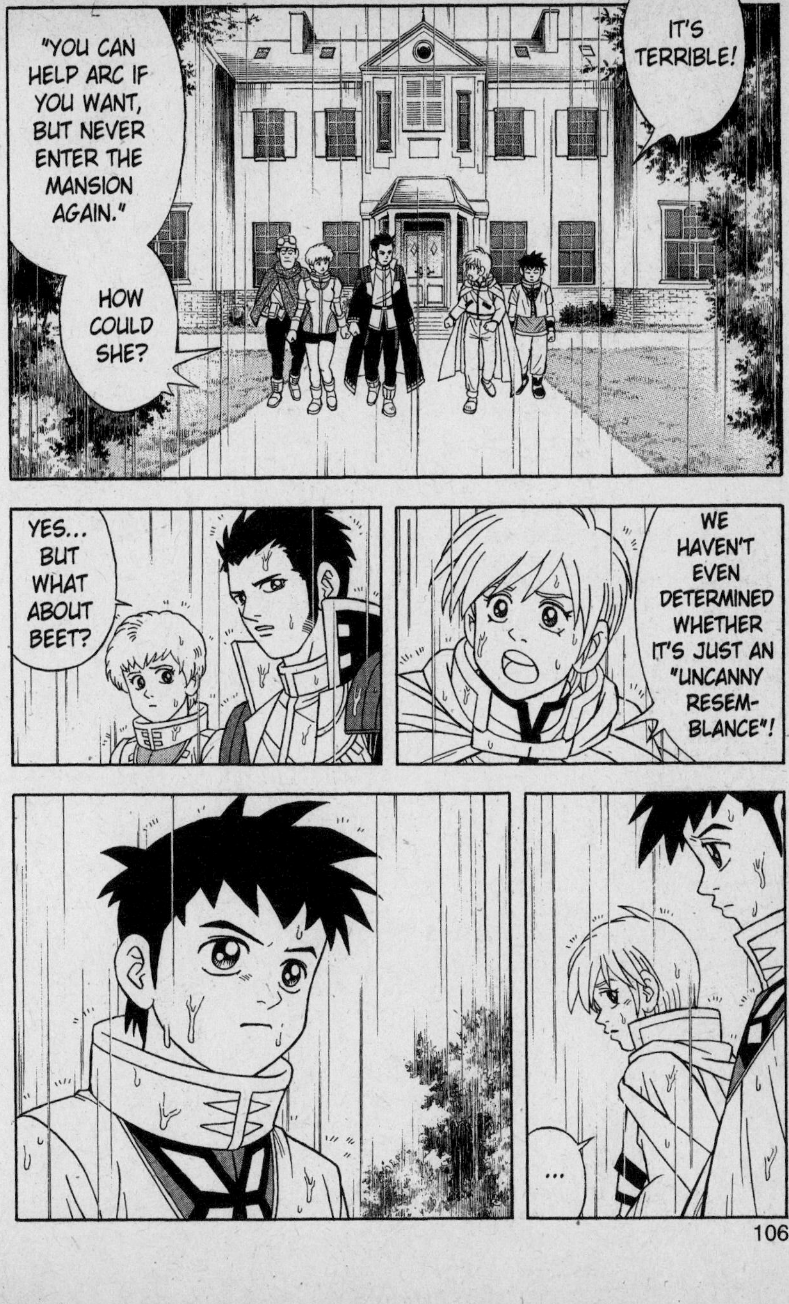
IT'S TERRIBLE!
"YOU CAN HELP ARC IF YOU WANT, BUT NEVER ENTER THE MANSION AGAIN."
HOW COULD SHE?
WE HAVEN'T EVEN DETERMINED WHETHER IT'S JUST AN "UNCANNY RESEMBLANCE"!
YES... BUT WHAT ABOUT BEET?
...

READ THIS WAY

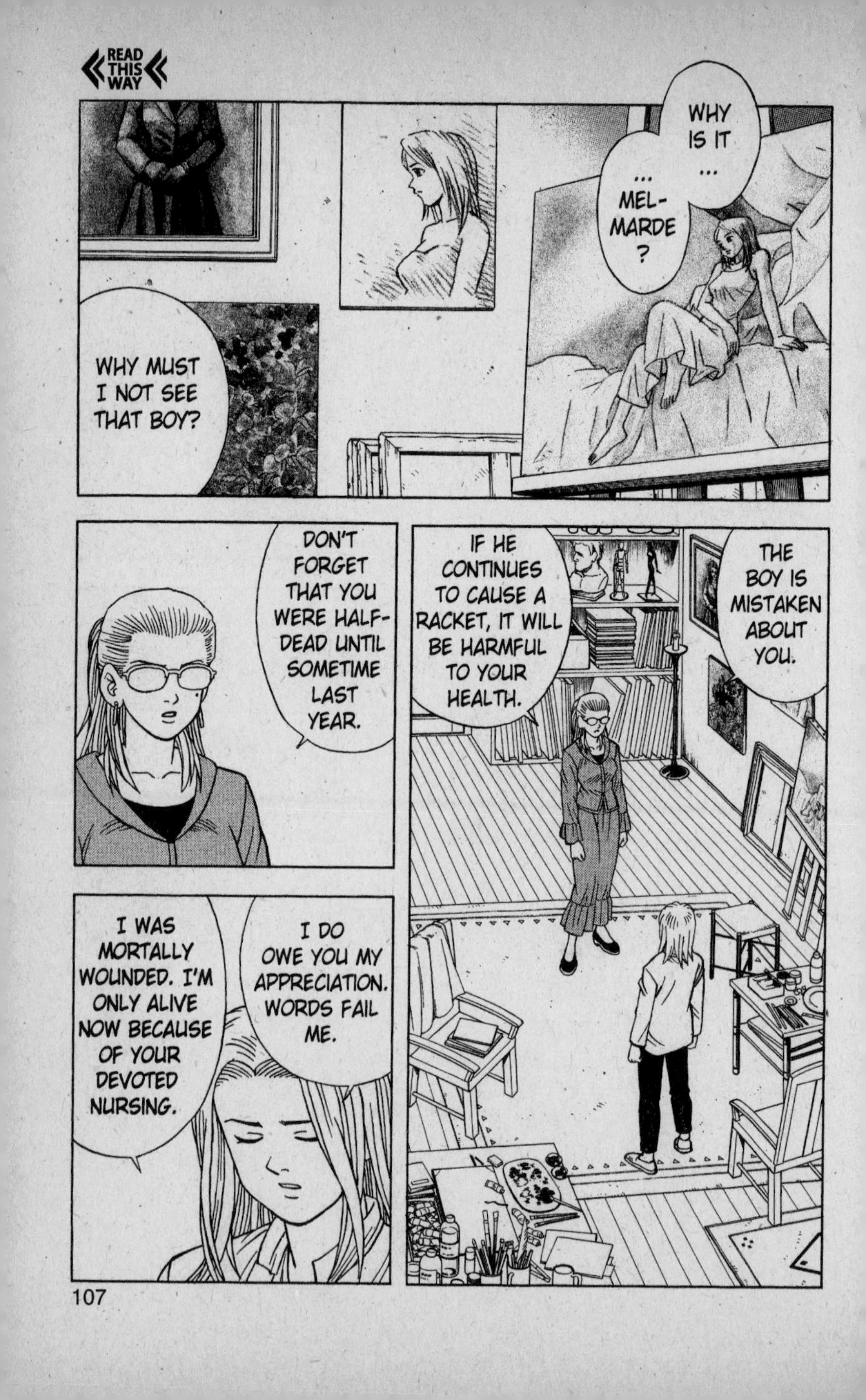
WHY IS IT ... ... MEL-MARDE?
WHY MUST I NOT SEE THAT BOY?
THE BOY IS MISTAKEN ABOUT YOU.
IF HE CONTINUES TO CAUSE A RACKET, IT WILL BE HARMFUL TO YOUR HEALTH.
DON'T FORGET THAT YOU WERE HALF-DEAD UNTIL SOMETIME LAST YEAR.
I DO OWE YOU MY APPRECIATION. WORDS FAIL ME.
I WAS MORTALLY WOUNDED. I'M ONLY ALIVE NOW BECAUSE OF YOUR DEVOTED NURSING.

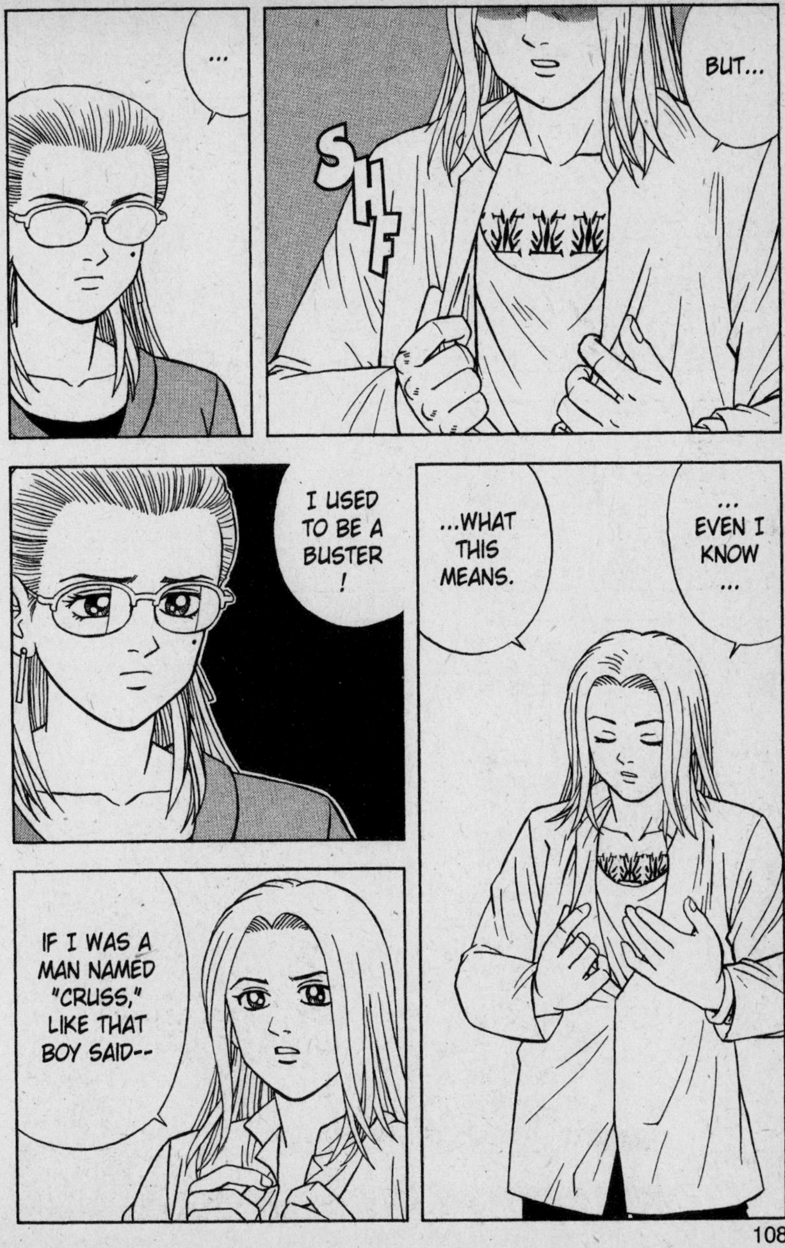
BUT...
SHF
...
... EVEN I KNOW ...
...WHAT THIS MEANS.
I USED TO BE A BUSTER!
IF I WAS A MAN NAMED "CRUSS," LIKE THAT BOY SAID--

READ THIS WAY

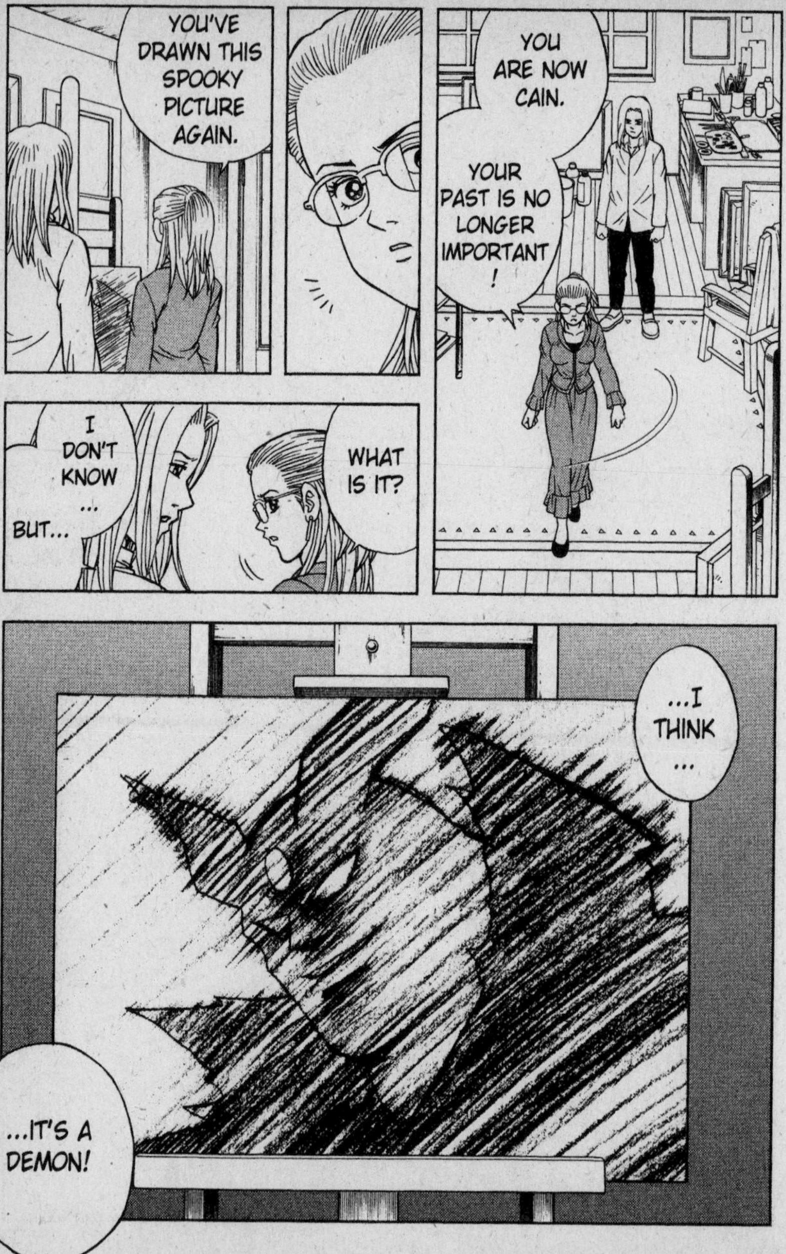
YOU ARE NOW CAIN.
YOUR PAST IS NO LONGER IMPORTANT!
YOU'VE DRAWN THIS SPOOKY PICTURE AGAIN.
WHAT IS IT?
I DON'T KNOW ... BUT...
...I THINK ...
...IT'S A DEMON!

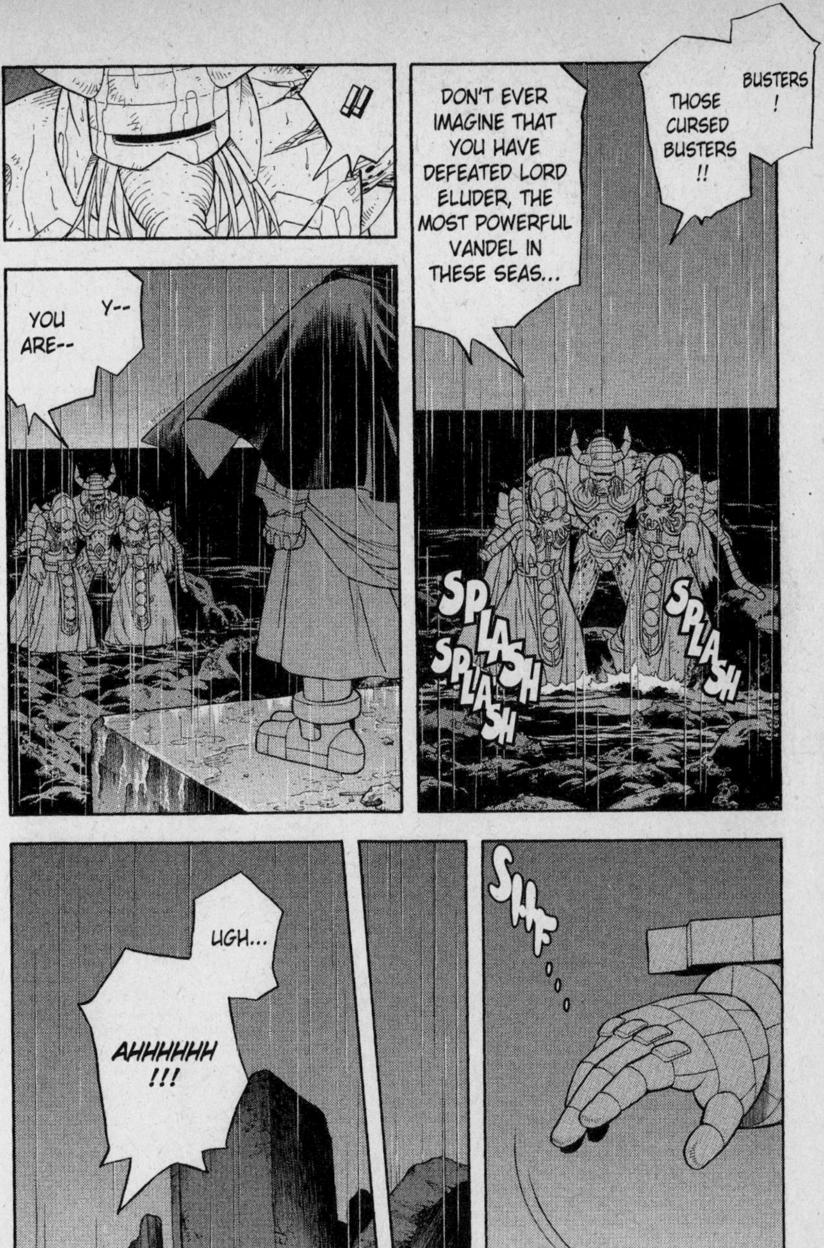
BUSTERS !
THOSE CURSED BUSTERS !!
DON'T EVER IMAGINE THAT YOU HAVE DEFEATED LORD ELUDER, THE MOST POWERFUL VANDEL IN THESE SEAS...
SPLASH
SPLASH
SPLASH
SPLASH
!!
Y--
YOU ARE--
SHF...
UGH...
AHHHHHH !!!

READ THIS WAY

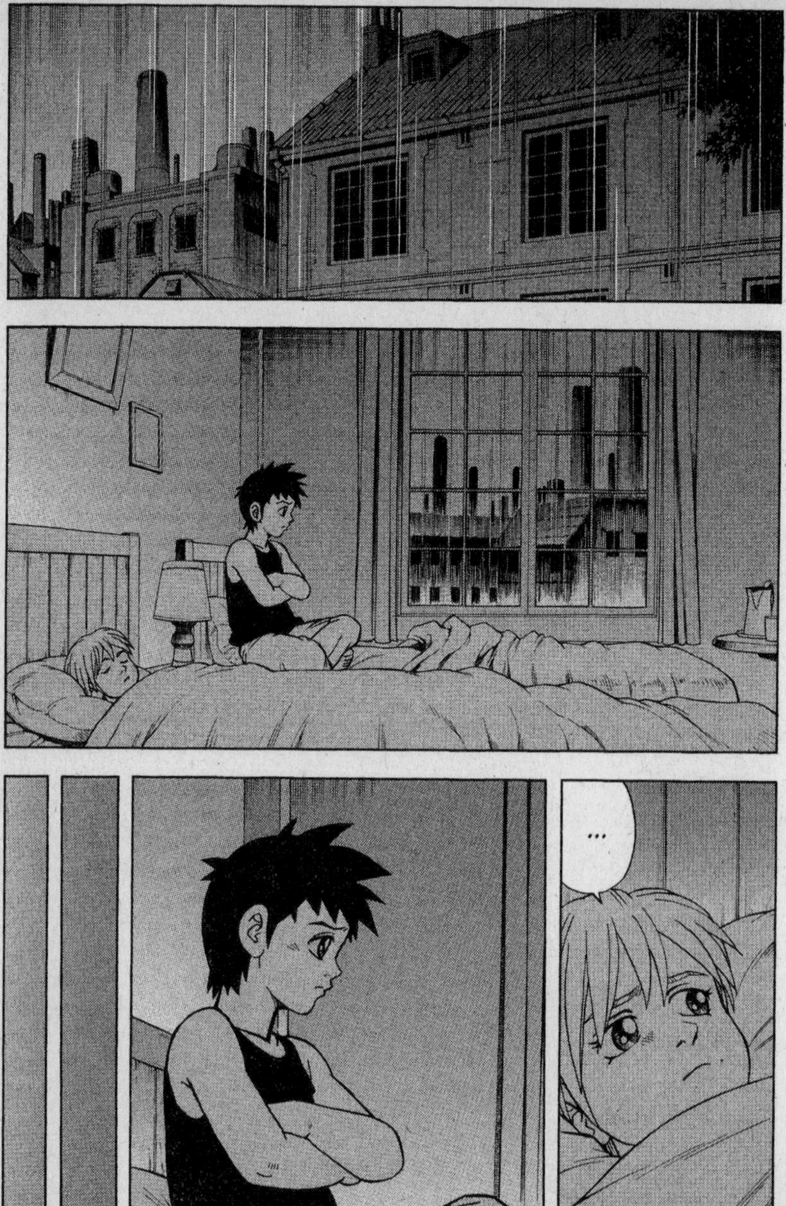
...

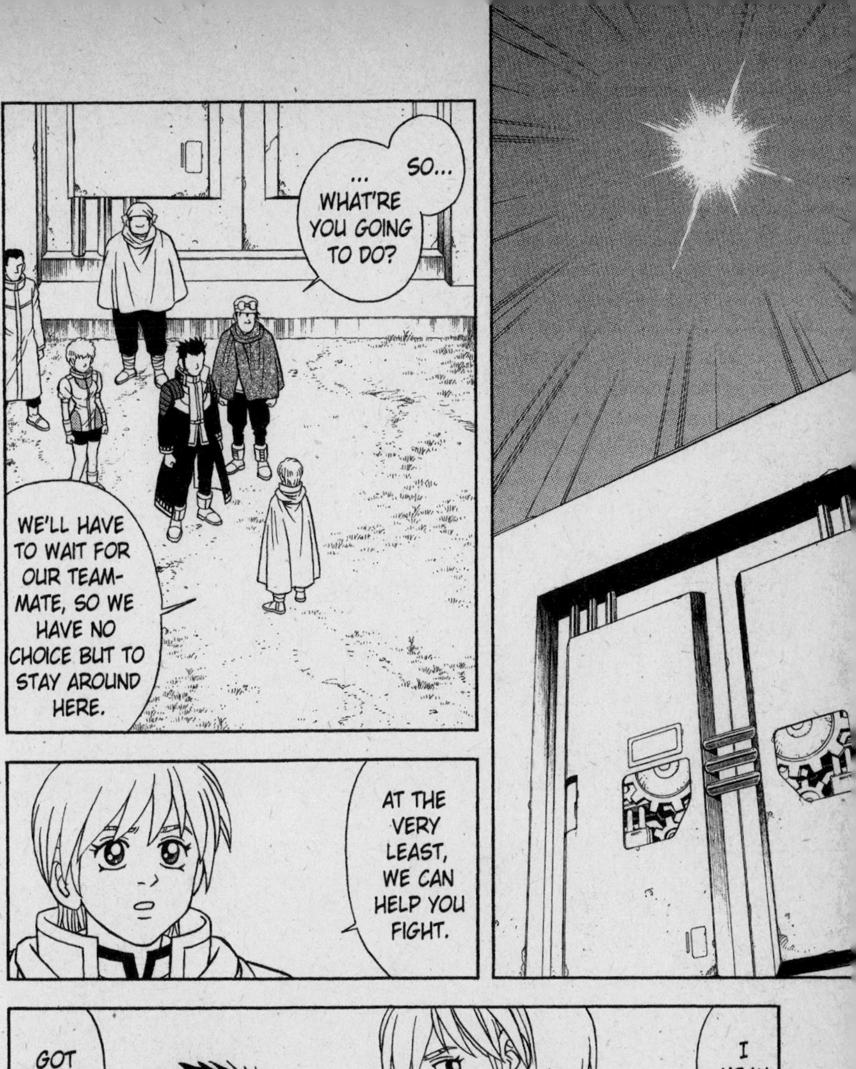
SO... ... WHAT'RE YOU GOING TO DO?
WE'LL HAVE TO WAIT FOR OUR TEAM-MATE, SO WE HAVE NO CHOICE BUT TO STAY AROUND HERE.
AT THE VERY LEAST, WE CAN HELP YOU FIGHT.
I MEAN... ...I WILL.
GOT IT.

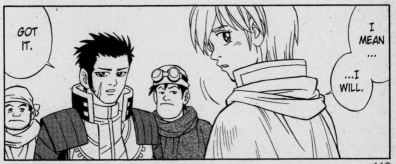

READ THIS WAY

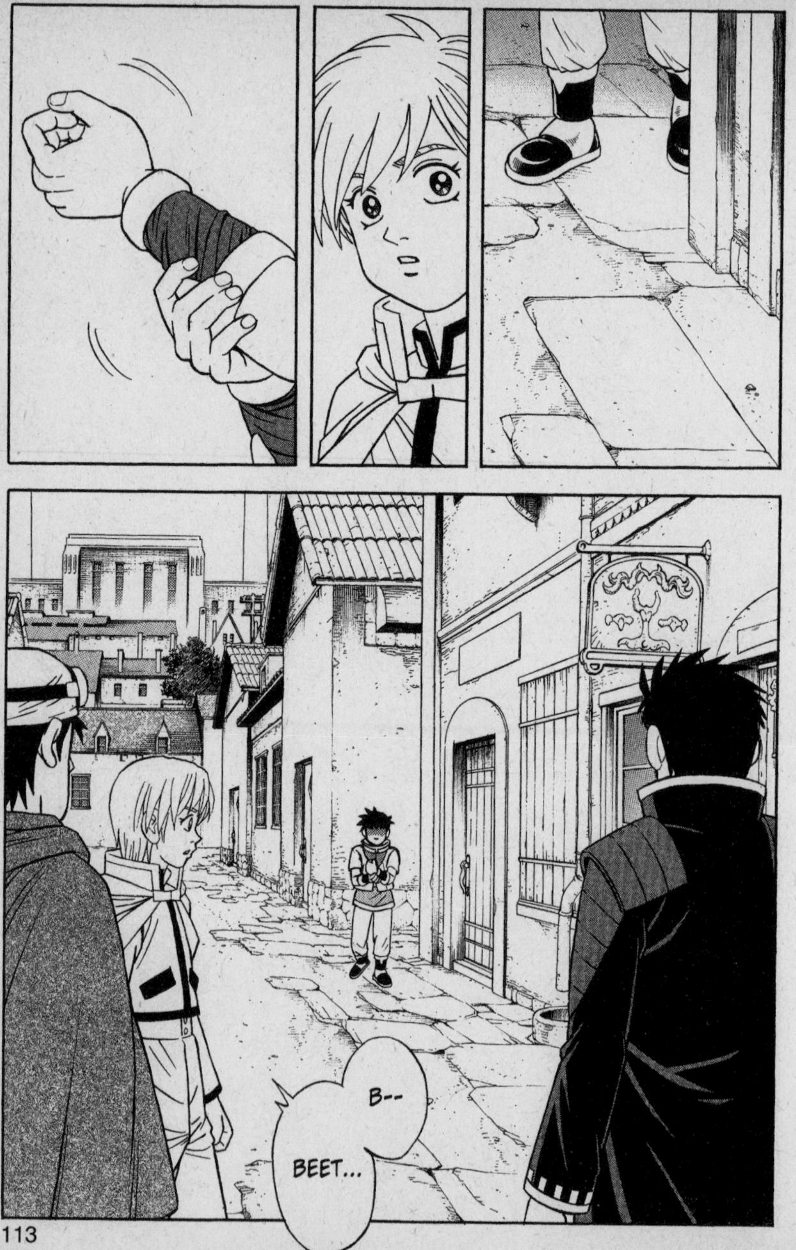
B--
BEET...

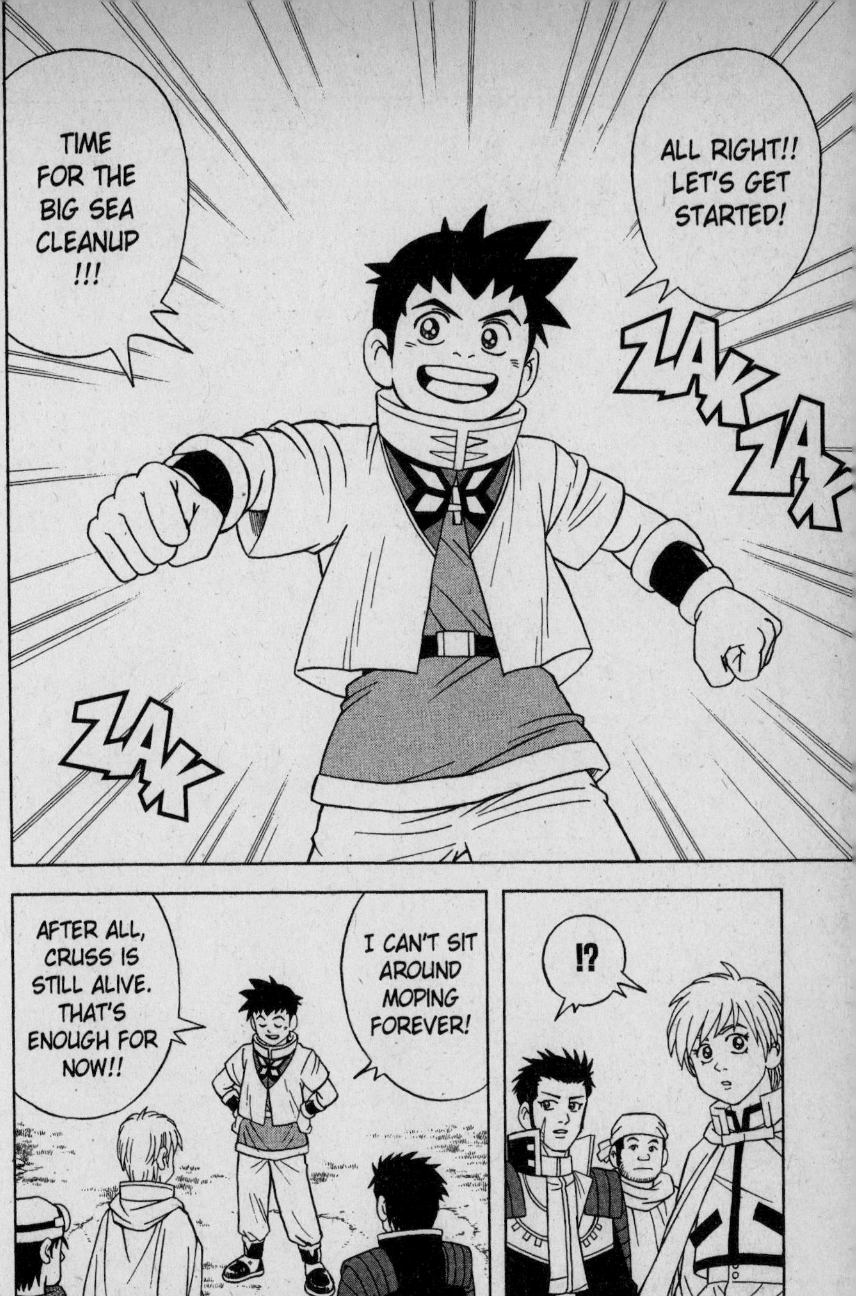
ALL RIGHT!! LET'S GET STARTED!
TIME FOR THE BIG SEA CLEANUP !!!
ZAK ZAK
ZAK
!?
I CAN'T SIT AROUND MOPING FOREVER!
AFTER ALL, CRUSS IS STILL ALIVE. THAT'S ENOUGH FOR NOW!!

READ THIS WAY

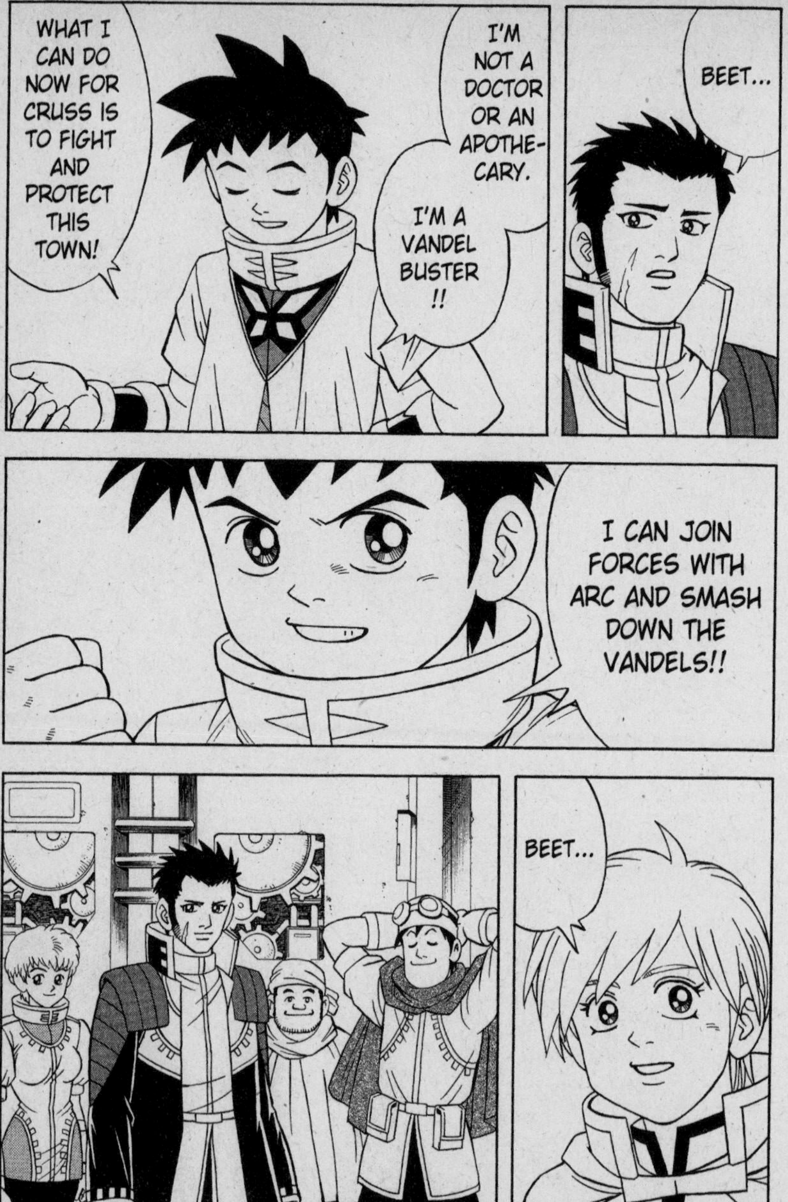
BEET...
I'M NOT A DOCTOR OR AN APOTHECARY.
I'M A VANDEL BUSTER!!
WHAT I CAN DO NOW FOR CRUSS IS TO FIGHT AND PROTECT THIS TOWN!
I CAN JOIN FORCES WITH ARC AND SMASH DOWN THE VANDELS!!
BEET...

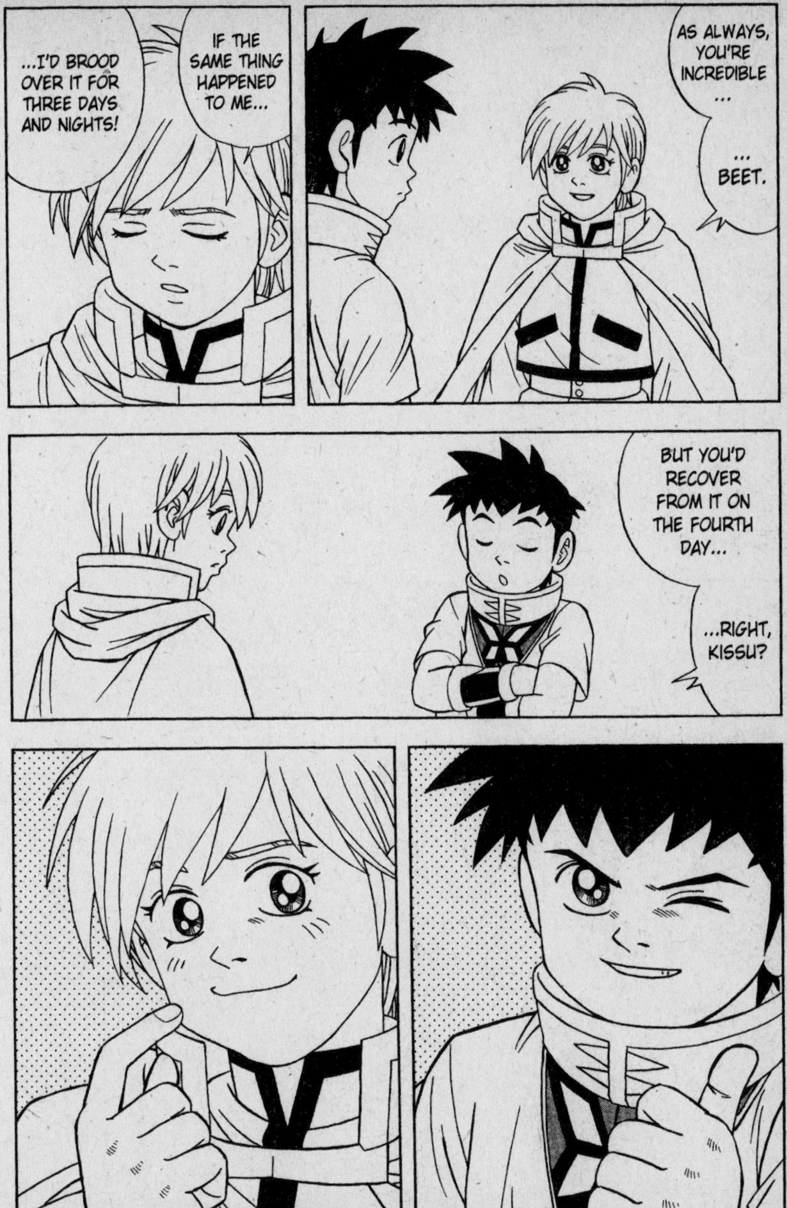
AS ALWAYS, YOU'RE INCREDIBLE ...
... BEET.
IF THE SAME THING HAPPENED TO ME...
...I'D BROOD OVER IT FOR THREE DAYS AND NIGHTS!
BUT YOU'D RECOVER FROM IT ON THE FOURTH DAY...
...RIGHT, KISSU?

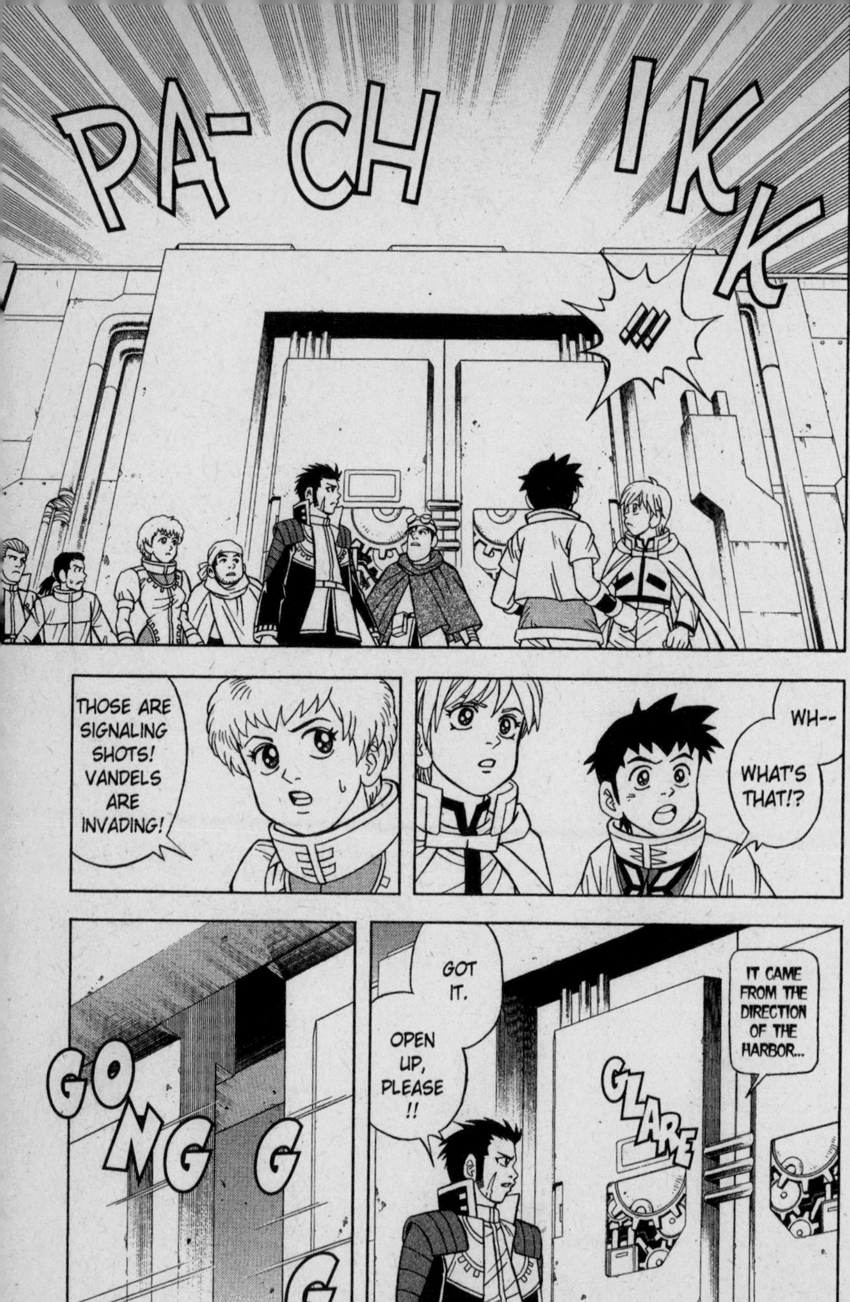
PA-CHIKK
WH-- WHAT'S THAT!?
THOSE ARE SIGNALING SHOTS! VANDELS ARE INVADING!
IT CAME FROM THE DIRECTION OF THE HARBOR...
GLARE
GOT IT.
OPEN UP, PLEASE !!
GONGGG

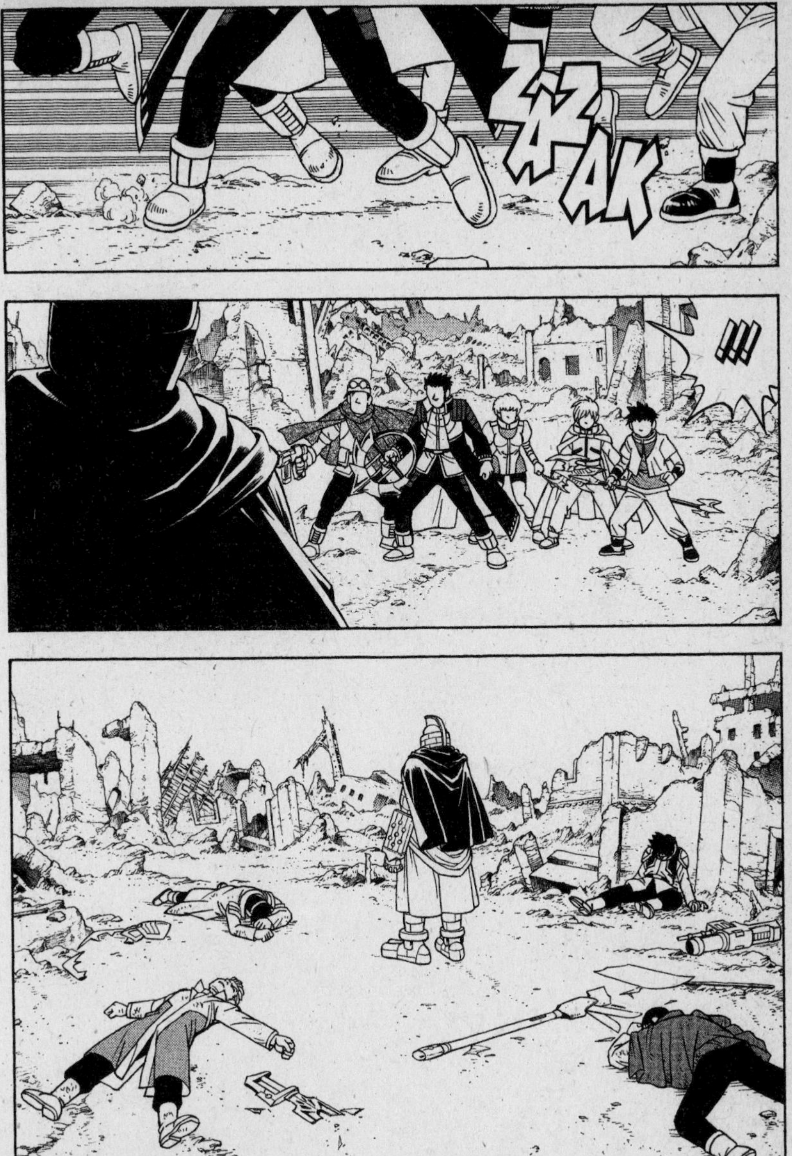
ZAZAK
!!!

READ THIS WAY

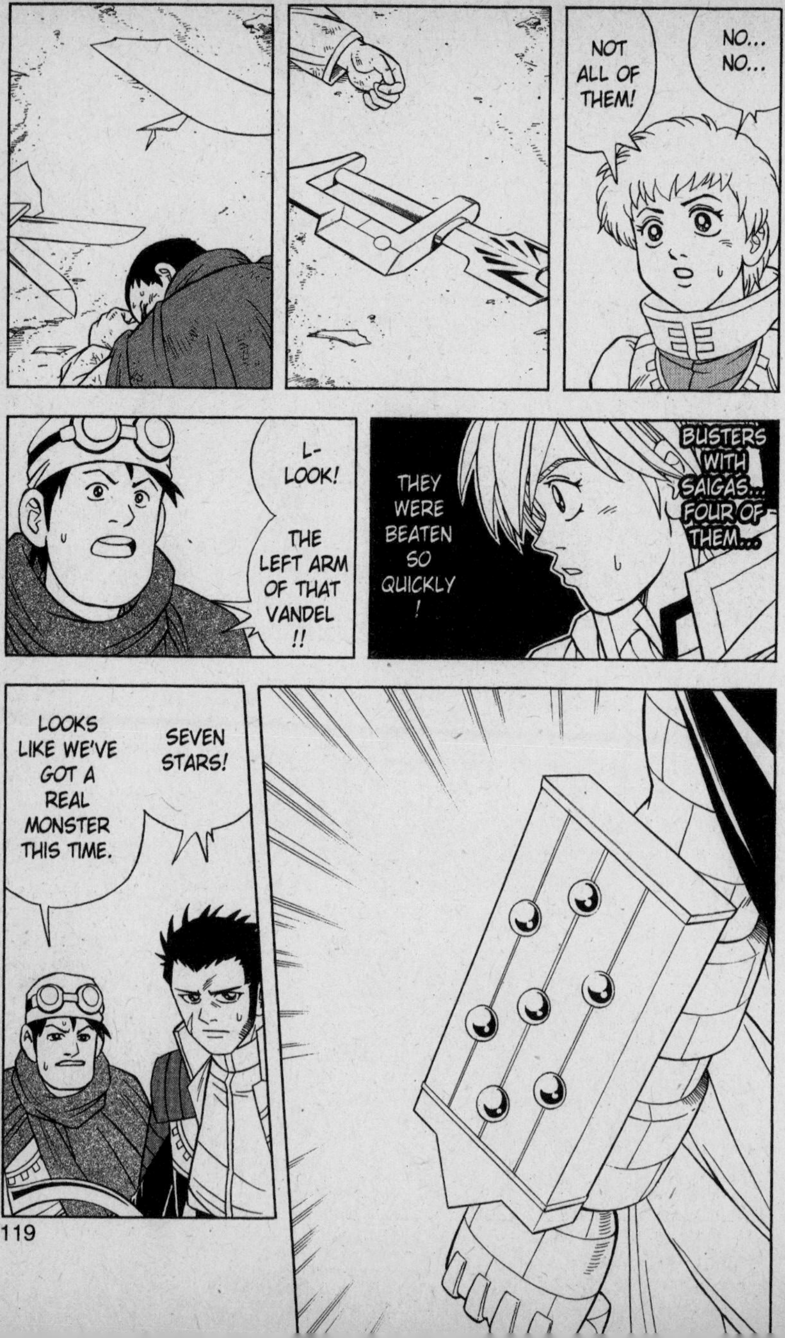
NO... NO...
NOT ALL OF THEM!
BUSTERS WITH SAIGAS... FOUR OF THEM...
THEY WERE BEATEN SO QUICKLY!
L- LOOK!
THE LEFT ARM OF THAT VANDEL!!
SEVEN STARS!
LOOKS LIKE WE'VE GOT A REAL MONSTER THIS TIME.

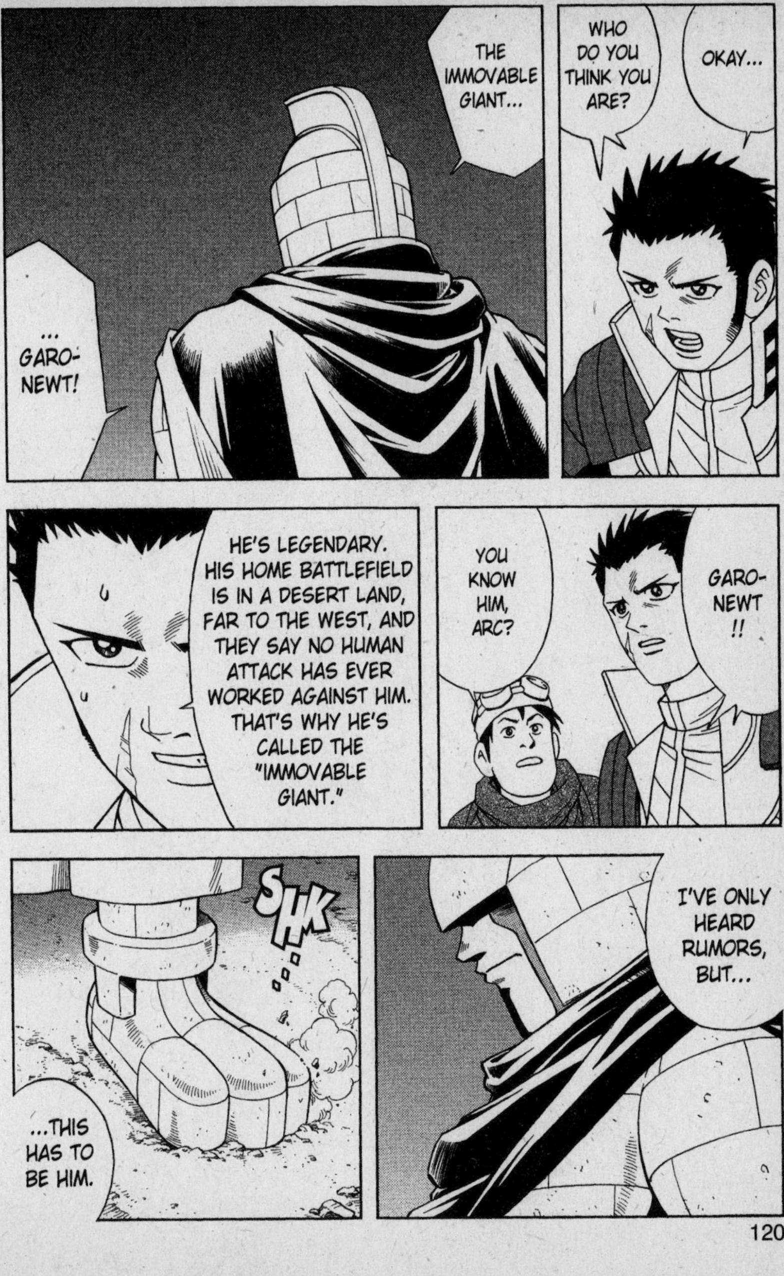
OKAY...
WHO DO YOU THINK YOU ARE?
THE IMMOVABLE GIANT...
...GARO-NEWT!
GARO-NEWT !!
YOU KNOW HIM, ARC?
HE'S LEGENDARY. HIS HOME BATTLEFIELD IS IN A DESERT LAND, FAR TO THE WEST, AND THEY SAY NO HUMAN ATTACK HAS EVER WORKED AGAINST HIM. THAT'S WHY HE'S CALLED THE "IMMOVABLE GIANT."
I'VE ONLY HEARD RUMORS, BUT...
SHK
...THIS HAS TO BE HIM.

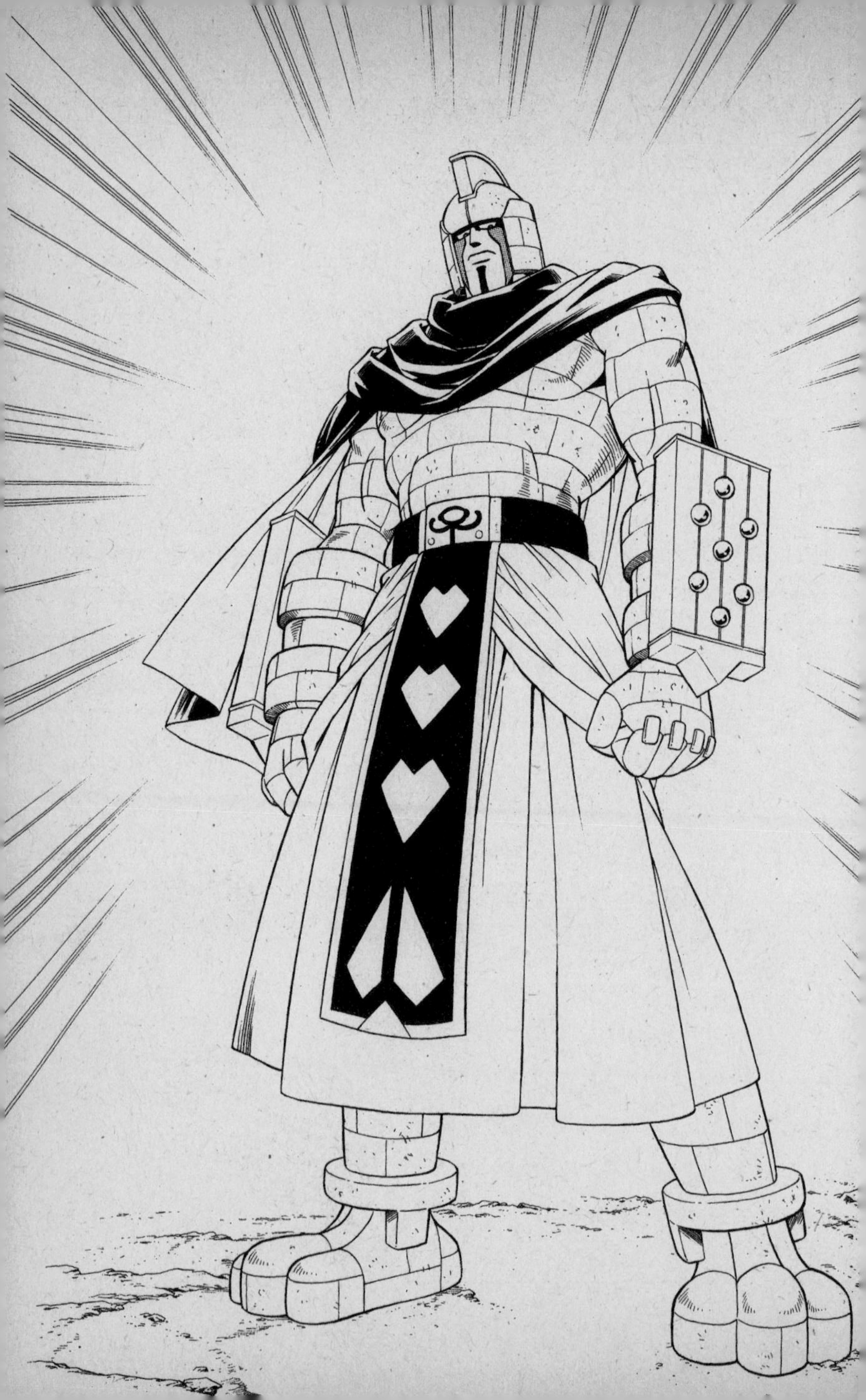

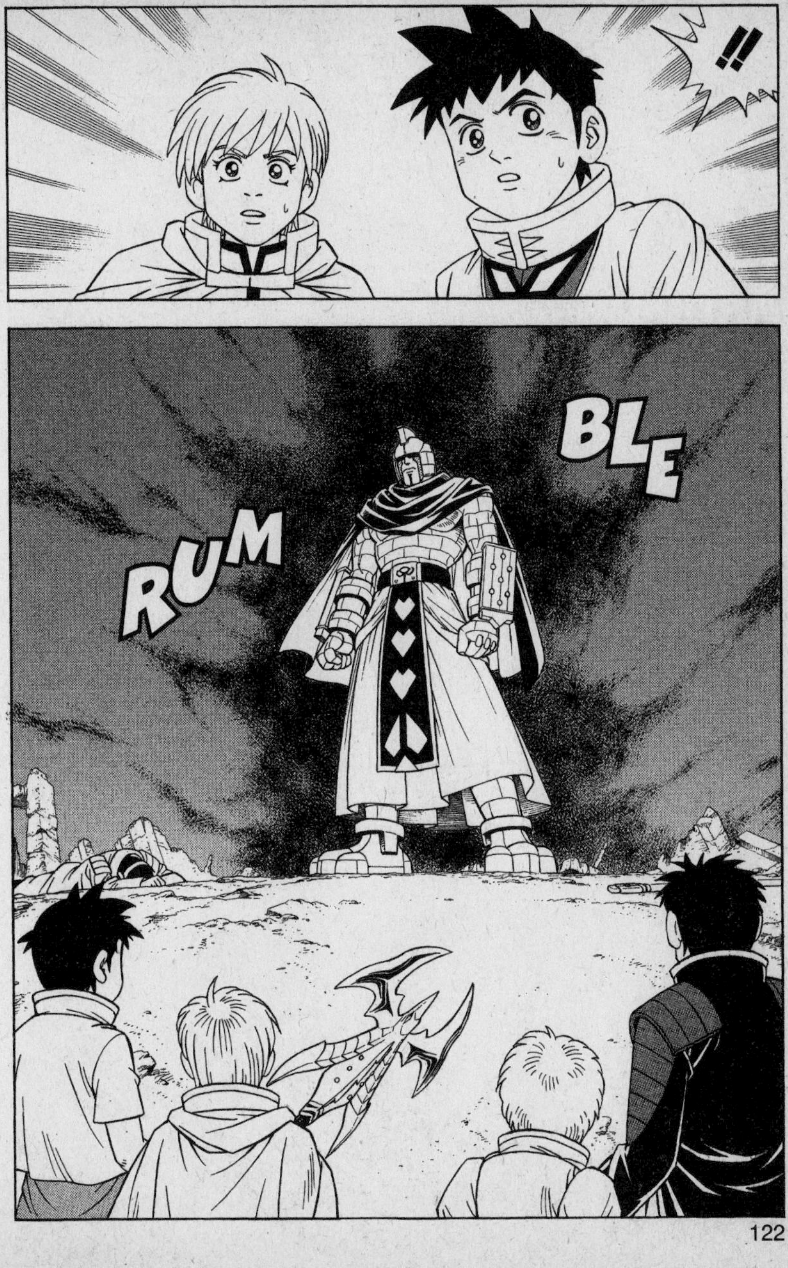
!!
RUM
BLE

READ THIS WAY

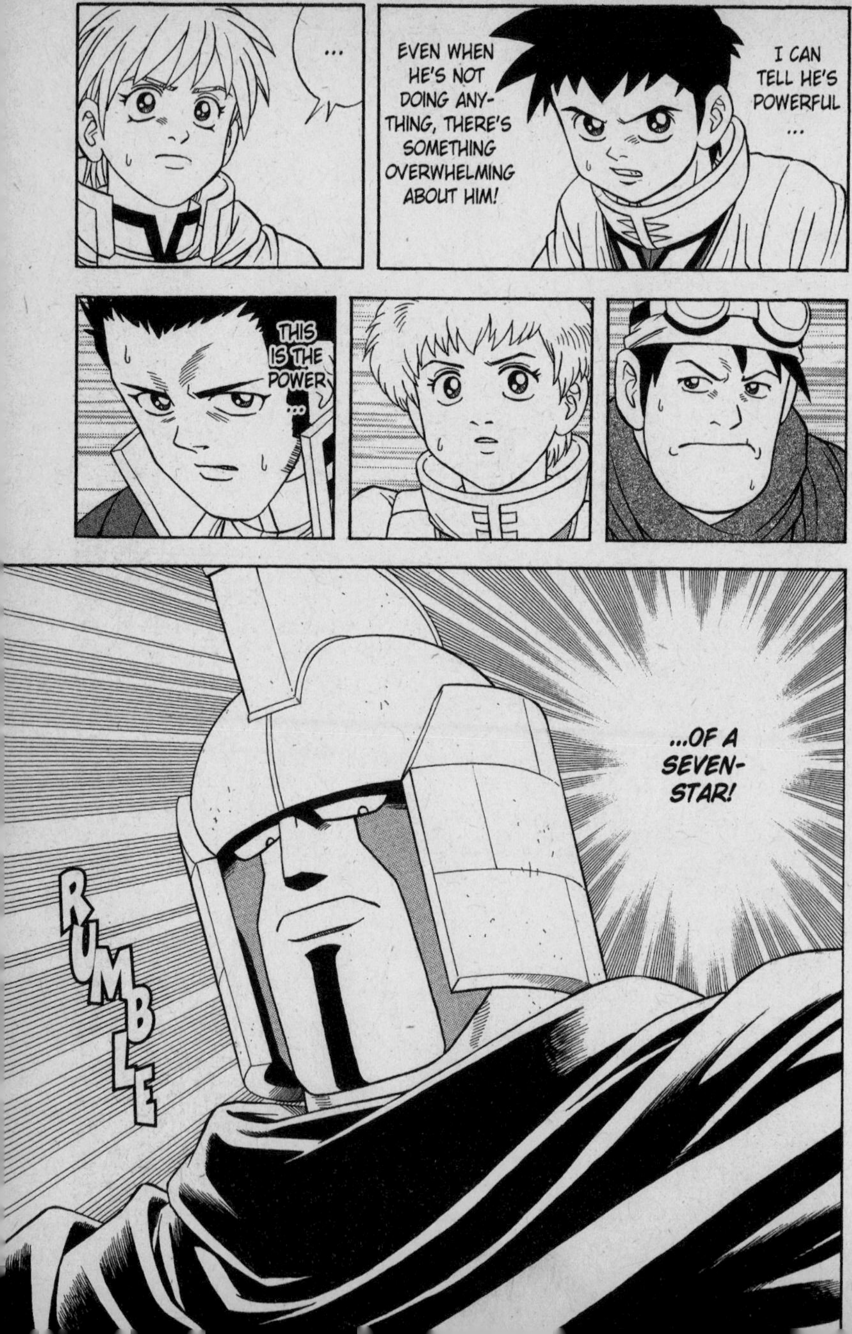
I CAN TELL HE'S POWERFUL ...
EVEN WHEN HE'S NOT DOING ANY-THING, THERE'S SOMETHING OVERWHELMING ABOUT HIM!
...
THIS IS THE POWER ...
...OF A SEVEN-STAR!
RUMBLE

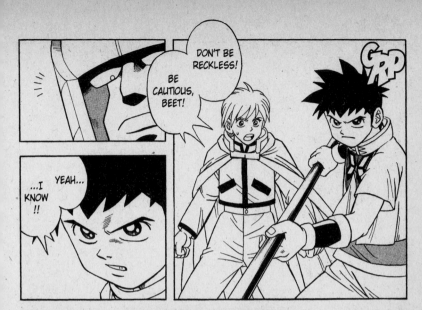

GRP

DON'T BE RECKLESS!

BE CAUTIOUS, BEET!

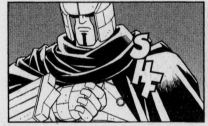

...I KNOW!!

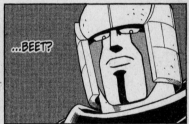

SHF

...BEET?

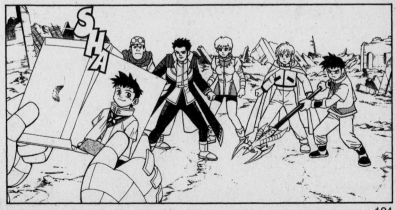

SHA

READ THIS WAY

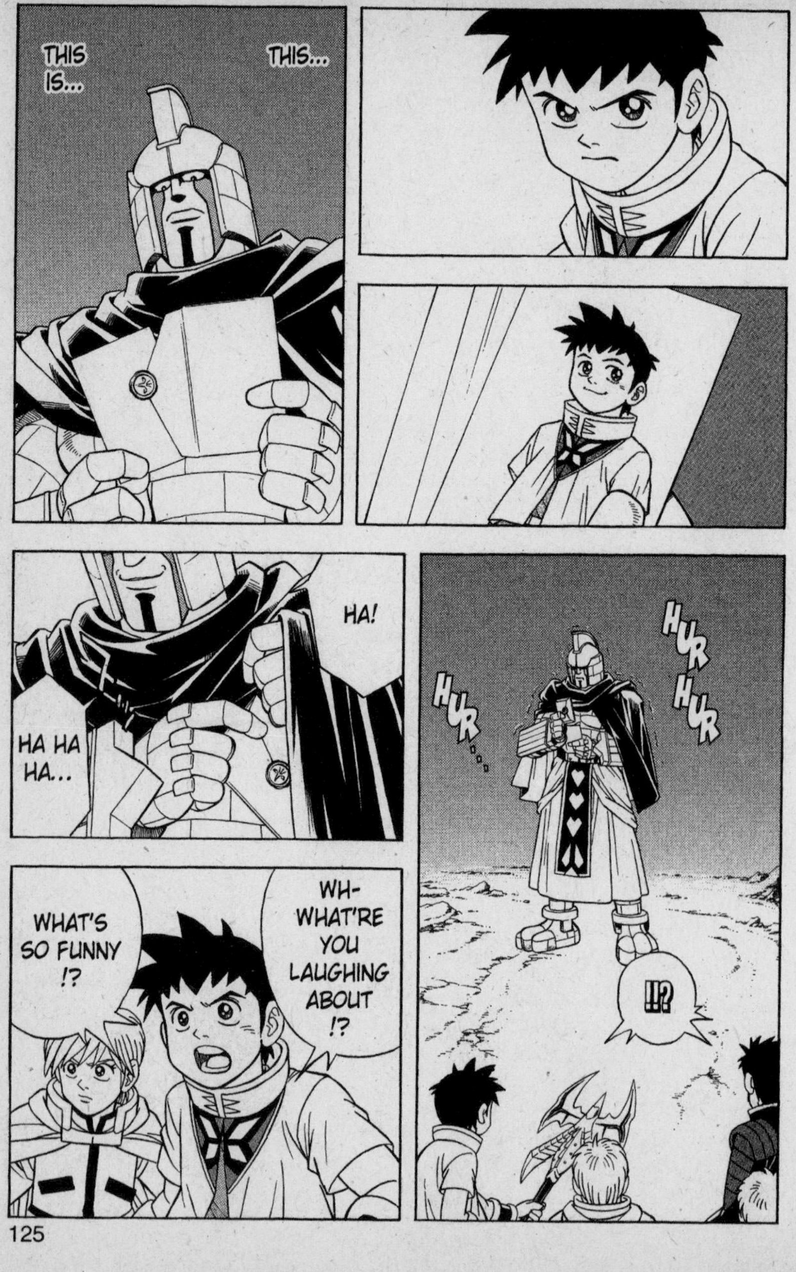
THIS...
THIS IS...
HUR HUR
HUR...
!!?
HA!
HA HA HA...
WH-WHAT'RE YOU LAUGHING ABOUT !?
WHAT'S SO FUNNY !?

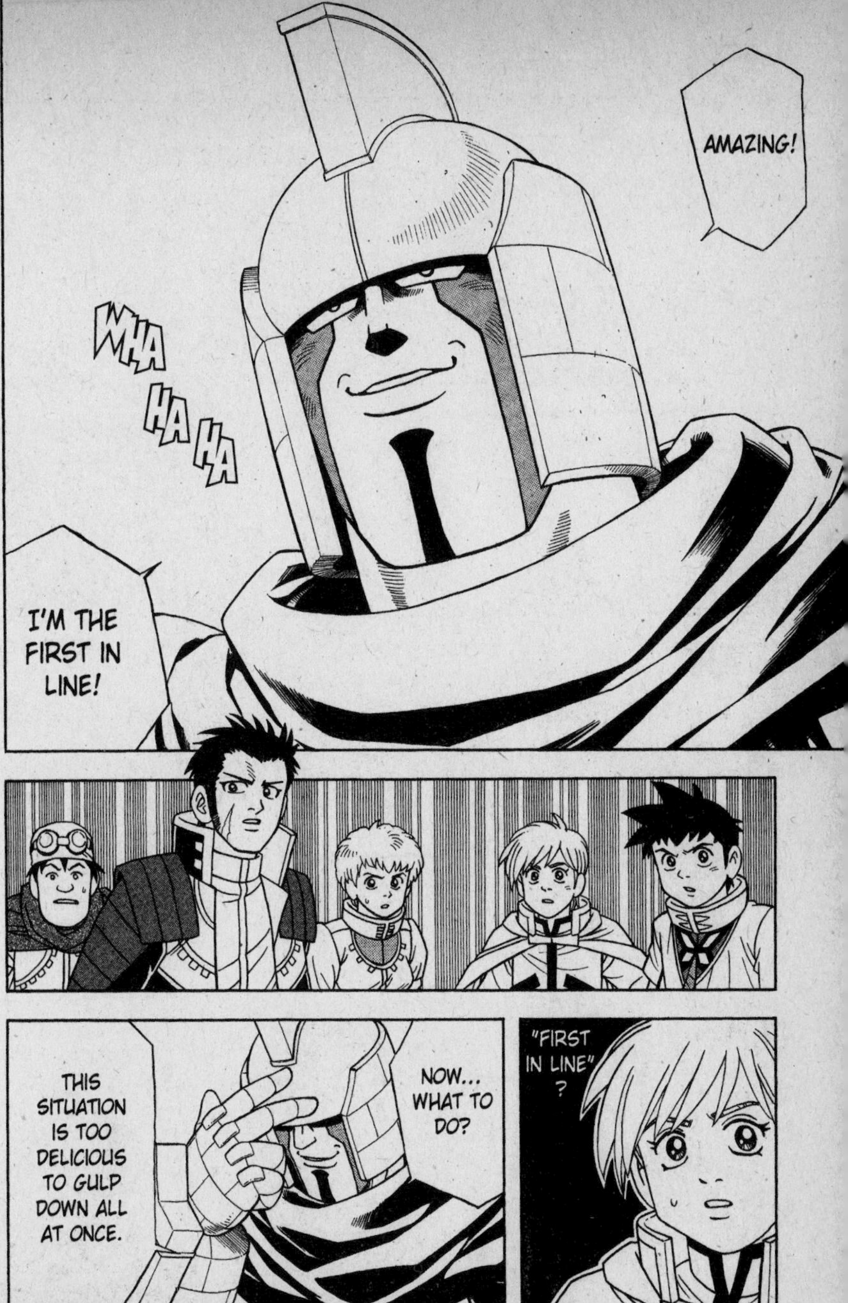
AMAZING!
WHA HA HA
I'M THE FIRST IN LINE!
"FIRST IN LINE"?
NOW... WHAT TO DO?
THIS SITUATION IS TOO DELICIOUS TO GULP DOWN ALL AT ONCE.

READ THIS WAY

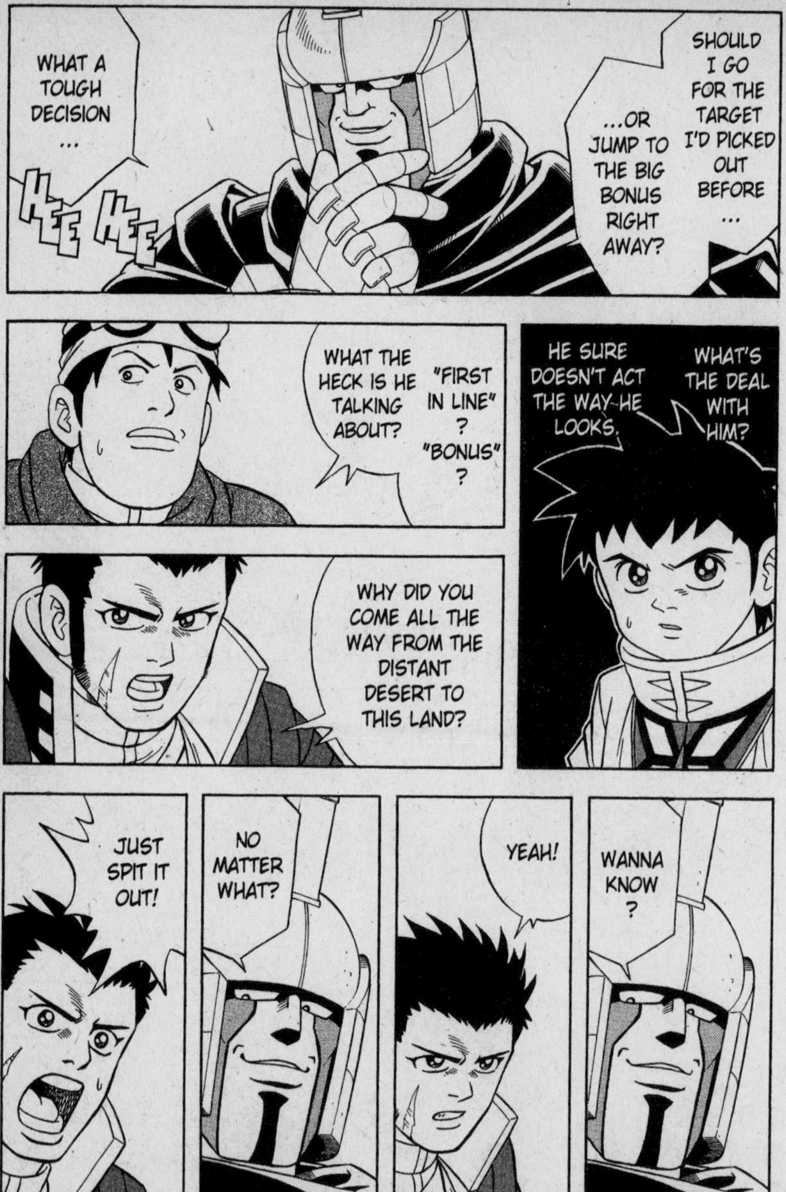

SHOULD I GO FOR THE TARGET I'D PICKED OUT BEFORE ...
...OR JUMP TO THE BIG BONUS RIGHT AWAY?
WHAT A TOUGH DECISION ...
HEE HEE
WHAT'S THE DEAL WITH HIM?
HE SURE DOESN'T ACT THE WAY HE LOOKS.
"FIRST IN LINE"? "BONUS"?
WHAT THE HECK IS HE TALKING ABOUT?
WHY DID YOU COME ALL THE WAY FROM THE DISTANT DESERT TO THIS LAND?
WANNA KNOW?
YEAH!
NO MATTER WHAT?
JUST SPIT IT OUT!

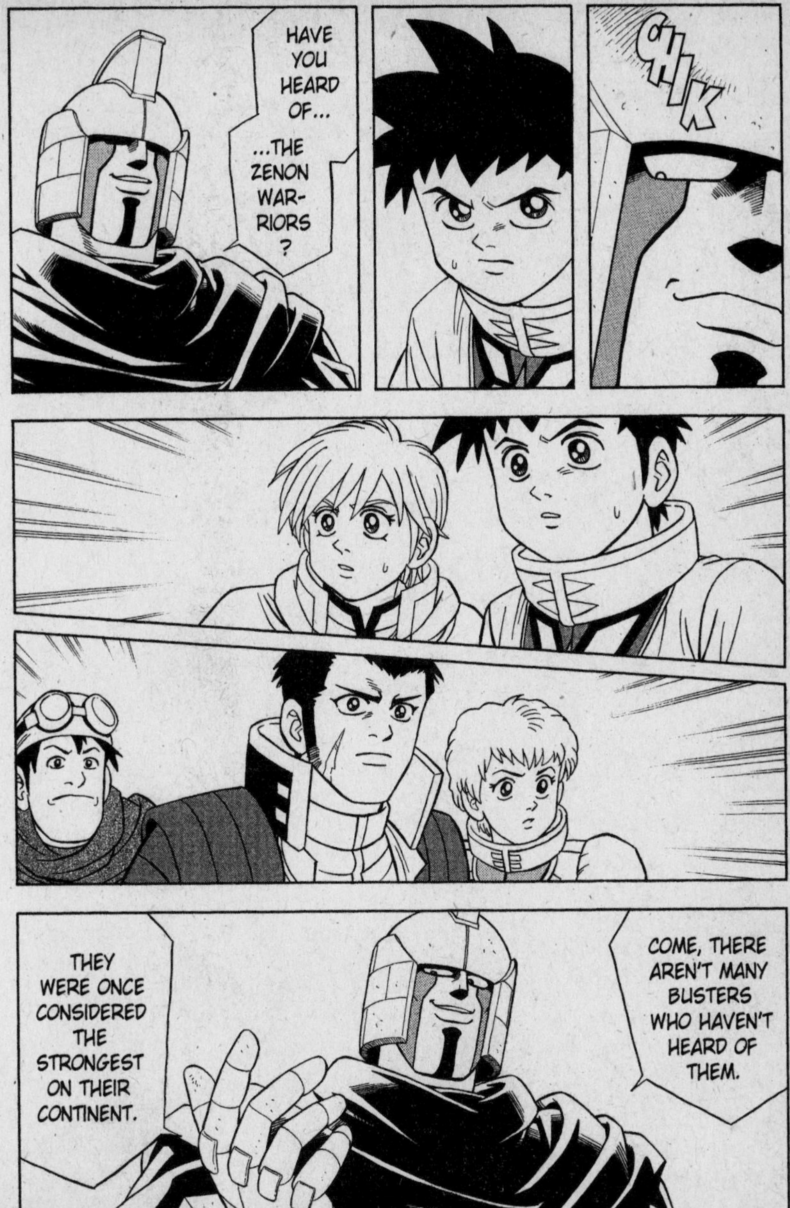
CHIK
HAVE YOU HEARD OF...
...THE ZENON WARRIORS?
COME, THERE AREN'T MANY BUSTERS WHO HAVEN'T HEARD OF THEM.
THEY WERE ONCE CONSIDERED THE STRONGEST ON THEIR CONTINENT.

READ THIS WAY

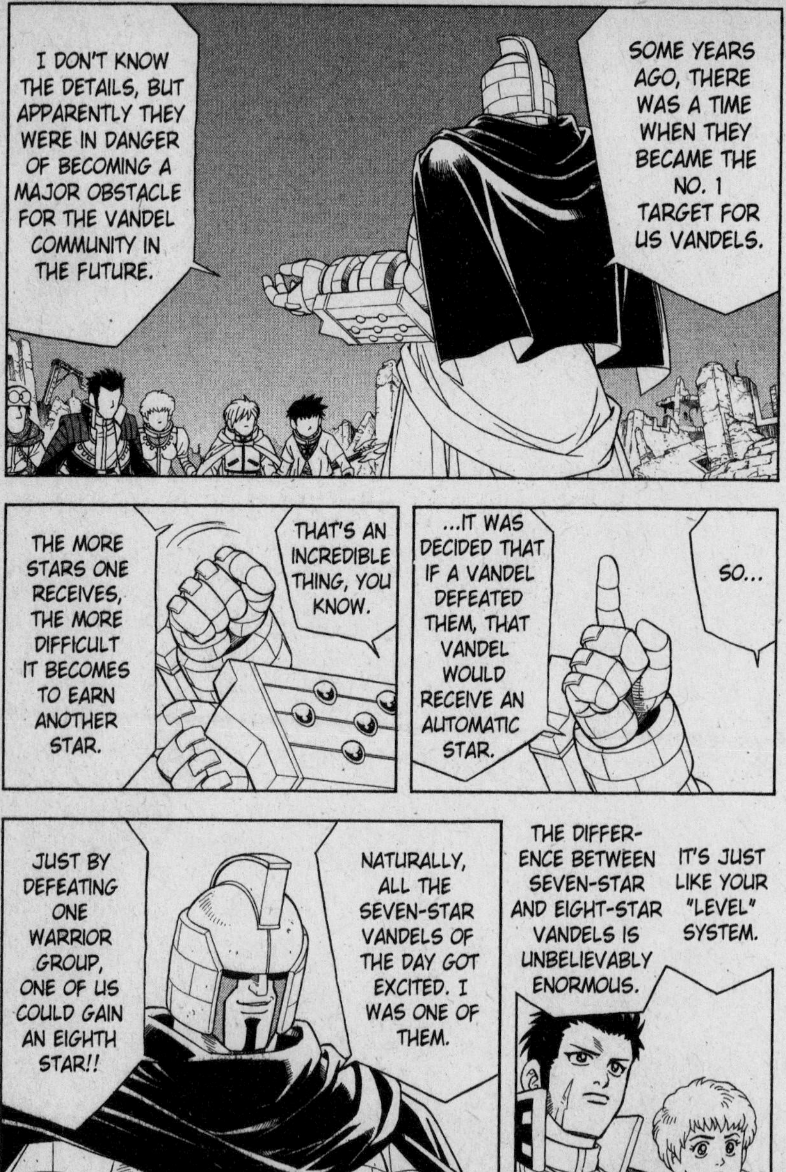
SOME YEARS AGO, THERE WAS A TIME WHEN THEY BECAME THE NO. 1 TARGET FOR US VANDELS.
I DON'T KNOW THE DETAILS, BUT APPARENTLY THEY WERE IN DANGER OF BECOMING A MAJOR OBSTACLE FOR THE VANDEL COMMUNITY IN THE FUTURE.
SO...
...IT WAS DECIDED THAT IF A VANDEL DEFEATED THEM, THAT VANDEL WOULD RECEIVE AN AUTOMATIC STAR.
THAT'S AN INCREDIBLE THING, YOU KNOW.
THE MORE STARS ONE RECEIVES, THE MORE DIFFICULT IT BECOMES TO EARN ANOTHER STAR.
IT'S JUST LIKE YOUR "LEVEL" SYSTEM.
THE DIFFER-ENCE BETWEEN SEVEN-STAR AND EIGHT-STAR VANDELS IS UNBELIEVABLY ENORMOUS.
NATURALLY, ALL THE SEVEN-STAR VANDELS OF THE DAY GOT EXCITED. I WAS ONE OF THEM.
JUST BY DEFEATING ONE WARRIOR GROUP, ONE OF US COULD GAIN AN EIGHTH STAR!!

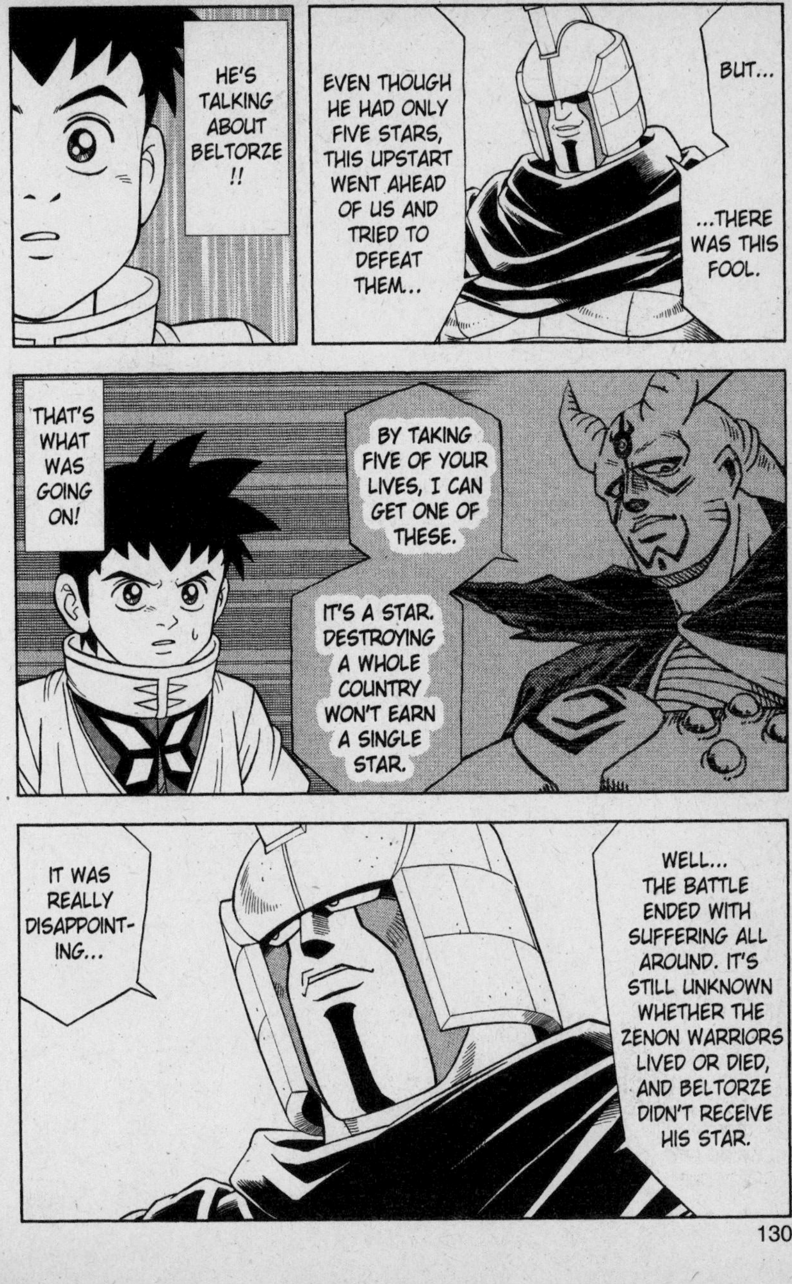
BUT...
...THERE WAS THIS FOOL.
EVEN THOUGH HE HAD ONLY FIVE STARS, THIS UPSTART WENT AHEAD OF US AND TRIED TO DEFEAT THEM...
HE'S TALKING ABOUT BELTORZE !!
BY TAKING FIVE OF YOUR LIVES, I CAN GET ONE OF THESE.
IT'S A STAR. DESTROYING A WHOLE COUNTRY WON'T EARN A SINGLE STAR.
THAT'S WHAT WAS GOING ON!
WELL... THE BATTLE ENDED WITH SUFFERING ALL AROUND. IT'S STILL UNKNOWN WHETHER THE ZENON WARRIORS LIVED OR DIED, AND BELTORZE DIDN'T RECEIVE HIS STAR.
IT WAS REALLY DISAPPOINT-ING...

READ THIS WAY

THE LEGENDARY WARRIOR GROUP WORTH A STAR.
THAT'S WHY I'VE WANTED TO MEET THEM FOR A LONG TIME...
....IF THEY'RE STILL ALIVE.
WHAT ABOUT YOU?
AREN'T YOU IN-TRIGUED?
HE... KNOWS...
HE KNOWS THAT CRUSS IS HERE!!
GRR
HO HO
LOOK AT HIS FACE. THERE'S NO MISTAKE.
THAT INFORMATION ABOUT AN AMNESIAC PAINTER BEING CRUSS OF THE ZENON WARRIORS... IT'S RIGHT ON!!
I'M SURE ALL THE ZENON WARRIORS ARE ALIVE, BUT ONLY THIS ONE GOT CAUGHT IN MY WEB OF INFORMATION! I HAD TO PICK THROUGH A LOT OF GROUNDLESS RUMORS...
...BUT IT WAS DEFINITELY WORTH LOOKING INTO EVERY ONE!

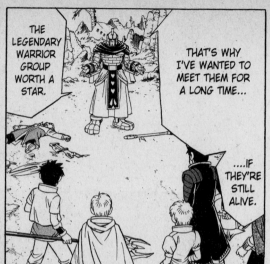

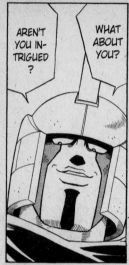

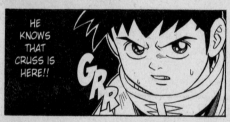

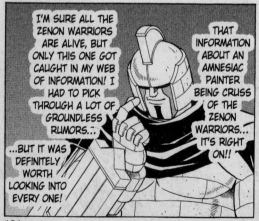

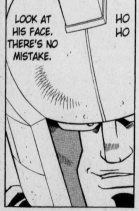

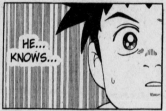

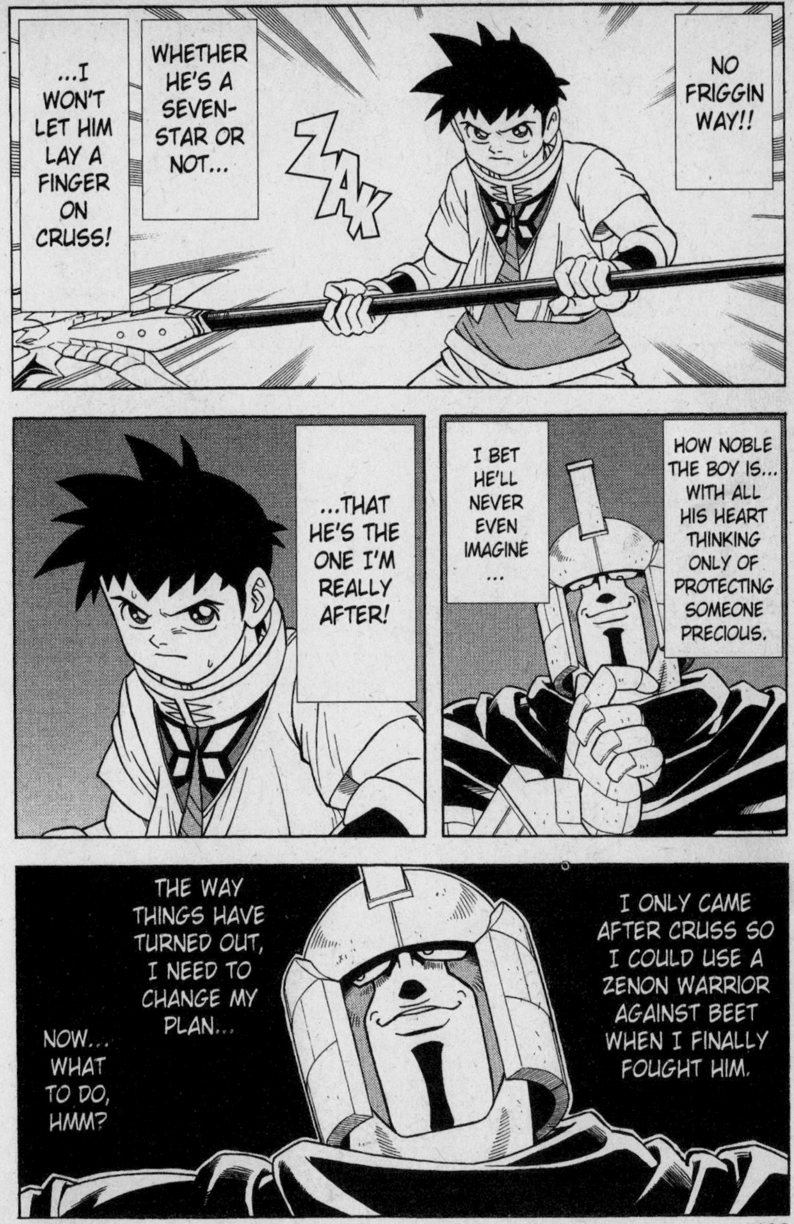
NO FRIGGIN WAY!!
WHETHER HE'S A SEVEN-STAR OR NOT...
ZAK
...I WON'T LET HIM LAY A FINGER ON CRUSS!
HOW NOBLE THE BOY IS... WITH ALL HIS HEART THINKING ONLY OF PROTECTING SOMEONE PRECIOUS.
I BET HE'LL NEVER EVEN IMAGINE...
...THAT HE'S THE ONE I'M REALLY AFTER!
I ONLY CAME AFTER CRUSS SO I COULD USE A ZENON WARRIOR AGAINST BEET WHEN I FINALLY FOUGHT HIM.
THE WAY THINGS HAVE TURNED OUT, I NEED TO CHANGE MY PLAN...
NOW... WHAT TO DO, HMM?

READ THIS WAY

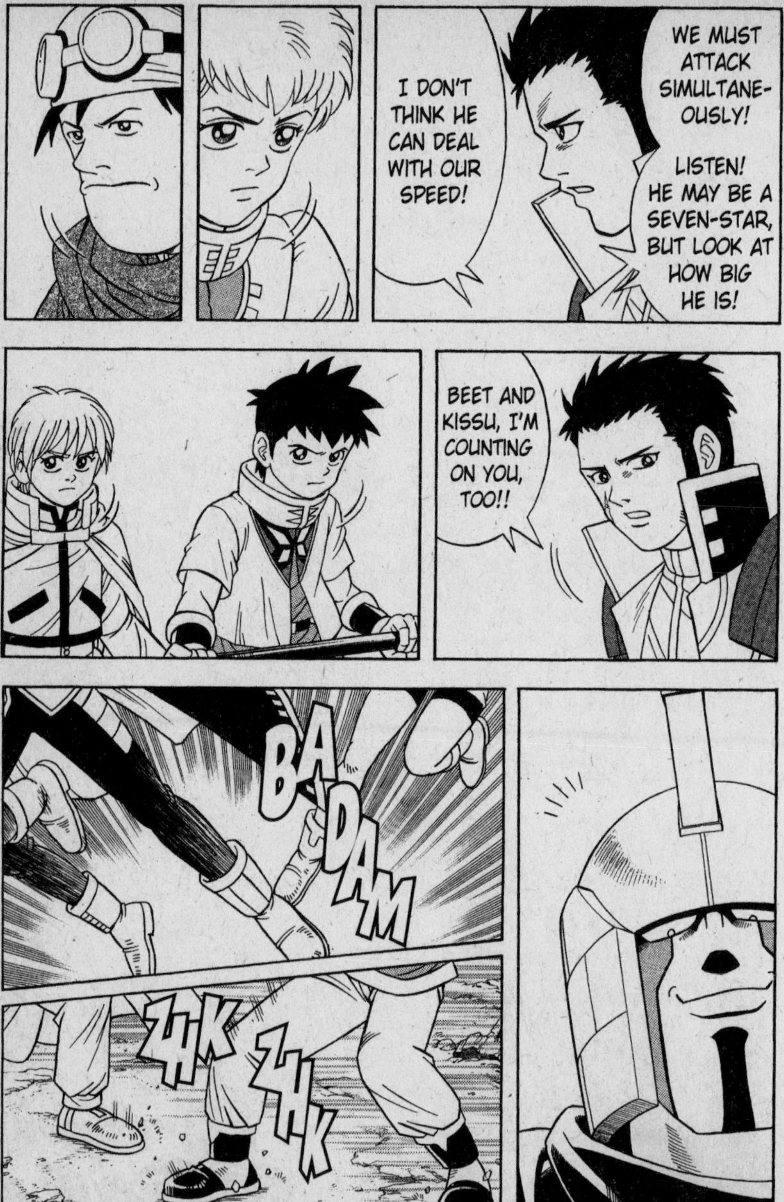
WE MUST ATTACK SIMULTANE-OUSLY!
LISTEN! HE MAY BE A SEVEN-STAR, BUT LOOK AT HOW BIG HE IS!
I DON'T THINK HE CAN DEAL WITH OUR SPEED!
BEET AND KISSU, I'M COUNTING ON YOU, TOO!!
BA DAM
ZHK
ZHK

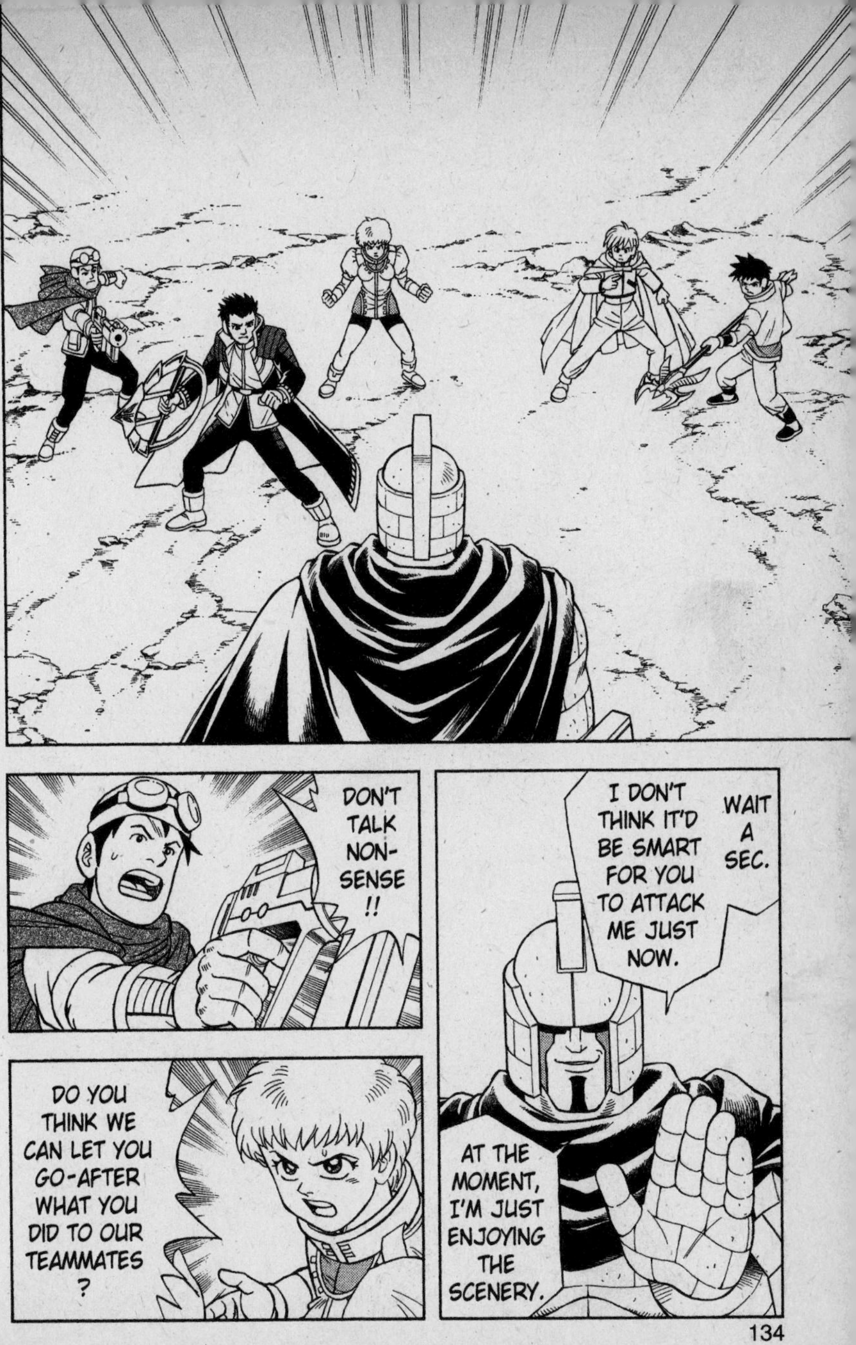
WAIT A SEC.
I DON'T THINK IT'D BE SMART FOR YOU TO ATTACK ME JUST NOW.
AT THE MOMENT, I'M JUST ENJOYING THE SCENERY.
DON'T TALK NON-SENSE !!
DO YOU THINK WE CAN LET YOU GO-AFTER WHAT YOU DID TO OUR TEAMMATES ?

READ THIS WAY

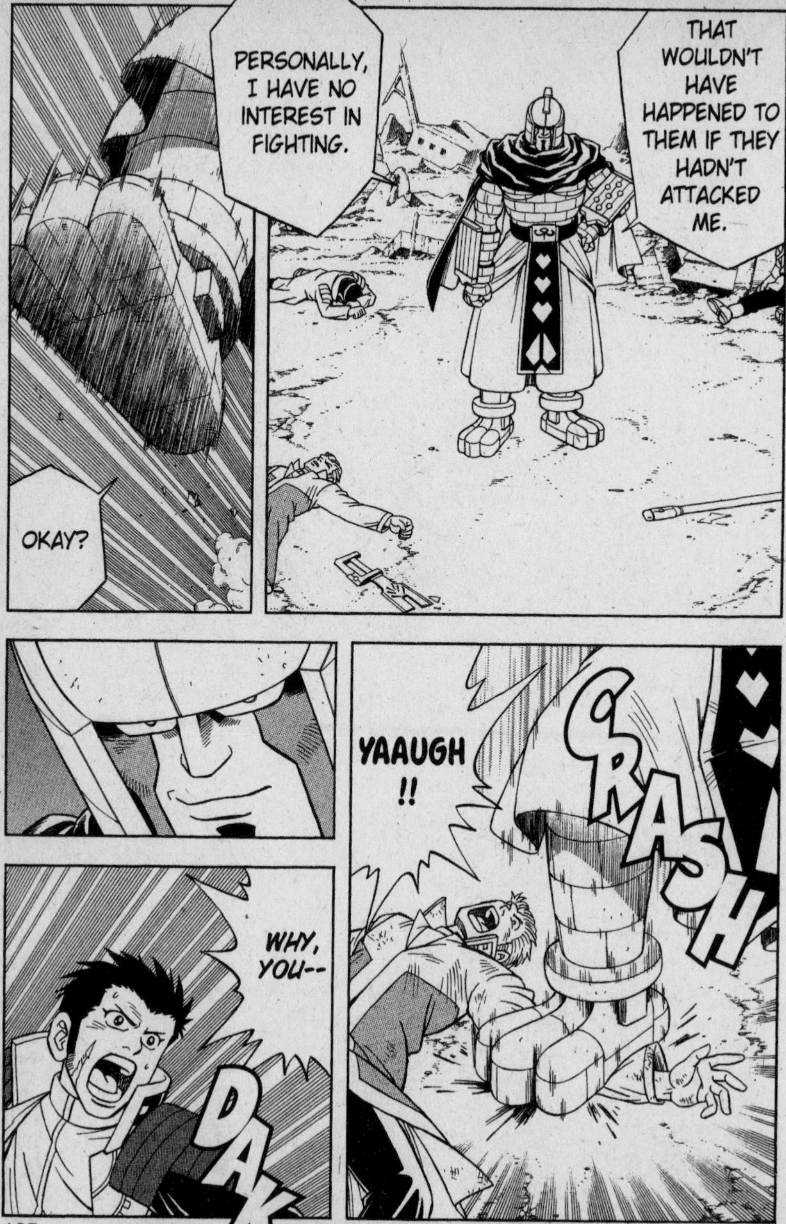
THAT WOULDN'T HAVE HAPPENED TO THEM IF THEY HADN'T ATTACKED ME.
PERSONALLY, I HAVE NO INTEREST IN FIGHTING.
OKAY?
CRASH
YAAUGH!!
WHY, YOU--
DAK

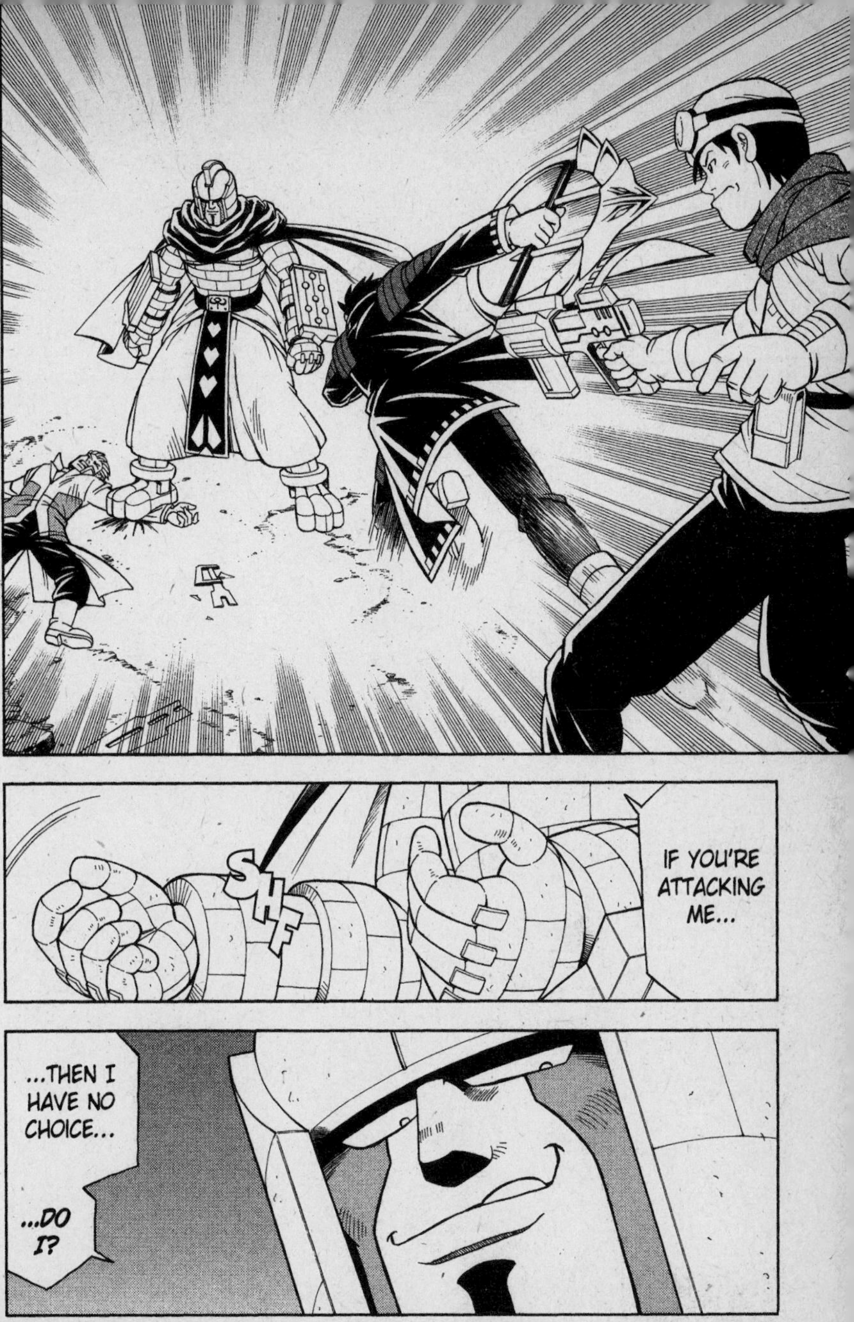
SHF
IF YOU'RE ATTACKING ME...
...THEN I HAVE NO CHOICE...
...DO I?

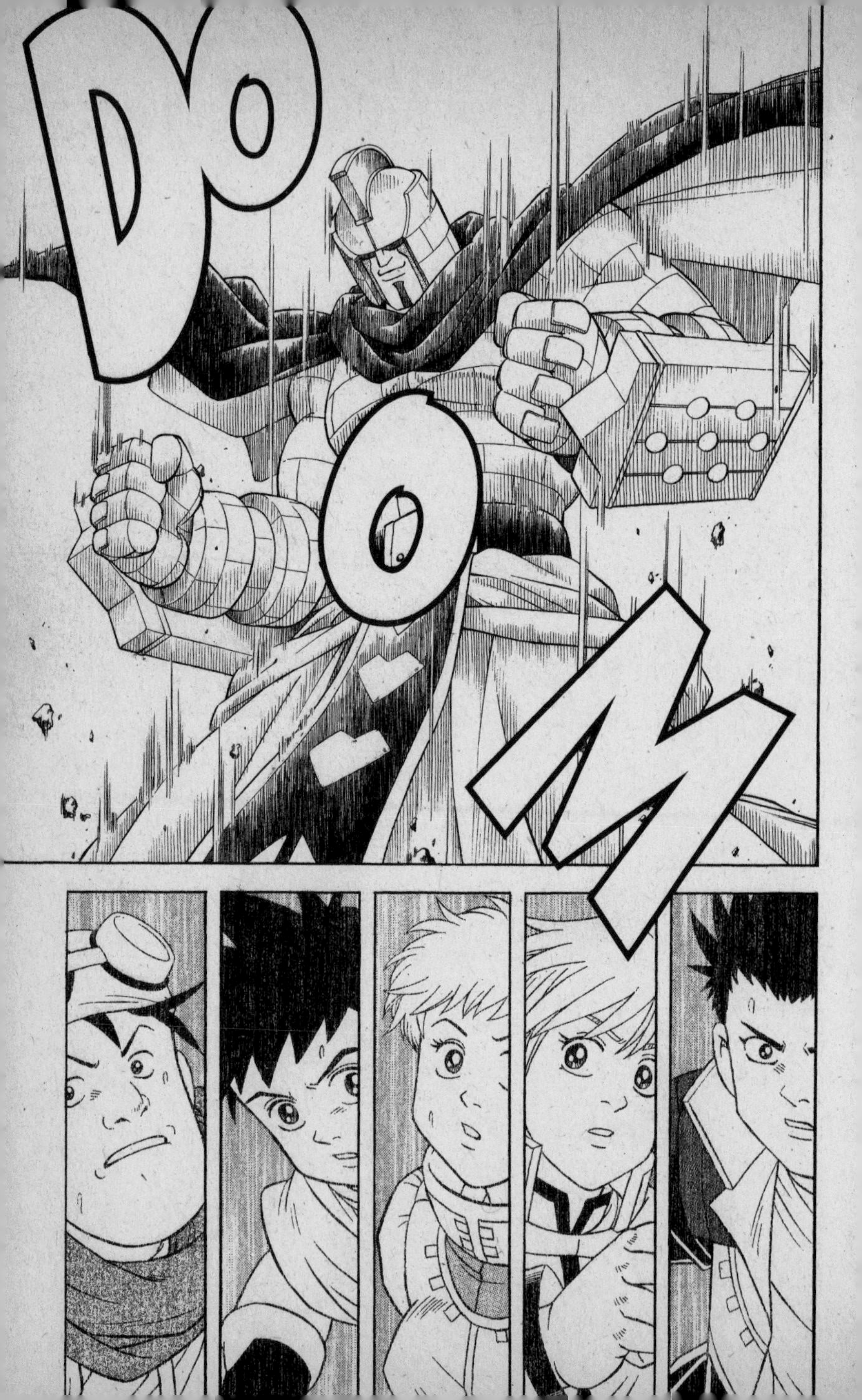
DOOM

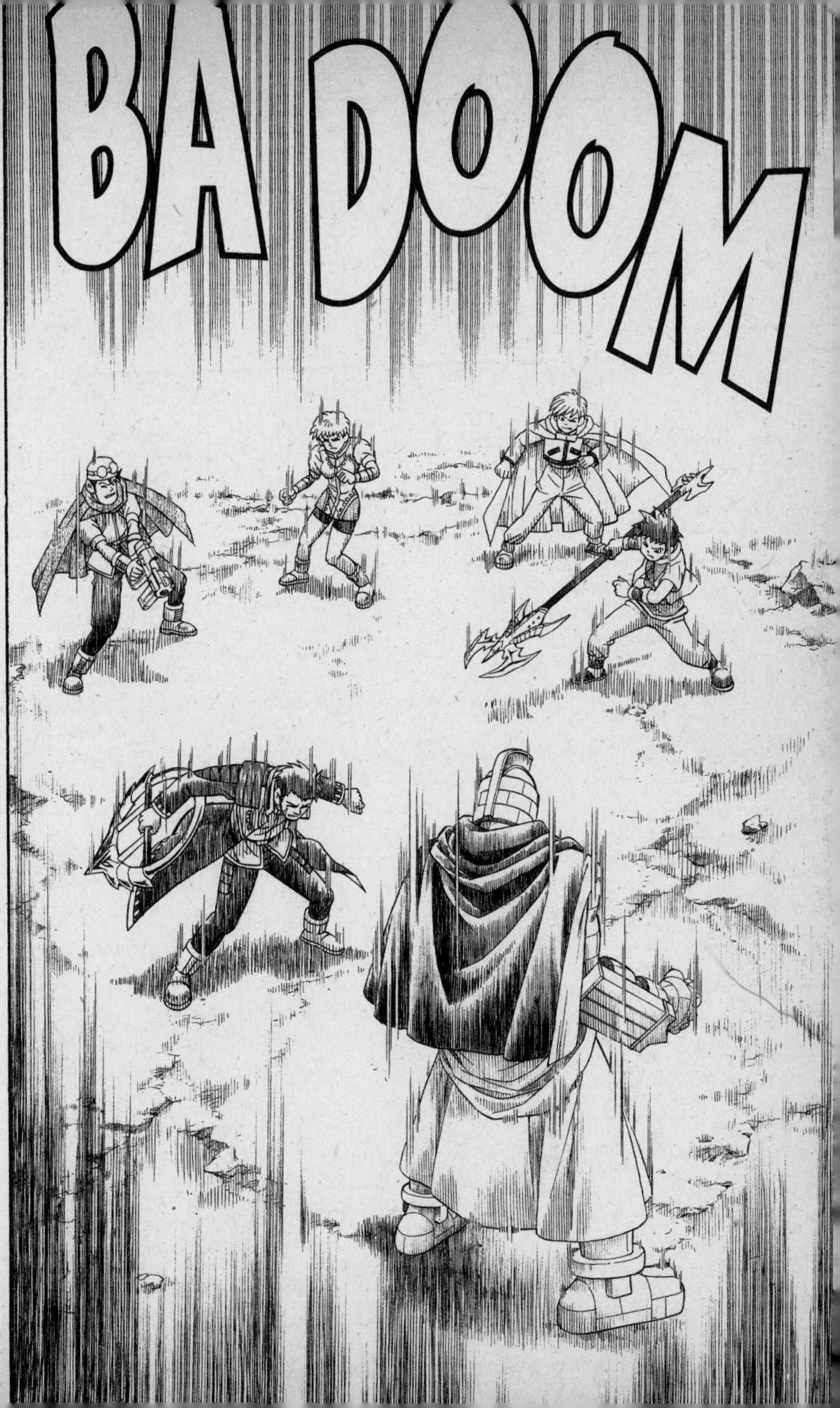
BA DOOM

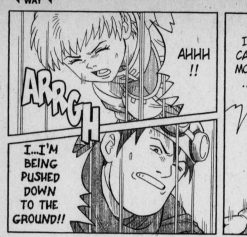

READ THIS WAY

WH- WHAT'S THIS!?
ARGH
I... CAN'T MOVE ...
AHHH !!
ARRGH
I...I'M BEING PUSHED DOWN TO THE GROUND!!
I SEE...HE HAS THE POWER TO CONTROL GRAVITY...! THIS IS HOW THE OTHER BUSTERS WERE DESTROYED!
BY THE SUPER GRAVITATIONAL POWER THAT COMES OUT OF HIS BODY, THEY WERE DEPRIVED OF THE ABILITY TO MOVE...
...AND...
ARRGH
NO... FRIGGIN ...
...WAY !!
IT'S TRUE I'M NOT ONE OF THE FASTER VANDELS.
THUD
!!

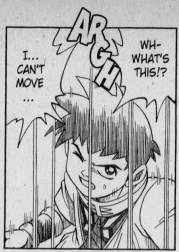

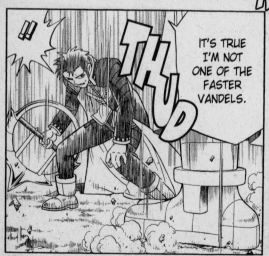

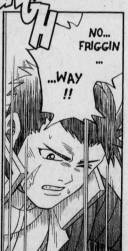

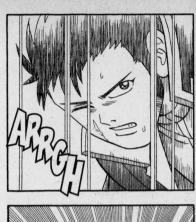

ARRGH

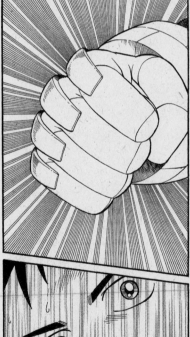

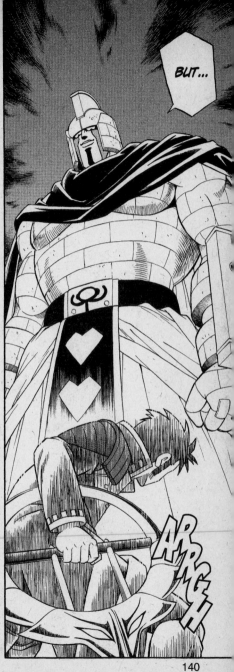

BUT...

AR RR GH

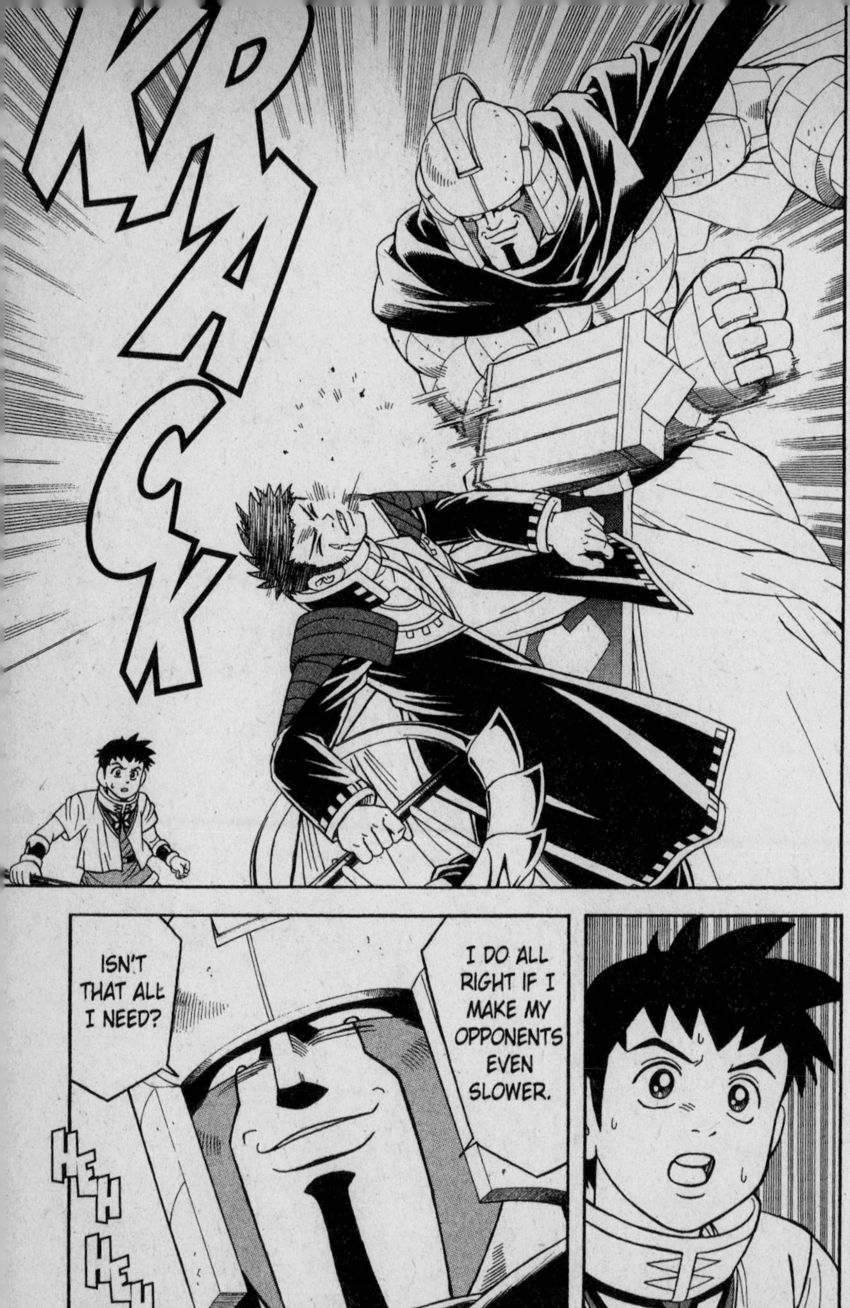
KRAACK
I DO ALL RIGHT IF I MAKE MY OPPONENTS EVEN SLOWER.
ISN'T THAT ALL I NEED?
HEH HEH

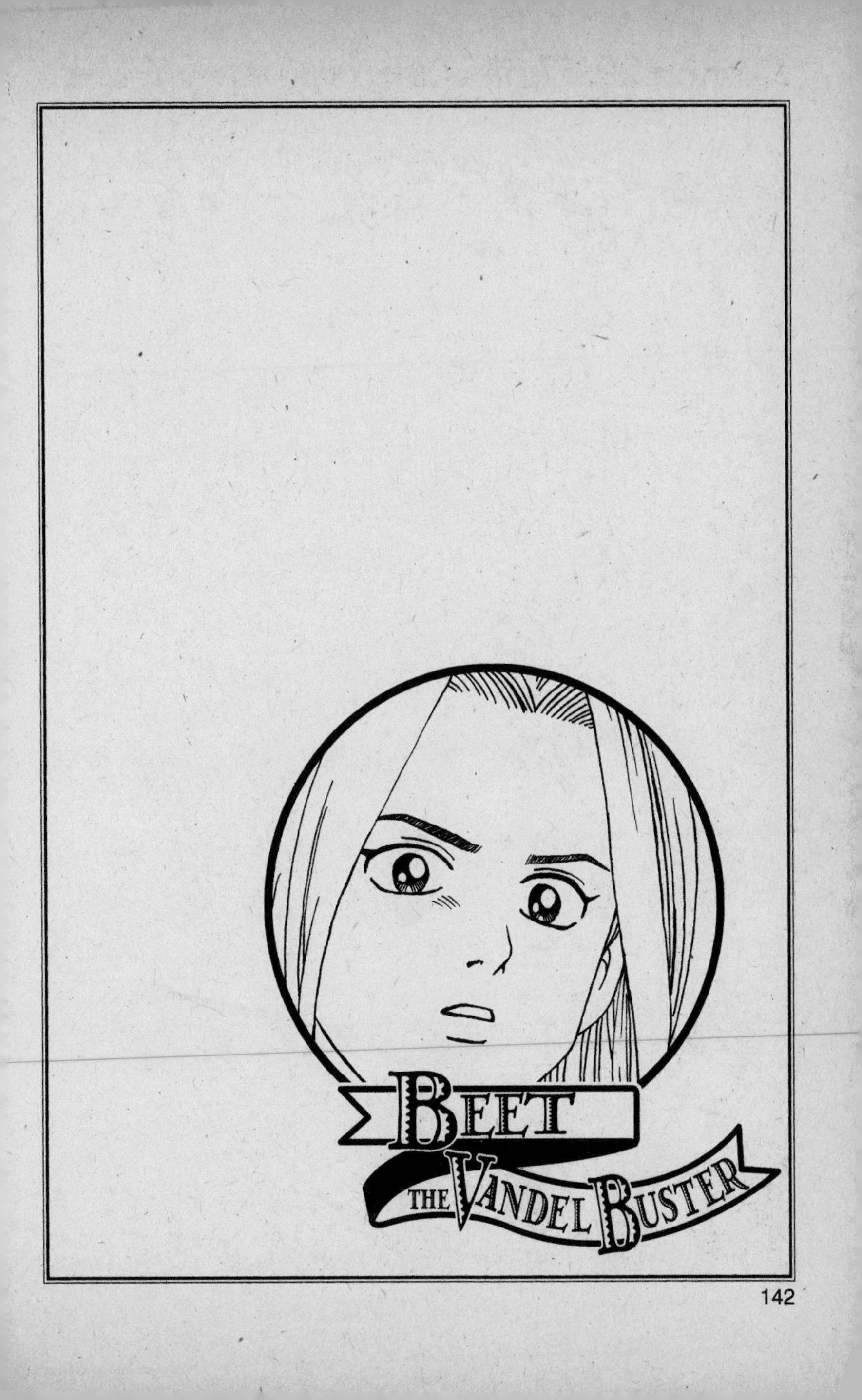
BEET THE VANDEL BUSTER

Chapter 29: Thrill of the Immovable Giant!!

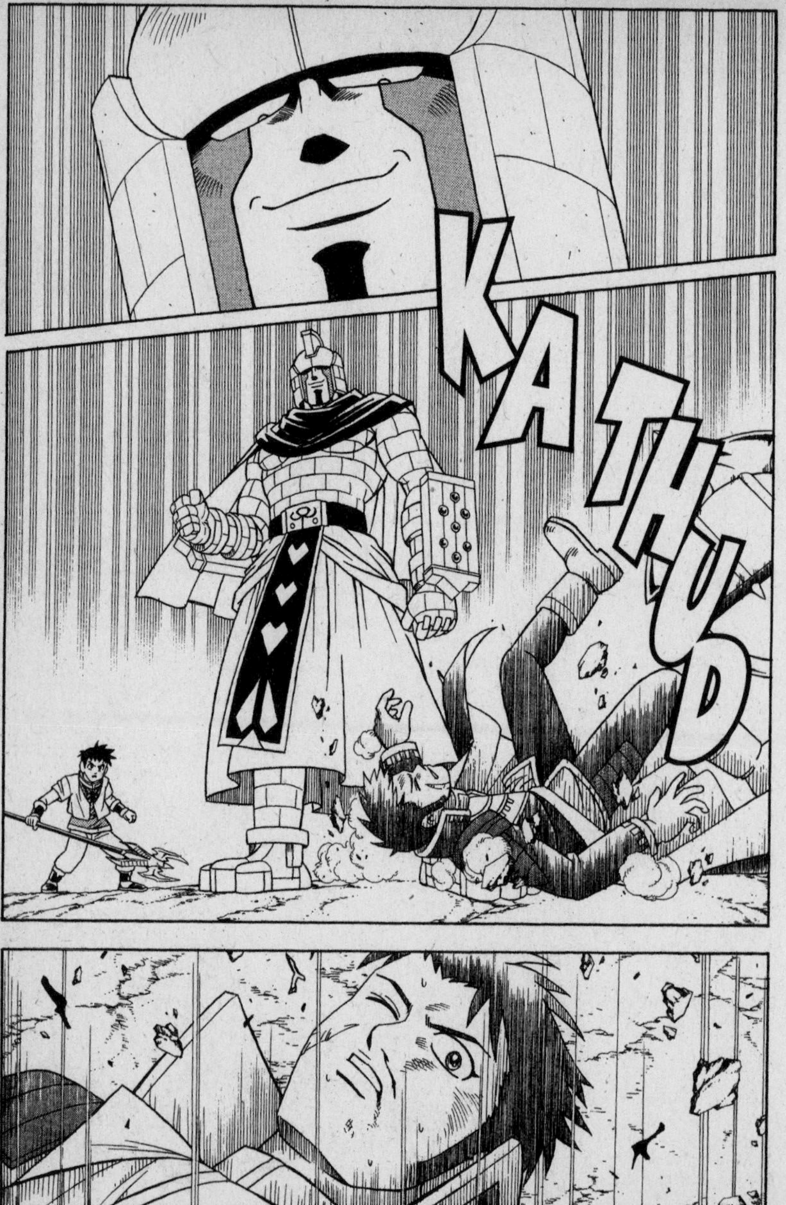
KATHUD

READ THIS WAY

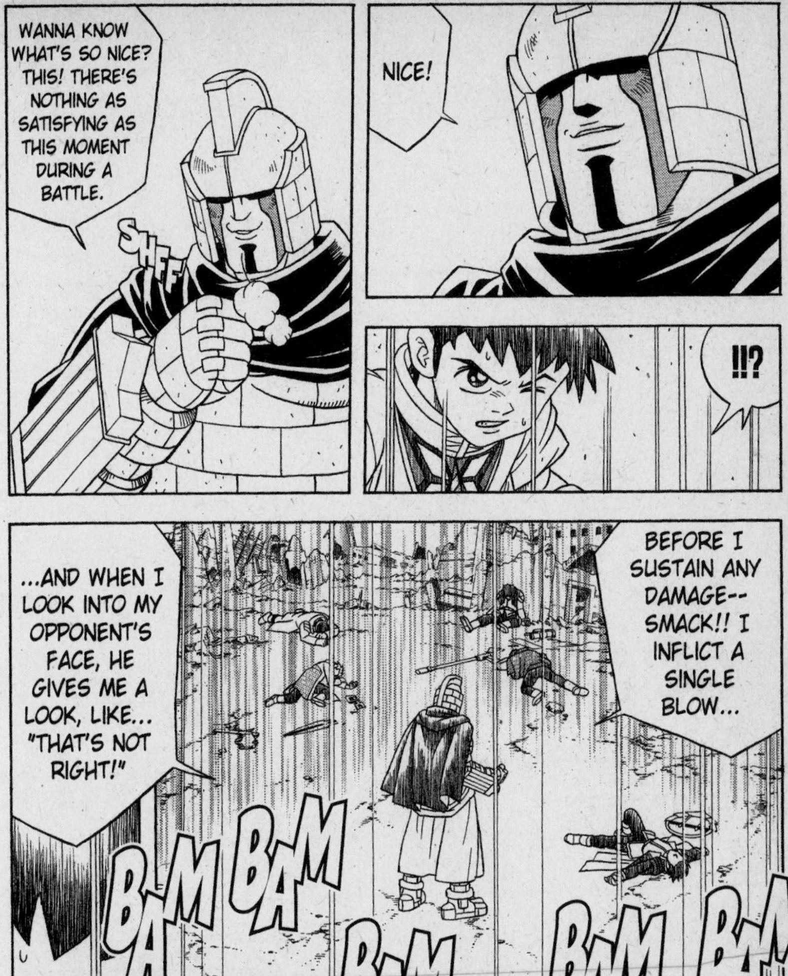
NICE!
!!?
WANNA KNOW WHAT'S SO NICE? THIS! THERE'S NOTHING AS SATISFYING AS THIS MOMENT DURING A BATTLE.
SHFF
BEFORE I SUSTAIN ANY DAMAGE-- SMACK!! I INFLICT A SINGLE BLOW...
...AND WHEN I LOOK INTO MY OPPONENT'S FACE, HE GIVES ME A LOOK, LIKE... "THAT'S NOT RIGHT!"
BAM BAM BAM BAM BAM BAM BAM

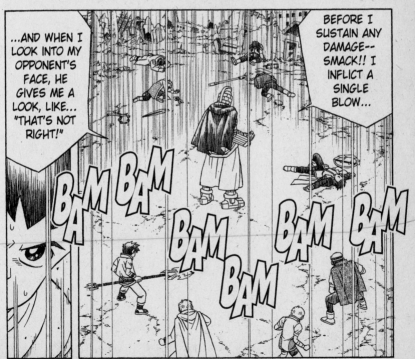

READ THIS WAY

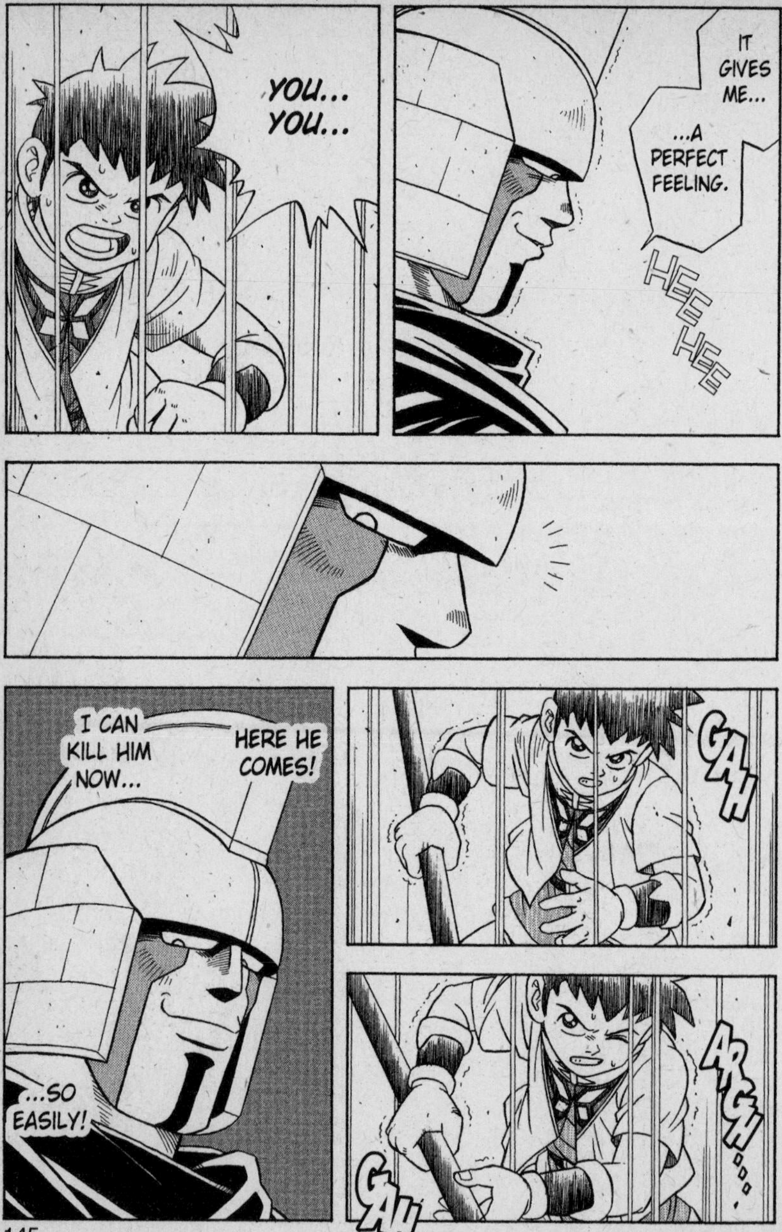
IT GIVES ME...
...A PERFECT FEELING.
HEE HEE
YOU... YOU...
GAH
ARGH...
GAH
HERE HE COMES!
I CAN KILL HIM NOW...
...SO EASILY!

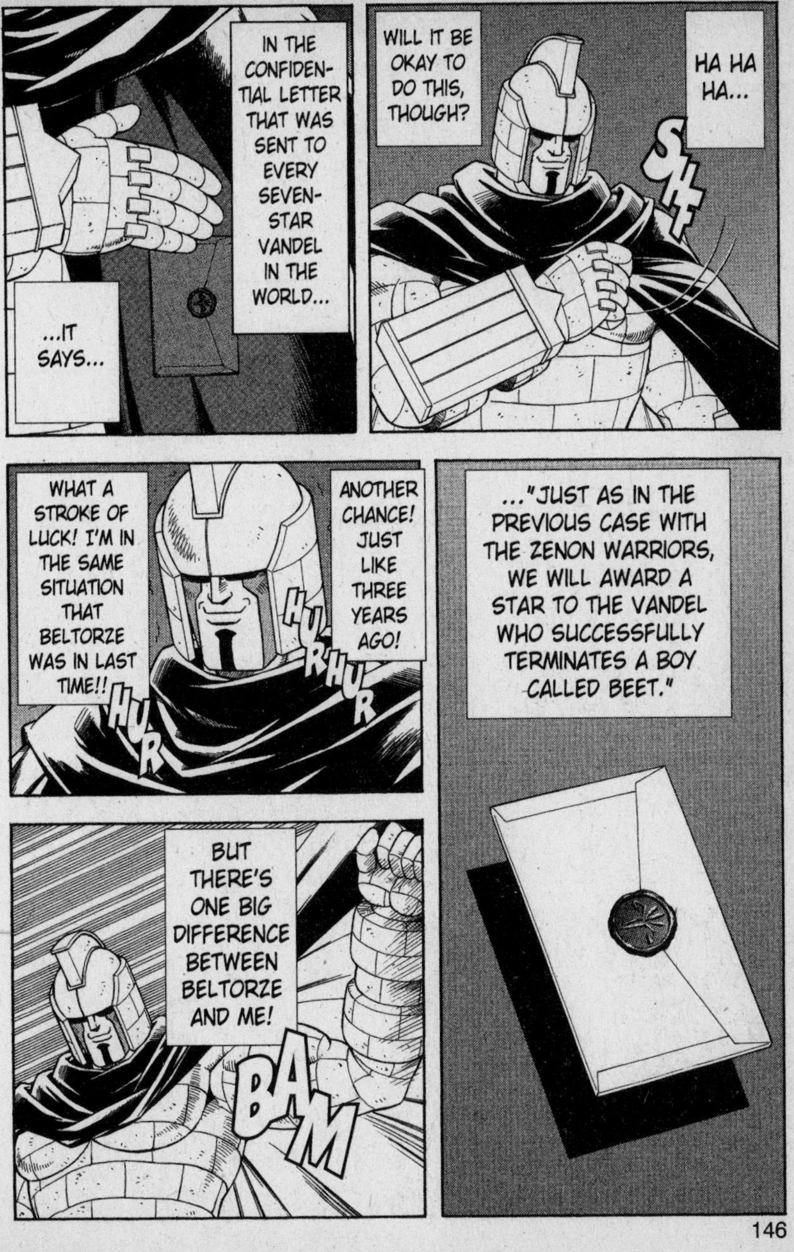
HA HA HA...
WILL IT BE OKAY TO DO THIS, THOUGH?
SHF
IN THE CONFIDENTIAL LETTER THAT WAS SENT TO EVERY SEVEN-STAR VANDEL IN THE WORLD...
...IT SAYS...
..."JUST AS IN THE PREVIOUS CASE WITH THE ZENON WARRIORS, WE WILL AWARD A STAR TO THE VANDEL WHO SUCCESSFULLY TERMINATES A BOY CALLED BEET."
ANOTHER CHANCE! JUST LIKE THREE YEARS AGO!
WHAT A STROKE OF LUCK! I'M IN THE SAME SITUATION THAT BELTORZE WAS IN LAST TIME!!
HUR HUR HUR HUR
BUT THERE'S ONE BIG DIFFERENCE BETWEEN BELTORZE AND ME!
BAM

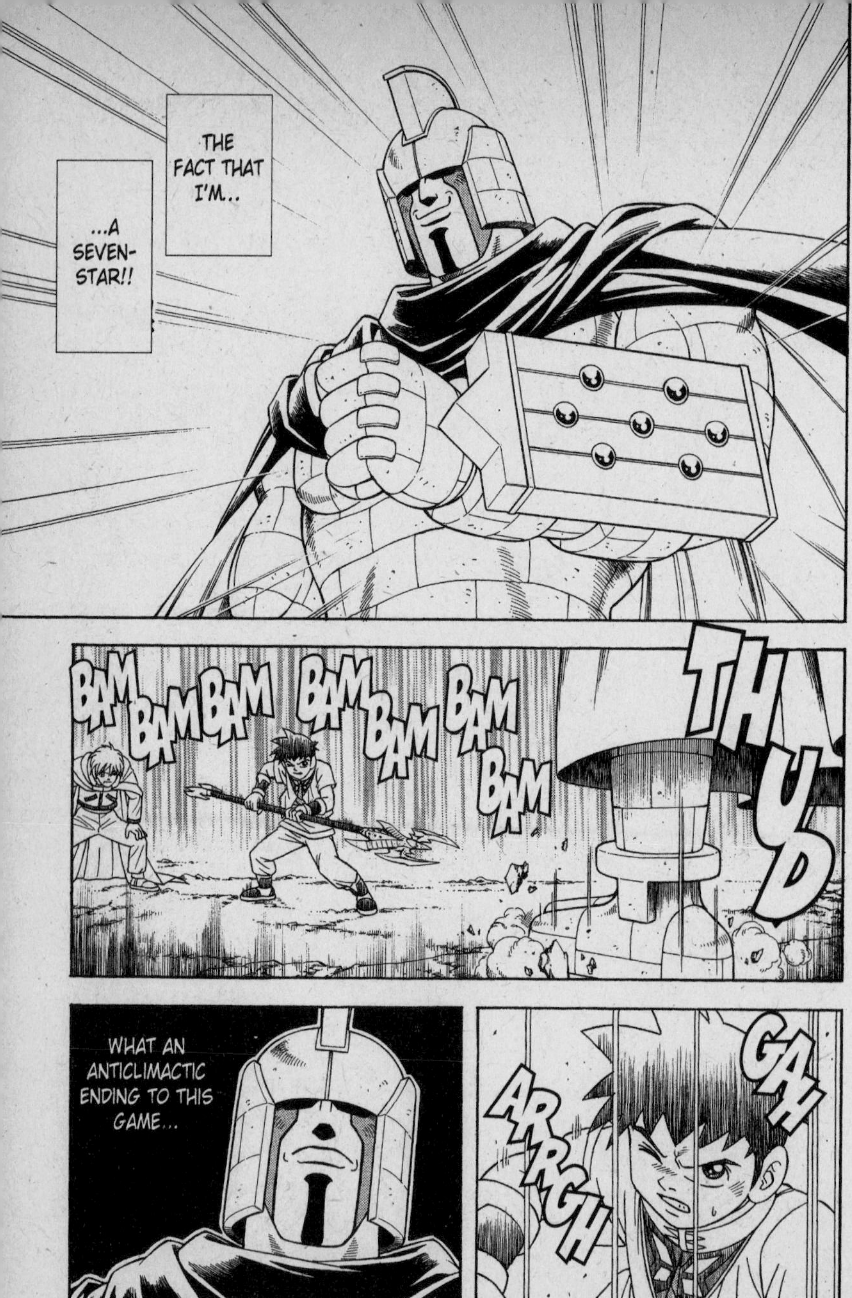
THE FACT THAT I'M...
...A SEVEN-STAR!!
THUD
BAM BAM BAM BAM
BAM BAM BAM
GAH
ARRGH
WHAT AN ANTICLIMACTIC ENDING TO THIS GAME...

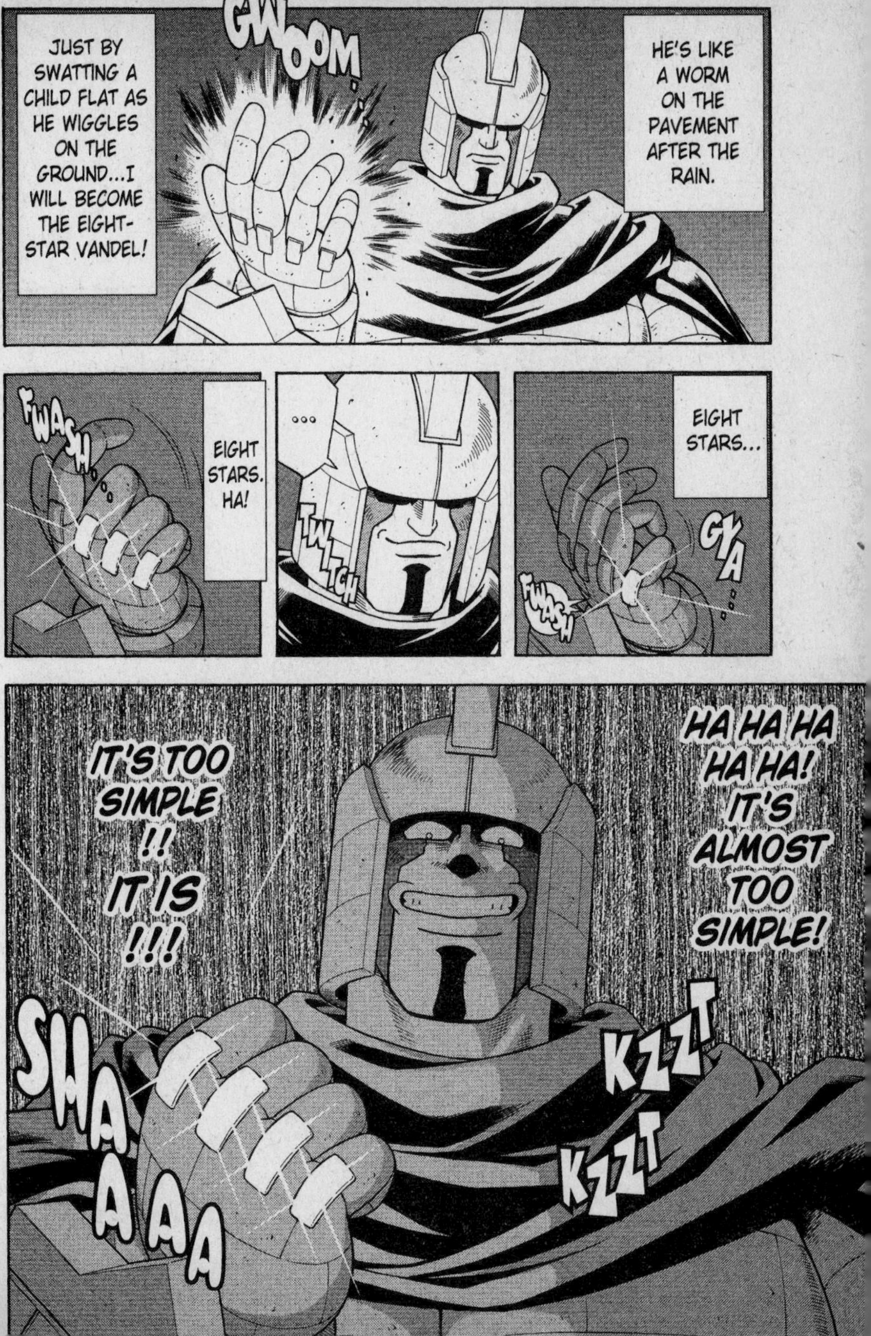
HE'S LIKE A WORM ON THE PAVEMENT AFTER THE RAIN.
GWOOM
JUST BY SWATTING A CHILD FLAT AS HE WIGGLES ON THE GROUND...I WILL BECOME THE EIGHT-STAR VANDEL!
EIGHT STARS...
GYA
FWASH
...
TWITCH
EIGHT STARS. HA!
FWASH
HA HA HA HA HA! IT'S ALMOST TOO SIMPLE!
IT'S TOO SIMPLE!! IT IS!!!
KZZT
KZZT
SHAAAAA

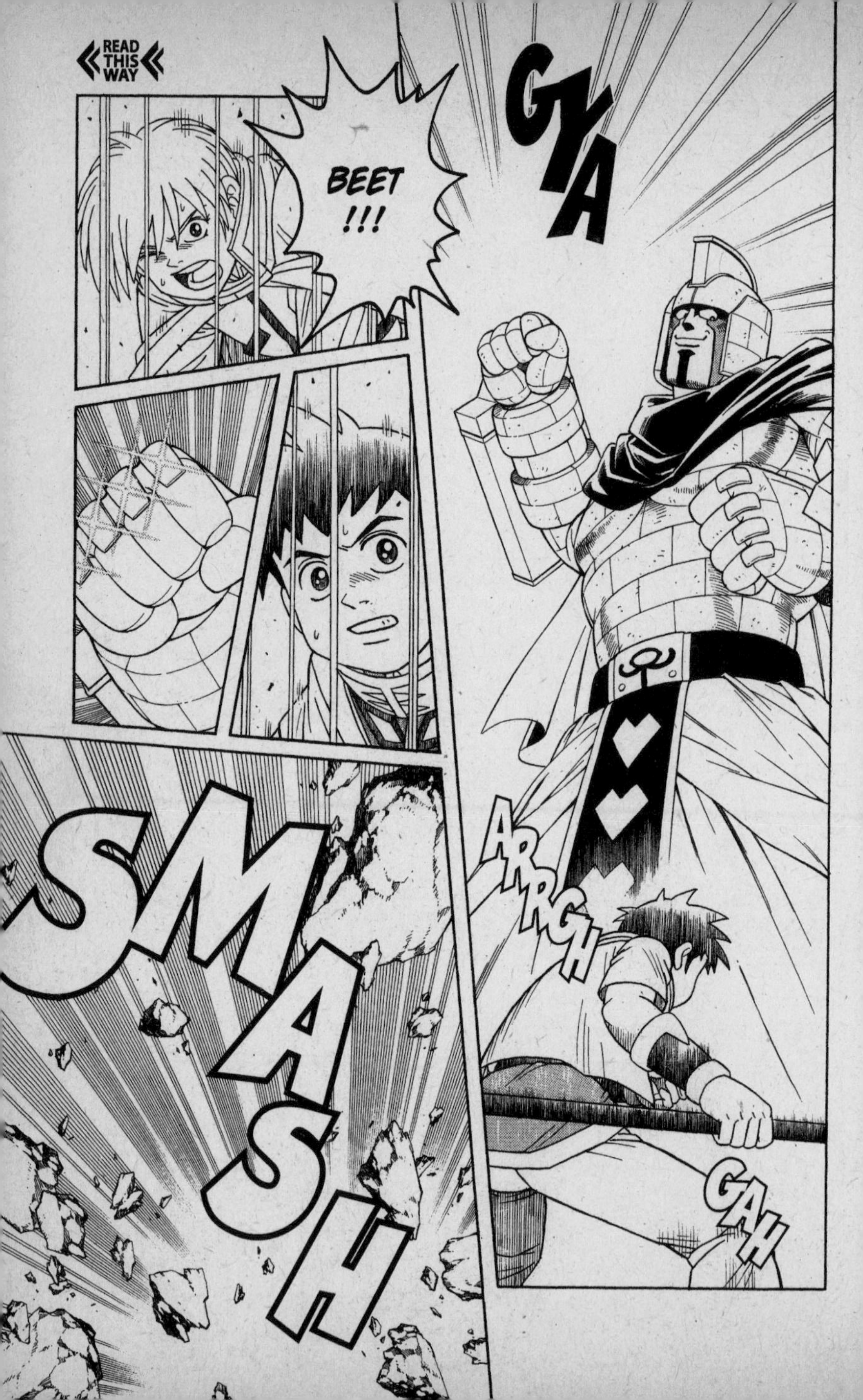
READ THIS WAY
GYA
ARRGH
GAH
BEET !!!
SMASH

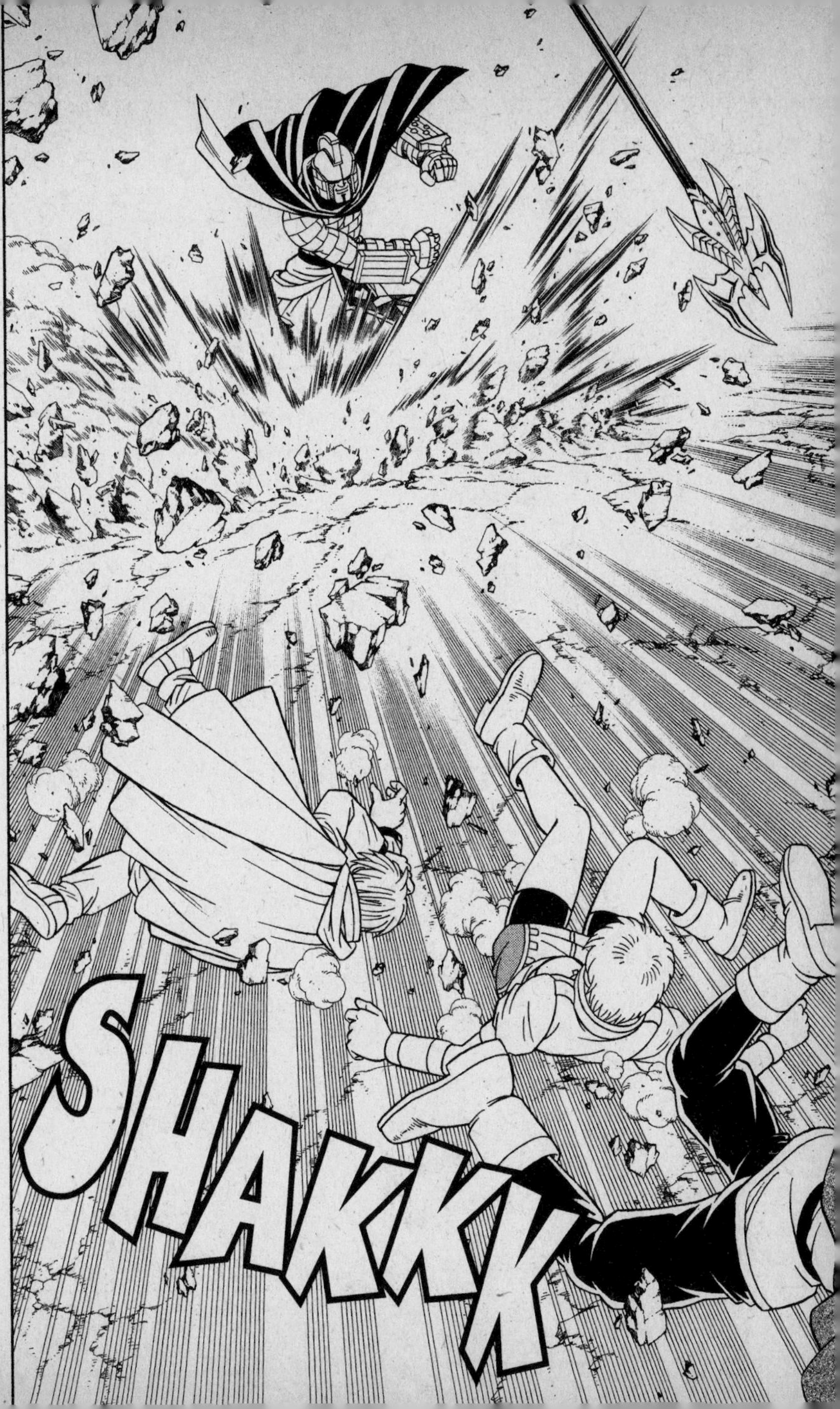
SHAKKK

READ THIS WAY

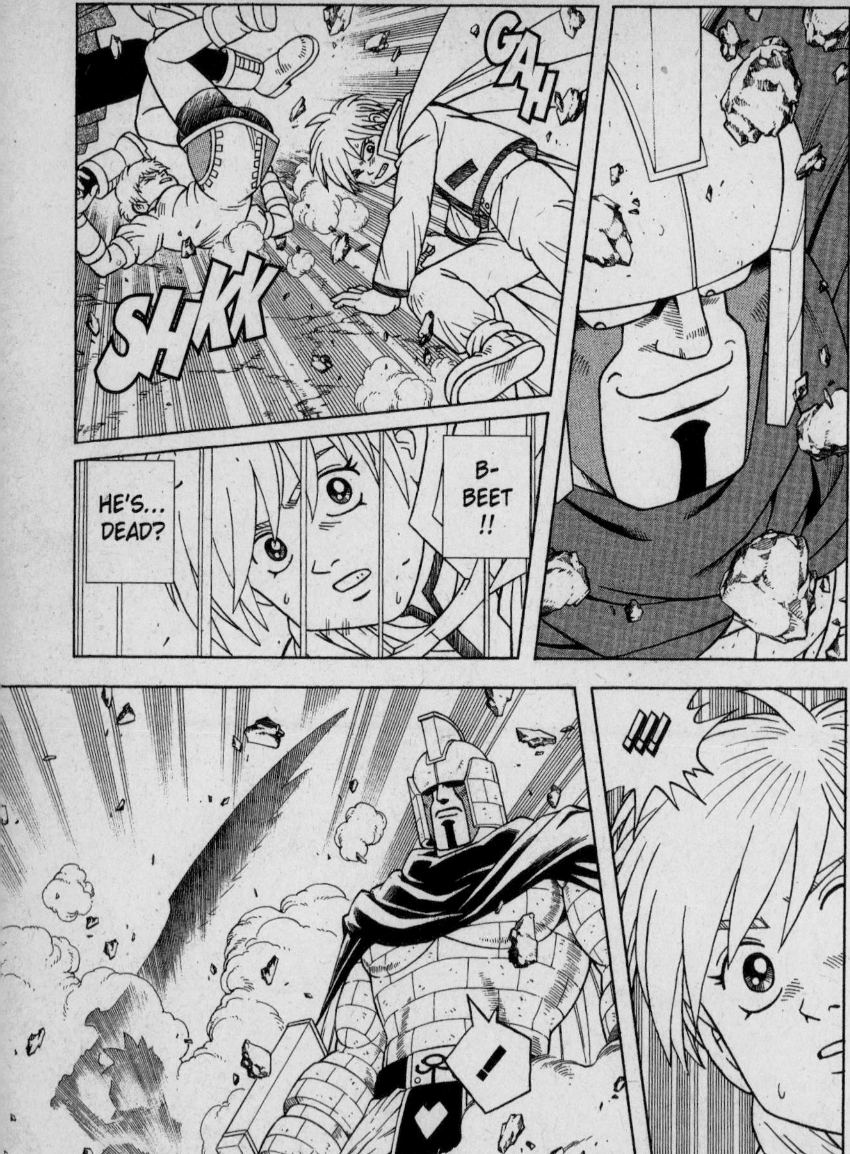
GAH
SHKK
B-BEET!!
HE'S... DEAD?
!!!
!

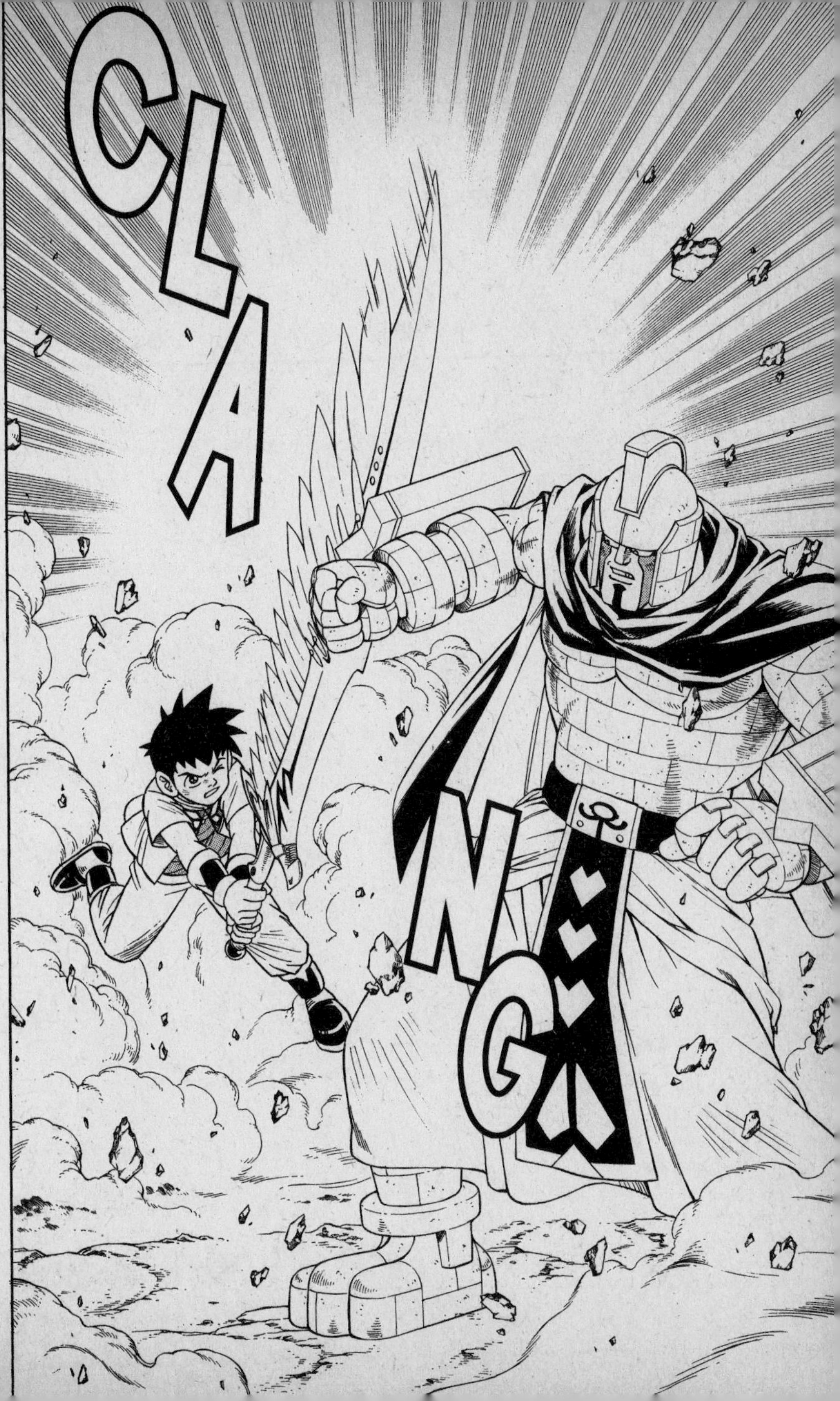
CLANG

READ THIS WAY

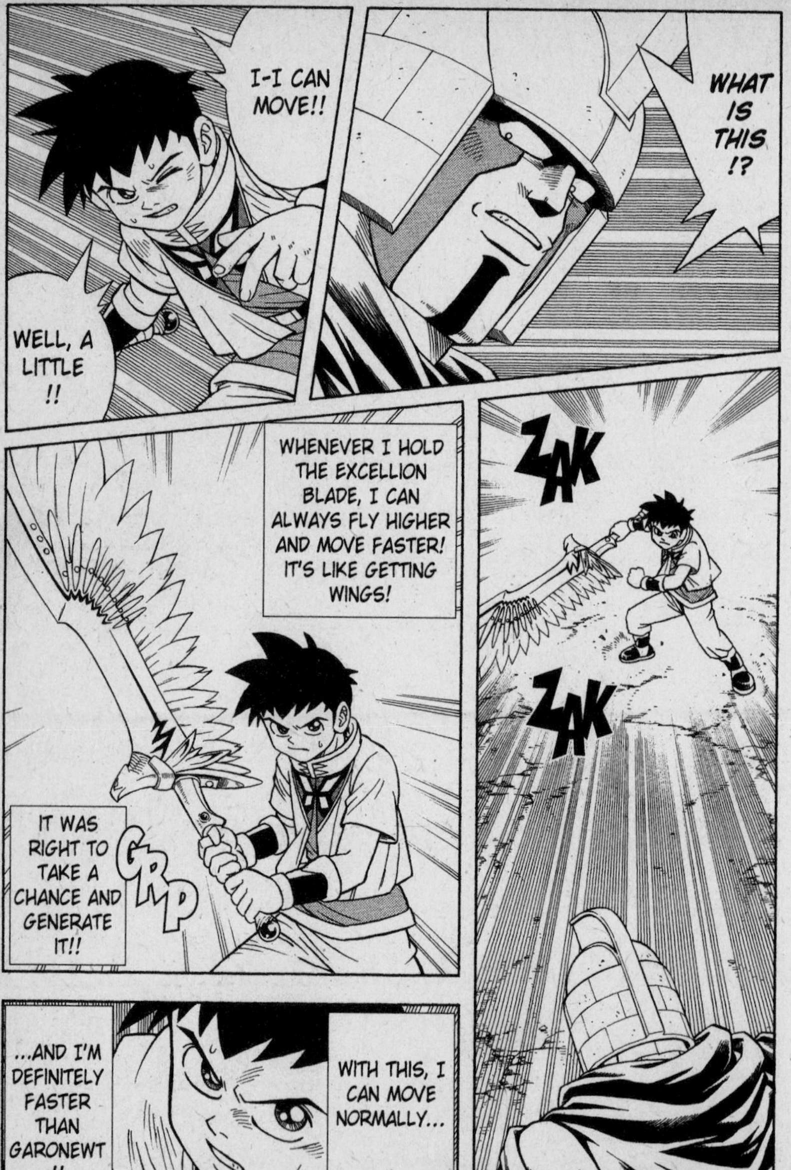
WHAT IS THIS !?
I-I CAN MOVE!!
WELL, A LITTLE !!
ZAK
ZAK
WHENEVER I HOLD THE EXCELLION BLADE, I CAN ALWAYS FLY HIGHER AND MOVE FASTER! IT'S LIKE GETTING WINGS!
GRP
IT WAS RIGHT TO TAKE A CHANCE AND GENERATE IT!!
WITH THIS, I CAN MOVE NORMALLY...
...AND I'M DEFINITELY FASTER THAN GARONEWT !!

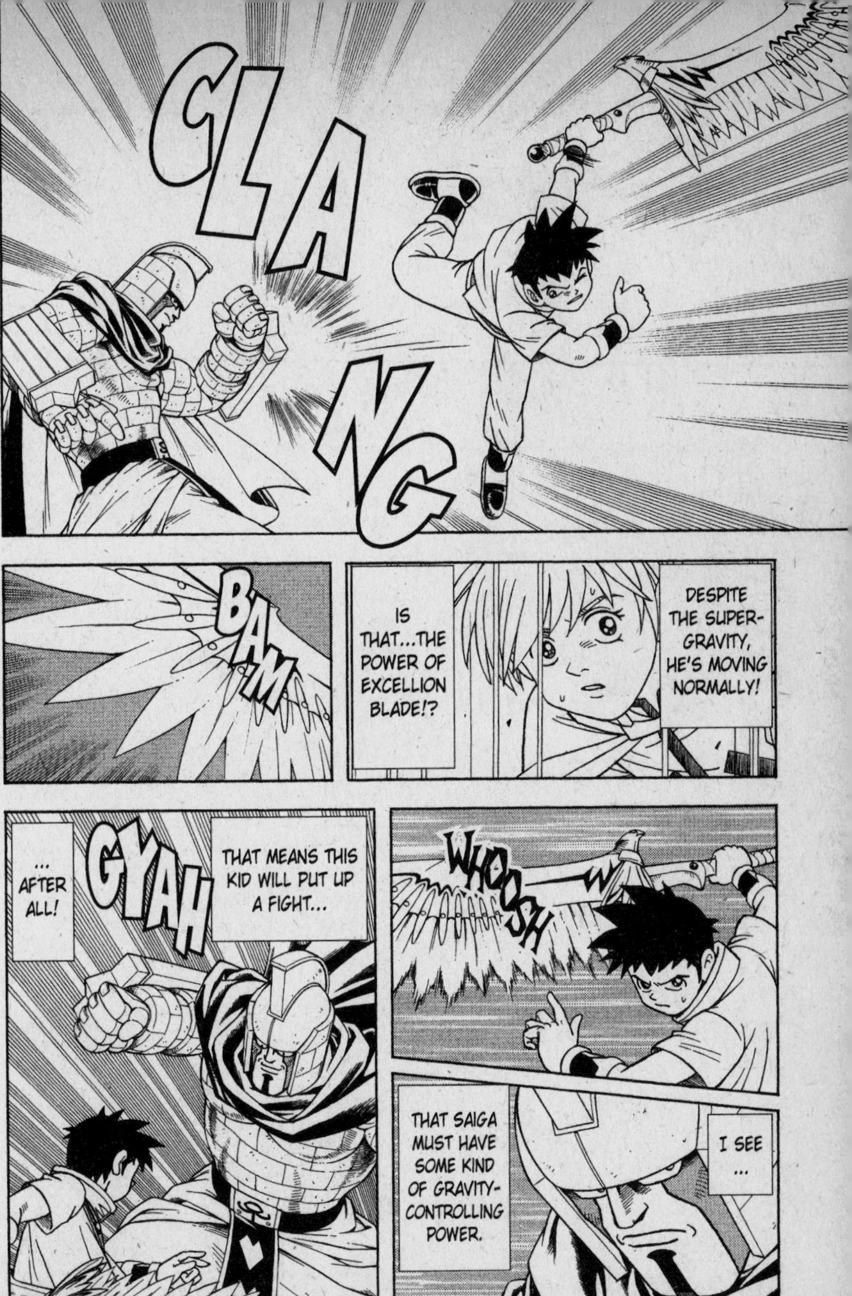
CLANG
DESPITE THE SUPER-GRAVITY, HE'S MOVING NORMALLY!
IS THAT...THE POWER OF EXCELLION BLADE!?
BAM
WHOOSH
I SEE ...
THAT SAIGA MUST HAVE SOME KIND OF GRAVITY-CONTROLLING POWER.
THAT MEANS THIS KID WILL PUT UP A FIGHT...
GYAH
... AFTER ALL!

READ THIS WAY

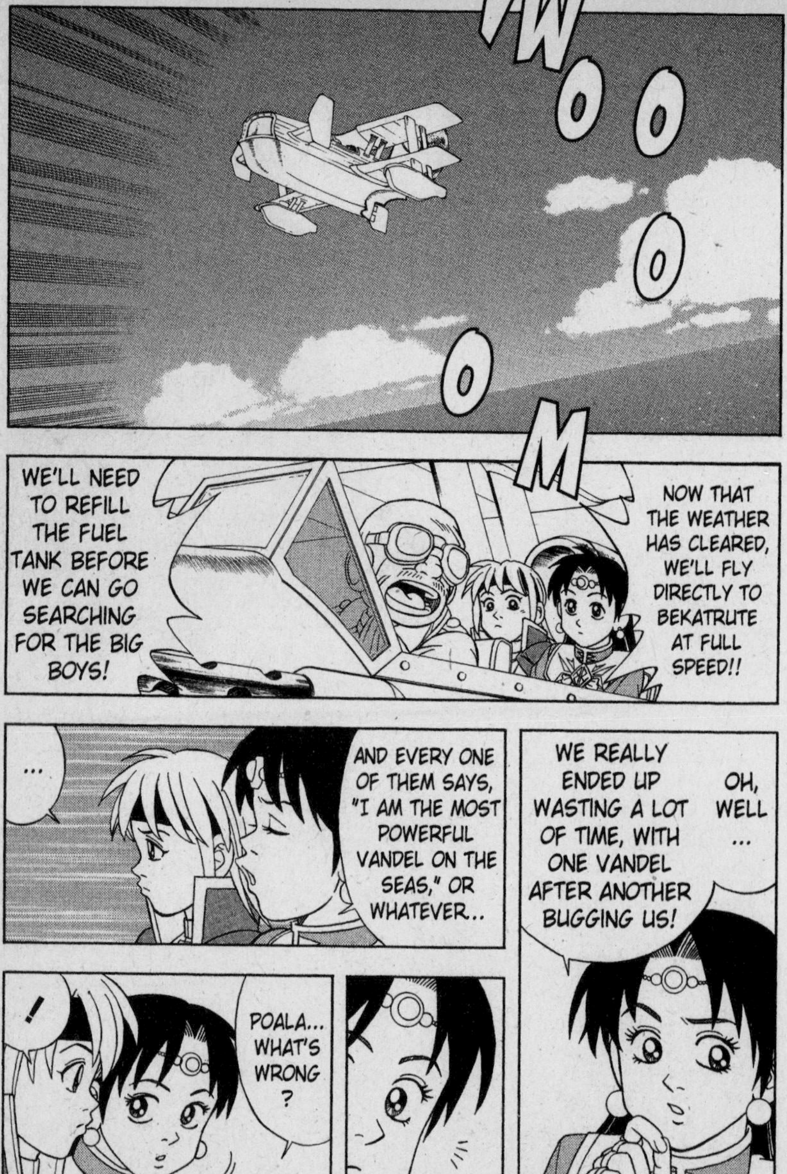
VWOOOOOM
NOW THAT THE WEATHER HAS CLEARED, WE'LL FLY DIRECTLY TO BEKATRUTE AT FULL SPEED!!
WE'LL NEED TO REFILL THE FUEL TANK BEFORE WE CAN GO SEARCHING FOR THE BIG BOYS!
OH, WELL...
WE REALLY ENDED UP WASTING A LOT OF TIME, WITH ONE VANDEL AFTER ANOTHER BUGGING US!
AND EVERY ONE OF THEM SAYS, "I AM THE MOST POWERFUL VANDEL ON THE SEAS," OR WHATEVER...
...
POALA... WHAT'S WRONG?
!

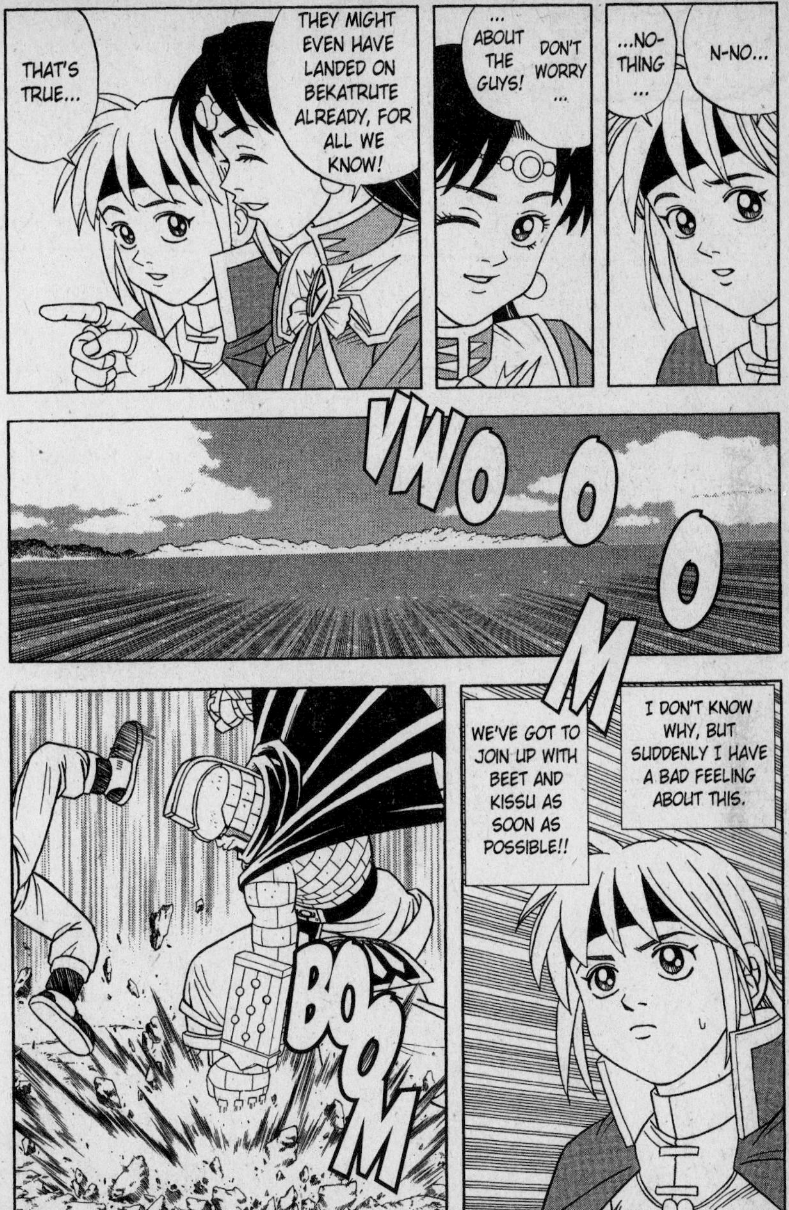
N-NO...
...NO-THING...
DON'T WORRY...
...ABOUT THE GUYS!
THEY MIGHT EVEN HAVE LANDED ON BEKATRUTE ALREADY, FOR ALL WE KNOW!
THAT'S TRUE...
VWOOOOM
I DON'T KNOW WHY, BUT SUDDENLY I HAVE A BAD FEELING ABOUT THIS.
WE'VE GOT TO JOIN UP WITH BEET AND KISSU AS SOON AS POSSIBLE!!
BOOOM

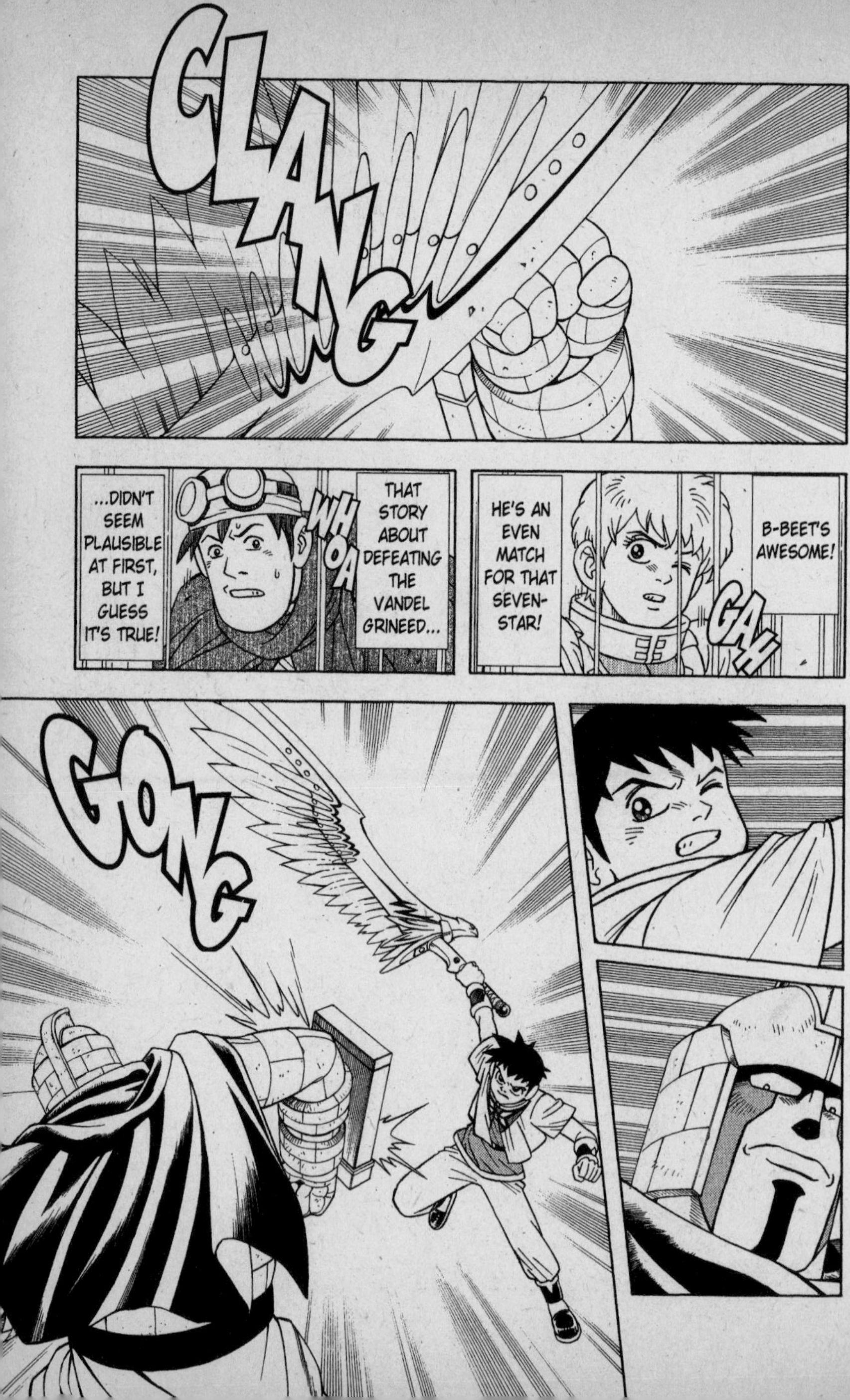
CLANG
B-BEET'S AWESOME!
GAH
HE'S AN EVEN MATCH FOR THAT SEVEN-STAR!
THAT STORY ABOUT DEFEATING THE VANDEL GRINEED...
WHOA
...DIDN'T SEEM PLAUSIBLE AT FIRST, BUT I GUESS IT'S TRUE!
GONG

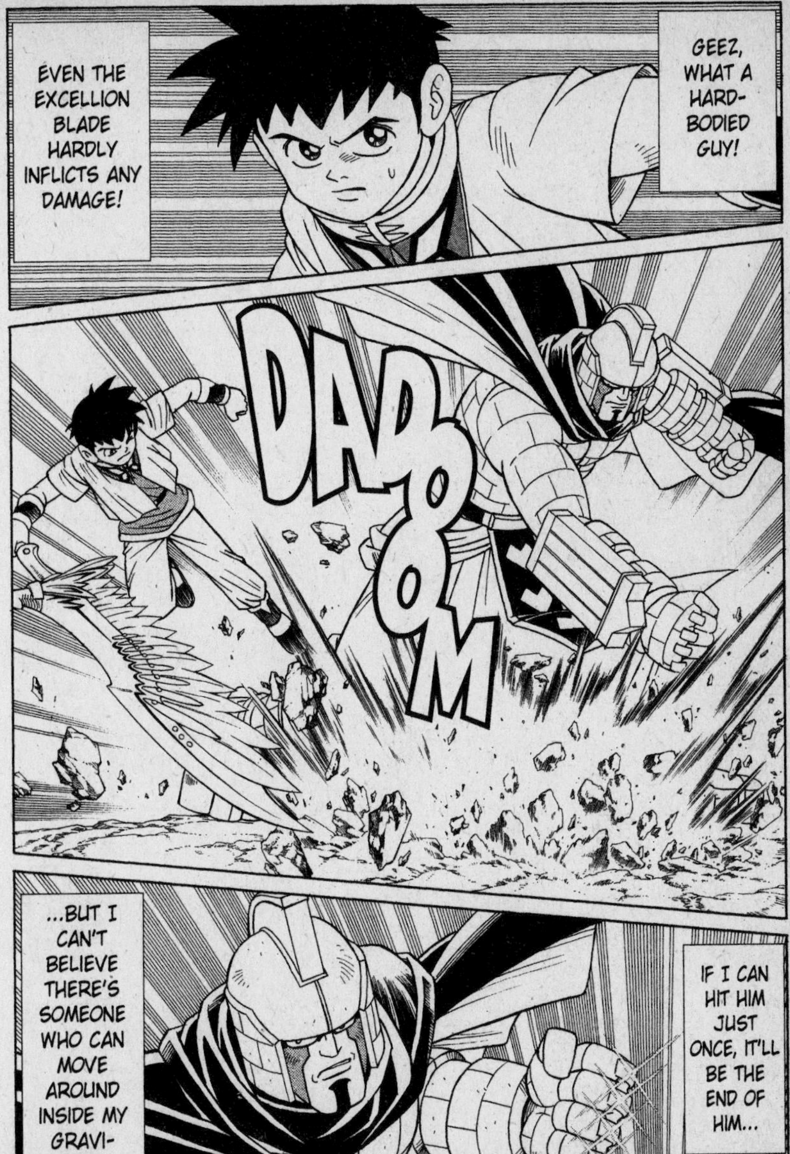
GEEZ, WHAT A HARD-BODIED GUY!
EVEN THE EXCELLION BLADE HARDLY INFLICTS ANY DAMAGE!
DADOOM
IF I CAN HIT HIM JUST ONCE, IT'LL BE THE END OF HIM...
...BUT I CAN'T BELIEVE THERE'S SOMEONE WHO CAN MOVE AROUND INSIDE MY GRAVI-ZONE!!

READ THIS WAY

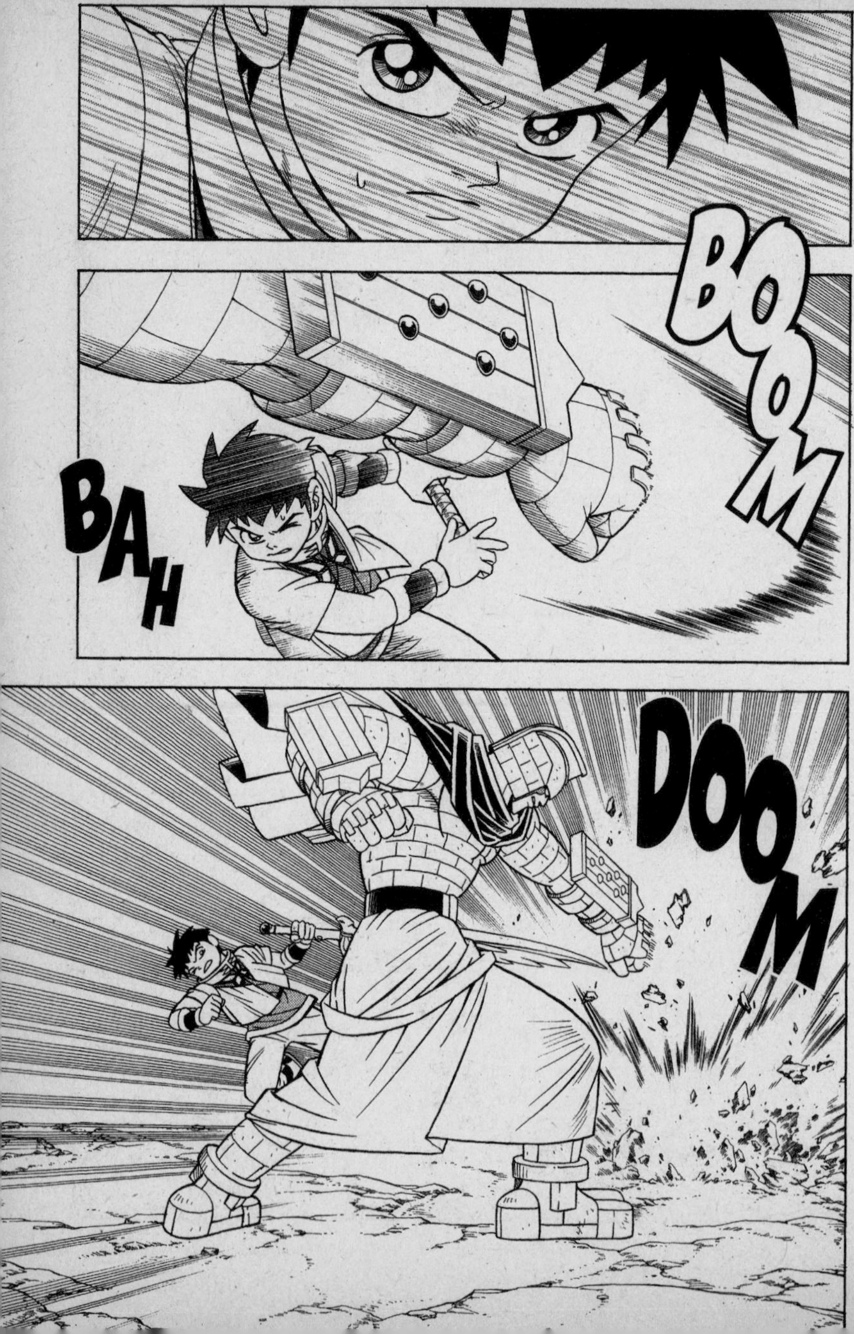
BOOM
BAH
DOOM

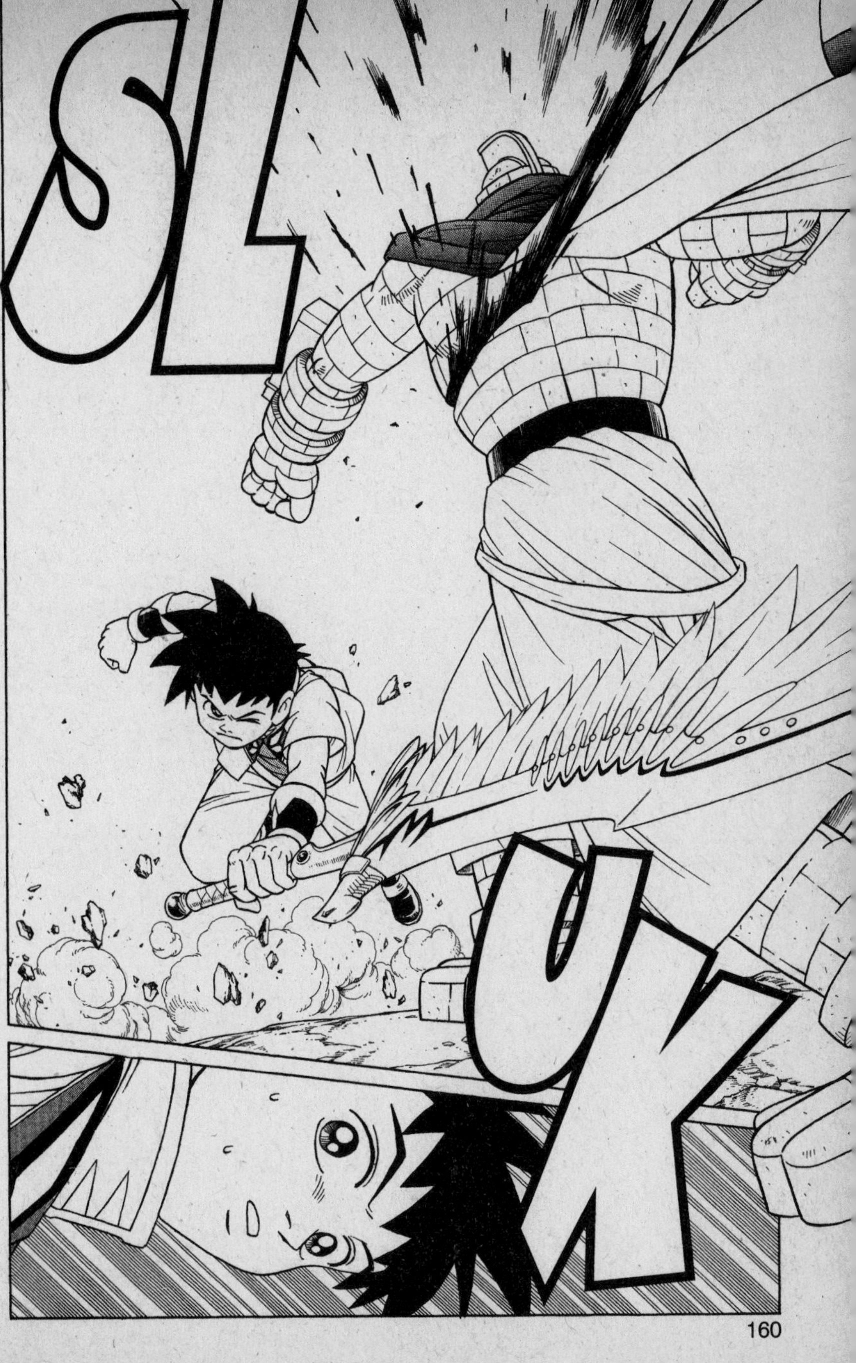
SLUK

READ THIS WAY

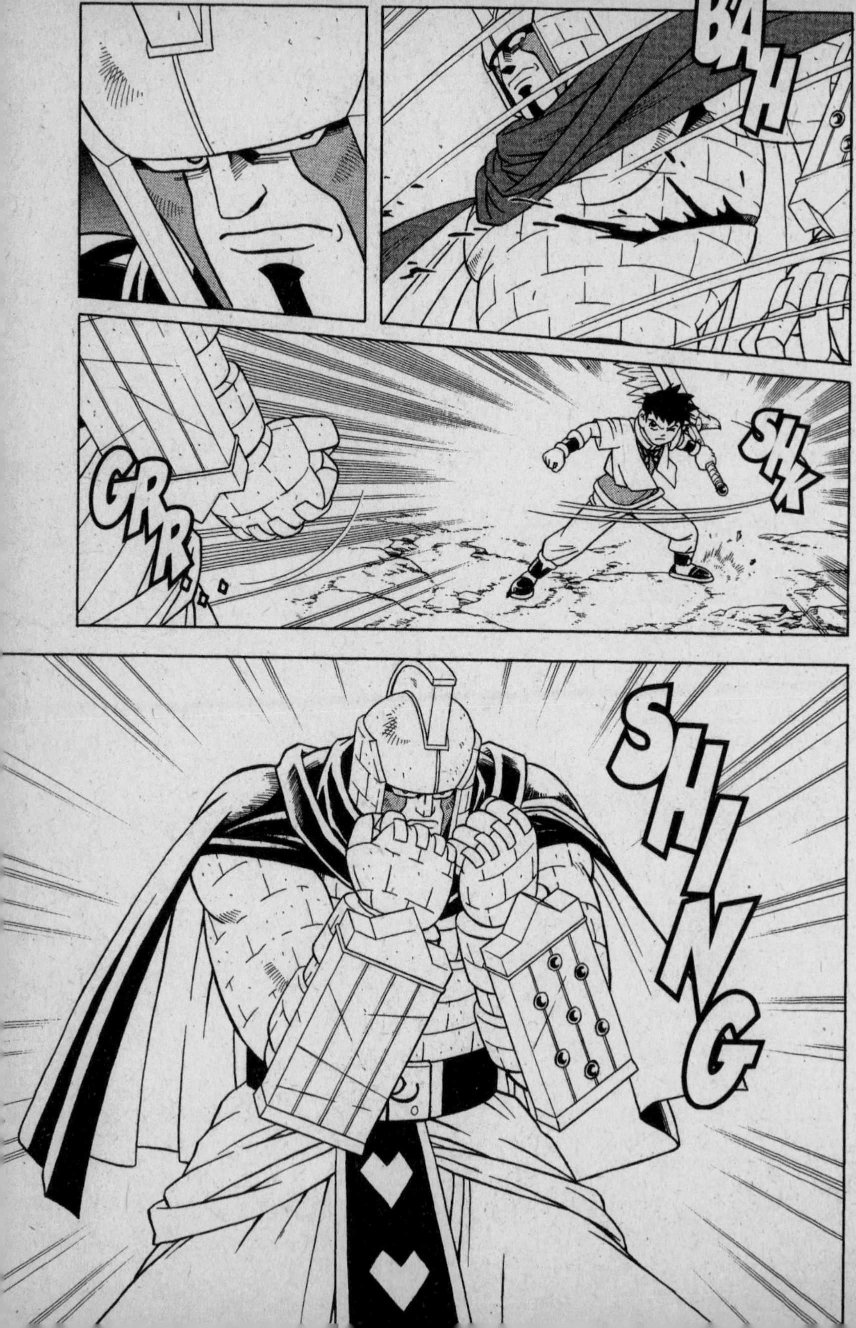
BAH
SHK
GRR...
SHING

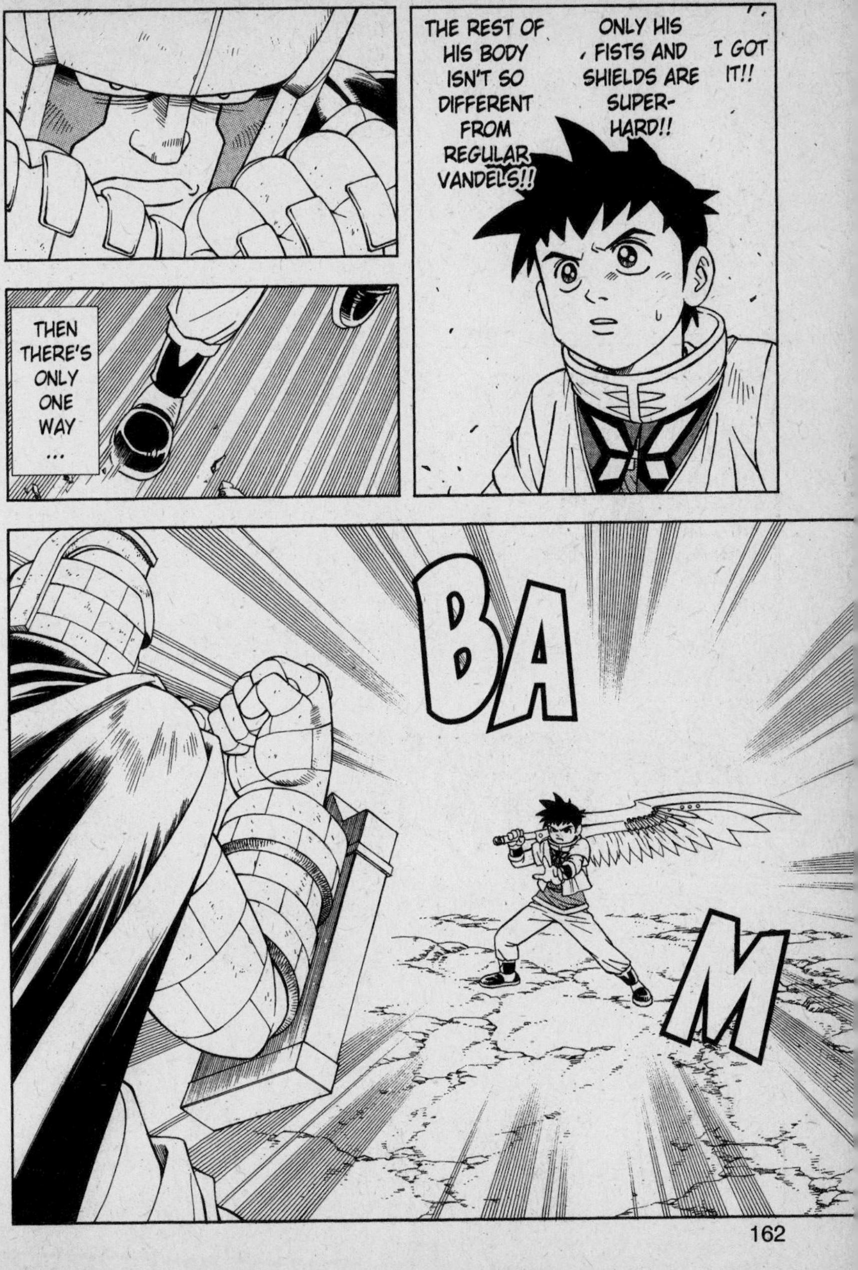
I GOT IT!!
ONLY HIS FISTS AND SHIELDS ARE SUPER-HARD!!
THE REST OF HIS BODY ISN'T SO DIFFERENT FROM REGULAR VANDELS!!
THEN THERE'S ONLY ONE WAY ...
BAM

READ THIS WAY

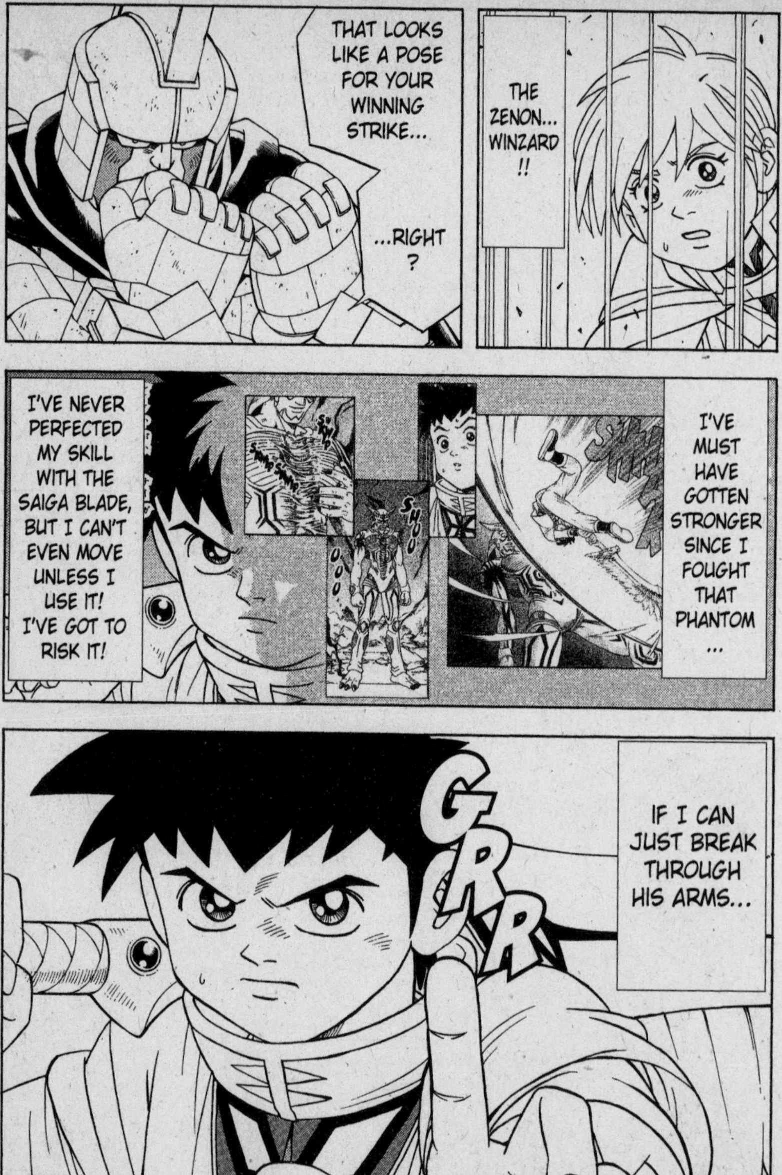
THE ZENON... WINZARD !!
THAT LOOKS LIKE A POSE FOR YOUR WINNING STRIKE...
...RIGHT ?
I'VE MUST HAVE GOTTEN STRONGER SINCE I FOUGHT THAT PHANTOM ...
I'VE NEVER PERFECTED MY SKILL WITH THE SAIGA BLADE, BUT I CAN'T EVEN MOVE UNLESS I USE IT! I'VE GOT TO RISK IT!
IF I CAN JUST BREAK THROUGH HIS ARMS...
GRRR

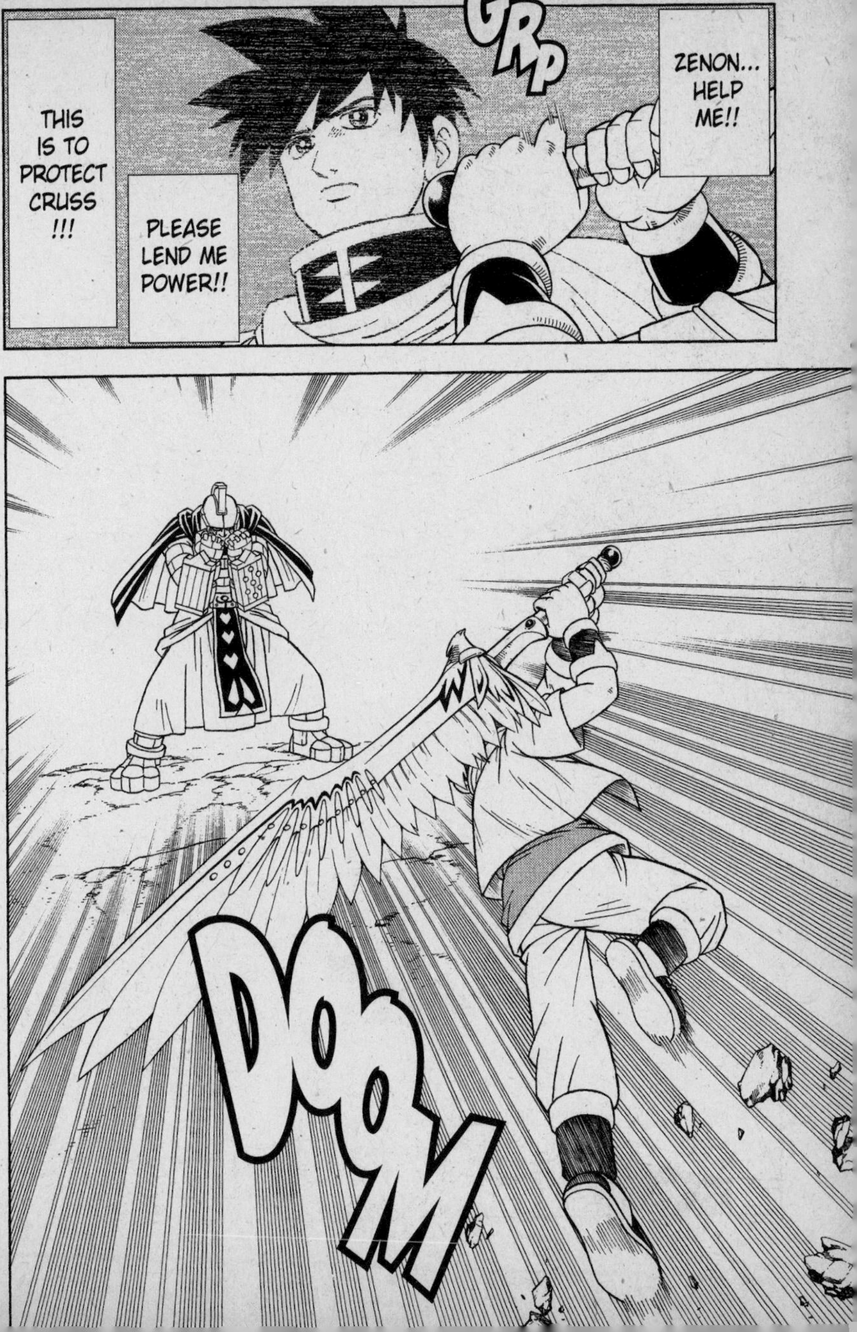
GRP
ZENON... HELP ME!!
PLEASE LEND ME POWER!!
THIS IS TO PROTECT CRUSS !!!
DOOM

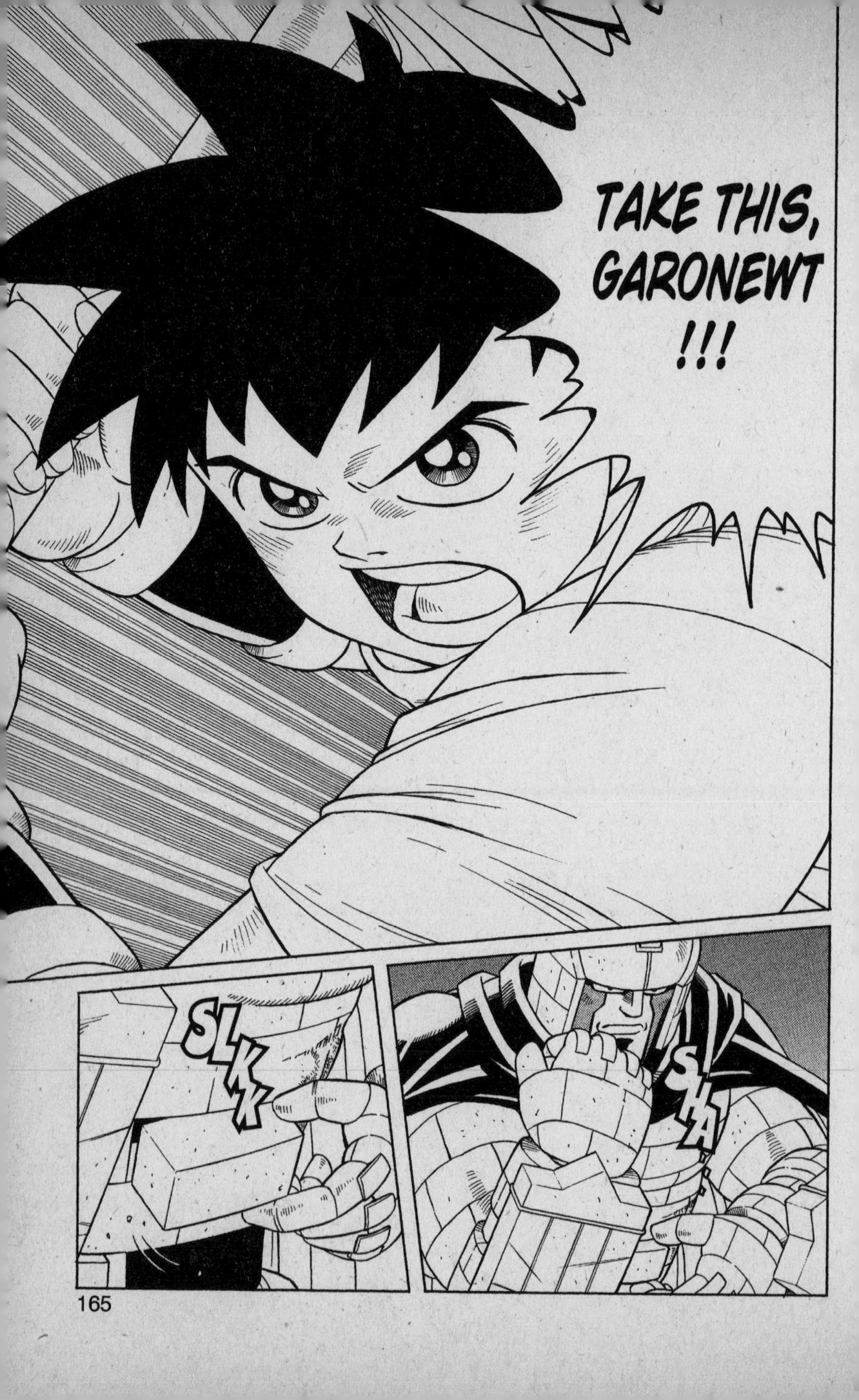
TAKE THIS, GARONEWT !!!
SHA
SLKK

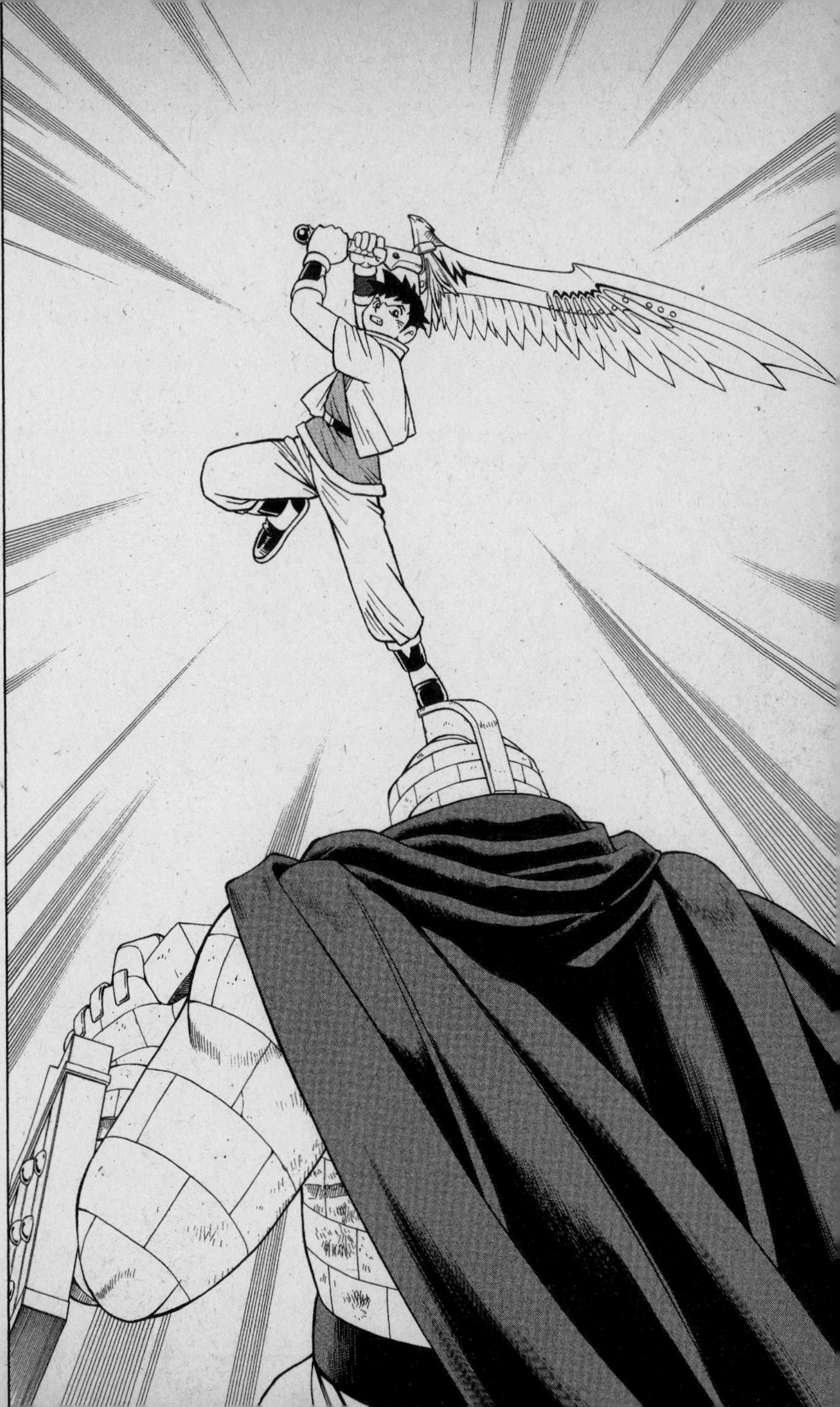

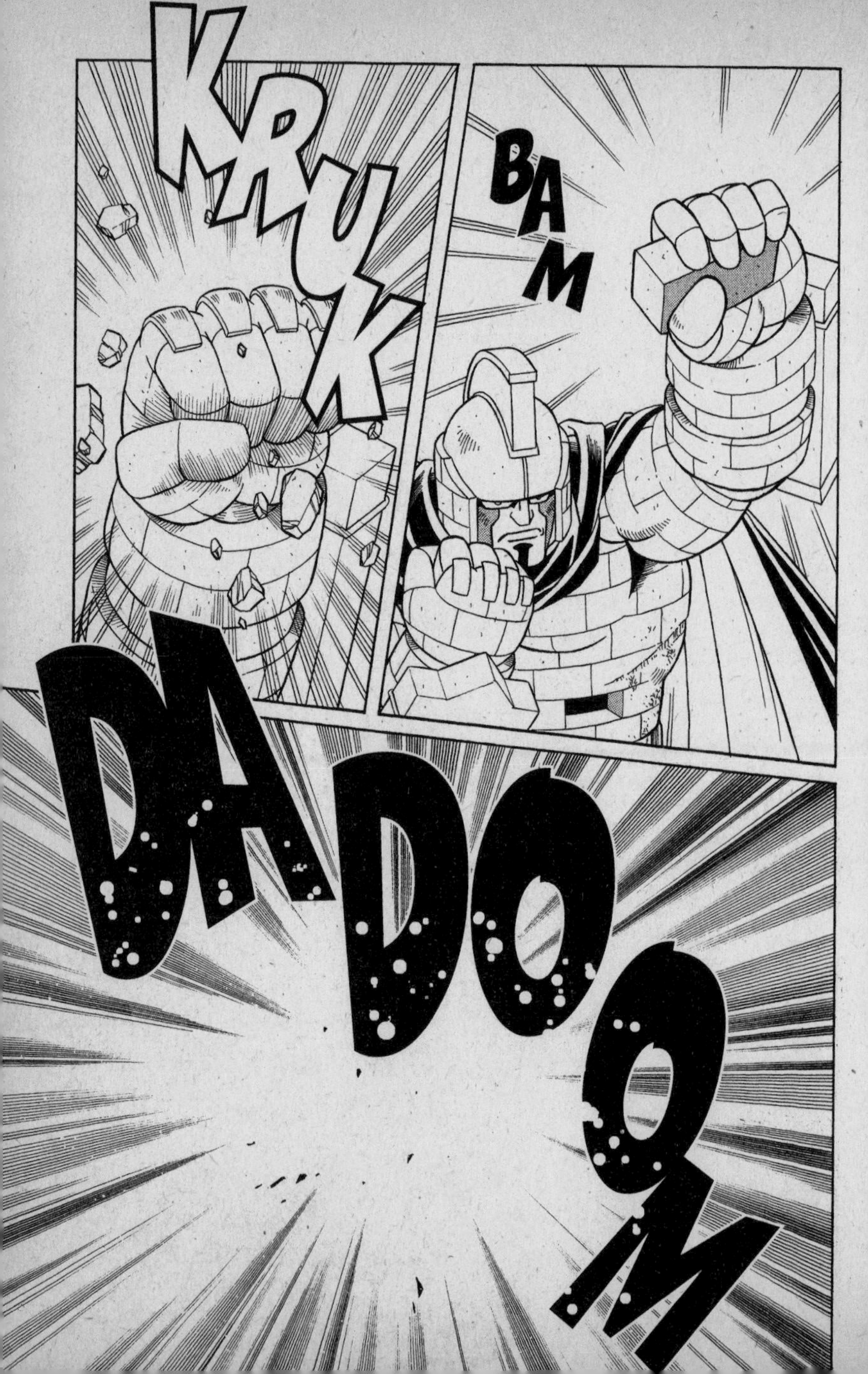
BAM
KRUK
DADOOM

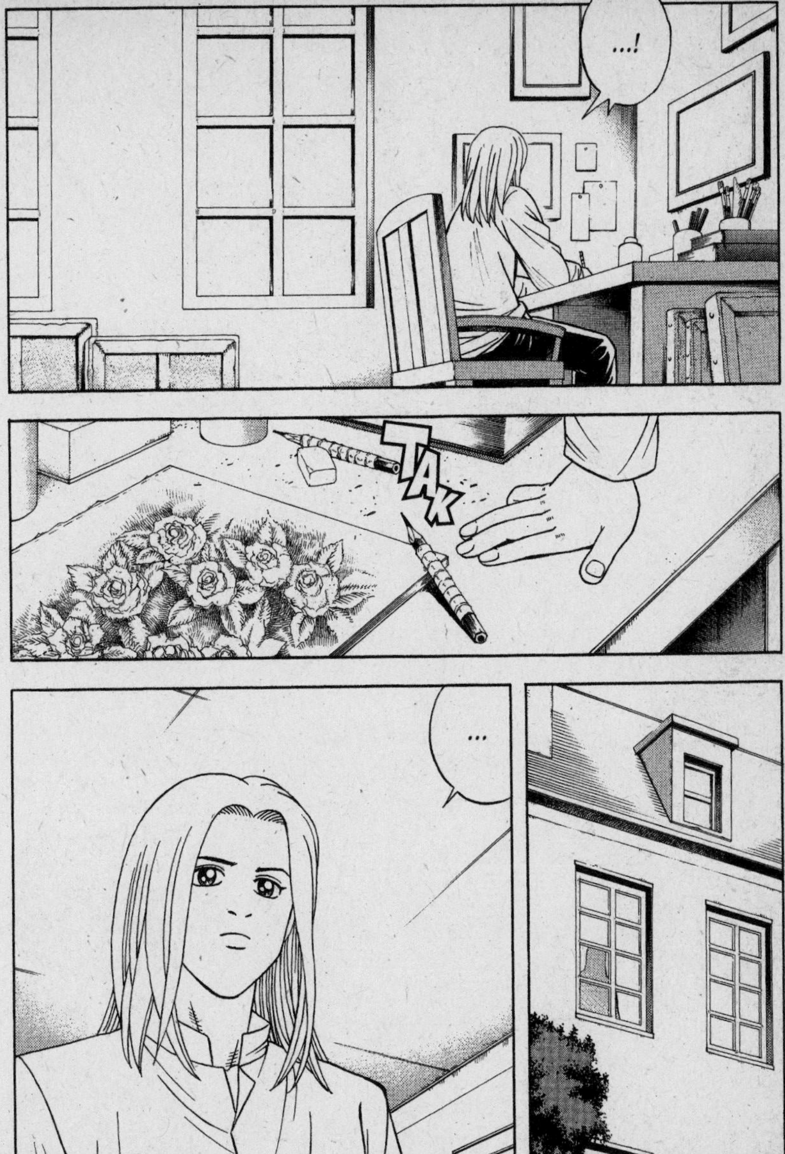
...!
TAK
...

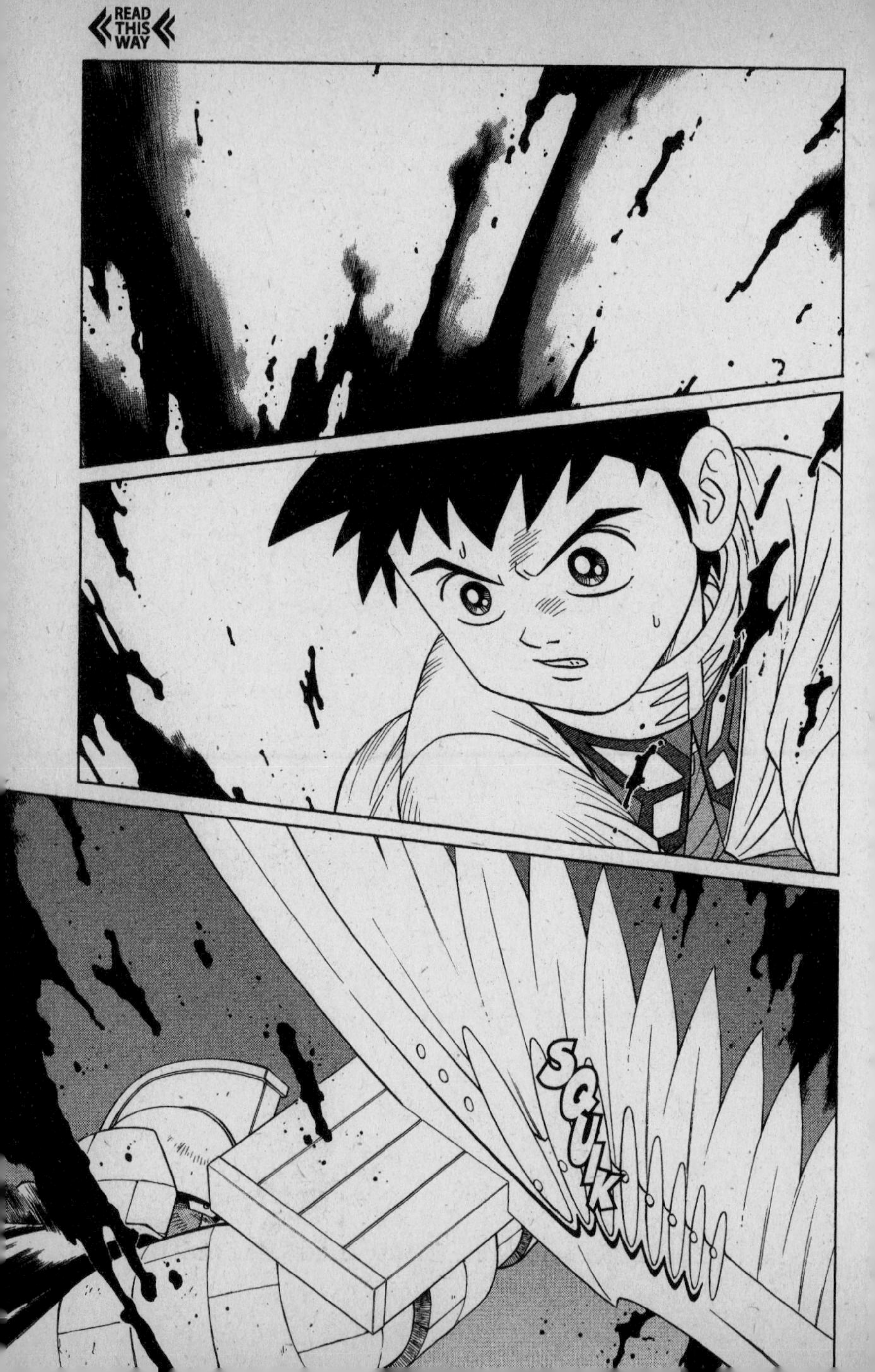
READ THIS WAY
SCUIK

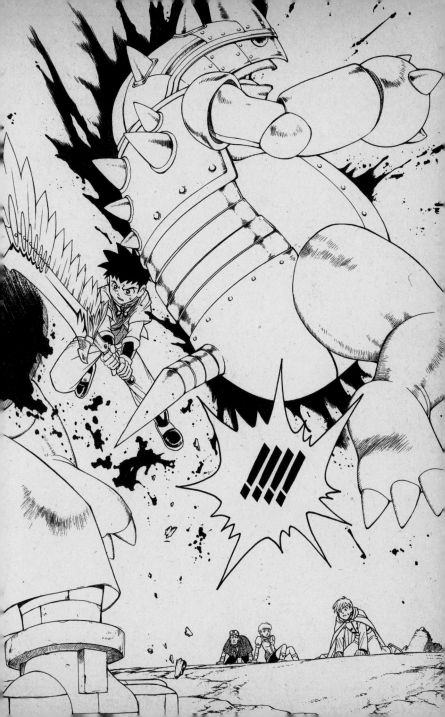

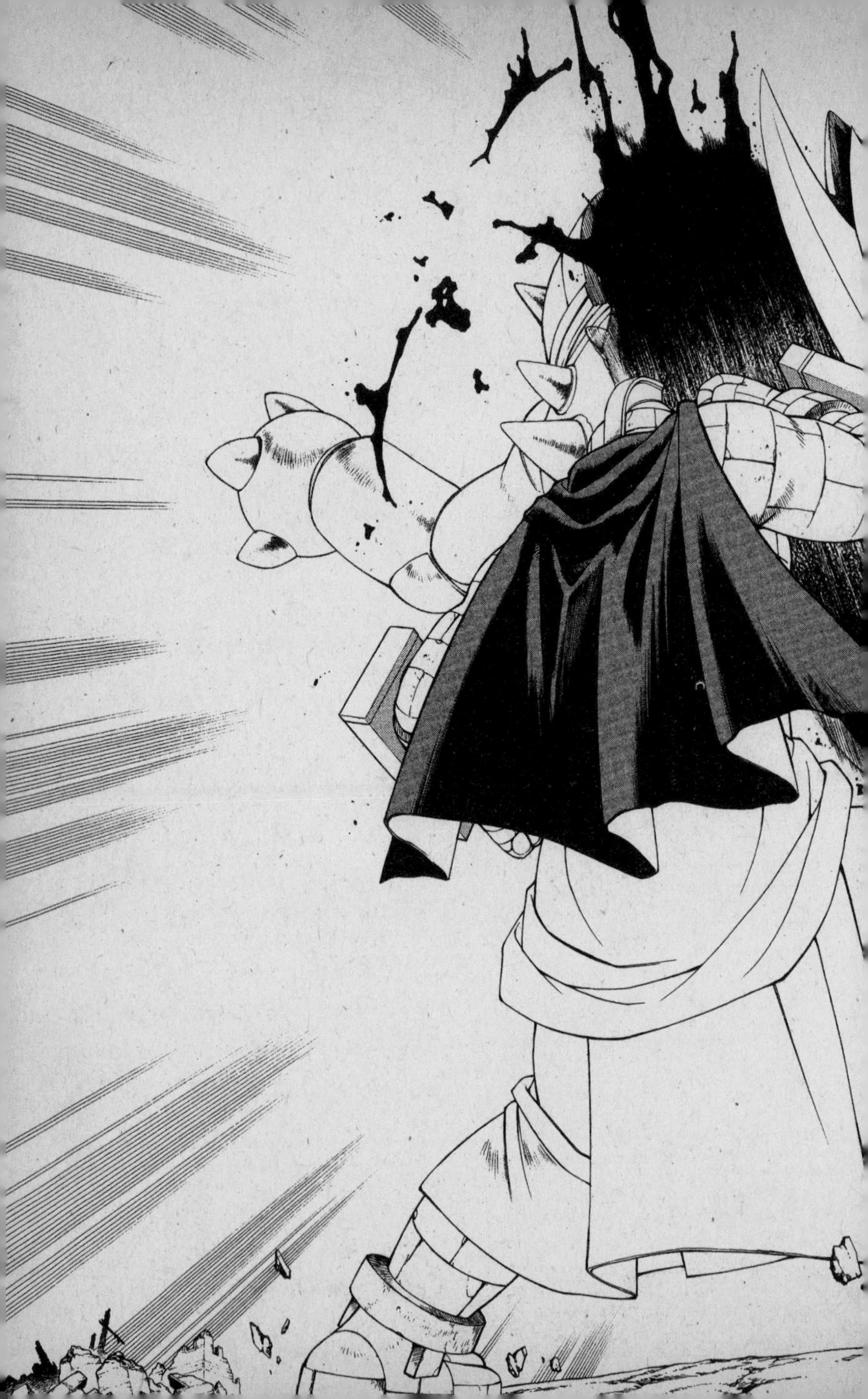

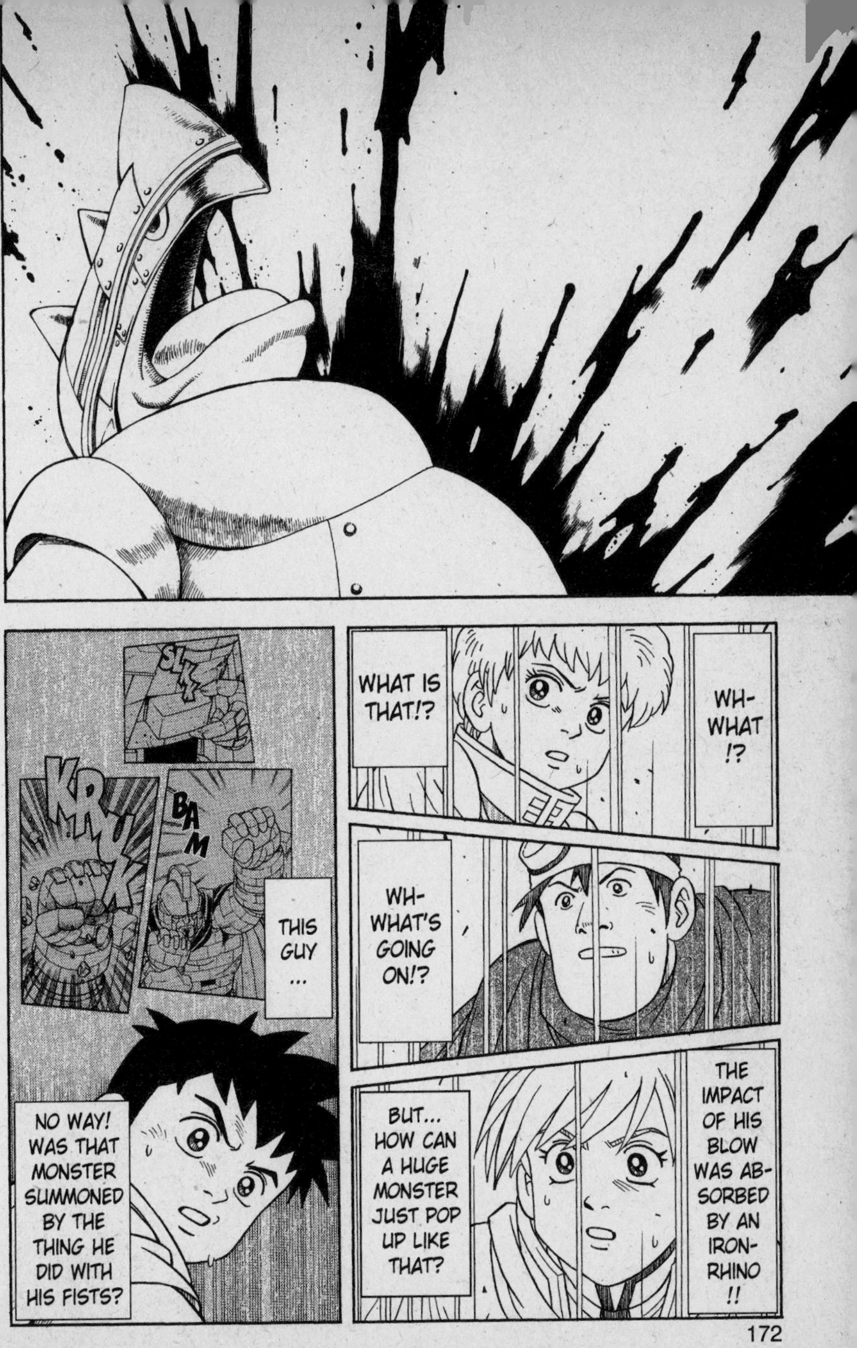
WH-WHAT!?
WHAT IS THAT!?
WH-WHAT'S GOING ON!?
THE IMPACT OF HIS BLOW WAS ABSORBED BY AN IRON-RHINO!!
BUT... HOW CAN A HUGE MONSTER JUST POP UP LIKE THAT?
SLK
BAM
KRUNK
THIS GUY...
NO WAY! WAS THAT MONSTER SUMMONED BY THE THING HE DID WITH HIS FISTS?

READ THIS WAY

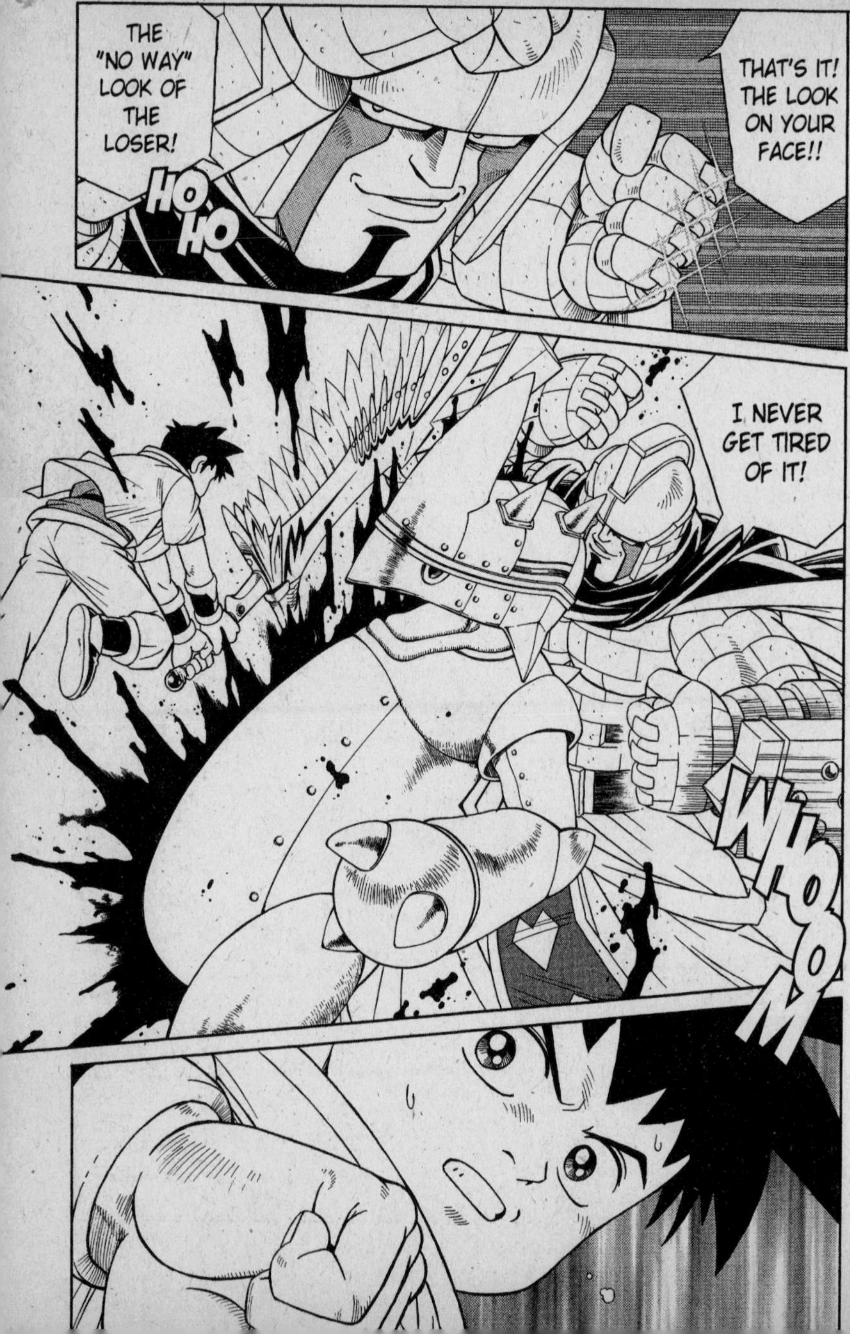
THAT'S IT! THE LOOK ON YOUR FACE!!
THE "NO WAY" LOOK OF THE LOSER!
HO HO
I NEVER GET TIRED OF IT!
WHOOOOM

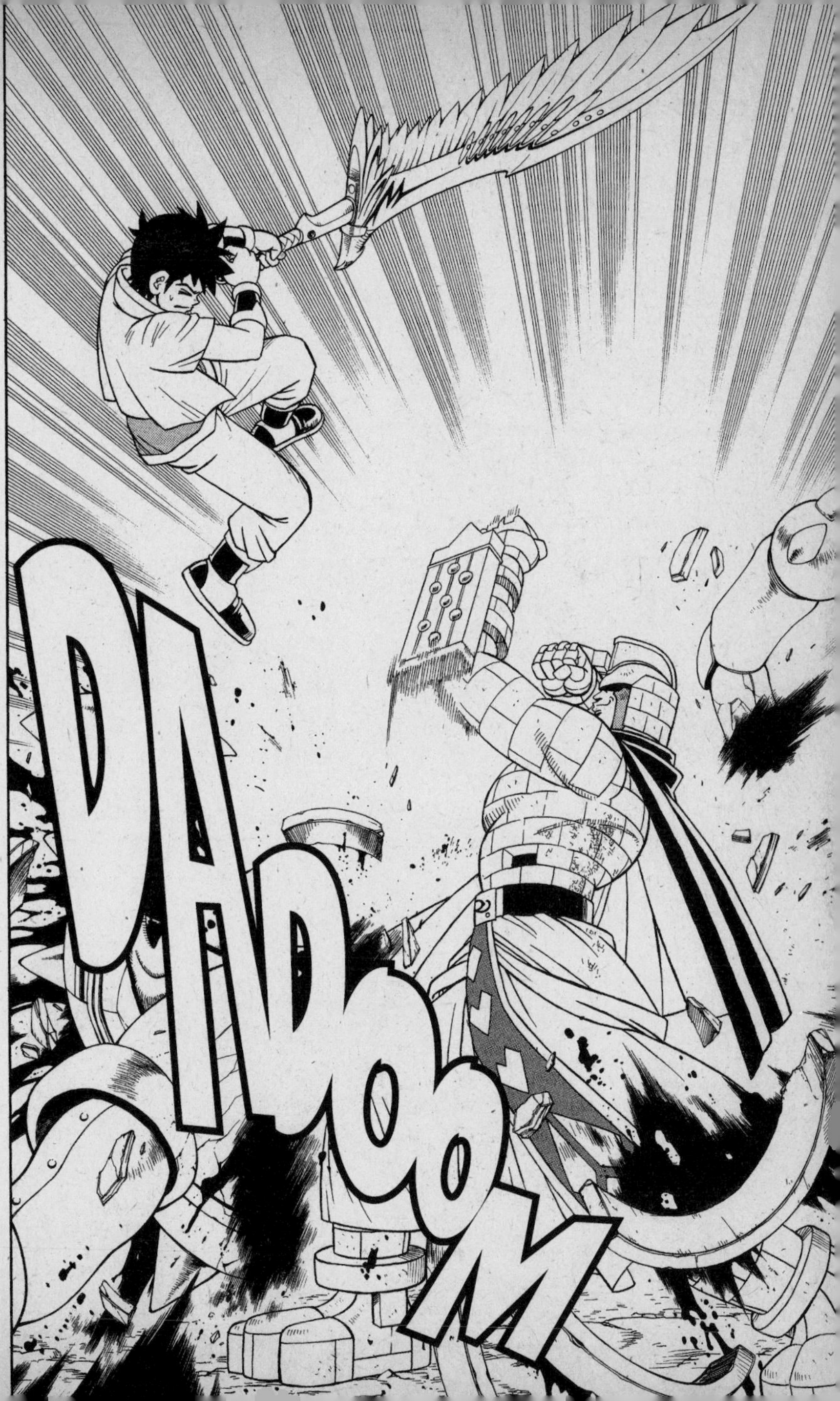
PADOOOM

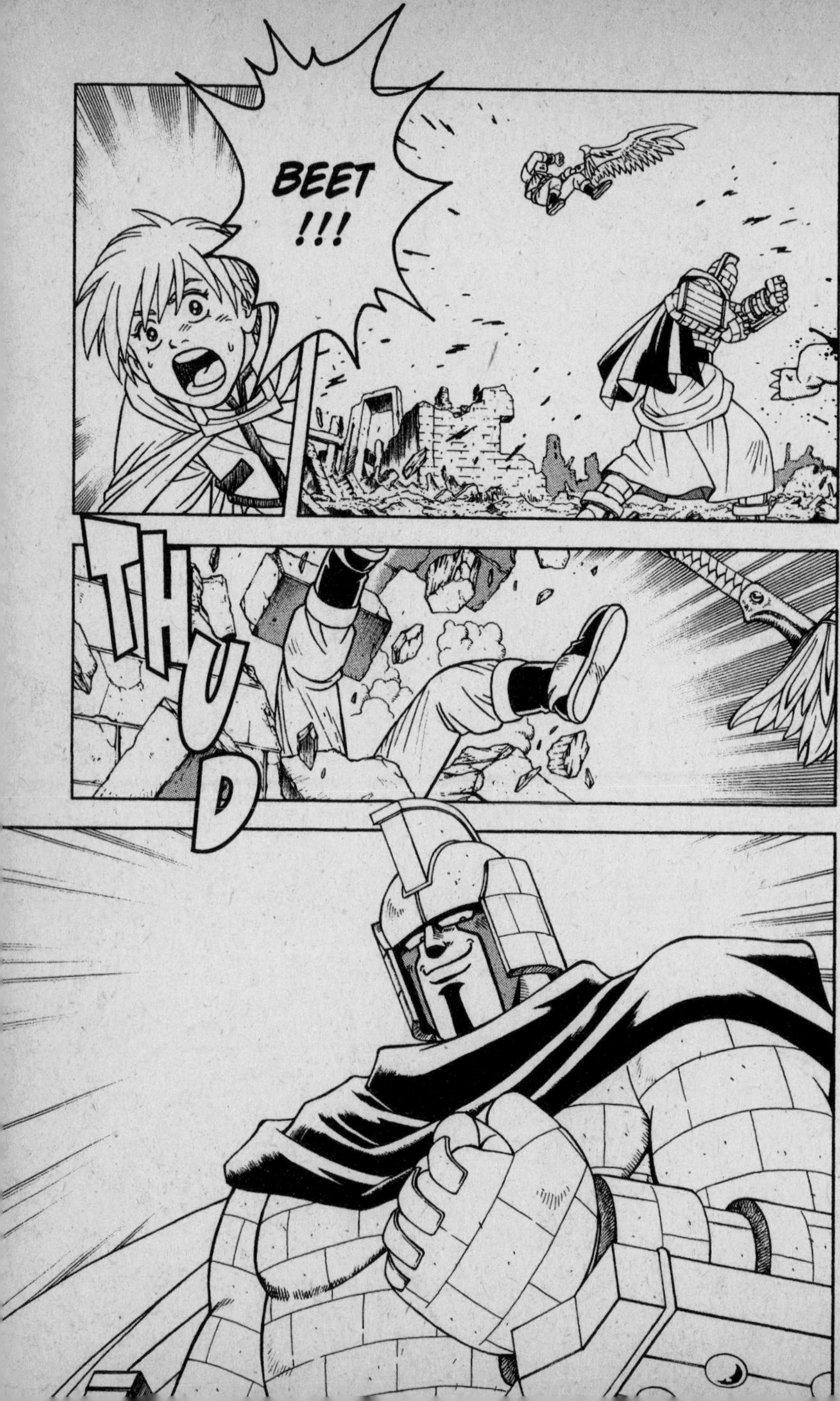
BEET !!!
THUD

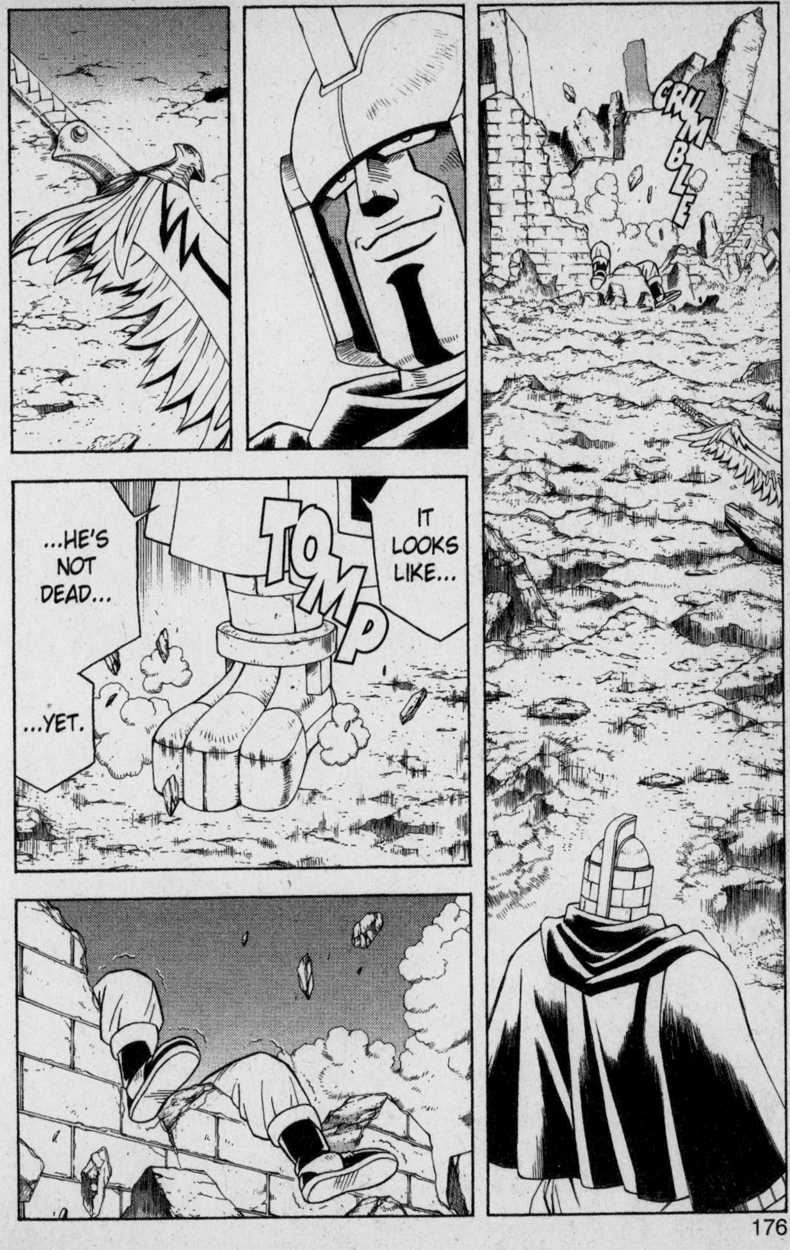
CRUMBLE
IT LOOKS LIKE...
TOMP
...HE'S NOT DEAD...
...YET.

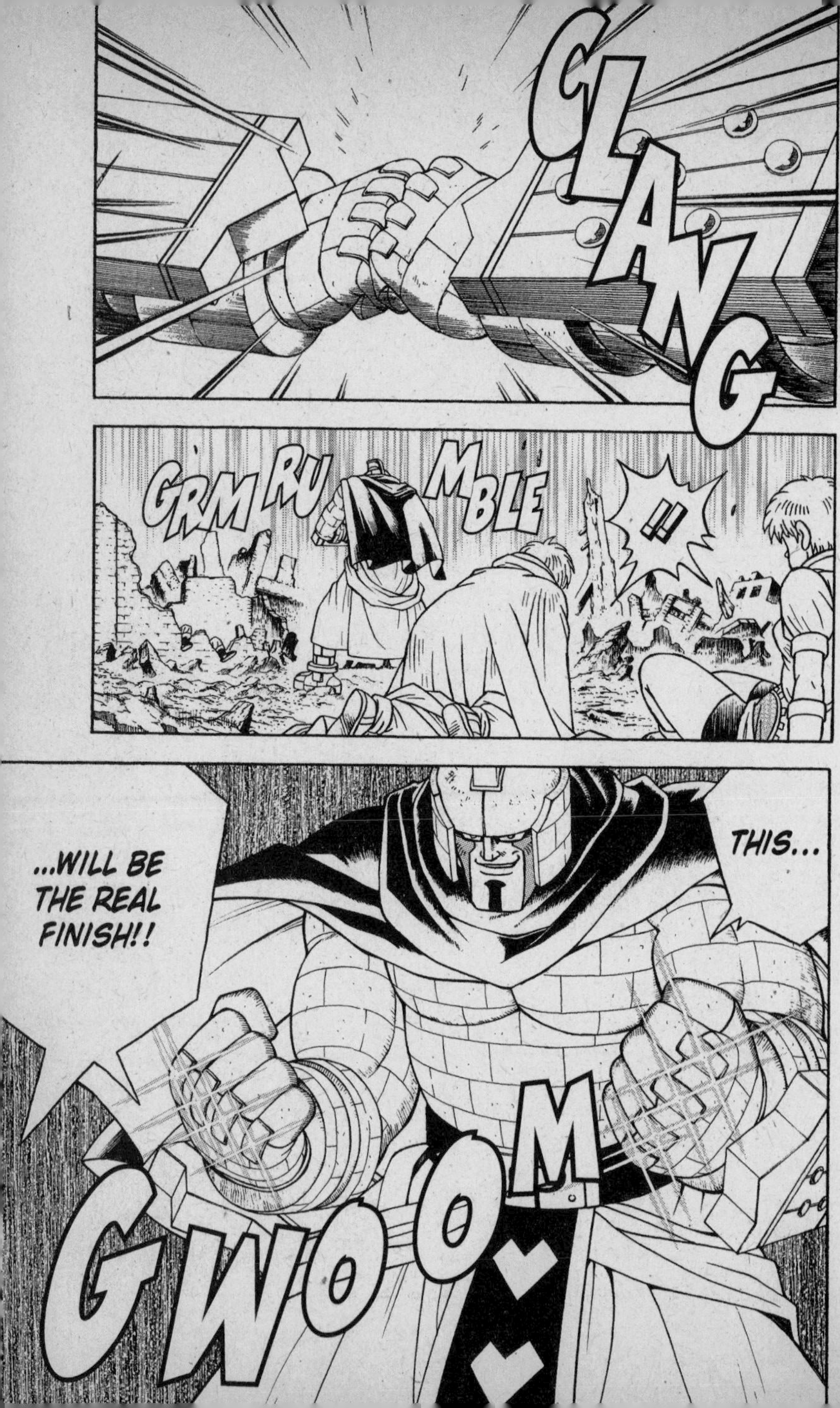
CLANG
!!
GRMRUMBLE
THIS...
...WILL BE THE REAL FINISH!!
GWOOOM

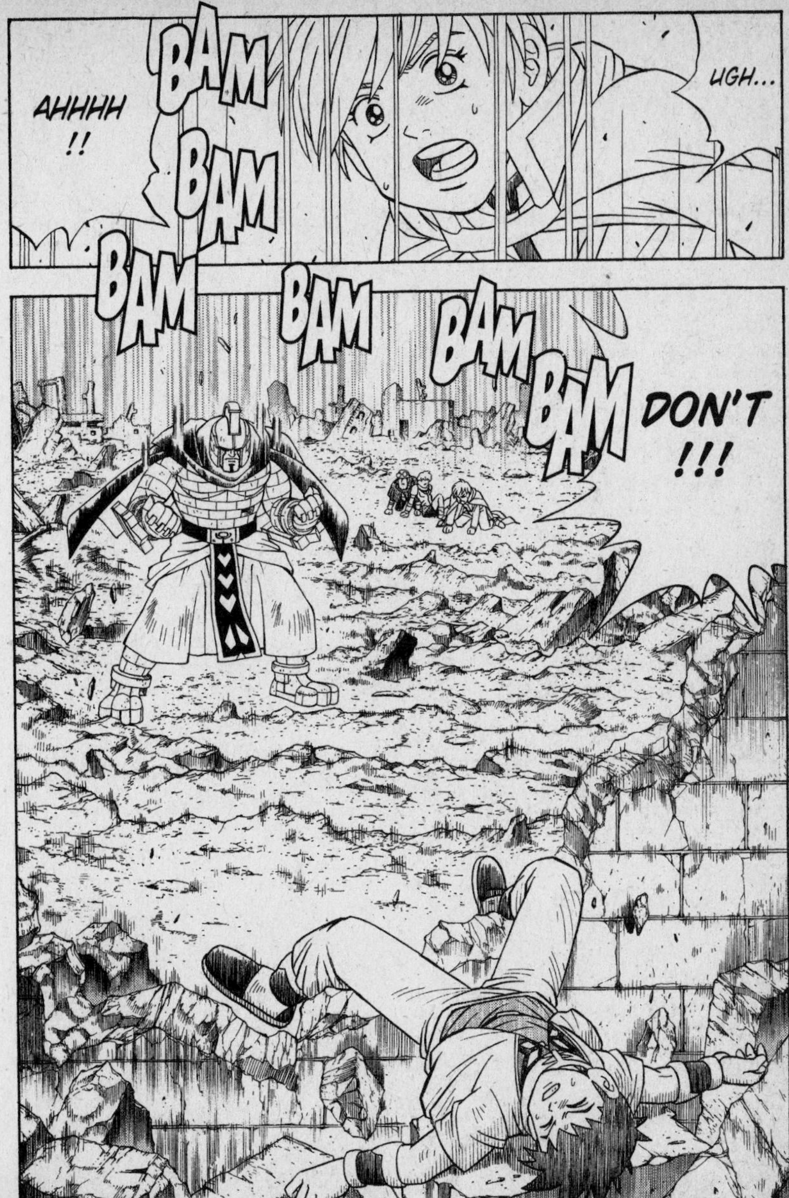
UGH...
BAM
BAM
BAM
AHHHH!!
DON'T!!!
BAM
BAM
BAM
BAM

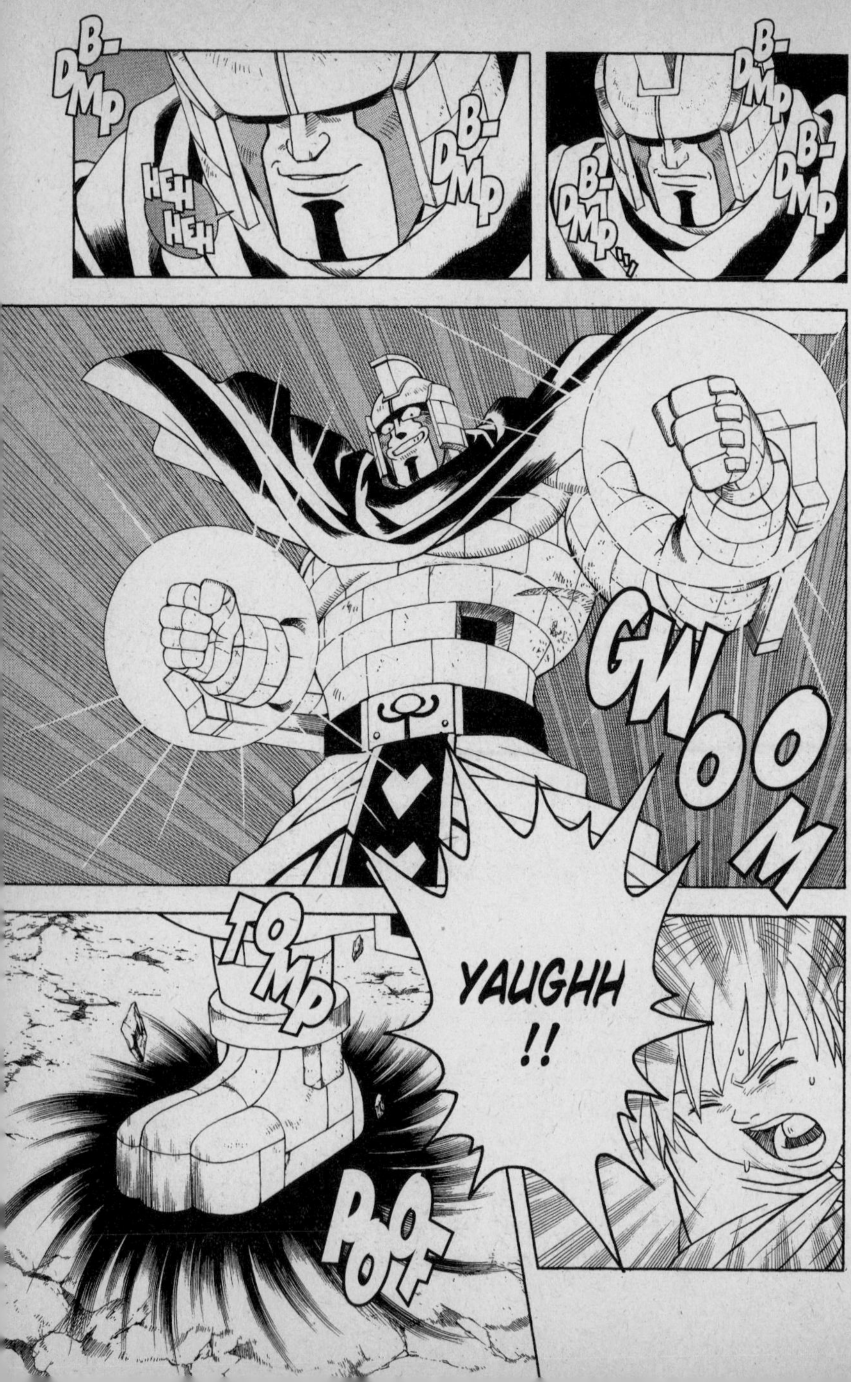
B-DMP
B-DMP
B-DMP...
B-DMP
HEH HEH
B-DMP
GWOOOM
YAUGHH!!
TOMP
POOF

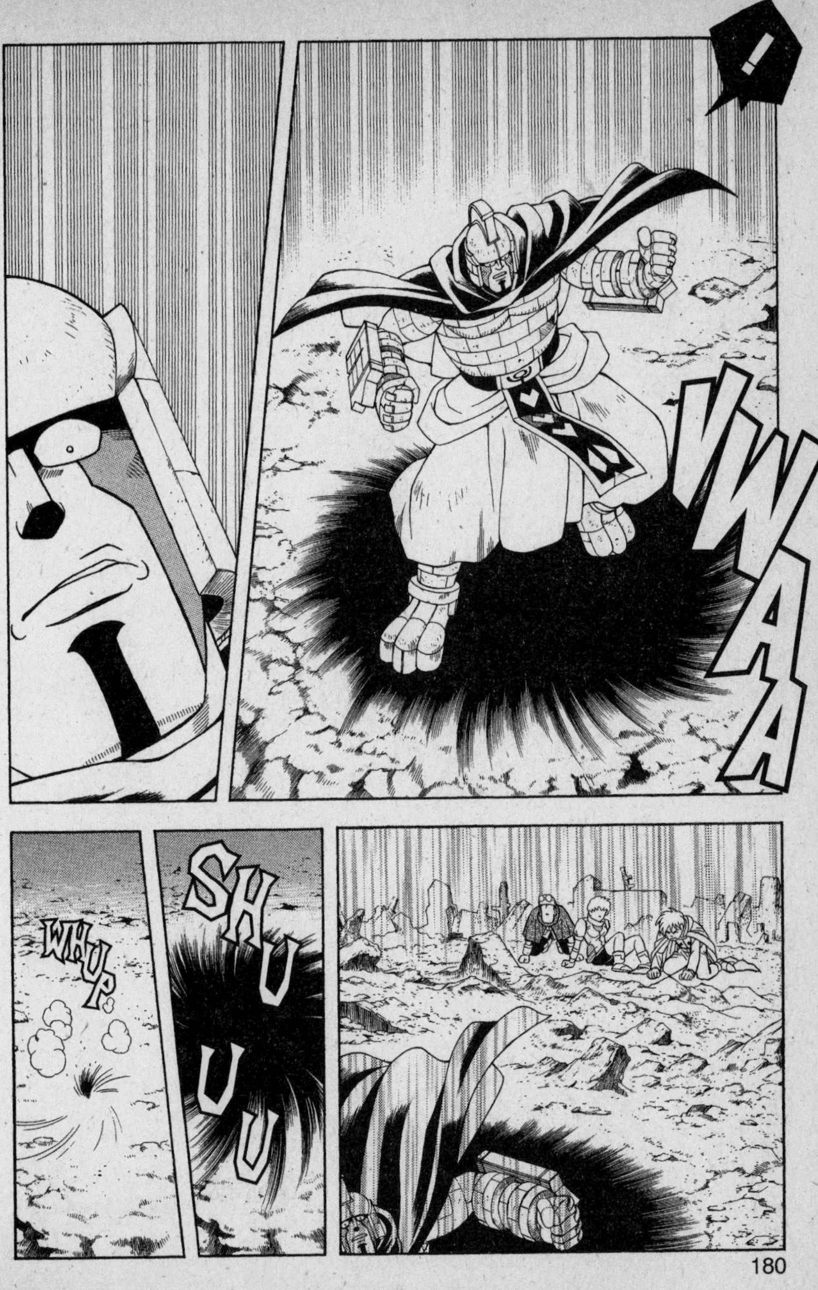
!
VWAAA
SHUUU
WHUP

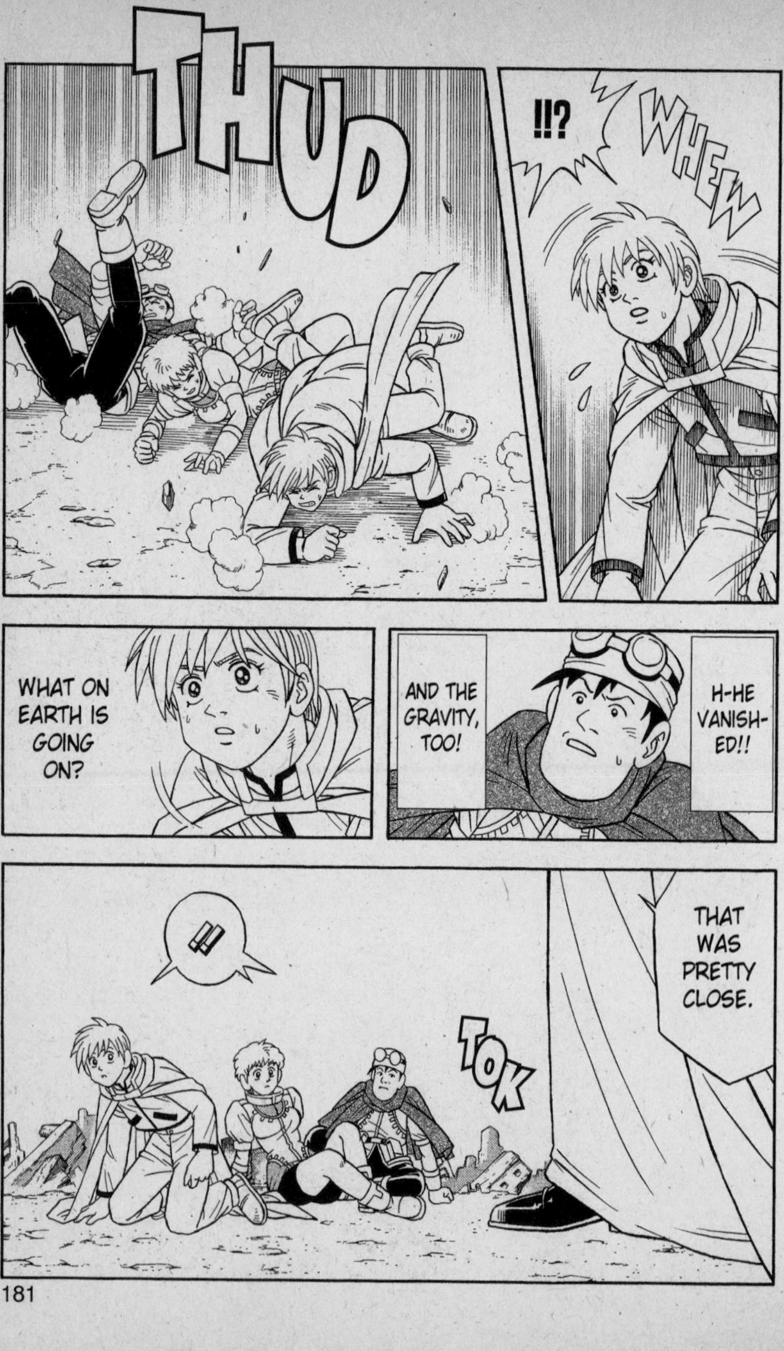

!!?
WHEW
THUD
H-HE VANISH-ED!!
AND THE GRAVITY, TOO!
WHAT ON EARTH IS GOING ON?
THAT WAS PRETTY CLOSE.
TOK
!!

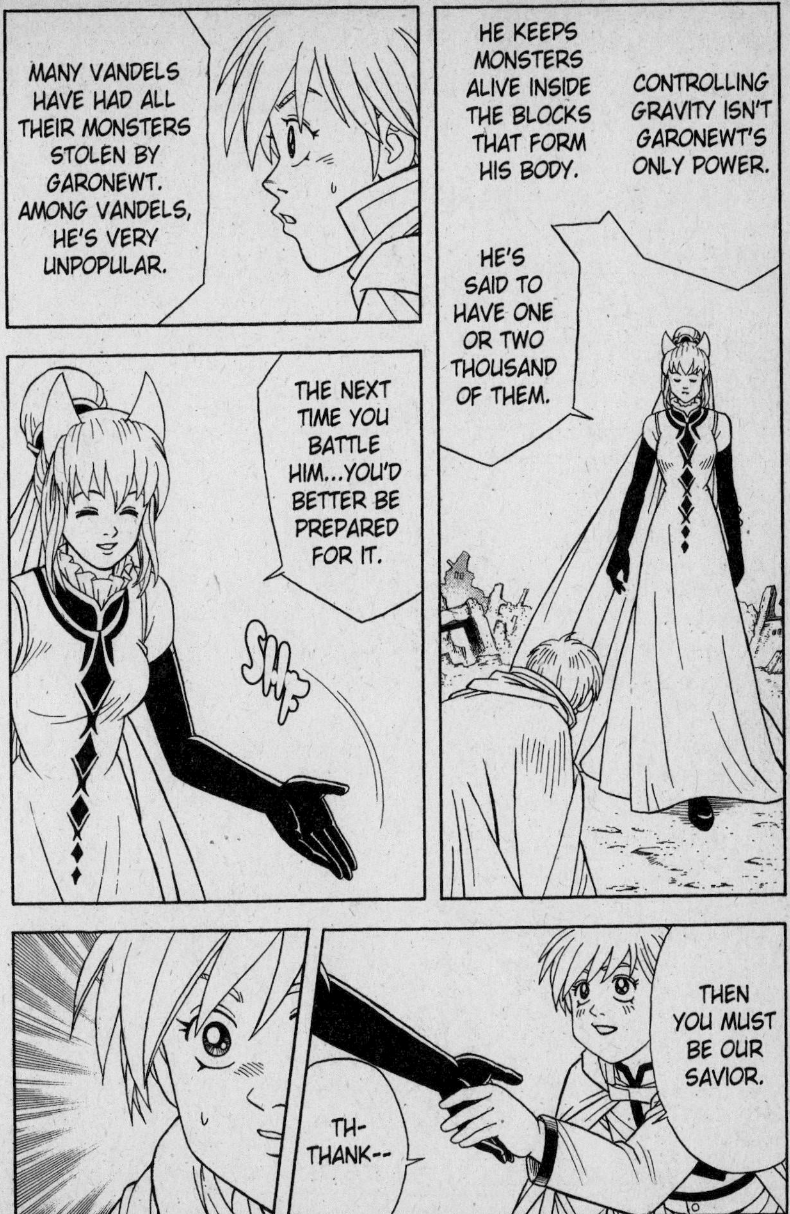
CONTROLLING GRAVITY ISN'T GARONEWT'S ONLY POWER.
HE KEEPS MONSTERS ALIVE INSIDE THE BLOCKS THAT FORM HIS BODY.
HE'S SAID TO HAVE ONE OR TWO THOUSAND OF THEM.
MANY VANDELS HAVE HAD ALL THEIR MONSTERS STOLEN BY GARONEWT. AMONG VANDELS, HE'S VERY UNPOPULAR.
THE NEXT TIME YOU BATTLE HIM...YOU'D BETTER BE PREPARED FOR IT.
SHF
THEN YOU MUST BE OUR SAVIOR.
TH- THANK--

READ THIS WAY

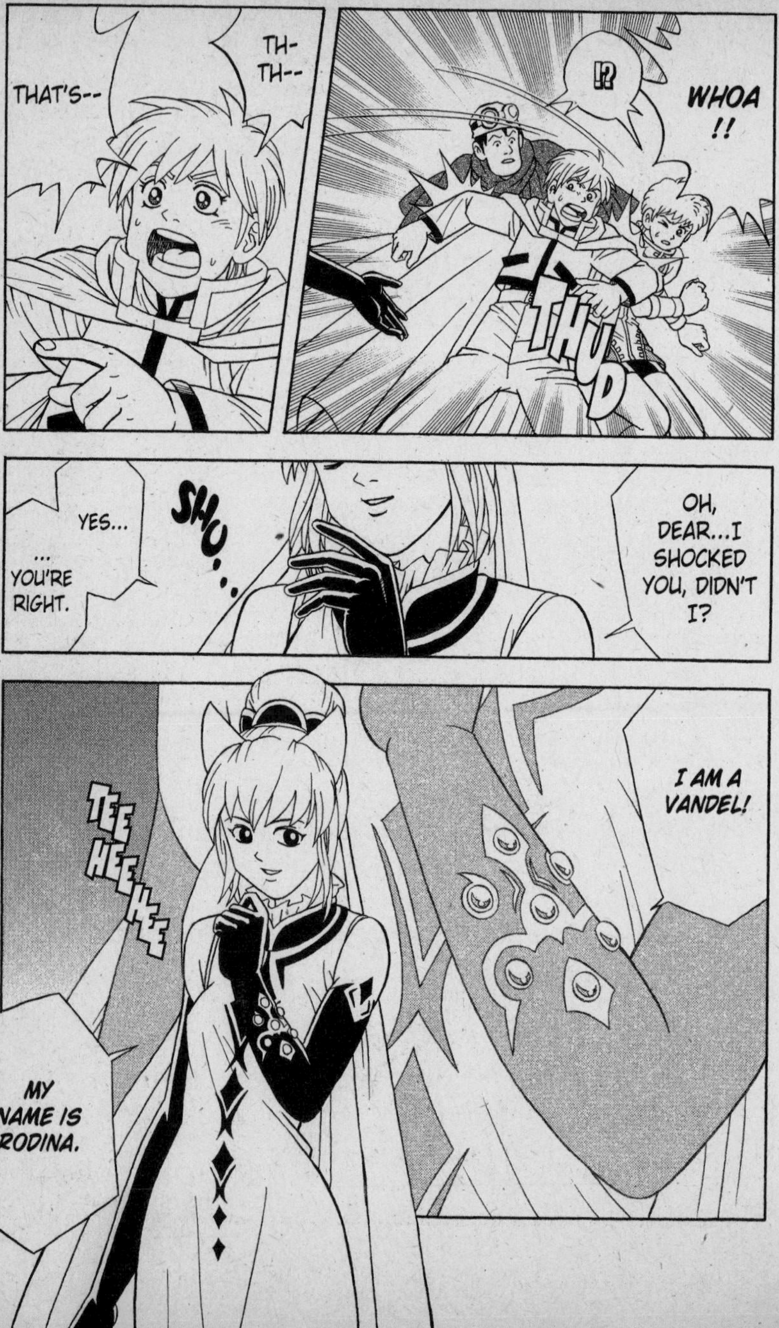
!?
WHOA !!
THUD
TH- TH--
THAT'S--
OH, DEAR...I SHOCKED YOU, DIDN'T I?
SHU...
YES...
...YOU'RE RIGHT.
I AM A VANDEL!
TEE HEE HEE
MY NAME IS RODINA.

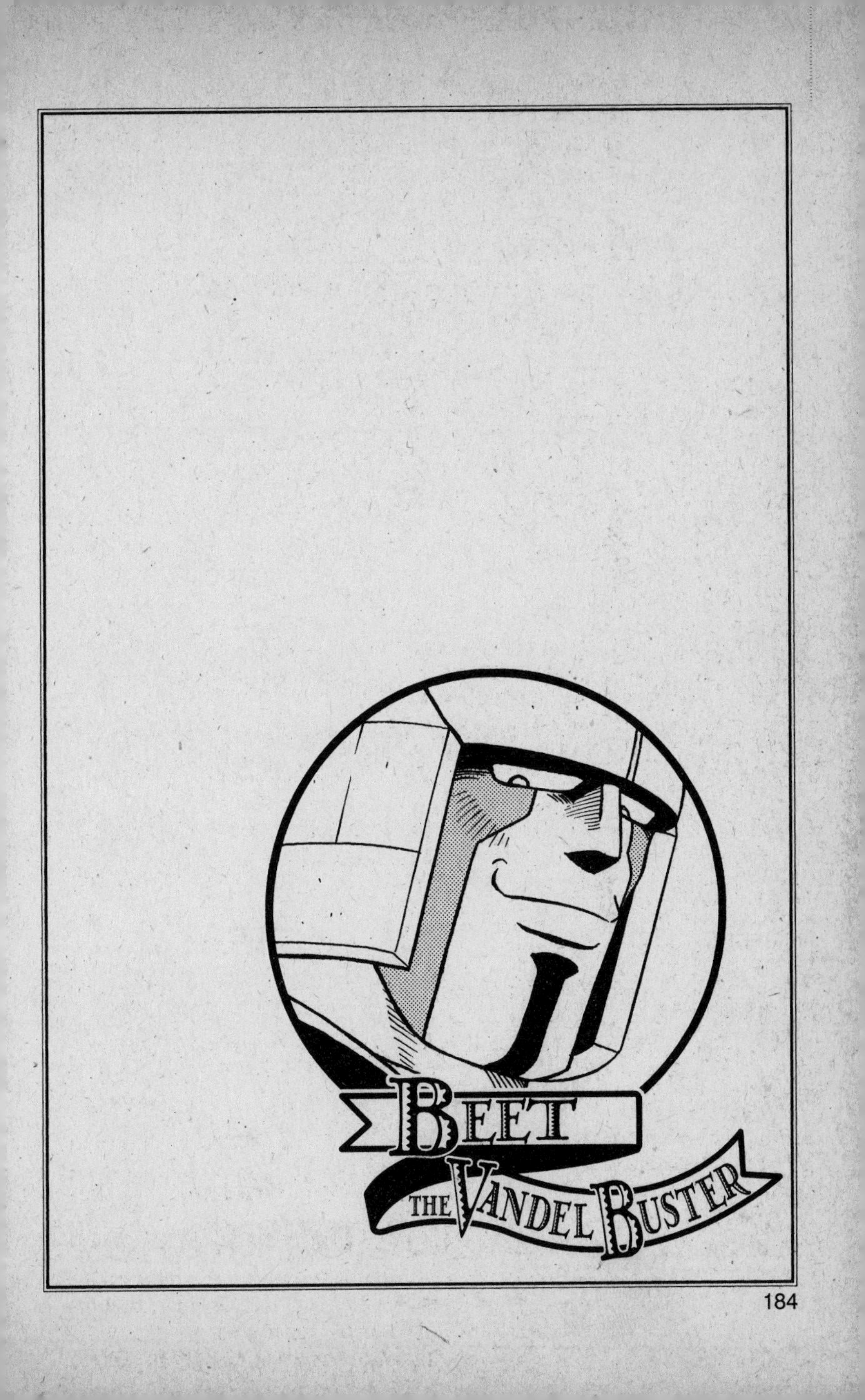
BEET
THE VANDEL BUSTER

BEET THE WORLD

THE WORLD OF
BEET the VANDEL BUSTER · PART 5

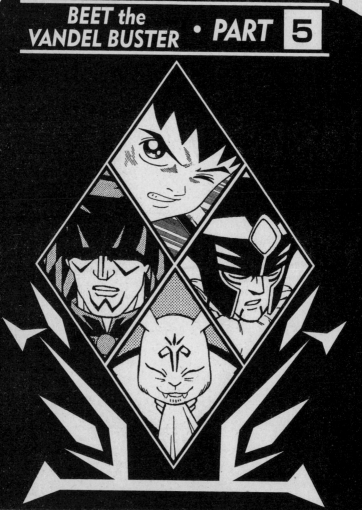

Powerful seven-star Vandels are congregating on Bekatrute, one after another!
This end-of-volume special examines the world of Beet as it heats up even more!
This edition is devoted to secret techniques!

HIDDEN STRENGTH

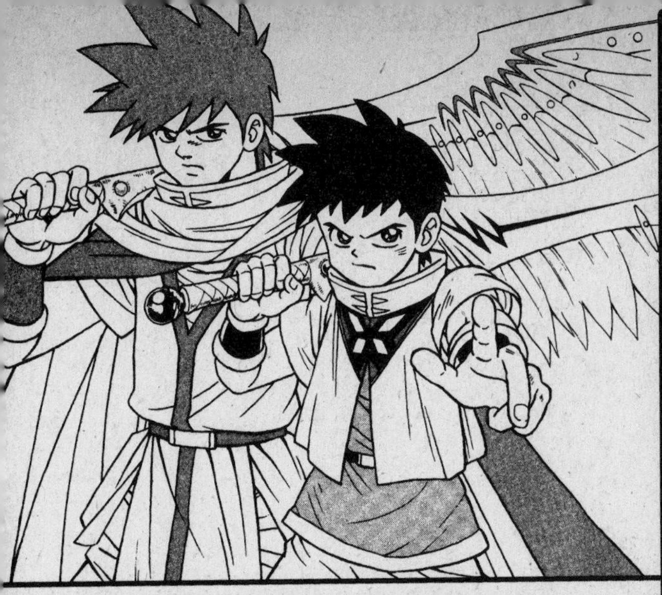

Both Saiga and Divine Attacks can be strengthened with special techniques. After Busters master a personal fighting style, they devise new techniques to multiply their power. Before anything else, Busters must perfect their Divine Attack and learn the skills that suit them best. A secret technique is used to increase or compress the Buster's Divine Power right at the moment when an attack explodes on the enemy. With it, the destructive power of the Divine Attack increases dramatically. Even against the tough bodies of Vandels, it can be fatal-in other words, it can work as a final winning strike. The best example of such a technique is the "Zenon Winzard" of Zenon, who was said to be the best Buster on the continent. Beet's greatest goal is to reproduce this ultimate technique.

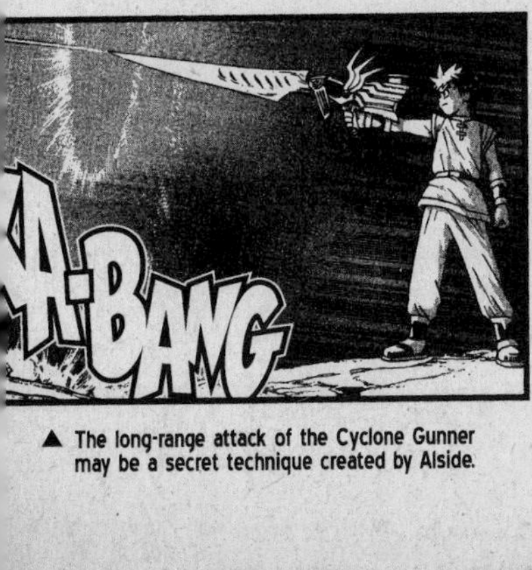
A-BANG

▲ The long-range attack of the Cyclone Gunner may be a secret technique created by Alside.

There are two types of secret techniques. One strengthens the attack of a Saiga; the other multiplies the power of a Divine Attack. Either way, one must have both talent and the strength of mind to control an enormous amount of Divine Power. Very few Busters reach this level. In other words, the ability to devise a secret technique is the sign of a first-class Buster!

FIRST CLASS BUSTERS DEVELOP WINNING SECRET TECHNIQUES, STRIKING EVIL WITH OVERFLOWING DIVINE POWER!

ZENON WINZARD
<ZENON • BEET>

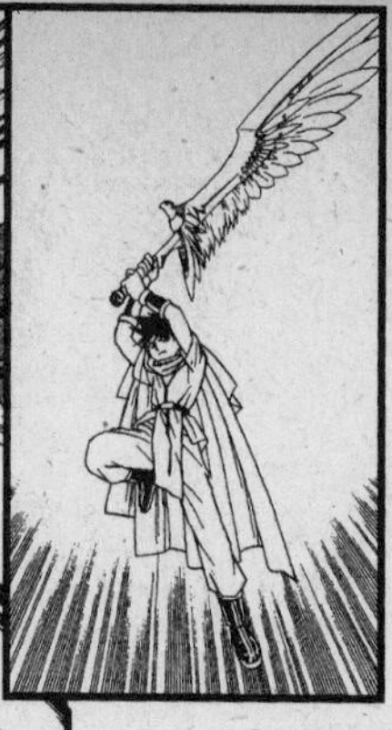

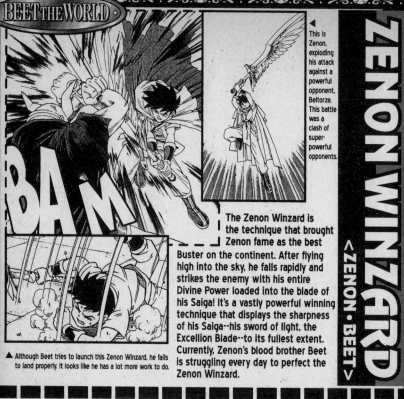

◀ This is Zenon, exploding his attack against a powerful opponent, Beltorze. This battle was a clash of super-powerful opponents.

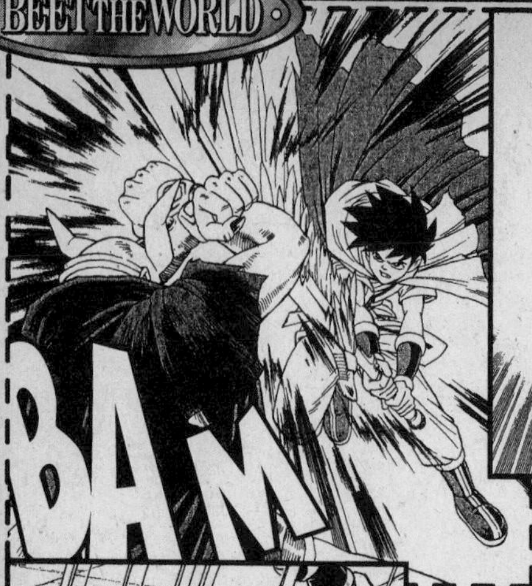
BAM

The Zenon Winzard is the technique that brought Zenon fame as the best Buster on the continent. After flying high into the sky, he falls rapidly and strikes the enemy with his entire Divine Power loaded into the blade of his Saiga! It's a vastly powerful winning technique that displays the sharpness of his Saiga--his sword of light, the Excellion Blade--to its fullest extent. Currently, Zenon's blood brother Beet is struggling every day to perfect the Zenon Winzard.

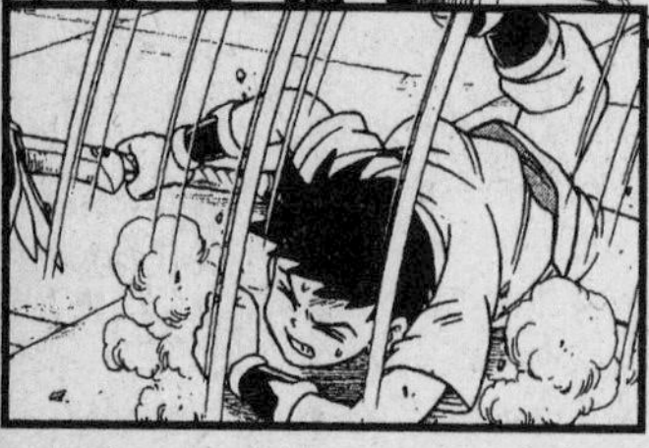

▲ Although Beet tries to launch this Zenon Winzard, he fails to land properly. It looks like he has a lot more work to do.

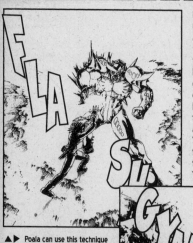

BURST END
<POALA>

Poala developed this technique using the Divine Attack of Fire by a stroke of luck during the battle with Grineed. It's a high-level technique that explodes the Divine Power of Fire after compressing it to its limit. Such compressed explosions of Divine Power are common secret techniques, so this technique has a general name, "Burst End." There are similar techniques for the Divine Power of Water and the Divine Power of Wind. They are all short-range attacks.

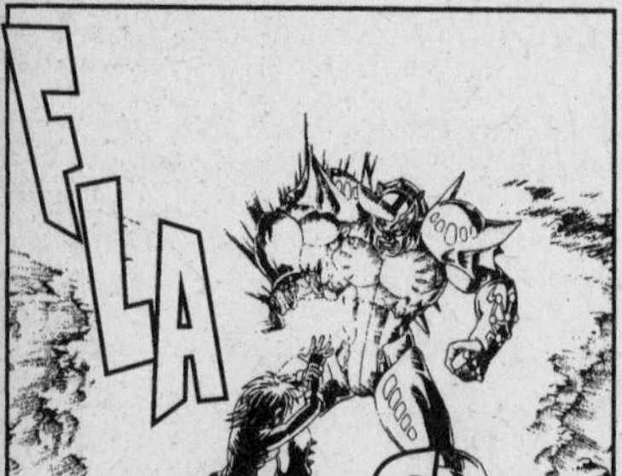
FLA

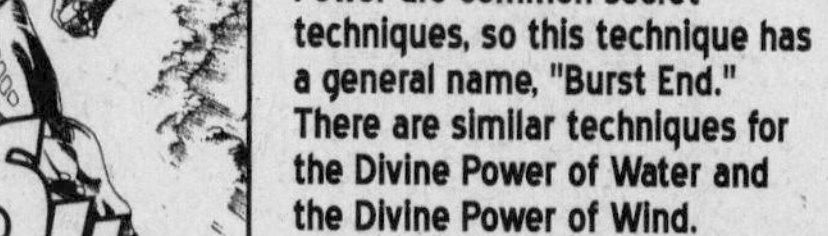
GYAA

▲▶ Poala can use this technique as a starting point to develop her own unique attacks!

HIDDEN STRENGTH: VANDELS

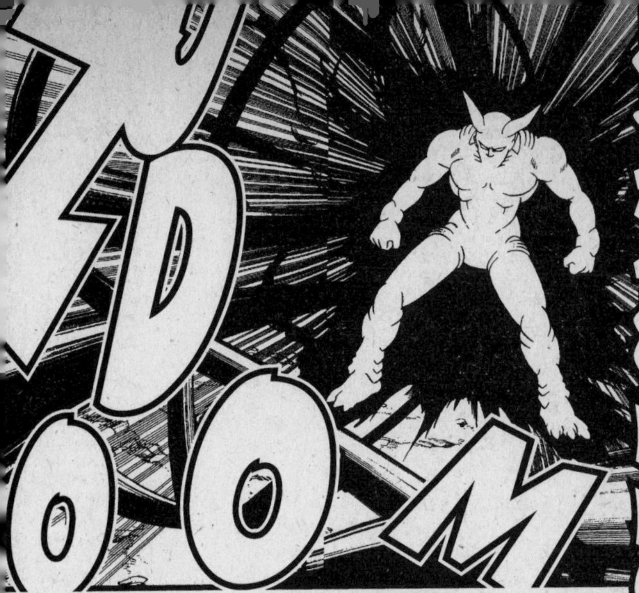
DOOM

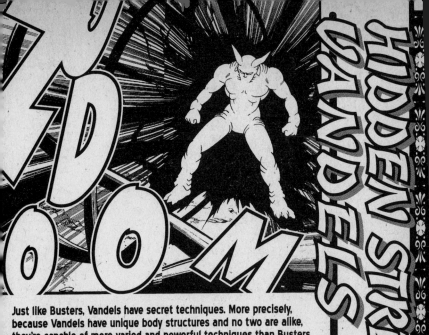

Just like Busters, Vandels have secret techniques. More precisely, because Vandels have unique body structures and no two are alike, they're capable of more varied and powerful techniques than Busters. Such a technique is a symbol of terror that forces every Buster who fights against it to face death. Just like a Buster's Divine Power, a Vandel's Dark Power is displayed to its maximum when a secret technique is used. However, unlike human techniques, which have similar basic styles, the Vandels' techniques are all different. The style of the technique will differ depending on each Vandel's physical characteristics and personality. There are styles that increase attack power by raising the Vandel's Dark Power, and styles that trap an opponent in the Vandel's unique "field." The possession of a secret technique is a major benchmark in measuring a Vandel's power.

▶ Some techniques, like Balleus' weapon-generating attack, utilize a unique characteristic of the Vandel's body.

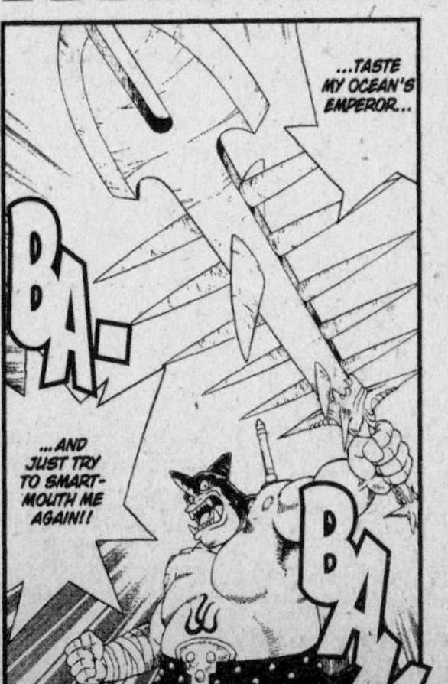
...TASTE MY OCEAN'S EMPEROR...
BA-
...AND JUST TRY TO SMART-MOUTH ME AGAIN!!
BA

Typical examples of Vandel techniques are Beltorze's "Phantom Explosion" and Grineed's "Fierce Wave of Infuriated Steel." As you can see, a secret technique can change the course of battle with a single stroke. It supports the battles of powerful Vandels and is used as a final resort to create attacks far beyond a Vandel's normal abilities or Dark Attacks.

A SECRET TECHNIQUE IS PROOF OF A POWERFUL VANDEL! IT IS A FATAL BLOW INTO WHICH A VANDEL'S ENTIRE DARK POWER IS LOADED!

ILLUSION MIST
<ROZZGOAT>

This is the Vandel Rozzgoat's secret technique. Using the Dark Power, he generates poisonous scales and scatters them around him, making it difficult for humans to launch Divine Attacks or Saiga. Although it appears to be a passive technique, it uses an enormous amount of Dark Power. Judging from the fact that Rozzgoat can use this technique as well as a first-class Dark Attack, his true ability is wondrous.

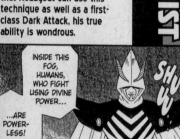

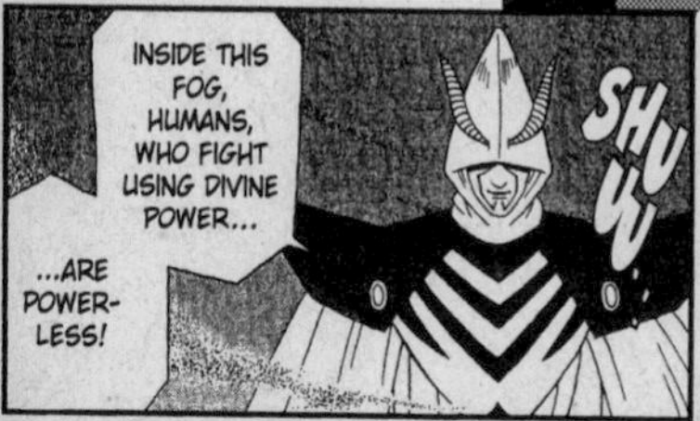
SHUW
INSIDE THIS FOG, HUMANS, WHO FIGHT USING DIVINE POWER...
...ARE POWER-LESS!

▲ Rozzgoat can perform this technique because he has a high level of Dark Power.

PHANTOM STROKE
<BELTORZE>

This is Beltorze's deadly secret technique. By compressing the Dark Power that shrouds his entire body into his fist, he launches a devastating blow to his opponent. It's called the "Phantom Stroke" because it causes a black shadow to attack the enemy, just as Beltorze's phantom would. The full-body version of this technique is an ultimate attack called the "Phantom Explosion."

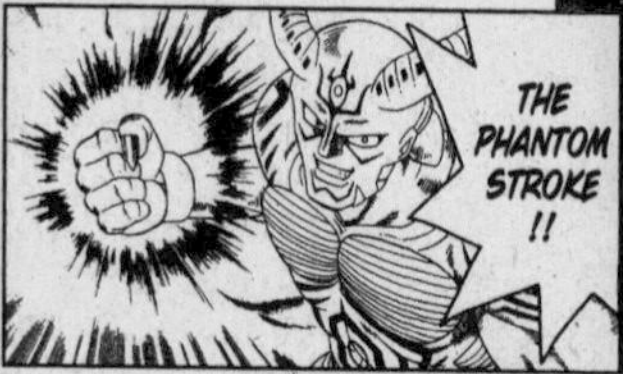
THE PHANTOM STROKE !!

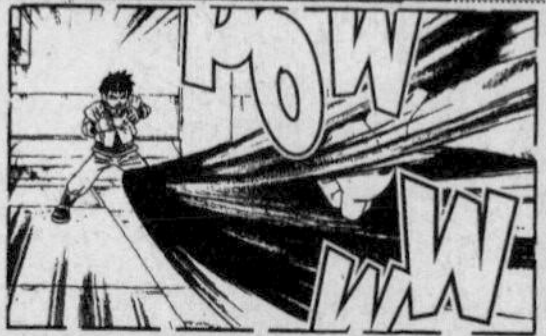
POW

▲▶ When released, his power approaches as if it has its own will.

GRAVI-ZONE
<GARONEWT>

This is just one of the techniques of the Vandel Garonewt. With the Dark Power generated from his body, he rapidly increases the gravitational pull of the area surrounding him, robbing his enemies of their ability to move freely. Not even a strong Buster can move inside such an area. Opponents caught in the Gravi-Zone soon suffer a fatal blow from Garonewt's powerful arm, of which he is very proud.

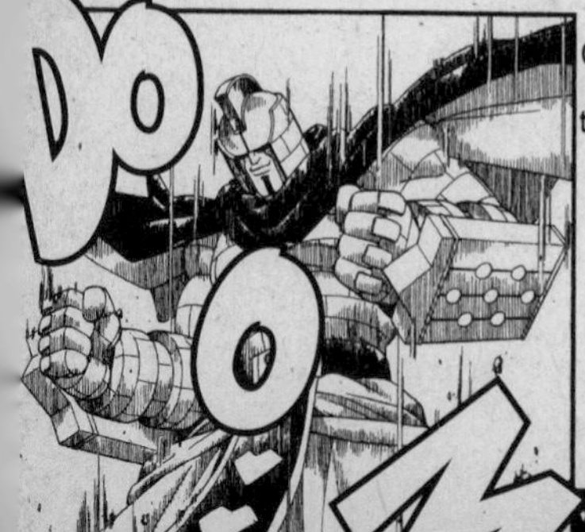
DOOM

◀ Garonewt uses this technique to compensate for his lack of speed.

FIERCE WAVE OF INFURIATED STEEL
<GRINEED>

This is the deadly technique that the Vandel Grineed launches--after revealing his true nature--applying his entire Dark Power toward strengthening his body. By vibrating every muscle at high speed, he releases a shock wave that annihilates the entire area surrounding him, slicing away everything except himself.
It's a technique that destroys everything, be it an opponent or teammate.

▼▶ His entire strength is pounded down onto the earth! Areas by his feet are completely annihilated!

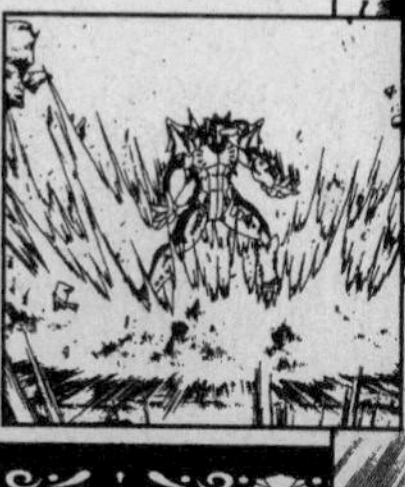

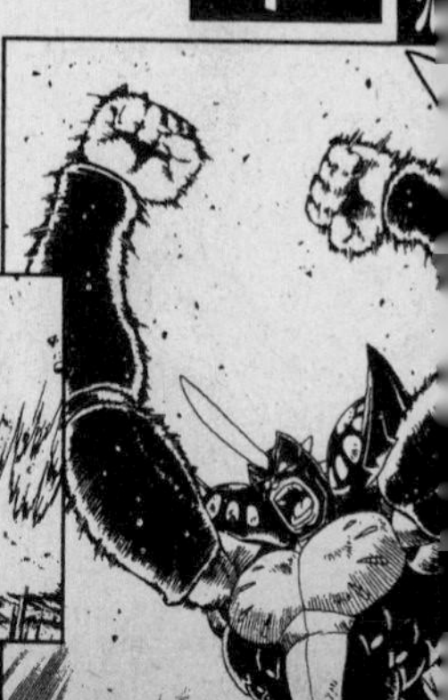

Coming Next Volume...

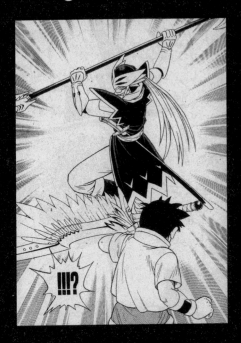

Having had their butts saved by a mysterious Vandel, Beet and his Beet Warriors have escaped doom once again. But wait, danger is back on the horizon as the mysterious rabbit-like Shaggy organizes all of the seven-star Vandels together for the sole purpose of defeating the Beet Warriors. Whoever can give Beet the beat-down will receive an incredible prize. Meanwhile a strange Vandel Buster suddenly shows up and challenges Beet to a duel. They clash, and not only does Beet get beaten, he finds out he has a whole lot more to learn about the true nature of Saigas! All that and more in the next explosive volume of *Beet the Vandel Buster*!

Available in February 2006!

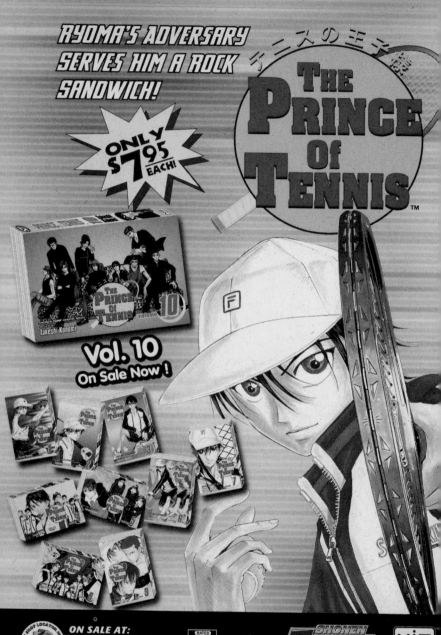

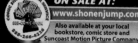

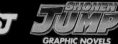

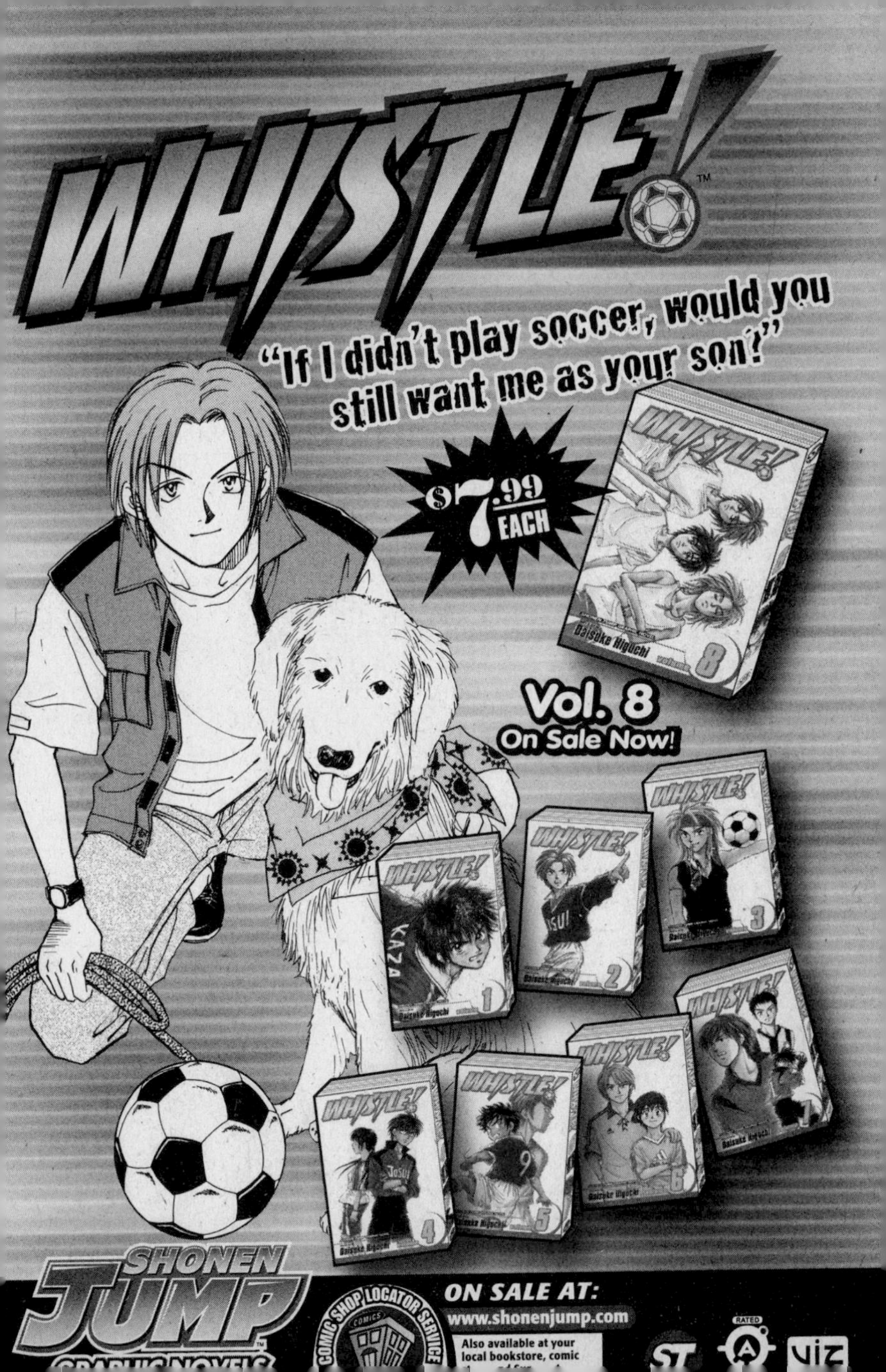
WHISTLE!™
"If I didn't play soccer, would you still want me as your son?"
$7.99 EACH
Vol. 8
On Sale Now!
SHONEN JUMP™
ON SALE AT:
www.shonenjump.com
COMIC SHOP LOCATOR SERVICE
Also available at your local bookstore, comic
RATED

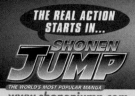
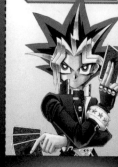

Check us out
on the web!

www.shonenjump.com

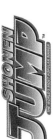

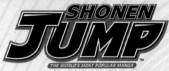

COMPLETE OUR SURVEY AND LET US KNOW WHAT YOU THINK!

☐ Please do NOT send me information about VIZ Media and SHONEN JUMP products, news and events, special offers, or other information.

☐ Please do NOT send me information from VIZ Media's trusted business partners.

Name: ______________________________

Address: ______________________________

City: ____________ **State:** ______ **Zip:** ________

E-mail: ______________________________

☐ **Male** ☐ **Female** **Date of Birth (mm/dd/yyyy):** ___/___/_____ **(Under 13? Parental consent required.)**

1 Do you purchase SHONEN JUMP Magazine?

☐ Yes ☐ No

If **YES**, do you subscribe?

☐ Yes ☐ No

If **NO**, how often do you purchase SHONEN JUMP Magazine?

☐ 1-3 issues a year ☐ 4-6 issues a year ☐ more than 7 issues a year

2 Which SHONEN JUMP Manga did you purchase this time? (please check only one)

☐ Beet the Vandel Buster ☐ Bleach ☐ Bobobo-bo Bo-bobo
☐ Death Note ☐ Dragon Ball ☐ Dragon Ball Z
☐ Dr. Slump ☐ Eyeshield 21 ☐ Hikaru no Go
☐ Hunter x Hunter ☐ I"s ☐ JoJo's Bizarre Adventure
☐ Knights of the Zodiac ☐ Legendz ☐ Naruto
☐ One Piece ☐ Rurouni Kenshin ☐ Shaman King
☐ The Prince of Tennis ☐ Ultimate Muscle ☐ Whistle!
☐ Yu-Gi-Oh! ☐ Yu-Gi-Oh!: Duelist ☐ Yu-Gi-Oh!: Millennium World
☐ YuYu Hakusho ☐ Other ______________

Will you purchase subsequent volumes?

☐ Yes ☐ No

3 How did you learn about this title? (check all that apply)

☐ Favorite title ☐ Advertisement ☐ Article
☐ Gift ☐ Read excerpt in SHONEN JUMP Magazine
☐ Recommendation ☐ Special offer ☐ Through TV animation
☐ Website ☐ Other ______________

4 **Of the titles that are serialized in SHONEN JUMP Magazine, have you purchased the paperback manga volumes?**

☐ Yes ☐ No

If **YES**, which ones have you purchased? (check all that apply)

☐ Hikaru no Go ☐ Naruto ☐ One Piece ☐ Shaman King
☐ Yu-Gi-Oh!: Millennium World ☐ YuYu Hakusho

If **YES**, what were your reasons for purchasing? (please pick up to 3)

☐ A favorite title ☐ A favorite creator/artist ☐ I want to read it in one go
☐ I want to read it over and over again ☐ There are extras that aren't in the magazine
☐ The quality of printing is better than the magazine ☐ Recommendation
☐ Special offer ☐ Other

If **NO**, why did/would you not purchase it?

☐ I'm happy just reading it in the magazine ☐ It's not worth buying the manga volume
☐ All the manga pages are in black and white, unlike the magazine
☐ There are other manga volumes that I prefer ☐ There are too many to collect for each title
☐ It's too small ☐ Other ____________

5 **Of the titles NOT serialized in the magazine, which ones have you purchased? (check all that apply)**

☐ Beet the Vandel Buster ☐ Bleach ☐ Bobobo-bo Bo-bobo ☐ Death Note
☐ Dragon Ball ☐ Dragon Ball Z ☐ Dr. Slump ☐ Eyeshield 21
☐ Hunter x Hunter ☐ I"s ☐ JoJo's Bizarre Adventure ☐ Knights of the Zodiac
☐ Legendz ☐ The Prince of Tennis ☐ Rurouni Kenshin ☐ Ultimate Muscle
☐ Whistle! ☐ Yu-Gi-Oh! ☐ Yu-Gi-Oh!: Duelist ☐ None
☐ Other ____________

If you did purchase any of the above, what were your reasons for purchasing?

☐ A favorite title ☐ A favorite creator/artist
☐ Read a preview in SHONEN JUMP Magazine and wanted to read the rest of the story
☐ Recommendation ☐ Other

Will you purchase subsequent volumes?

☐ Yes ☐ No

6 **What race/ethnicity do you consider yourself? (please check one)**

☐ Asian/Pacific Islander ☐ Black/African American ☐ Hispanic/Latino
☐ Native American/Alaskan Native ☐ White/Caucasian ☐ Other

THANK YOU! Please send the completed form to:

VIZ Media Survey
42 Catharine St.
Poughkeepsie, NY 12601

All information provided will be used for internal purposes only. We promise not to sell or otherwise divulge your information.

BEET THE VANDEL BUSTER
VOL. 8
The SHONEN JUMP Graphic Novel Edition

STORY BY RIKU SANJO
ART BY KOJI INADA

English Adaptation/Shaenon K. Garrity
Translation/Naomi Kokubo
Touch-Up & Lettering/Mark McMurray
Graphics & Cover Design/Andrea Rice
Editor/Urian Brown

Managing Editor/Elizabeth Kawasaki
Director of Production/Noboru Watanabe
Vice President of Publishing/Alvin Lu
Vice President & Editor in Chief/Yumi Hoashi
Sr. Director of Acquisitions/Rika Inouye
Vice President of Sales & Marketing/Liza Coppola
Publisher/Hyoe Narita

Printed in the U.S.A.

Published by VIZ Media, LLC
P.O. Box 77064
San Francisco, CA 94107

SHONEN JUMP Graphic Novel Edition
10 9 8 7 6 5 4 3 2 1
First printing, November 2005

www.viz.com

THE WORLD'S
MOST POPULAR MANGA

www.shonenjump.com

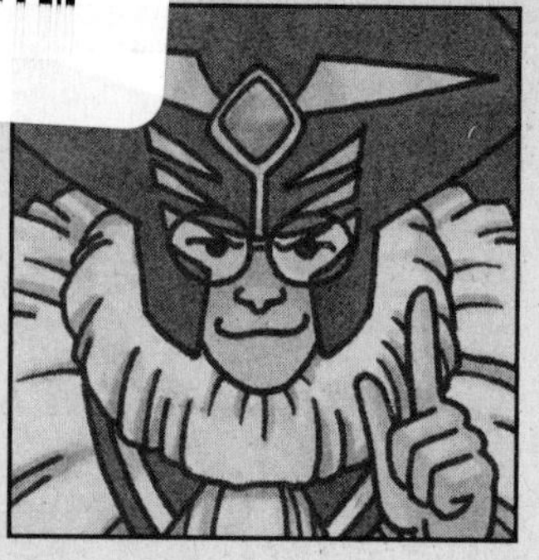

By the time this volume is published, the "Beet" TV series should be on Japanese television. Mr. Katsuyoshi Nakatsuru, who has been collaborating with us on the designs of the Vandels and monsters since this manga started, is in charge of the animated character designs, which is his professional occupation. Since he's been involved with this project as a staff member for the original manga, there's nothing as promising as having him work on the anime production. Just as you support the manga version, please support the anime version too!
— Riku Sanjo

Author Riku Sanjo and artist Koji Inada were both born in Tokyo in 1964. Sanjo began his career writing a radio-controlled car manga for the comic **Bonbon**. Inada debuted with **Kussotare Daze!!** in **Weekly Shonen Jump**. Sanjo and Inada first worked together on the highly successful **Dragon Quest—Dai's Big Adventure**. **Beet the Vandel Buster**, their latest collaboration, debuted in **Monthly Shonen Jump** in 2002 and was an immediate hit, inspiring an action-packed video game and an animated series on Japanese TV.